MACROECONOMIC SYSTEMS

Keith Cuthbertson and
Mark P. Taylor

Basil Blackwell

For our children:

Theo and Leon
and
Benjamin and Oliver

Copyright©Keith Cuthbertson and Mark P. Taylor 1987

First published 1987

Basil Blackwell Ltd
108 Cowley Road, Oxford, OX4 1JF, UK

Basil Blackwell Inc.
432 Park Avenue South, Suite 1503
New York, NY 10016, USA

British Library Cataloguing in Publication Data

Cuthbertson, Keith
  Macroeconomic systems.
  1. Economic policy   2. Macroeconomics
  I. Title   II. Taylor, Mark P.
  339   HD87

  ISBN 0-631-14341-6
  ISBN 0-631-14342-4 Pbk

Library of Congress Cataloging in Publication Data

Cuthbertson, Keith.
  Macroeconomic systems.

  Bibliography: p.
  Includes index.
  1. Macroeconomics.   I. Taylor, Mark P.
1958 May 17–   .   II. Title.
HB172.5.C87   1987   339   87-10332
ISBN 0-631-14341-6
ISBN 0-631-14342-4 (pbk.)

Typeset in 10 on 11½ pt Times
by Dobbie Typesetting Service, Plymouth, Devon
Printed in Great Britain by Page Bros (Norwich) Ltd

Contents

Foreword   v

Acknowledgements   x

1 Closed-economy models   1

1.1 Introduction   1
1.2 The Determinants of Demand: IS–LM Analysis   3
1.3 Monetary and Fiscal Policy in the IS–LM Fixed-Price Model   9
1.4 Real Balance and Wealth Effects   14
1.5 The Supply Side: an Introduction   21
1.6 Automatic Full Employment?   29
1.7 The Phillips Curve   32
1.8 Summary and Conclusion   36

2 Quantity-constrained macroeconomics   53

2.1 Introduction   53
2.2 Non-Market-Clearing and the Dual Decision Hypothesis   54
2.3 Further Analysis of Keynesian Unemployment   67
2.4 'Bootstraps' Effects   70
2.5 The Model in a Simple Open Economy   72
2.6 The Role of Money and Assets in Quantity-Constrained
     Macroeconomics   74
2.7 Endogenous Prices in Quantity-Constrained Models   75
2.8 Summary and Conclusion   76

3 Rational expectations and the new classical view   79

3.1 Introduction   79
3.2 Basic Tenets of the Rational-Expectations Hypothesis   80
3.3 Axioms of RE   84

3.4   Surprise Supply Functions and the Phillips Curve   89
3.5   Policy Ineffectiveness   95
3.6   Policy Evaluation: the Lucas Critique   109
3.7   Cyclical or Persistence Effects   111
3.8   Partly Rational Models   113
3.9   Adaptive and Rational Expectations   120
3.10 Summary   122

**4   New theories of employment: implicit contracts and
      adverse selection**   135

4.1   Introduction   135
4.2   Implicit Contracts   136
4.3   Adverse Selection in the Labour Market   161

5   Open-economy models   175

5.1   Introduction   175
5.2   The Mundell–Fleming Model   178
5.3   The Current Account Monetary (CAM) Model   196
5.4   Capital Account Monetarist (KAM) Models   202
5.5   Interest Rates and the Exchange Rate   212
5.6   The Portfolio Balance Model   216
5.7   Summary   226

6   Models and policy design   239

6.1   Introduction   239
6.2   Analytical and 'Real-World' Models   239
6.3   Models, Instruments and Targets   245
6.4   Optimal Control Theory   247
6.5   Optimal Control in Practice: a Comparative Simulation
      Exercise   250
6.6   Policy Optimization with Rational Expectations   253
6.7   Summary and Conclusion   260

References   264

Index   274

Foreword

Macroeconomics is, to say the least, currently in a state of flux, both at a theoretical and at a practical level. The neo-Keynesian consensus of the 1950s and 1960s has disintegrated, partly under pressure arising from the advent of new theories and partly because it is vociferously asserted by some that the practical difficulties of demand management are unlikely to be overcome. At present, in Western industrialized economies, there is a drift towards 'non-intervention' by governments at a macro level: 'demand management is dead'. According to some economists, this philosophy has, ironically, generated a massive rise in unemployment in a number of industrialized nations: precisely the outcome suggested by Keynes in the 1930s and for which the General Theory (Keynes 1936) was to provide the antidote. For others, it was the very failure of Keynesian macroeconomic policy to contain inflation and unemployment that led to its abandonment. What is certain is that there are now a plethora of competing analytic and macroeconometric models that purport to 'explain' the macroeconomy and the appropriate role for government policy. In some cases, these competing analytic models yield diametrically opposed policy conclusions and often empirical evidence does not (or indeed, logically cannot) discriminate decisively between them.

Given the state of crisis in which macroeconomics finds itself, this book is the outcome of the authors' experience in at least two areas. Firstly, much of the material has been derived from advanced courses in macroeconomic theory and policy that we have given to graduates, undergraduates and civil servants over a number of years. There seemed to be a very real need for a macroeconomics text that was at once up to date, reasonably comprehensive and at a level suitable for advanced undergraduates and beginning postgraduate students. Secondly, a large part of the analysis has been motivated by our experience not as teachers but as working economists attempting to analyse the macroeconomy and provide practical policy advice. Thus, the book can also be used as a guide to current policy debates by practising economists seeking, for example, a concise account of what exactly are 'time inconsistency', 'the Lucas critique' or 'an implicit labour contract', and what the policy implications of these phenomena are.

The essence of good economic theorizing and policy analysis is to decide exactly which features one wishes to analyse and which can be discarded as excess baggage for the purpose in hand. In the main, the book therefore deals with small analytic models and the light they throw on contemporary debates. However, the link between such models and (usually larger) macro-econometric forecasting models is also dealt with in the final chapter.

We begin in chapter 1 with the basic 'building blocks' of a number of analytic models. Thus the interaction of monetary and fiscal policy is examined in a fix-price, closed-economy IS–LM model – from a pedagogic point of view, this chapter also serves as a bridge between the level of economic knowledge one might expect of a typical student using this text and what follows. We then consider the impact of wealth effects on the demand side of the model, working via the government budget constraint. An elementary 'supply side' is then added to the model and, together with the aggregate demand curve, this allows an analysis to be made of the neutrality of money and the 'crowding-out' effects of fiscal policy. The possibility that prices adjust sluggishly allows the Phillips curve to be interpreted as a form of 'supply curve'. This leads naturally to the so-called 'neoclassical synthesis', where Keynes's contribution to the theory of unemployment is viewed solely as an assumption that nominal wages are sticky downwards in the neoclassical model. In the appendices to chapter 1 we adopt a more formal approach to the solution of conventional macromodels. In particular, we formally demonstrate the method of comparative statics and the use of the so-called 'Correspondence Principle'.

The inexorable logic of the fully specified neoclassical synthesis – namely that unemployment can only be generated by wage rigidities – leads naturally into an analysis of the implications of price and wage rigidities for the behaviour of output and employment, and this is the subject of chapter 2 on quantity-constrained macroeconomic. Moreover, part of this chapter is devoted to an alternative interpretation of the economics of Keynes – that is, given parametrically sticky wages and prices, the Keynesian consumption function and typically Keynesian policy prescriptions can be derived within a standard, neoclassical optimizing framework. The chapter also gives some space to a discussion of the so-called 'bootstraps effect' – the notion that agents' expectations (e.g. that they will be unemployed) can be self-fulfilling.

It is often stated that the new revolution in macroeconomics is that of rational expectations (RE). In chapter 3, we cover the main elements in this approach in a closed-economy context. When the assumption of RE is added to a market-clearing, neoclassical framework one can obtain startling policy conclusions. Such models are called New Classical models. First, the Lucas critique of econometric policy evaluation (Lucas 1976) asserts that 'conventional' macromodels are likely to yield incorrect policy decisions if agents are 'rational' when forecasting the future because the change in policy is likely to change the structure of the economy. Policy simulations on conventional models are, therefore, useless. Second, in some New Classical models it can be shown that the authorities cannot alter the mean level of real variables (e.g. output and employment) by using systematic policy rules (e.g. increasing government expenditure when output is low). This is the policy ineffectiveness proposition and is the basis of one argument that 'demand management (or discretionary policy) is dead', and that the authorities should set policy instruments according to fixed rules (e.g. the money supply should grow at k per cent per annum). Third, in RE models, announced (anticipated) changes in policy variables have a different short-run impact (on say output or inflation) than unanticipated changes. In fact with RE, the course of the economy may alter after the *announcement* of a new policy, and well in advance of any actual change in the policy variables. These possibilities do not arise in conventional models and make the interpretation of past policy changes somewhat problematic. In the appendix to chapter 3 we discuss the various solution methods for RE models.

In chapter 4 we carry out a rigorous analysis of the labour market in an attempt to explain a number of empirical phenomena, and in particular why sticky wages and layoffs may coexist. Rather than taking sticky prices as parametric, as we did in chapter 2, in chapter 4 we attempt to provide an explanation for quantity rather than price adjustment in the labour market over the business cycle, in terms of optimizing behaviour on the part of firms and workers. Because of the importance attached to explaining unemployment as a macroeconomic aggregate, and because much of this literature is technically demanding, we devote a considerable amount of space to expositing two broad approaches to the sticky-wages–layoffs phenomenon. Firstly, we examine the theory of implicit contracts where relatively sticky wages result from less risk-averse firms effectively insuring more risk-averse workers against wage variation. Secondly, we examine the notion of adverse selection in the labour market, where sticky wages basically occur because if the firm were to cut the wage (rather than the workforce) during a slump 'the best workers would quit'. In the appendix to chapter 4 we discuss the nature of implicit contracts under asymmetric information – when only the firm can observe which phase of the business cycle is prevailing. This situation tends to lead to socially deficient levels of employment since the firm typically has to lay off extra workers in order to convince the workforce that times really are bad and that they should accept even a small wage cut.

In chapter 5 we introduce trade and capital flows into the analysis. The behaviour of a small open economy is discussed first, in the Mundell–Fleming fix-price model to which we add wealth effects. The efficacy of monetary and fiscal policy is found to depend crucially on the degree of capital mobility and whether the economy is operating under fixed or flexible exchange rates. We then informally introduce flexible prices in the Mundell–Fleming model and compare this model with the flex-price current account monetary (CAM) model. A defect of these open-economy models is the absence of any explicit account of exchange rate expectations, which are a crucial determinant of capital flows. The Dornbusch (1976) overshooting model remedies this defect.

The interaction between monetary and fiscal policy, and movements in output, inflation and the exchange rate is then amenable to analysis. In the final part of this chapter, we discuss reasons for the rather volatile movements in nominal exchange rates before extending our range of RE solution techniques by presenting the detailed solution of certain Dornbusch-type models in an appendix.

In chapter 6 we bring together the main elements of the models discussed in previous chapters and indicate how these ideas are steadily being incorporated in applied macroeconomic models. We then outline how a large-scale model may be used for forecasting and policy analysis, before going on to discuss a number of topics in the theory of optimal policy design. In particular, we analyse how the government may wish to choose trade-offs between macroeconomic targets, when it is impossible to achieve them all simultaneously, by formally applying optimal control techniques – that is, maximizing a particular objective function with respect to a given model in order to derive optimal policy rules (the formal solution technique of dynamic programming is outlined in the appendix). From our preview of chapter 3, it should be clear that no discussion of optimal policy would be complete without a discussion of the impact of rational expectations. We therefore discuss in further detail the Lucas (1976) critique of econometric policy evaluation, as well as problems that may arise in choosing a macro policy that is consistently optimal at all points in time (i.e. 'time consistent') when agents are 'rational' and therefore know that the government has an incentive to 'surprise' them.

Although, in chapters 2 and 4, we have not shield away from delving into microfoundations in an attempt to analyse particular problems ('what are the macroeconomic consequences of non-clearing markets?', 'why may sticky wages and layoffs coexist?') for the main part the book concentrates on the systems aspects of macroeconomics, and we often spend little time on the detailed derivation of individual behavioural equations. This is a conscious choice on our part. It is the systems aspect that are probably the greatest source of confusion to students and non-specialists and that form the basis of contemporary policy debates and policy recommendations.

The reader turning to this book in an attempt to find out 'the truth' about macroeconomics will certainly be disappointed, not least because truth, like beauty, often seems to lie in the eye of the beholder. This is not an admission of mendacity but a statement of our efforts to avoid taking sides in any particular macroeconomic debate (although the reader will, at times, inevitably discern in which directions our sympathies lie). Rather, we have attempted an objective exposition of macro theory and policy by making clear the assumptions made at each stage, and leaving it to the reader (or the instructor) to decide which he or she finds more plausible. In that sense, the book is offered as an up-to-date, reasonably comprehensive manual of macroeconomics, which we hope provides a useful blend of academic rigour and practical application.

Finally, we should perhaps mention our assumptions concerning the economic and quantitative background of students using this book. As noted above, apart from its appeal to practising economists, the book is aimed at advanced undergraduates and graduate students beginning taught Master's and PhD courses. Thus, we assume a general knowledge of economic theory that one would expect of a second-year economics major, although chapter 1 serves largely as a revision and extension of the 'basic macro model'. As far as mathematical background is concerned, we assume that the reader has followed a basic course in quantitative methods (including elementary statistics) of a standard one would expect to find in a second-year undergraduate economics programme, and we often give references to an appropriate text such as Chiang 1984. Moreover, quantitatively more demanding material is generally relegated to appendices, so that it may be used on more advanced courses or followed up by the interested student without overloading the main body of the text.

Acknowledgements

We would like to thank Mike Artis, John Black, David Cobham, John Hutton, and Eric Pentecost, all of whom read and commented on various parts of the manuscript. Special thanks are due to John Black for his rapid and very detailed comments on the entire book. We also owe a debt to a number of students who have been exposed to and commented upon much of the material presented here in various courses. We also thank Sue Kirkbride at LSE for typing the manuscript cheerfully and efficiently; and Phillip Thompson who prepared the indices and checked the references. Naturally, all of the above-mentioned people are exonerated from responsibility for any errors or omissions which may remain. Part of the book was written while Cuthbertson was a Hallsworth fellow at the University of Manchester. Any views expressed in this work are those of the authors and are not necessarily those of the Bank of England. Finally, we are grateful to our wives, June and Anita, for encouragement, and to our children for light relief.

1   Closed-economy models

1.1   Introduction

In this chapter we present the basic 'building blocks' of a simple macroeconomic model which deals with simultaneous equilibrium in the goods, money and labour markets. This general framework is widely used in discussing the relative merits of fiscal and monetary policy and may be encapsulated in the theoretical constructs of the IS–LM curves and the aggregate-demand–aggregate-supply diagram. A recurring debate in macroeconomics concerns the ability of the economy to achieve *automatically* a full-employment level of output without the aid of discretionary government fiscal and monetary policy. Broadly speaking, the classical view supports the notion of automatic full employment, whilst 'Keynesians' deny the proposition. The so-called neoclassical synthesis suggests that Keynesian ideas are not 'general' but merely add a special assumption to the classical model, namely that nominal wages are rigid in a downwards direction. Put another way, a Keynesian assumption would be that the labour market does not clear. We agree with the logic of the neoclassical synthesis. However, this begs the question of *how* in a decentralized market system prices move quickly to equate supply and demand in all markets. The neoclassical view invokes a fictional Walrasian auctioneer who 'announces' prices and no trading takes place until the announced prices are those that exactly equate supply and demand in all markets. If we assume that some trading takes place at non-market-clearing prices we enter the world of quantity-constrained macroeconomics and this is dealt with in chapter 2. In the present chapter we deal (in the main) with static *equilibrium* models – all markets clear in all periods. We also consider only closed-economy models – there are no trade or capital flows and for the most part we assume that agents' behaviour is not influenced by expectations of economic variables (e.g. the rate of inflation). We relax the latter assumption when discussing the Phillips curve in 1.6 and we investigate 'expectations' in detail in chapter 3.

The neutrality proposition, namely that in the long run increases in the money supply are reflected one-for-one in price changes and do not alter the path of real variables (e.g. real output and unemployment), is one of the oldest propositions in monetary economics. We investigate the conditions under which the neutrality proposition holds. It is frequently asserted that increases in government expenditure will be wholly or partly offset by falls in private investment (and perhaps consumption). Our model allows us to analyse this phenomenon of financial 'crowding out'.

The price expectations augmented Phillips curve (PEAPC) appears in numerous macroeconomic models and provides a link between changes in aggregate demand (and unemployment) and wage and price inflation. Under certain circumstances the PEAPC is vertical in the long run. This has two powerful policy implications. First the authorities may only reduce unemployment below its equilibrium (or 'natural') rate if people continually underestimate the rate of inflation. The latter condition is likely to be the case only if inflation is accelerating. Hence the PEAPC embodies the 'accelerationist hypothesis': permanently lower unemployment is only possible if the authorities engineer an accelerating rate of inflation. This contrasts sharply with the naïve Keynesian view that permanently lower unemployment may be obtained with a higher (but non-accelerating) rate of inflation. The second policy implication of the vertical PEAPC is that at the equilibrium (or natural) level of unemployment any (perfectly anticipated) rate of inflation is possible. Monetarists would further add that the rate of inflation is determined solely by the rate of monetary growth. The reader may have noticed that there appears to be a link between the neutrality proposition and the PEAPC. The common element is the interpretation of the PEAPC as a reformulation of the neoclassical model of the labour market. We are able to examine a number of alternative interpretations of the PEAPC relationship.

A prerequisite for using either the money supply or fiscal policy to alter the level of output or the rate of inflation is an understanding of the transmission mechanism from these policy instruments to the chosen policy targets. The primary aim of this chapter is to demonstrate the conditions under which monetary and fiscal policy have either a short-run or long-run impact on these policy variables. This is a necessary condition for the use of such instruments in a discretionary manner. However, detailed discussion of the use of models in aiding policy choice is dealt with in chapter 6.

In the rest of the chapter, we proceed as follows. We begin with a simple closed-economy IS–LM model which deals with simultaneous equilibrium in the goods and money market. The model determines the level of *planned* (*ex ante*) demand (or expenditure) in the economy; but with the naïve 'supply side' assumption that firms supply whatever is demanded, at a fixed price level, the model determines *actual* (*ex post*) output. The link between the goods and money market is provided by the interest rate on bonds and interest rate effects are a key element in the transmission mechanism of monetary and fiscal policy. It turns out that the relative size of the interest elasticity of the demand for money and the demand for investment goods determines whether it is monetary or fiscal policy that has the major impact on output. We extend the channels by which fiscal and monetary policy operate by adding real balance and wealth effects (which in a closed economy emanate from the government budget constraint) to the basic model.

In the next section we introduce the labour market and develop the neoclassical theory of the supply of output based on profit maximization under perfect competition. Prices are assumed to be perfectly flexible and move to equate planned supply and planned expenditures (demand). However, in this simplified neoclassical labour market the equilibrium level of employment is determined solely by relative factor prices (such as the real wage) and is independent of monetary and fiscal policy. (This yields a vertical aggregate supply curve.) Hence, monetary and fiscal policy although influencing *planned* expenditure have no effect on planned (and actual) supply in the long run: changes in demand are reflected solely in changes in the price level (and the rate of inflation). Hence the neutrality of money holds. In addition, fiscal policy is 'crowded out' because the supply of output by firms does not respond to increased government expenditure (this is often referred to as physical crowding out).

In the neoclassical model of the labour market, prices and wages are perfectly flexible. We retain the assumption of profit-maximizing firms but in the next section we assume that the labour market does not clear, because there are downwardly rigid nominal wages. Here the neutrality of money does not hold and monetary and fiscal policy influence both output and prices. However we do not discuss the microeconomic theory of 'sticky' wages until chapter 4.

In the final section we discuss the relationship between the aggregate supply curve and the Phillips curve, together with the acceleration hypothesis. Appendix 1.1 provides a mathematical representation of the main results. Appendix 1.2 then formally sets out the method of comparative statics and the so-called 'correspondence principle', while in appendix 1.3 we extend our mathematical treatment of 'wealth effects'.

1.2   The Determinants of Demand: IS–LM Analysis

IS–LM analysis is a device widely used to discuss the efficacy of fiscal and monetary policy. Its role as the centrepiece of economic analysis has been superseded as models have become more complex and more realistic. However, for many models IS–LM analysis forms the basic framework and it is therefore a useful place to start our macroeconomic analysis. It was first introduced by Hicks (1937) as an interpretation of the economics of Keynes.

The basic IS–LM model deals with simultaneous equilibrium in two markets, the goods market and the money market. It embodies the simple Keynesian multiplier analysis but allows interaction with the money market. The model deals either with an under-employment situation where prices are fixed and the model determines the level of real output, or it deals with full-employment situations where the level of real output is given and the model explains price changes. We will concentrate initially on the fixed-price model. Here the efficacy of monetary and fiscal policy in influencing real output is seen to depend crucially on the relative size of two parameters, the interest elasticity of (investment) expenditure and the interest elasticity of the demand for money. The model therefore deals with the (financial) crowding-out debate – that is, whether fiscal policy can influence the level of real output if the money supply is held constant. We shall first discuss equilibrium in the goods market, then deal with equilibrium in the money market before looking at the efficiency of fiscal and monetary policy under alternative assumptions about elasticities. Our exposition will be somewhat terse as we expect that most readers will already be reasonably familiar with this model.

1.2.1 The Goods Market and the IS Curve

The goods market may be represented by the following set of equations:

$$AD \equiv C + I + G + X - Z \tag{1.1}$$
$$Y^s = AD \tag{1.2}$$
$$Y \equiv Y^s \tag{1.3}$$
$$I = I(r) \qquad (i_r = \partial I / \partial r < 0) \tag{1.4}$$
$$C = C(Y - T) \qquad (c_y = \partial C / \partial Y > 0) \tag{1.5}$$
$$T = T(Y) \qquad (t_y = \partial T / \partial Y > 0) \tag{1.6}$$
$$Z = Z(Y) \qquad (z_y = \partial Z / \partial Y > 0) \tag{1.7}$$

where for completeness we have included exports and imports of goods, but for simplicity we exclude *indirect* taxes.

The first equation is an *identity* which defines desired expenditure or 'aggregate demand' for *domestic* output, AD. The demand for domestic output arises from consumption, C, from a demand for investment goods, I, demands by the government, G, demands for exports by foreigners, X, net of imports purchased, Z.[1] The second equation defines *equilibrium in* the goods market, where desired or aggregate demand is equal to output supplied, Y^s, by producers of goods.[2] The third equation is an *identity* which says that all output supplied yields income, Y, to the suppliers. We assume a 'fix-price' model – that is, supply is forthcoming at the going price level (even though it may be unprofitable for firms to ensure this). Fluctuations in output are therefore determined solely by aggregate demand. In most texts these first three equations are collapsed into a single equation which has $Y = C + I + G + X - Z$, but the advantage of presenting the three equations separately is to make the distinction between (i) behavioural relationships, definitions or identities and (ii) equilibrium equations as clear as possible.

Equation (1.4) is a behavioural equation and indicates that investment depends negatively on the rate of interest, r. The rate of interest measures the cost of borrowing for investment purposes: the lower the cost of borrowing the greater the level of real investment. As we shall see, it is the interest rate that provides the link between the goods market and the money market. Equation (1.5) is the consumption function – consumption depends positively upon disposable income. Equation (1.6) relates income taxes to the level of income. Equation (1.7) shows imports depending positively on the level of domestic output or income. Exports and government expenditure are exogenous variables (i.e. not determined by the model).

The IS schedule shows the relationship between the interest rate and the level of output, which yields equilibrium in the goods market when the exogenous variables in the goods market are held constant.[3] A lower interest rate leads to increased investment expenditures, increased supply (initially of investment goods, via equation (1.2)) and to increased incomes in the investment goods industries (equation (1.3)). Increased income leads to increased consumption which in turn brings forth an increase in supply of consumption goods and a further increase in income to those who work in consumption industries. Thus we have the familiar multiplier process. A lower interest rate therefore leads to a higher level of output in order to maintain equilibrium in the goods market. The IS curve is therefore downward-sloping and in our conceptual experiment we have moved from A to B (figure 1.1).

If investment does not respond to changes in the interest rate (i.e. is perfectly inelastic) then the IS curve is vertical. The converse also applies and the IS curve is horizontal if investment is highly interest-elastic.

The IS curve $\text{IS}(G_0)$ is drawn under the assumption that the exogenous variables G and X are held constant. If any of these 'other variables' change, the IS curve shifts to the right or to the left. Anything that increases aggregate demand at a given interest rate will shift the IS curve to the right via the familiar multiplier process. Thus, starting from point A, an increase in government expenditure or in exports or in *autonomous elements* of

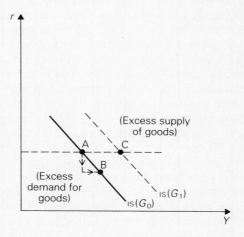

Figure 1.1   The IS curve $(G_1 > G_0)$

consumption and investment will move the IS curve to the right: at any given interest rate we move from point A to point C. For example, if a devaluation of the exchange rate leads to an increase in exports (and a fall in imports) this will increase demand for British goods and shift the IS curve to the right. (The latter mechanism will come to the fore when we extend the IS–LM analysis to include a more complete foreign sector.) An autonomous increase in government expenditure has a similar effect.

It is worth noting that for a given interest rate this shift in the IS curve is given by the familiar simple Keynesian multiplier. The distance AC (figure 1.1) is therefore given by

$$\mathrm{d}G/[1 - c_y(1 - t_y) + z_y]$$

where $\mathrm{d}G$ = the increase in government expenditure (see appendix 1.1).

1.2.2   The Money Market and the LM Curve

The money market may be represented by the following three equations:

$$M^s = \overline{M} \tag{1.8}$$
$$M^d = M(Y, r)\, P \qquad m_y > 0,\ m_r < 0 \tag{1.9}$$
$$M^s = M^d \tag{1.10}$$

The first equation indicates that the money supply is assumed to be exogenous and determined by the monetary authorities. The second equation indicates that the desired demand for money by the private sector depends upon three factors. If money is used for transactions purposes we expect more to be held when the level of (real) transactions is higher; this level is here measured by the level of real output – hence $m_y > 0$. The higher the opportunity cost of holding money, that is, the interest rate on bonds, the less money we can be expected to hold, $m_r < 0$; this is somewhat imprecisely referred to as the 'speculative demand'. Finally, we assume that the demand for money in nominal terms is proportional to the price level which, for the moment, we assume exogenous to the model. The third equation expresses equilibrium in the money market which pertains when the supply of money is equal to the desired demand for money.

In this model of the money market it is implicitly assumed that wealth is held in both money and bonds. The demand for bonds is the mirror image of the demand for money. An increase in the rate of return on bonds encourages substitution into bonds and out of money.

The LM curve shows the combinations of the interest rate and the level of output that yield equilibrium in the money market.[4] Suppose the money supply and the price level are fixed and that output and the interest rate are at such a value that the demand for money just equals the exogenous supply (point A in figure 1.2). Suppose income now rises, which increases the desired demand for money at the going interest rate. With a fixed money supply, to

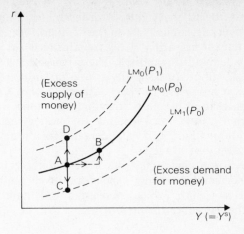

Figure 1.2 The LM curve ($P_1 > P_0$, $M_1 > M_0$)

obtain more 'transactions money' the private sector must sell bonds. The increased supply of bonds causes the price of bonds to fall and the interest rate on bonds to rise. On receiving money in exchange for bonds, some members of the private sector note that the interest rate on bonds is now higher. The higher interest rate is just sufficient to reduce the speculative demand and offset the increase in the transactions demand for money caused by the higher output. For a higher level of output one therefore requires a higher interest rate in order to maintain equilibrium in the money market, with a fixed money supply. In terms of figure 1.2, we have moved from point A to point B.

Consider two polar 'special cases' for the slope of the LM curve. First if the interest elasticity of the demand for money is very small it takes a large rise in r to reduce the speculative demand for money and the LM curve is steeper than that of figure 1.2 (in the limit it is vertical). Second, if the interest elasticity is very large, the increase in r required to reduce the speculative demand is very small and the LM curve is very flat (in the limit it is horizontal); this is an implication of the so-called Keynesian 'liquidity trap'.

By analogy with the IS curve it should be obvious that any variable other than r or Y that influences either the supply or demand for money will *shift* the LM curve. For example, consider the following conceptual experiment. Assume the government increases the money supply by open-market operations, that is, by purchasing bonds from the non-bank private sector. To encourage the non-bank private sector to hold more money and less bonds the authorities must offer a higher price for the bond in the market, that is, a lower interest rate. Thus, with a higher money supply and a given level of output, money market equilibrium requires a lower interest rate. We therefore move from point A (on figure 1.2) to point C to maintain money market equilibrium. With a higher money supply the LM curve therefore shifts downwards (or to the right) in order to maintain money market equilibrium. Conversely, an increase in the demand for money will shift the LM curve to the left (or upwards). A higher price level for example increases the 'transactions demand' for money. The private sector sell bonds, which with an unchanged supply of bonds leads to a fall in bond prices and a rise in interest rates (at any given level of output). Again, the induced rise in interest rates reduces the 'speculative demand' for money sufficient to offset the increase in the 'transactions demand' for money caused by the higher price level (A to D in figure 1.2). The demand for money is now equal to the unchanged supply of money.

As an introduction to our discussion of wealth effects in §1.4 it is worth noting that if the demand for money depends positively on the level of wealth, then an increase in wealth, which increases the demand for money, will therefore shift the LM curve to the left.

Equilibrium: Uniqueness and Stability Equilibrium in both money and goods markets is given by point A at interest rate r_0 and output Y_0 (figure 1.3). It can be shown that this equilibrium is unique. Dynamic stability requires that a small perturbation from A will result in a return to equilibrium. This can be demonstrated graphically (figure 1.3) by considering the direction of changes in r and Y that ensue in the 'four quadrants' around the equilibrium point A. When $M^d > M^s$, individuals sell bonds and interest rates rise and when $AD > Y^s$, demand and output increase. The converse also applies. These areas are marked in the four quadrants of figure 1.3 and it can be seen that the resulting direction of motion of r and Y (indicated by the broken arrows) is towards A. Hence the system is stable.[5] (See appendices 1.1 and 1.2 for a more formal exposition.)

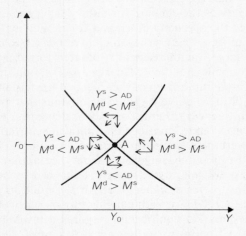

Figure 1.3 Equilibrium in the goods and money market

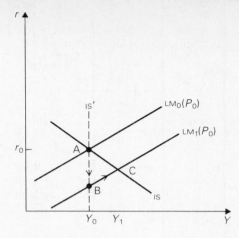

Figure 1.4 Monetary policy (impotent for $|E_r^I| = 0$ or $|E_r^M| = \infty$)

1.3 Monetary and Fiscal Policy in the IS–LM Fixed-Price Model

1.3.1 Monetary Policy

Initial equilibrium in both the goods and money market is given by point A in figure 1.4 where the interest rate is r_0 and output is Y_0. To increase the money supply by open-market operations the authorities must purchase bonds from the private sector. This requires an increase in the price of bonds, that is, a fall in the interest rate (A to B). The fall in the interest rate reduces the cost of borrowing and investment rises. Output then increases to Y_1 via the multiplier (B to C). Thus, with 'normal' IS–LM curves, monetary policy is potent and increases the equilibrium level of real output.

Monetary Policy Impotent: Inelastic Investment and the Liquidity Trap
Suppose, however, that investment did not respond to changes in the cost of borrowing. Then the fall in the interest rate would not trigger changes in investment expenditures and output. In this case we would move from A to B and the level of output would remain unchanged. The interest–inelastic investment schedule produces a vertical IS curve which passes through A and B (it is shown by the broken line IS'). Consider another special case. Suppose the interest elasticity of the demand for money (and incidentally the demand for bonds) is infinite. Under these circumstances when the government purchases bonds it need not offer a higher price (or it offers an infinitesimally higher price). The private sector is therefore willing to increase its money holdings (and reduce its bond holdings) at the existing interest rate. Under this assumption the LM curve is therefore a horizontal line passing through the point A for *all* values of the money supply. The horizontal LM curve

Table 1.1   Closed-economy fix-price IS–LM model (E_r^I is the interest elasticity of investment (absolute value) and E_r^M is the interest elasticity of the demand for money)

Policy	$E_r^I = 0$	$E_r^M = \infty$	$E_r^I = \infty$	$E_r^M = 0$	Normal elasticities
Fiscal: $\Delta G > 0$	'Full' Keynesian multiplier	'Full' Keynesian multiplier	0	0	Some crowding out, but $\Delta Y > 0$
Monetary: $\Delta M^s > 0$	0	0	'Full' money multiplier	'Full' money multiplier	$\Delta Y > 0$

implies that, for any value of the money supply, the private sector will willingly hold this money at an unchanged rate of interest r_0. This is the Keynesian *liquidity trap*. Because an increase in the money supply does not alter interest rates it does not influence investment and the level of output. The final equilibrium is the same as the initial equilibrium at A. Both the interest rate and the level of output remain unchanged. Monetary policy is therefore impotent if either the interest elasticity of investment is zero or the interest elasticity of the demand for money is infinite. These results are summarized in table 1.1.

1.3.2   Fiscal Policy: Partial Crowding Out

With normal IS–LM curves fiscal policy is effective in influencing the level of output. An increase in government expenditure increases incomes and via the multiplier leads to a higher level of output at any given interest rate (A to B in figure 1.5). This is the full 'simple' Keynesian multiplier. However, at point B we have an excess demand for money. The higher level of income at B increases the demand for transactions (money) balances. If the authorities keep the money supply fixed and there are only two assets held by the private sector then an increase in the demand for money implies that the private sector must sell bonds. An increase in bond sales with a fixed bond and money supply leads to a fall in bond prices and a rise in the interest rate. It is this rise in interest rate that reduces the speculative demand for money so demand again equals the fixed supply. However the rise in the interest rate leads to a fall in investment and output (B to C). Thus government expenditure is partially *crowded out* by a fall in private expenditure and the final equilibrium is at Y_2. The degree of crowding out could be measured by the ratio of 'distances' $Y_2 Y_1$ to $Y_0 Y_1$. In this case, crowding out occurs entirely because of changes in *demand* via the interest rate mechanism, and so is often referred to as financial crowding-out.

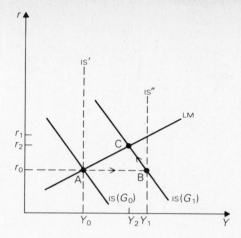

Figure 1.5   Fiscal policy, partial crowding out and a 'full' Keynesian multiplier

Full Keynesian Fiscal Multipliers   Assume the demand for money is infinitely interest-elastic. The LM curve is then a horizontal line through AB (figure 1.5). Because the interest rate is unchanged the full Keynesian multiplier prevails and there is no crowding out. The final equilibrium is point B.

If investment is interest-inelastic (the lines IS' and IS" in figure 1.5) but we also have a normal upward-sloping LM curve, then the final equilibrium is also at a level of output Y_1 although the interest rate will be higher at r_1. At output Y_1, money market equilibrium still requires a rise in the interest rate. However, if investment is interest-inelastic the rise will not reduce the level of investment and therefore Y_1 is the final equilibrium level of output. In terms of the diagram the vertical IS curve moves from IS' to IS".

To summarize our results so far, we note that monetary policy is impotent when either investment is interest-inelastic or when the demand for money is infinitely interest-elastic (the liquidity trap). Such conditions are precisely those under which fiscal policy has a full Keynesian multiplier effect and there is no crowding out (table 1.1).

1.3.3   Other Special Cases

Fiscal Policy Impotent: Monetary Policy Potent   The question arises as to whether there are circumstanes in which fiscal policy is impotent yet monetary policy is effective in influencing output. It is not surprising that the conditions under which fiscal policy is impotent are the reverse of those under which monetary policy is impotent. Thus, fiscal policy is impotent if the interest elasticity of the demand for money is zero (inelastic) or if the interest elasticity of investment is infinite (table 1.1).

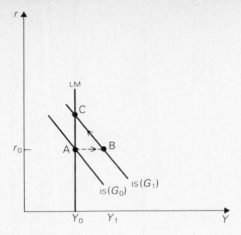

Figure 1.6   Fiscal policy impotent, $E_r^M = 0$ (full crowding out)

Full Crowding Out   Consider the case of a zero interest elasticity of the demand for money, $E_r^M = 0$ (figure 1.6). An increase in government expenditure initially expands output to Y_1 and increases the transactions demand for money. If the money supply is fixed the speculative demand for money must fall. If the interest elasticity of the demand for money is small it takes a large change in the interest rate to reduce the speculative demand. Therefore, at point B (figure 1.6) it takes a large rise in the interest rate to equate the supply and demand for money. The large rise in the interest rate due to changes in the money market causes a large fall in investment expenditure which completely *crowds out* government expenditure (B to C). The final equilibrium level of output is unchanged. (The composition of output has changed: there is a higher level of government expenditure and an equal fall in private investment.) Diagrammatically this case is represented by a vertical LM curve, the final equilibrium point being C.

The Full Money Multiplier   When $E_r^M = 0$ output is completely determined by the money supply and the income elasticity of the demand for money, $\Delta Y = (1/m_y)\Delta(M^s/P)$. Monetary policy is therefore potent and the 'full' money multiplier $1/m_y$ applies (figure 1.7).

The transmission mechanism in this case is not entirely transparent (figure 1.7). Since the money supply does not directly appear in the expenditure functions (and the IS curve) and *initially* the interest rate does not have to fall to equate the supply and demand for money, how does the rise in output occur? Diagrammatically, we note that the interest rate does fall and hence investment expenditures are higher but this does not really tell us how this comes about. Some economists add some elementary dynamics to the IS curve to model this process. The resulting models are often referred to as

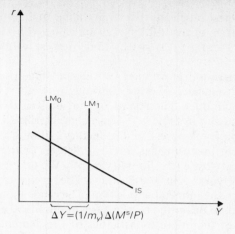

Figure 1.7 Monetary policy potent, $E_r^M = 0$ and a 'full' money multiplier

'disequilibrium monetary models'. The *change* in demand (or output) is determined by 'excess money' and the IS curve becomes

$$\Delta Y_t = Y(r_t, Y_t) + \gamma \left[\left(\frac{M}{P}\right)^s_t - \left(\frac{M}{P}\right)^d_t \right] .$$

The term $Y(r_t, Y_t)$ is the static IS curve. Hence disequilibrium money triggers off the *change* in output and when output reaches its new higher level the money market is again in equilibrium ($M^s/P = M^d/P$). Empirically this type of approach has worked reasonably well (see, for example, Laidler et al. (1980) and Davidson (1984) for the UK, Laidler et al. (1983) for Canada and Laidler and Bentley (1983) for the US). Without the 'disequilibrium money' scenario, we can merely note that output *must* rise for money market equilibrium and, given that G (and X) are exogenous, this can only be triggered off by a fall in the interest rate and a rise in investment expenditures.

More for the sake of completeness than economic realism we consider the case of an infinitely elastic demand for investment goods. In the normal IS/LM case an increase in government expenditure puts upward pressure on interest rates in order to maintain money market equilibrium (see point C in figure 1.5). If investment is infinitely elastic this modest rise in the interest rate will reduce investment by a large amount. In fact for $|E_r^I| = \infty$, government expenditure is completely crowded out by the fall in private investment. Diagrammatically the IS curve is horizontal and does not alter when government expenditure exchanges.

With an infinite elasticity of investment it is easy to see that monetary policy will be highly effective in influencing output. With a normal LM curve an increase in the money supply requires a fall in the interest rate (at any given level of output) to maintain equilibrium in the money market. If $|E_r^I| = \infty$, this fall in the interest rate leads to a large change in investment expenditure. Output rises by effect of the 'full' money multiplier. This is easily seen using equations (1.9) and (1.10) with the interest rate held constant, $\Delta Y = (1/m_y)\Delta(M^s/P)$.

In our verbal description we have introduced some pseudo-dynamics by implying a causal sequence of events, although strictly speaking our model is a timeless static model. The results of our analysis of the simple IS–LM model are summarized in table 1.1. If we characterize Keynesians with the view that fiscal policy is potent and monetary policy is impotent then this requires either that investment is interest-inelastic or that the demand for money is infinitely elastic (the liquidity trap). (We take up this point again when discussing Keynes versus the Classics). The reverse applies for our crude characterization of the monetarist position. The crude monetarist–Keynesian debate is therefore to be settled on the basis of empirical evidence about the relative strength of the interest elasticities of the demands for money and for investment goods. On the latter the evidence is rather ambiguous and on the former it is difficult to establish; however, there is ample evidence to suggest that the interest elasticity of the demand for money is neither zero nor infinite (see, for example, Cuthbertson 1985).

There is an alternative method of resolving the monetarist–Keynesian debate as set out above. With normal IS–LM curves the equilibrium level of real output is determined solely by exogenous changes in fiscal policy instruments (government expenditure and tax rates and allowances) and the exogenous money supply (appendix 1.1). A regression of output on the real money supply (M^s/P) and real government expenditure should provide statistically significant coefficients on both variables if the normal IS–LM model is correct. In the extreme Keynesian case the coefficient on government expenditure is expected to be large and that on the (real) money supply zero. The converse would be expected to apply for the monetarist case (although as we shall see, after adding an aggregate supply curve, monetarists would expect the *real* output effect of changes in M^s to be zero in the long run).[6] Empirical tests on such reduced-form models to discriminate between the two extreme positions are frequently undertaken although interpretation of results is fraught with difficulties and this evidence cannot be said to have resolved this particular debate (see inter alia Anderson and Jordan 1969, Sims 1972, Matthews and Ormerod 1978, Goodhart et al. 1976).

1.4   Real Balance and Wealth Effects

A limitation of the simple closed-economy model analysed above is that it fails to consider the possibility that the (real) stock of assets held by agents might have a *direct* effect on expenditures and hence on the IS curve. In addition, the demand for money (and bonds) is likely to depend on the level of wealth (e.g. as the risk-aversion model of Tobin 1958) and hence changes in the latter will influence the position of the LM curve and the equilibrium level of output in our fix-price model. Clearly, if the above conjectures are correct our model must be amended to take account of equilibrium in the holding of asset stocks. If we consider all financial wealth as being held in either 'money' or 'bonds', then how might wealth (in the aggregate) alter? Within the private sector, *as a whole*, there can be no generation of additional wealth except in real capital assets (e.g. houses, plant, machinery and buildings) and the 'equity claims' on these real assets (e.g. receipts of dividends). For simplicity we rule out this source of growth in real wealth.

If some agents within the private sector issue bonds that are purchased in exchange for money by other members of the private sector, then total wealth is unchanged. A similar argument applies if a member of the private sector borrows money (i.e. bank deposits) in the form of a bank advance (a liability). His or her *net* worth (wealth) is unchanged. Since we are in a closed economy the only possible source of *additional* money or bonds comes from the authorities. The mechanism takes place via the budget deficit which must be financed by either issuing money (cheques) or selling bonds to the non-bank private sector (NBPS).[7] The consequence of introducing 'wealth effects' into the IS–LM model is to alter radically the short-run and long-run impact of monetary and fiscal policy. In addition it is possible that financing a budget deficit by bond issues may lead to a cumulative fall in output with the latter having no long-run equilibrium level. Wealth effects arising from the government budget constraint also provide an analytic model that is consistent with the 'monetarist' view that a budget deficit caused by a fiscal expansion (say), coupled with a fixed-money-supply policy (to control inflation) will lead to ever-spiralling interest rates and hence full crowding out of government expenditure. (This mechanism as we shall see does not require a vertical IS curve as in our 'simple' IS–LM model.) This policy result is often presented in general terms as 'you cannot spend your way out of a recession'. In an *open economy* this argument applies *a fortiori* because of exchange rate overshooting (see chapter 5). Given a fixed monetary target a corollary of the above is that to avoid a destabilizing fall in output, the budget should be in balance over a run of years. Fiscal policy becomes subordinate to the monetary target, and 'sound finance' becomes the order of the day. This general philosophy has gained much credence in the latter half of the 1970s and in the 1980s.

A simple example of a wealth effect concerns the impact that changes in the price *level* may have on the *real* value of money holdings. This is the 'real balance' or 'Pigou effect' (Pigou 1943), which we now describe.

Suppose agents consider the money supply,[8] as part of wealth and that *real* money balances (M^s/P) have a direct effect on (consumers') expenditure. If the authorities increase the nominal money supply (without altering the other component of wealth, bond holdings) and the price level is fixed, then aggregate demand will increase, and the IS curve shifts to the right. This is known as the 'real (money) balance' or Pigou effect. As we shall see in §1.5 it provides one riposte to Keynes's critique of the classical assertion of an automatic full-employment equilibrium.

1.4.1   The Government Budget Constraint

In this section we consider wealth effects that arise solely from the government budget constraint in a fix-price closed-economy model.

The normal IS–LM, closed-economy, fiscal multiplier is unlikely to constitute the long-run equilibrium of the system. After an exogenous increase in government expenditure (i.e. an unbalanced budget expansion) the higher level of tax payments, consequent on the higher level of output, falls short of the increase in government expenditure. At C in figure 1.5 there is a *permanent* budget deficit which is financed by continuously issuing bonds to the NBPS. The deficit cannot be financed by increases in money since the 'normal' IS–LM analysis assumes that the money supply under fiscal policy remains fixed. Thus the NBPS are assumed to be willing to acquire bonds continuously at an *unchanged interest rate* r_2 (if C in figure 1.5 really is the equilibrium position) even though the ratio of bonds to money approaches infinity in the long run. Also, if interest-bearing government bonds are considered by the NBPS to be net wealth, then the equilibrium at C involves a continuous increase in the ratio of the stock of financial wealth to expenditure (or output), *without any repercussions on expenditure decisions*.[9]

If bonds are net wealth for the NBPS then the normal IS–LM equilibrium at C assumes that the wealth coefficient in the demand for bonds is unity and in the demand for money is zero. A more plausible assumption is that wealth influences both the demand for money and the demand for bonds, as well as influencing expenditure decisions. However, there are ways in which the normal IS–LM equilibrium at C (figure 1.5) can be considered a full equilibrium (for a closed economy), although these rather special cases would not necessarily occur in practice. First, for a balanced budget fiscal change, $\Delta G = \Delta T$, there is no change in wealth and therefore there are no wealth effects to consider. C in figure 1.5 is a full equilibrium even if the demand for money and expenditure functions depend on wealth. Second, if a budget deficit is financed by bonds and money in such proportions as to satisfy the increased *demand* for bonds and money, consequent on this increase in wealth, then there would be no tendency for interest rates to change because of asset market disequilibrium. If, in addition, there are no wealth effects in the expenditure function, and IS and LM curves would not shift due to this change in wealth and the 'normal' IS–LM equilibrium at C would be a long-run equilibrium, even in the presence of wealth effects. This second 'special case' seems most unlikely to occur in practice and balanced budgets are somewhat of a rarity even over a run of years. Other than for the rather special cases discussed above, the need to 'finance' a budget deficit leads to wealth effects and a different equilibrium position to the normal IS–LM closed-economy case. Again when dealing with wealth effects, the number of possible combinations of different assumptions is enormous. We shall limit the number considered. Our preliminary assumptions are as follows.

1   Expenditure and the demand for money depend positively upon wealth. Wealth must be held in some financial asset: either bonds or money in our simple model. The life cycle hypothesis assumes that consumption depends on net wealth (Ando and Modigliani 1963).
2   Government bonds (and money) are considered to be net wealth by the NBPS. The NBPS, therefore, does not believe (or take into account) that 'bond wealth' will be reduced by future tax liabilities to pay for higher total coupon payments consequent on a higher stock of bonds.[9]
3   Money refers to high-powered money, that is, a liability of the monetary authorities. Money held as deposits that are not backed by high-powered money have a liability counterpart, for the NBPS (mostly bank advances) and do not form part of (net) wealth.
4   We ignore any influence of changes in *physical* wealth, due to real investment. We can either assume these are small in relation to the outstanding stock or that the 'wealth effects' in the expenditure and demand for money functions depend only on net *financial* wealth.
5   We ignore the change in wealth caused by *changes* in interest rates and the price of marketable (long-term) debt. Such valuation changes do not affect 'long-run' results where interest rates are constant by definition.
6   Unless otherwise stated we ignore interest payments (net of income tax receipts) on the outstanding stock of bonds. We assume these interest receipts are offset by changes in government transfers, so there is no net change in *incomes* of the NBPS from this source.
7   The price level is exogenous and fixed (although we can allow parametric changes in the price level) and hence we ignore the 'inflation loss' on the outstanding stock of government debt held by the NBPS.[10]

1.4.2   Unbalanced Budget Expansion

We begin at A in figure 1.8 in full equilibrium; the budget is balanced $G_0 = T(Y_0)$ and therefore wealth is constant and the IS and LM curves are stationary. An unbalanced budget expansion caused by an increase in government expenditure, G, leads to a 'normal' IS–LM temporary equilibrium at B in figure 1.8. At B we have a higher level of output and a budget deficit with wealth therefore increasing. We now demonstrate that pure bond or mixed money–bond financing *may* lead to instability (no equilibrium level of output being attained) whereas money financing produces a stable system.

Instability and Bond Finance   Pure bond financing leaves the money supply unchanged but increases the demand for money as wealth, W, increases (in the form of a higher outstanding bond stock). The LM curve shifts to the left and *for a given IS curve* (through B) output tends to fall (to C) as interest rates rise to maintain equilibrium in the money market. However, the increase in wealth also shifts the IS curve to the right tending to increase output (C to D). If the *net* effect of these two wealth effects is negative, that is output falls from Y_B to Y_D, then bond financing is unstable. The fall in

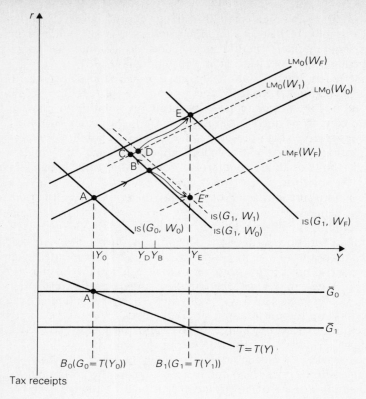

Figure 1.8 Unbalanced budget fiscal expansion (E = bond finance, E'' = money finance)

output to Y_D reduces income tax receipts, $T = T(Y)$, and increases the budget deficit, reinforcing the contractionary 'negative' wealth effects described above and output falls continuously. The negative wealth effect is more likely, the larger the wealth coefficient in the demand for money relative to that on expenditure. It is therefore important to establish the size of the wealth elasticity of the demand for money and expenditure, empirically.

Unless stated otherwise we shall from now on assume that bond-financed deficits have a 'positive' wealth effect on output – that is, the positive wealth effect in the IS curve exceeds the negative wealth effect on the demand for money and from Y_B we move to a higher level of output. Tax receipts are therefore higher than at B, the budget deficit and the increase in wealth are attenuated until we reach the long-run equilibrium at Y_E where the budget is again balanced (with higher G and T) and the change in wealth is again zero.

Money-Financed Deficit   For a money-financed deficit arising from the unbalanced budget expansionary policy, the wealth effect on output is always positive. The increase in the money supply outweighs the increase in the wealth-induced rise in the demand for money, given the plausible assumption $\partial M^d/\partial W < 1$. The LM curve at B therefore shifts to the right (LM_F) along with the IS curve and output rises, raising tax receipts. The budget deficit becomes smaller and the wealth effects are attenuated as output reaches its new higher equilibrium value (B→E''). Clearly *mixed* money and bond finance could be unstable, although instability is less likely than under pure bond finance.

1.4.3   Methods of Financing the Deficit

We now digress for a moment to consider the literature in chronological order and analyse whether the *method of financing* deficits influences the *size* of the output multiplier (Christ 1968). Note that *without wealth effects* in the IS–LM curves, a bond-financed deficit gives the 'normal' equilibrium at B (figure 1.8) but a purely money-financed deficit gives a higher level of output as the LM curve shifts to the right. Ignoring the fact that this 'normal' equilibrium is implausible (see above) this appears to show that money-financed deficits are more expansionary than bond-financed deficits. Thus in the 'normal' IS–LM model the size of the unbalanced budget fiscal multiplier *does depend* upon the method of financing the deficit.

With the inclusion of wealth effects (but ignoring interest payments) we can show that the size of the fiscal multiplier is *independent* of the method of finance (Christ 1968). In long-run equilibrium, wealth must be constant and therefore the budget must balance (we assume we start from a balanced budget position); hence

$$dG - t_y\, dY = 0 \qquad\qquad\qquad (1.11)$$
$$dY/dG = 1/t_y \qquad\qquad\qquad (1.12)$$

The multiplier is equal to $1/t_y$ regardless of the bond–money mix used in financing the deficit. This is shown in figure 1.8, where in the lower quadrant we have taxes as a positive function of income and government expenditure, exogenous. The final equilibrium at Y_E must lie on the balanced budget line $B_1(.)$. Wealth effects ensure the IS and LM curves eventually intersect at the level of output Y_E. For pure bond financing the LM curve shifts to the left and the final equilibrium is at E above the original LM curve; the converse applies for pure money finance where the final equilibrium could be at a point such as E'' (below and to the right of the temporary equilibrium at B).

Let us now make the model more realistic (and more complex) by introducing *net interest payments into the budget constraint* while still retaining our wealth effects. In such circumstances a bond-financed deficit increases the stock of bonds and thus interest payments on the debt, whereas a money-financed deficit does not. Interest payments increase (interest) *income* and hence aggregate demand. Thus under these conditions a bond-financed deficit (if stable) is more expansionary than a money-financed deficit (Blinder and Solow 1973), and the method of financing is again an important determinant of the long-run level of output.[11]

Our main conclusions from this discussion of fiscal policy are threefold. First, in a model with debt interest payments endogenous, the method chosen to finance the deficit influences the value of the fiscal multiplier. Second, an unbalanced budget expansion has different output effects from a balanced budget expansion (which gives rise to no wealth effects in a closed economy). Third, bond financing or 'mixed financing' may give rise to instability. These conclusions, which are specific to the above model, remain true in more complex models as we shall see below.

1.4.4   Monetary Policy in a Closed Economy with Wealth Effects

To simplify matters we revert to our simplifying assumption that interest payments are offset by changes in government transfer payments. Since the long-run output multiplier is determined entirely by the government budget constraint $(dG - dT = 0)$, it follows that pure monetary policy is impotent (figure 1.9). Assuming bonds as well as money are considered as net wealth, an open-market purchase of bonds to increase the money supply ($LM_0 (W_0)$ to ($LM_1 (W_0)$)) does not directly alter net wealth. The expansion of output in the normal IS–LM model (A to B in figure 1.9) yields increased tax receipts, a budget surplus and hence a fall in wealth at B. If wealth effects are 'positive', the fall in wealth leads to a shift to the left in the IS curve to $IS(W')$ and a shift to the right in the LM curve to $LM_1 (W')$ and a fall in output. The fall in output continues until C is reached, where $G_0 = T(Y_A)$ at the initial

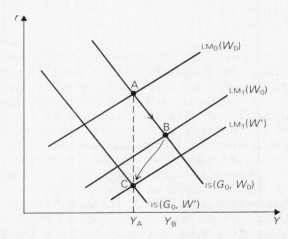

Figure 1.9   Monetary policy impotent with 'wealth effects' $(W' < W_0, M_1 > M_0)$

level of output. Monetary policy is therefore impotent when wealth effects are added to the IS–LM closed-economy model.

1.4.5 Conclusions for Wealth Effects and the Government Budget Constraint

For a fix-price closed-economy model our conclusions are that with wealth effects, an unbalanced-budget, bond-financed fiscal expansion, if stable, is more powerful than in the 'normal' IS–LM model. The converse applies for pure monetary policy which has a zero multiplier when wealth effects are included (and government bonds are considered as net wealth). The real balance or Pigou effect is a simplified 'wealth effect' in which only money is considered as wealth (i.e. government bonds are *not* net wealth) and 'wealth effects' only occur in the expenditure function (the IS curve).

The above are all long-run results for a closed-economy fix-price model and are therefore somewhat unrealistic. In the *short run* it is quite possible that monetary policy in the form of an open-market operation influences output. Also, if government bonds are *not* net wealth then an open-market purchase of bonds will yield a positive money multiplier even in the long run. Finally, note that an unbalanced-budget fiscal expansion financed by an increase in the money supply or, if wealth effects are positive, by an increase in bond sales, is expansionary. All of our analysis so far in this chapter assumes a fix-price world, an assumption we now relax.

1.5 The Supply Side: an Introduction

So far, our macromodels have been 'demand side' models: firms willingly supply any level of output demanded at the going fixed price level even though it may be unprofitable to do so because of rising costs of production. In the very short term this may be a realistic assumption. Firms sell part of their stocks of finished goods as demand rises and then expand production to replenish stock levels. However, if firms face rising marginal costs of production, and are profit maximizers in perfect competition, then additional 'supply' will only be forthcoming at a higher price level. Once we recognize the possibility of independent supply decisions then equilibrium in the goods market depends on the equality of planned supply and planned demand: the former no longer acts passively to changes in the latter.

In this section we discuss the impact of monetary and fiscal policy under different assumptions about the shape of the aggregate supply (AS) curve. Our model determines equilibrium price and output. We are able to demonstrate the conditions necessary for the neutrality proposition to hold and to discuss possible impediments to 'automatic full employment'. The Keynes versus the Classics debate and the neoclassical synthesis are also analysed. We wish to concentrate on the systems aspects – that is, the interaction between supply and demand factors. We therefore present a schematic account of the AS curve and reserve our detailed analysis of the various interpretations of this function for §1.7, on the Phillips curve.

1.5.1   *IS–LM, the Price Level and the Aggregate Demand Curve*

We must now consider the IS–LM construct as determining planned *demand* (aggregate demand); the latter depends on variations in the price level (as well as government expenditure and the money supply). Changes in the price level affect aggregate demand directly (i.e. the IS curve) via the real balance effect and indirectly via the demand for money and the money market (§1.2). A rise in the price level (*ceteris paribus*) leads to a fall in aggregate demand as the LM and IS curves both shift to the left. Hence the AD curve in figure 1.10 is negatively sloped. It shifts to the right when there is an increase in the money supply or government expenditure, if the IS and LM curves have their normal slope (A to B in figure 1.10).

The multipliers analysed above for the fixed-price IS–LM model are likely to be smaller if an expansion in demand involves a rise in the price level (A to B to C in figure 1.10). Thus even with 'normal' IS–LM curves the impact of policy on output *depends crucially on the behaviour of the price level*. Initially we assume that the rate of change in the price level is determined by excess demand (i.e. a type of Phillips curve):

$$\Delta P = \alpha(\text{AD} - \text{AS}) \qquad \alpha > 0 \qquad (1.13)$$

where AD is (desired) aggregate demand and AS the desired supply. Equilibrium, with no change in the price level (and hence in output via the shifting LM curve), therefore ensues when AD = AS.

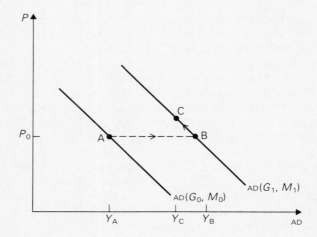

Figure 1.10   The aggregate demand curve

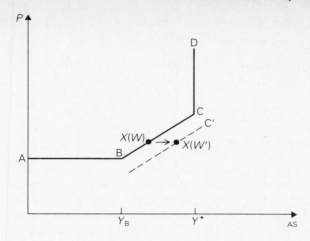

Figure 1.11   The aggregate supply curve

1.5.2   *Alternative Aggregate Supply Curves*

The first point to note about our theory of supply is that we assume a one-to-one (technical) relationship between labour input and output supplied. This is the production function. Profit-maximizing firms in perfect competition have a representative supply curve (the marginal cost curve) given by ABCD (in figure 1.11). Along the portions AB and BC we assume that factor prices (e.g. nominal wages) are constant. Along AB, firms have constant returns to scale; they can double output by doubling all inputs, which with fixed factor prices implies average variable costs are constant (and equal to marginal cost). They are willing to supply output to a level Y_B at a constant price level and still earn 'normal' profits. This is the implicit assumption about 'supply' used in our fix-price model.

Along BC, firms face fixed factor prices but there is diminishing marginal productivity of labour and hence marginal costs of production rise. Firms therefore require an 'incentive' of a higher price level before they will *supply* more output. Hence the *real* wage (W/P) falls as we move along BC and is equal to the falling marginal physical product of labour. The supply curve BC is therefore directly related to the *demand*-for-labour schedule for a perfectly competitive firm.

If the firm is at $X(W)$ and there is a fall in the nominal wage to W' but prices remain constant then this fall in the real wage (or increase in the profit margin P/W) will lead to an increase in the demand for labour and an increase in the supply of output to $X(W')$. This is nothing more than a shift to the right in the marginal cost curve as nominal wages (factor prices) fall. The portion of the AS curve 'ABC' may be considered as the horizontal summation of individual firm's marginal cost curves. The mathematics of this portion of the AS curve is simply that firms choose labour input L to maximize profits, Π:

$$\max \Pi = PY(K,L) - WL - RK \tag{1.14}$$
$$P\,\partial Y/\partial L - W = 0 \tag{1.14a}$$

or

$$P = W\,\partial L/\partial Y \equiv \mathrm{MC} \tag{1.14b}$$

or

$$W/P = \partial Y/\partial L = \mathrm{MPP}_L \tag{1.14c}$$

where $Y(K,L)$ is the production function depending upon the capital stock K and labour input L, and where W is the nominal wage rate and R the rental price of capital. The first-order conditions yields either equality of price and marginal cost or equivalently equality of the real wage and the marginal physical product of labour. If the latter is assumed to be a decreasing function of the level of labour input we have a downward-sloping curve (BC in figure 1.12). If the marginal product of labour is constant, then as labour input varies we have the portion of the curve AB. The portion ABC of the aggregate supply curve (figure 1.11) corresponds to the portion ABC of the demand-for-labour schedule (figure 1.12). One is the mirror image of the other, as they are linked via the production function. Note also that the section of the AS curve labelled ABC could be labelled 'Keynesian' since we assume fixed money wages.

So far we have discussed only the demand for labour. To complete our analysis and derive the *neoclassical* supply curve (the portion CD in figure 1.11) we need to add the supply curve for labour and an assumption of perfectly flexible wages and prices.

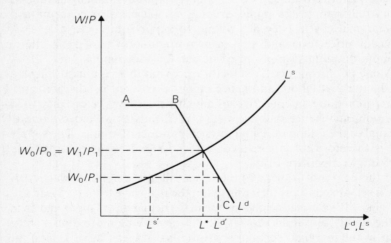

Figure 1.12   Demand and supply of labour in the neoclassical model (W/P is the real wage)

The Supply of Labour   The simplest static neoclassical theory of labour supply has each individual maximizing utility, which depends positively on leisure hours (per week, say) and income from work (in the current period only). As usual in such models, diminishing marginal utility from leisure and income is assumed. The constraint is that work-hours plus leisure-hours per week cannot exceed a fixed amount (e.g. 90 hours per week if six non-leisure-hours of sleep are required per day and there are only five (working) days per week). The nominal wage rate is exogenous to the individual. The second constraint (or budget identity) is that real income is equal to the real wage rate multiplied by hours worked.

Interest usually centres on the response of hours worked (i.e. labour supply) to an increase in the real wage. *A priori*, this effect is ambiguous, depending on the strength of the 'income' and 'substitution effects'. A higher real wage increases the cost (in terms of goods foregone) of an additional hour of leisure and hence individuals tend to substitute work for leisure. However, with a higher hourly wage rate the individual can earn more income for an unchanged level of hours worked. The individual is better off in real terms and if leisure is a 'normal good' this will tend to reduce work hours. In the short run it is usual to assume that the substitution effect outweighs the income effect, so the real wage and *desired* labour supply (i.e. hours worked) are positively related.

For those in work who have a fixed minimum working week the model as it stands determines overtime hours. Potential new entrants to the labour force (e.g. married women, the self-employed) should also respond to changes in the real wage. An exogenous change in wealth is likely to reduce labour supply as it generates a pure 'income effect' (which we assume is positive). Other exogenous influences on labour supply such as population growth and sociological factors such as attitudes to working wives may also shift the labour supply curve.

The model can be extended in a number of ways. Income tax is easily incorporated into the model: the supply curve shifts *to the left* when (i) the income tax rate increases (strictly speaking pivots to the left); (ii) the absolute level of welfare benefits increases (an income effect); (iii) when *means tested* benefits increase for a given wage rate – this involves the usual substitution and income effects; (iv) increases in government expenditure lower the cost of activities that are complementary to leisure time (e.g. subsidized entertainment).

A neoclassical *intertemporal* model in which individuals maximize current and *future* income and leisure yields richer results (Killingsworth 1983, Lucas and Rapping 1969). In particular a temporary increase in wage rates gives a larger short-run increase in the labour supply than arises from an equal permanent increase in wages. However we do not explore this approach further.

1.5.3   Market Clearing, the Neoclassical Labour Market and Aggregate Supply

The key assumptions of the neoclassical labour market are that (i) the supply of labour is positively related to the real wage (*ceteris paribus*); (ii) the demand for labour is determined in a perfectly competitive environment where firms face fixed factor prices (the demand for labour is negatively related to the real wage, is independent of the level of output (or expected output) and only shifts when labour productivity alters); (iii) wages and prices are perfectly flexible and move to eliminate excess demand in the market.

With perfectly flexible wages and prices the labour market 'clears', in that all those who wish to work at the equilibrium real wage rate $(W/P)_0$ (figure 1.12) may do so; in this sense there is 'full employment'. However, in this neoclassical model there may still be people classified as unemployed because they voluntarily leave employment to devote more 'search time' to obtaining information on wage rates and general job prospects. This frictional or structural unemployment means that in general there will be a positive 'natural rate' of unemployment even when the labour market is in equilibrium; this 'search unemployment' is voluntary. With a welfare benefits system, some (unskilled) workers may find it more conducive to be unemployed rather than work for wages that are little greater than the level of benefits. Again there are no involuntary unemployed.

Neoclassical Supply Curve   In the neoclassical model of the labour market a sudden increase in the price level leads to a fall in the real wage (to W_0/P_1, figure 1.12), an excess demand for labour and a tendency for the *nominal* wage rate to rise and restore the real wage to its initial equilibrium level $(W_1/P_1 = W_0/P_0)$ and labour utilization to L^*. Hence, via the production function, output remains at Y^* (figure 1.11) and the neoclassical supply curve in $P-Y$ space is vertical in the long run (CD in figure 1.11). This arises because of the assumption of perfectly flexible wages and prices and hence market clearing in the labour market.

Another key factor to bear in mind concerning the neoclassical supply function is that it is independent of monetary and fiscal policy; changes in

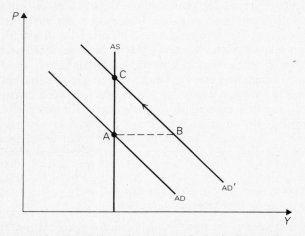

Figure 1.13   Neutrality of money and physical crowding out

the money supply and government expenditure do not affect the position or slope of the neoclassical AS curve (we return to the question of taxes below).[12]

Superimposing our neoclassical AS curve with the AD curve (figure 2.13) makes it clear that in this neoclassical world output is supply determined. Changes in AD merely result in changes in the price level and this is the origin of the neutrality of money.

1.5.4 Neutrality of Money

An increase in the money supply shifts the AD (and LM) curve to the right to AD' (figure 1.13). Excess demand for goods causes an equiproportionate rise in the price level (and the LM curve shifts back to its original position). The money supply affects only nominal variables such as the price level and does not influence real output. This is sometimes termed the 'classical dichotomy' – all real variables are determined on the real side of the economy, leaving only nominal variables to be determined on the financial side (i.e. in the money market).

Physical Crowding Out   An increase in government expenditure also causes excess demand (at B in figure 1.13) which again raises the price level and the demand for money (so the LM curve shifts to the left). The rise in interest rates (as the LM curve shifts to the left) leads to a fall in investment and output. The final equilibrium is at C with unchanged output, a higher interest rate and a higher price level. (The rise in the interest rate offsets the increase in the demand for money caused by the higher price level such that money demand equals the unchanged money supply in the final equilibrium.)

Here an increase in government expenditure is completely 'crowded out' by a fall in private investment caused by the induced rise in the interest rate which is itself a consequence of the rise in the price level (and wages) in the neoclassical labour market. This is often referred to as *physical crowding out*. (It does not depend on the shape of the IS curve, unlike 'financial' crowding out.)

There are physical limits to the possible increase in *real* government expenditure but the money supply is easily increased (and may increase as a consequence of budget deficits). This is the origin of the assertion that a *continuous* rise in the price level – that is inflation – is 'always and everywhere a monetary phenomenon' (Friedman 1968).

Further Aspects of the Neoclassical Model   If money is neutral and government expenditure is crowded out then what causes changes in output in the long run in the neoclassical model? The equilibrium level of output (often called the 'natural rate' alters only if the supply or demand curves for labour shift, which, in turn, via the production function, leads to shifts in the vertical aggregate supply curve.

For example, an increase in labour productivity increases aggregate supply (shifts the demand curve for labour to the right) as does a cut in employers' taxes on labour (e.g. national insurance contributions). Increases in labour supply might be brought about by a cut in income tax rates or a cut in unemployment benefits and this in turn shifts the aggregate supply curve to the right.

Notice that here fiscal policy in the form of tax cuts only affects output to the extent that it affects supply decisions made by firms. It is not the *demand* effects of tax cuts that are important in a neoclassical world. To re-establish labour market equilibrium, the increase in labour supply leads to a fall in wages and prices (and the real wage) and it is the fall in the price level that stimulates *demand* via the money market (LM shifts to the right) and any real balance effects. Hence, it is not the change in disposable income and the multiplier that is of importance but the supply response of firms (and workers). If supply decisions determine output and the rate of growth in the money supply determines the rate of inflation, what influences the interest rate in this neoclassical world?

A *step* increase in the money supply of x per cent leads to a change of x per cent in the price *level* which restores money market equilibrium. Hence there is no change in the interest rate (point A in figure 1.14). Since the price level is constant at its new higher level this implies no change in the real interest rate. (The *real* interest rate is the nominal rate less the (expected) rate of inflation.) Hence, again, the money supply does not influence real variables. The interest rate in a non-inflationary world is determined by the intersection of the IS curve and the vertical neoclassical aggregate supply curve (figure 1.14). It is therefore determined by the 'real' factors that influence the positions of these curves. For example, an increase in real government expenditure will raise the equilibrium real interest rate to r_1 (figure 1.14). On the IS curve planned saving equals planned investment and hence the

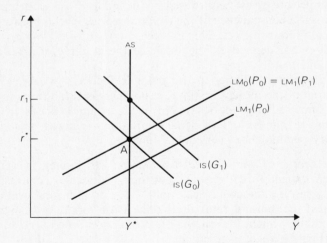

Figure 1.14 The determination of the interest rate in the neoclassical (full-employment) model

(real) interest rate is determined by 'loanable funds' (and is *not* influenced by 'Keynesian' liquidity preference and the money market).

With a constant growth in the money supply and hence constant inflation the *nominal* rate of interest, in a neoclassical world, will move one-for-one with the (perfectly anticipated) rate of inflation (the hypothesis of Fisher (1911)). The *real* rate of interest will therefore remain constant and independent of the money supply, in line with the 'classical dichotomy'.

1.6 Automatic Full Employment?

The debate between Keynes and the Classical economists over the possibility of automatic full employment may be conducted at two broad levels of generality. The first accepts the neoclassical assumption of perfectly flexible wages and prices; the second assumes that nominal wages are sticky in a downward direction. For both strands of the argument we accept the neoclassical labour demand and labour supply schedules.

Consider the neoclassical case. With perfectly flexible wages and prices, and the 'normal' IS–LM curves which underlie the AD curve, full-employment equilibrium exists, at Y^* (figure 1.15). If demand falls to AD' (say due to a fall in private investment expenditure) then at a price level P^*, desired supply exceeds aggregate demand (by an amount $Y_B Y^*$). The latter causes prices to fall and as the *real* money supply increases demand rises along BC (i.e. the IS and LM curves (real balance effect) move to the right), restoring full employment without any change in fiscal or monetary policy by the authorities.

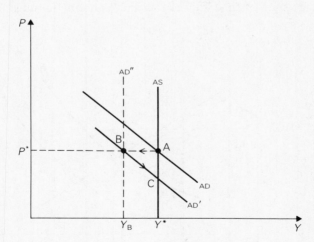

Figure 1.15 Automatic full employment: the neoclassical model, perfectly flexible wages and prices

One argument contradicting this scenario is to assume (i) there is no real balance effect *and* either (ii) the IS curve is vertical (i.e. interest-inelastic investment) at some under-employment level of output or (iii) the demand for money is infinitely interest-elastic (the liquidity trap) at the current under-employment level of output.

In case (ii) the fall in the interest rate consequent on the increase in the real money supply does not alter the level of demand (figure 1.4) (and the AD curve AD″ is vertical at a level of output Y_B; figure 1.15). Excess supply (of $Y_B Y^*$) persists indefinitely. A similar argument applies in the liquidity trap case where an increase in the real money supply leads to no change in the interest rate and hence no stimulus to investment demand (again the AD is vertical through B). Even if we have cases (i) and (ii) we can reassert the tenet of automatic full employment by adding a real balance or Pigou effect. Falling prices then shift the IS curve to the right, raising demand (this is reflected in the negative slope BC of the AD curve AD′ of figure 1.15) to the full-employment level of output Y^*.

Thus, with perfectly flexible prices (and wages) the neoclassical model (with the Pigou effect) firmly establishes the existence of an automatic full-employment level of output. Even without the Pigou effect, failure to attain full employment rests on Keynes's two 'pathological' cases of the 'liquidity trap' and inelastic investment expenditure. For those not steeped in recent economic history the debate may seem a little rarified, having little to do with the 'real world'. To some extent this insight is correct. Nevertheless, it is clearly of importance to establish the conditions for the existence of a unique full-employment market equilibrium level of output. That said, we are still left with the major problem of determining whether such an equilibrium is stable and the time path between equilibrium positions, including the length of time it takes to achieve automatic full employment.

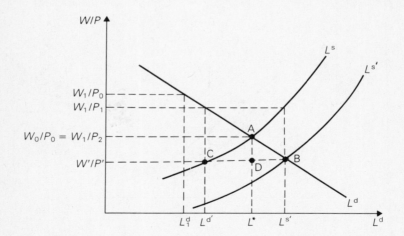

Figure 1.16 Supply and demand for labour (W/P is the real wage)

It is in this context that it is now thought that Keynes's real insights lay. If we do not instantaneously (and safely!) jump to the new equilibrium position (A to C in figure 1.15) then it is possible the agents undertake transactions (e.g. hiring labour) at non-market-clearing prices. This may lead to a further 'chain reaction' with 'quantities' (e.g. output, employment) providing the signals to agents in the market and taking the brunt of the adjustment rather than prices (as in the neoclassical model). This is the subject matter of the next chapter.

Finally in this section we wish to consider the Keynesian case of downwardly rigid nominal wages, but staying within the framework of the static equilibrium approach of this chapter.

1.6.1 Sticky Nominal Wages

If nominal wages increase, say due to the increased bargaining power of unions, to W_1 then with an unchanged price level P_0, firms will cut back labour demand (to L_1^d in figure 1.16) and the Keynesian aggregate supply curve shifts to the left, AS (W_1) (figure 1.17). Excess demand (at price level P_0) causes prices to rise to P_1 (B in figure 1.17) but by less than wages, and hence real wages rise to W_1/P_1 (figure 1.16). There is an excess supply of labour and *involuntary* unemployment (indicated by $L^{s'} L^{d'}$ in figure 1.16), but this disequilibrium in the labour market is assumed not to put immediate downward pressure on *nominal* wages. The goods market (and money market) are in equilibrium at B (figure 1.17) but the labour market is not. If nominal wages are rigid in a downward direction then we have an impasse and full employment will not be achieved automatically. Keynes believed this assumption of sticky nominal wages to be a realistic one. He therefore advocated that the authorities undertake an expansionary fiscal or monetary

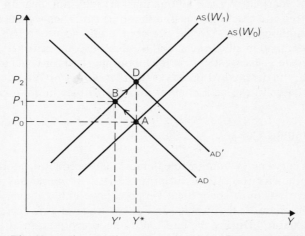

Figure 1.17 The Keynesian cut in real wages via an expansion of demand; no automatic full employment

policy, shifting the aggregate demand curve to AD', to achieve full employment (B to D in figure 1.17). This expansion is accompanied by a rise in the price level to P_2 and (for given nominal wages W_1) a fall in the *real* wage (to W_1/P_2 in figure 1.16). Hence, full employment in the Keynesian sticky wage case, requires a cut in real wages but this is achieved by an induced rise in the price level, rather than an attempt to cut nominal wages.

It is clear that the risk in such a policy is that nominal wages respond to the induced rise in prices as workers try to maintain their living standards ('real-wage resistance'). If so, there is a danger of a wage price spiral. Indeed if workers are unwilling to accept cuts in *real* wages in an expansionary period then the policy may end in stagflation as the AS curve continuously shifts further to the left as the AD curve moves to the right. This process could be reinforced by large welfare payments to the unemployed who may then be voluntarily unemployed even though the authorities' expansionary policy assumes they are involuntarily unemployed. In addition 'monetarists' would assert that a *continual* shift to the left of the AD curve may only be accomplished by a (continuous) rise in the money supply – hence their conclusion that the latter is the most important source of inflationary pressure. The whole process may also be aggravated by rises in prices of raw materials (e.g. oil) which increase marginal costs of production and again lead to a shift to the left in the aggregate supply (marginal cost) curve. To the extent that a rise in oil prices renders 'oil-intensive' plant and machinery economically obsolete, this reinforces any adverse 'supply side' consequences.

Thus, although 'sticky wages' provide the most cogent reason for the failure to achieve the neoclassical 'automatic route' to full employment, nevertheless 'Keynesian' expansionary monetary and fiscal policy are not without their attendant real-world dangers. If we are to develop this insight of Keynes – that markets (particularly the labour market) may not clear in all periods because 'prices' are 'sticky' at least in the short run, then we need to analyse (i) why 'optimizing agents' might not continually adjust 'prices' to equate supply and demand in all markets; and (ii) the consequences of 'false trading' in one market (e.g. excess supply in the labour market) for behaviour in other markets (e.g. the demand for goods) – in other words 'spillover effects'. We discuss the latter in the next chapter and the former in chapter 4.

1.7   The Phillips Curve

The Phillips curve plays a major role in most macroeconomic models, linking the real sector with the rate of inflation. There are numerous varieties of Phillips curve but most theoretical versions have either unemployment or output as the main 'real variable' and either wage or price changes as the 'inflation variable'. During the late 1960s one interpretation of the Phillips curve relationship implied that in the long run there was no trade-off between inflation and unemployment: this was the so-called vertical Phillips curve.

At a particular level of unemployment (known sometimes as the 'natural rate', sometimes as the non-accelerating inflation rate of unemployment, the NAIRU) inflation could take on any constant value, which for monetarists is determined by the rate of growth in the money supply. The authorities could only reduce unemployment below the natural rate, or NAIRU, if it was willing to engineer an *acceleration* in the rate of inflation. This 'accelerationist hypothesis' seemed to suggest that the authorities' scope for altering the level of unemployment by Keynesian expansionary policy is severely limited. The trade-off between inflation and unemployment, as represented for example in the early Phillips curve literature, was deemed to be only a short-run phenomenon (Friedman 1968).

We do not have space to develop theories of the Phillips curve in great detail and therefore we merely wish to concentrate on the relationship between the Phillips curve and the AS–AD analysis of the previous section. This 'systems aspect' allows us to outline the accelerationist thesis, the idea of the natural rate or NAIRU, and the interpretation of the Phillips curve as a surrogate (some would add a very imperfect surrogate) for the 'supply side'.

1.7.1 The Neoclassical Market-Clearing View

In the neoclassical model of the labour market (figure 1.12) the real wage and the natural (frictional) rate of unemployment are determined simultaneously by the (exogenous) determinants of the supply and demand for labour. The natural rate of unemployment, U_n (and the real wage), therefore depends on such 'real' factors, 'Z' as labour productivity, the level of welfare benefits, labour taxes and the growth in the population of working age. Let us represent these influences as $U_n(Z)$. Wages and prices are perfectly flexible and therefore, at *any* equal rate of wage and price inflation,

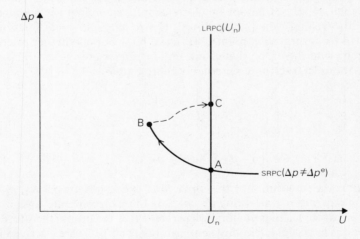

Figure 1.18 Short and long run Phillips curves (ΔP is the inflation)

the real wage is constant and unemployment is at the natural rate; in short, the labour market remains in equilibrium. In inflation–unemployment ($\Delta p, U$) space this would be represented by the vertical Phillips curve (LRPC(U_n) in figure 1.18). In (P, Y) space it is represented by the vertical aggregate supply curve. How might the neoclassical labour market give rise to the short-run trade-off between inflation and unemployment? The answer lies in misperceptions about the price level and the rate of inflation.

Friedman (1968) was one of the first economists to propound the following 'search model' which requires the crucial assumption of *asymmetric information* between workers and employers. Suppose we are in equilibrium at L^* in figure 1.16 with a *natural rate* of 'search' unemployment U_n consistent with an underlying, perfectly anticipated rate of wage and price inflation. A positive 'shock' to aggregate demand will cause the price level to rise faster to P'. Suppose the price rise is *perfectly perceived by employers* who then increase nominal wages but by less than the increase in prices. Hence, the *actual* real wage falls to W'/P' (figure 1.16) and employers increase their desired demand for labour by DB. If workers do not *fully perceive* the increase in prices they may believe that the increase in nominal wages is an increase in their *real* wage. They therefore supply more labour by reducing their search time as the current *perceived* real-wage offer now appears generous. (The supply curve shifts to $L^{s'}$ in figure 1.16.) Hence both the desired supply and demand for labour increase by DB and 'search unemployment' falls. We therefore have a negative association between unemployment and an increase in the price level; that is, we move along AB on the short-run Phillips curve (SRPC, figure 1.18). Also, via the production function, output supplied increases and this is consistent with an upward-sloping AS curve (e.g. AS(W_0) in figure 1.17). If there are no further shocks to the system it is assumed that workers eventually fully perceive the increase in prices, recognize that their real wages are unchanged and hence voluntarily reduce their supply of labour by, for example, extending the average time spent 'in searching' when unemployed. Hence unemployment (and output) returns to its natural rate (point C in figure 1.18) but at a higher price level. In the long run, therefore, the AS and Phillips curves are vertical. This model of the labour market may be crudely represented as

$$U - U_n(Z) = -a[(w - p^e)_t - (w - p)_t] \tag{1.15a}$$

or

$$U - U_n(Z) = -a(p - p^e)_t \tag{1.15b}$$

or

$$U - U_n(Z) = -a[(p - p_{t-1}) - (p^e - p_{t-1})] \tag{1.15c}$$

where p^e is the (logarithm of the) price *level* expected by workers, $p_t - p_{t-1}$ is the actual rate of inflation, $p_t^e - p_{t-1}$ is the expected rate and w is the (logarithm of the) actual nominal wage rate. Price 'surprises' therefore cause fluctuations in actual unemployment around its natural rate. Derived in this manner the PEAPC assumes equilibrium in the labour market at all times and full employment is automatically restored by flexible wages and prices as soon as workers correct their expectational errors about the price level. Cyclical (or serially correlated) movements in unemployment around the natural rate depend upon expectational errors for the price level persisting over a number of periods. (As we shall see in chapter 3, rational expectations deny the latter possibility and hence unemployment is always at the natural rate, apart from during the usual random shocks that disturb equilibrium relationships in the very short run.)

Equations (1.15b) and (1.15c) show a simultaneous relationship between price 'surprises' (or expectational errors) and movements in $U - U_n$. To speak of a direction of causation from $p - p^e$ to $U - U_n$ is not strictly correct although this model is often interpreted as such. All equations (1.15) do is to impose a severe constraint on the relationship between the two variables: unemployment can only be below the natural rate if the actual price level is above the expected price level (or, equivalently, actual inflation exceeds expected inflation). If workers eventually come to anticipate fully a *constant* rate of inflation and make no expectational errors, then the authorities can only cut unemployment by engineering *accelerating* inflation (which it is assumed will only be perceived with a lag); this is the accelerationist policy implication of the Phillips curve.

The key policy element in this neoclassical interpretation of the Phillips curve is therefore that only if expectational errors persist is there scope for discretionary policy, in principle at least. For example, policy may be used to push unemployment back towards its natural rate quicker than the free market might do. Of course the free market will accomplish the task given time: automatic full employment is back on the agenda. The search literature implies that fluctuations in unemployment around the natural rate are caused by 'price surprises' and this seems far less of a problem than the 'Keynesian' view that it is the result of wage rigidities and long-run disequilibrium. We discuss 'surprise' supply functions and the Phillips curve in greater depth in chapter 3.

1.7.2 The NAIRU

Suppose we now abandon the formal model of the neoclassical labour market and merely assert that there is a relationship between nominal wage inflation Δw_t (in logarithms), the expected rate of inflation $\Delta p^e \equiv p_t^e - p_{t-1}$ and the deviation of unemployment from some 'equilibrium rate', U_0. However, suppose we remain somewhat agnostic about the determinants of U_0, which may include 'bargaining factors' as well as 'market-orientated' variables such as the level of welfare benefits. Denoting the latter variables Z_0, our agnostic 'theory' may be represented by

$$\Delta w_t = \alpha - \beta(U - U_0(Z_0)) + \gamma \Delta p_t^e. \tag{1.16}$$

In addition, suppose we assert that in the long run workers do not suffer from money illusion – hence $\gamma = 1$ – and they obtain secular real-wage increases of α, equal to the (constant) rise in labour productivity. In our closed economy, price inflation is determined by unit labour costs:

$$\Delta p_t = \Delta w_t - \alpha \tag{1.17}$$

where α is the rate of growth of labour productivity. In such a model, when inflation is *constant* and *perfectly anticipated* we have

$$\Delta p_t = \Delta w_t - \alpha = \Delta p_t^e. \tag{1.18}$$

Substituting in (1.18) for Δw_t from (1.16) and assuming $\gamma = 1$,

$$0 = -\beta(U - U_0(Z_0)) \qquad \text{or} \qquad U = U_0(Z).$$

Thus, for the above conditions of a constant (i.e. non-accelerating) rate of inflation which is perfectly anticipated, actual unemployment will equal $U_0(Z)$. Note that, unsurprisingly, in such a framework $U_0(Z)$ is termed the non-accelerating inflation rate of unemployment, the NAIRU.

The accelerationist hypothesis and the vertical long-run Phillips curve apply to this 'NAIRU' model, but unlike in the neoclassical model the 'equilibrium' rate of unemployment is not necessarily determined in an atomistic market-clearing framework where all unemployment is *voluntary*. In the NAIRU framework the determinants of Z_0 may embody non-market-clearing variables and for example can be made consistent with wage bargaining models and firms operating in imperfectly competitive output markets (Nickell 1984, Layard and Nickell 1985).

1.8   Summary and Conclusion

We have analysed the key elements in a basic closed-economy model. We began in a fix-price framework and discussed the relative efficacy of fiscal and monetary policy in terms of the interest elasticity of investment expenditures and the demand for money and then proceeded to add wealth effects operating via the government budget constraint. We then added an elementary 'supply side' to our model and discussed the conditions under which the model yields 'automatic full employment'. We noted that, in the context of the neoclassical synthesis, Keynes's main contribution is to be found in his assumption that when nominal wages are 'sticky downwards' this may lead to agents undertaking transactions at non-market-clearing prices; quantity adjustments then bear the burden of adjustment rather than prices. This may lead to a negative multiplier effect and the possibility of involuntary unemployment. The corollary of this is that, as a practical matter, it may be safer to reduce the real wage and hence expand employment by increasing aggregate demand and the price level, rather than waiting for nominal wages to fall. We explore these possibilities more formally in the next chapter. In the final part of this chapter we examined the relationship between the Phillips curve, a construct widely used in macroeconomic models, and the more textbook-orientated concept of the aggregate supply curve.

Notes

1   The demand for *domestic output Y* comprises demands for *domestically produced* consumption, investment, government, and export goods, C^d, I^d, G^d, X respectively, where the superscript d indicates demands for domestically produced goods only. Aggregate *expenditure* by domestic residents comprises expenditures on *domestically produced* goods and on *imports*; denoting aggregate expenditures by C, I, G and imports by C^m, I^m, G^m we have $C = C^d + C^m$ etc. Hence

$$Y = C^d + I^d + G^d + X$$
$$= C + I + G + X - (C^m + I^m + G^m)$$
$$= C + I + G + X - Z$$

where Z = aggregate imports = $(C^m + I^m + G^m)$.

2   We implicitly assume that *desired* supply by producers equals actual output supplied – that is, there are no unintended changes in stocks and all output plans are met.

3   In fact the IS schedule is simply

$$Y - C(Y - T(Y)) - I(r) - G - X + Z = 0.$$

Note that this is a *flow equilibrium* condition, since it says that the flow of output produced *over a certain period* is equal to the flow of demand over the same period.

4   The LM curve is in fact

$$\overline{M}/P - M(Y, r) = 0.$$

Note that this is a *stock equilibrium* condition, since it says that the stock of money made available by the authorities *at a certain point in time* is equal to stock agents' collective wish to hold for a given level of prices, income and interest rates, at the same point in time.

5   More formally, we implicitly endow the model with some elementary dynamics of the form $\dot{Y} = \phi_1(Y, r)$ and $\dot{r} = \phi_2(Y, r)$ where $\dot{Y}$ is the (absolute) change in Y etc. We can then apply Samuelson's correspondence principle to the partial derivatives of ϕ_1 and ϕ_2 as in appendix 1.2. Note that the IS–LM model, as set out above, really tells us very little about *how* we move from one equilibrium to another, leaving us to rely on informal 'stories' to explain how output and the interest rate move over 'time' (this is sometimes referred to as the 'pseudo-dynamics' of the IS–LM model – Chick 1977). This is because the IS–LM system is, in line with much of economics, couched within the framework of *comparative statics* – see appendix 1.2.

6   These tests usually use real output and nominal output as alternative dependent variables. In the 'extreme' monetarist case we expect a unit long-run elasticity of the money supply with respect to *nominal* output or the price level and a zero elasticity with respect to real output.

7   The deficit leads initially to an increase in the money supply as the authorities pay for goods and services; but the authorities may then sell bonds to the NBPS to return the money supply to its initial level. A constant positive budget deficit constitutes a constant *flow* of excess expenditure and therefore requires a *continuous* issue of government debt, be this money or bonds.

8   Most bank deposits have a counterpart liability for the NBPS (e.g. commercial bills or bank advances). Hence only those deposits that are 'backed' by 'bank reserves' (or high-powered money), a liability of the monetary authority, constitute net 'money wealth'. Since the quantity of high-powered money is relatively small, it is argued that the Pigou effect will be small. However, the appropriate definition of net 'money wealth' is still subject to debate (Laidler 1973, 1982, 1985).

9   The idea that government bonds are not net wealth (i.e. debt neutrality) arises because the (discounted present) value of future coupon receipts may be entirely offset by higher expected tax liabilities (this is sometimes termed the 'Ricardian equivalence theorem'). There is a thriving debate on this issue (Barro 1974, Laidler 1982, Buiter 1980).

10 If nominal wealth at the end of period $t-1$ is W_{t-1} and the interest rate earned from $t-1$ to t is r_t then real wealth at time t is $W_{t-1}(1+r_t)/P_t$, where P_t is the price level at time t. The *change* in real wealth is

$$\Delta \text{RW} = (W_{t-1}(1+r_t)/P_t) - (W/P)_{t-1}.$$

Substituting the identity $P_t/P_{t-1} = 1 + g$ where g is the proportionate rate of inflation in this equation and using $(1+g)^{-1} \simeq (1-g)$ we have the change in real wealth given by

$$\Delta \text{RW} = (W_{t-1}/P_t)(r_t - g).$$

Interest receipts are added to income but the erosion in the purchasing power of the outstanding stock, namely $g(W_{t-1}/P_t)$, is not usually deducted from income. The latter is known as the 'inflation loss', and on government debt can be substantial in periods of 'high' inflation (see Taylor and Threadgold 1979 and Cuthbertson 1982).

11 A perpetuity (an irredeemable bond) pays a *fixed* coupon £C per annum. If B is the number of bonds outstanding, the annual interest payments are £CB. If C is fixed at £1 then interest payments are £B. B is both the number of bonds outstanding and the *value* of interest payments. Assume interest and other income are both taxed at the same rate. In long-run equilibrium the budget must balance ($\Delta W = 0$); hence

$$G + B - T(Y + B) = \Delta W = 0$$
$$dG + dB - T' \, dY - T' \, dB = 0$$
$$dY/dG = 1/T' + (dB/dG)(1 - T')/T'.$$

For bond finance $dB/dG > 0$ and therefore the multiplier exceeds that for money finance (where $dB/dG = 0$ and $dY/dG = 1/T'$). See appendix 1.3 for further details.

12 This is true only under rather strong assumptions. If a change in the money supply affects the price level *and* the outstanding stock of bonds are considered as net

wealth by the private sector, then changes in real wealth may shift the (neoclassical) labour supply curve and hence alter the supply of output. Thus, money 'neutrality' also requires an assumption of debt neutrality. Similarly, fiscal changes (e.g. changes in tax rates) may influence the supply and demand for labour and shift the vertical neoclassical supply curve. Neoclassical economists accept that fiscal changes might slowly alter the natural rate of output but usually argue in favour of debt neutrality (see note 9).

Appendix 1.1   The Algebra of IS–LM and AS–AD Models

Fix-Price IS–LM Models   Equilibrium in the goods market, using (1.1)–(1.8) (excluding indirect taxes), and assuming linearity of all functions, is given by

$$Y = C + I + G + X - Z$$
$$Y = c_y(1 - t_y)Y - i_r r + G + X - z_y Y. \qquad (A1.1.1)$$

On rearranging we have the IS curve:

$$r = -\left(\frac{k}{i_r}\right) Y + \frac{(G+X)}{i_r} \qquad (A1.1.2)$$

where $k = 1 - c_y(1 - t_y) + z_y$ is the inverse of the simple Keynesian expenditure multiplier. The slope of the IS curve is $-k/i_r$.

Equilibrium in the money market is given by

$$M^s/P = m_y Y - m_r r \qquad (A1.1.3)$$

which on rearranging gives the LM curve:

$$r = \left(\frac{m_y}{m_r}\right) Y - \frac{1}{m_r}\left(\frac{M^s}{P}\right) \qquad (A1.1.4)$$

with a positive slope (m_y/m_r).

Equating (A1.1.2) and (A1.1.4) and rearranging yields the *reduced-form equation for output* (i.e. output expressed solely as a function of the exogenous variables and parameters):

$$Y = k_f(G+X) + k_m(M^s/P) \qquad (A1.1.5)$$

where $k_f = [k + (i_r m_y/m_r)]^{-1}$ is the fiscal multiplier and $k_m = [m_y + (km_r/i_r)]^{-1}$ is the money supply multiplier. Substituting (A1.1.5) in (A1.1.2) or (A1.1.4) and rearranging gives the *reduced-form equation for the interest rate*:

$$r = \left(\frac{km_r}{m_y} + i_r\right)^{-1}(G+X) - \left(m_r + \frac{i_r m_y}{k}\right)^{-1}\left(\frac{M^s}{P}\right). \qquad (A1.1.6)$$

An alternative method of solution, which is sometimes useful when there are a large number of equations, is to put the IS and LM equations (A1.1.2) and (A1.1.4) in matrix form:

$$\begin{bmatrix} k & i_r \\ m_y & -m_r \end{bmatrix} \begin{bmatrix} Y \\ r \end{bmatrix} = \begin{bmatrix} G+X \\ M^s/P \end{bmatrix} \tag{A1.1.7}$$

which may be written in obvious notation as

$$\mathbf{B}Z = R \tag{A1.1.8}$$

where $R = [G+X, M^s/P]'$ and the solution for Z is

$$Z = \begin{bmatrix} Y \\ r \end{bmatrix} = \mathbf{B}^{-1}R. \tag{A1.1.9}$$

The inverse of $\mathbf{B}$ is easily shown to be (Chiang 1984)

$$\mathbf{B}^{-1} = -(km_r + m_y i_r)^{-1} \begin{bmatrix} -m_r & -i_r \\ -m_y & k \end{bmatrix} \tag{A1.1.10}$$

and after some simple manipulation (A1.1.9) yields equations (A1.1.5) and A1.1.6).

Special Cases   We shall refer to m_r etc. as elasticities, although strictly speaking they are partial derivatives.

Consider for example an inelastic demand-for-money function ($m_r \to 0$). Equation (A1.1.4) indicates that the LM curve becomes vertical while from (A1.1.5) we have $\partial Y/\partial M^s = (1/m_y)$ and $\partial Y/\partial G = 0$; the latter indicates complete financial crowding out. A similar analysis reveals that an inelastic investment schedule ($i_r \to 0$) yields a vertical IS curve (equation (A1.1.2)) and, using (A1.1.5), $\partial Y/\partial M^s = 0$ and $\partial Y/\partial G = (1/k)$, the latter being the full Keynesian multiplier. Other special cases, noted in table 1.1, are left as an exercise for the reader.

Simple lagged responses are easily introduced into the fix-price IS–LM model for example by using (first-order) partial adjustment (Tucker 1966) or adaptive expectations (e.g. permanent income in the consumption function; Laidler 1968) or both (Laidler 1973). If a second- or higher-order difference equation ensues then 'impact (output) multipliers' may exceed their long-run values; that is, 'overshooting' occurs. Addition of the government budget constraint introduces rather complex dynamics (see, e.g. Blinder and Solow 1973, and Christ 1978, 1979) which we do not consider (see, e.g. Turnovsky 1977 for a detailed exposition).

Aggregate Supply and the Phillips Curve   Assume that we can represent the 'supply side' by a Phillips curve relationship (in logarithms):

$$p = \lambda p^e + \beta(y - y_0) \qquad 0 < \lambda < 1 \qquad\qquad\text{(A1.1.11)}$$

where p is the price level and p^e the expected price level. If one assumes a neoclassical labour market, y_0 is the natural rate of output and depends on the exogenous determinants of the supply and demand for labour (e.g. labour productivity). The natural rate is independent of government expenditure and the money supply. Alternatively one may view y_0 as the 'non-accelerating rate of output' and not specify its precise determinants (which could therefore include bargaining variables; see Layard and Nickell 1985).

If there is no money illusion, $\lambda = 1$, we have the vertical Phillips curve and we can rewrite the equation in terms of the rate of inflation:

$$p_t - p_{t-1} = p_t^e - p_{t-1} + \beta(y - y_0). \qquad\qquad\text{(A1.1.12)}$$

For a given level of p_t^e, equations (A1.1.11) and (A1.1.12) yield a positive relationship between p_t and y_t – the 'supply curve'.

For ease of exposition, assume the aggregate demand curve (A1.1.5) is linear in logarithms:

$$y = k_f g + k_m(m^s - p) \qquad\qquad\text{(A1.1.13)}$$

where lower-case letters indicate logarithms of the variables (and $X = 0$, for convenience). Note that $\partial y / \partial p < 0$ as required by the aggregate *demand* relationship.

Substituting (A1.1.13) into (A1.1.11) and rearranging we obtain the reduced-form equation for the price level:

$$p = \frac{\lambda}{1 + \beta k_m} p^e + \frac{\beta}{1 + \beta k_m}(k_f g + k_m m^s) - \frac{\beta}{1 + \beta k_m} y_0. \qquad\text{(A1.1.14)}$$

If expectations are correct in some steady state, then $p = p^e$ and hence

$$p = \frac{\beta}{1 + \beta k_m - \lambda}(k_f g + k_m m^s) - \frac{\beta}{1 + \beta k_m - \lambda} y_0. \qquad\text{(A1.1.15)}$$

The reduced-form solution for output may be found by substituting (A1.1.15) into (A1.1.13) (or (A1.1.11)):

$$y = \frac{1 - \lambda}{1 + \beta k_m - \lambda}(k_f g + k_m m^s) + \frac{\beta k_m}{1 + \beta k_m - \lambda} y_0. \qquad\text{(A1.1.16)}$$

It is easy to see that with money illusion (i.e. $0 < \lambda < 1$) then $\partial y / \partial m^s$, $\partial y / \partial g$, $\partial p / \partial g > 0$ and $1 > \partial p / \partial m^s > 0$. Hence money is *not* neutral and government expenditure has a positive multiplier effect on output. Graphically these results are represented by a shift to the right of the aggregate demand curve with a 'normal' upward-sloping aggregate supply curve. The Keynesian 'sticky wage' model is consistent with these results.

Absence of money illusion on the supply side (i.e. $\lambda = 1$) gives $\partial p/\partial m^s = 1$, $\partial y/\partial m^s = \partial y/\partial g = 0$; hence money is 'neutral' and fiscal policy (i.e. a change in g) is completely crowded out (physical crowding out). The equilibrium level of output only changes if the determinants of y_0 alter ($\partial y/\partial y_0 = 1$) – a supply side response.

The above analysis ignores (i) wealth effects and (ii) an analysis of equilibrium under a constant growth rate (for example, a constant *growth* in the money supply and the issue of the super-neutrality of money). Buiter 1980 provides a succinct analysis of the latter case.

Appendix 1.2   The Method of Comparative Statics and the Correspondence Principle

Introduction   Comparative statics is not a topic in macroeconomics as such, but a method widely used throughout economic theory. Usually, the method is applied informally. The purpose of this appendix is to attempt to clarify what is going on when comparative statics is applied and to help you in using the method. To do this we develop the method formally and then show how it can be applied to one or two specific macroeconomic examples.

Comparative statics is a method used by economists to analyse changes in the equilibrium of an economic model that result from changes in exogenous variables. In terms of the calculus, comparative statics is concerned with determining the derivative of each of the endogenous variables with respect to the exogenous variables when the system-wide effects of the model are taken into account and equilibrium is maintained – i.e. the reduced-form partial derivatives (e.g. $\partial Y/\partial G$, $\partial r/\partial m^s$ above).

An obvious use of the reduced-form partial derivatives, particularly in the macro context, lies in the formulation of policy prescriptions – the reduced-form partial derivative of income with respect to autonomous expenditure in a Keynesian macromodel, for example, is the familiar Keynesian multiplier. Further, if economic theory is to be meaningful it must have empirical content. In other words it must, at least in principle, be capable of being refuted empirically. By predicting the nature of changes in the endogenous variables resulting from a change in one or more of the exogenous variables in a model, the method of comparative statics describes features of that model that could, even if only under ideal circumstances, be tested. Samuelson writes

> The usefulness of our theory emerges from the fact that by our analysis we are often able to determine the nature of changes in our unknown variables resulting from a designated change in one or more parameters. In fact, our theory is meaningless in the operational sense unless it does imply some restrictions upon empirically observable quantities, by which it could conceivably be refuted. (1947, p. 7)

Keynesian economics, for example, predicts that, in a situation of unemployment, an autonomous increase in investment will, *ceteris paribus*, bring about an increase in income and employment. Now it is possible to conceive of an experiment where this prediction is put to the test. In the real world, of course, the experiment could not be performed, not least because of the impossibility of realizing the *ceteris paribus* assumption. Nevertheless, the theory is clearly more meaningful than a macro theory that says nothing at all about the changes in income and employment brought about by an increase in investment.

Unlike our example in appendix 1.1, the method of comparative statics can be used when the structural equations are non-linear.

The Method of Comparative Statics Generally, an economic model consists of *n structural* equations in *n* endogenous variables y_i, $i = 1, \ldots, n$, and *m* exogenous variables x_i, $i = 1, \ldots, n$:

$$f_i(y_1, y_2, \ldots, y_n, x_1, x_2, \ldots, x_n) = 0 \qquad i = 1, \ldots, n. \qquad \text{(A1.2.1)}$$

In our previous example (appendix 1.1), $y_i = (Y, r)$ and $x_i = (G, M^s/P)$ for $i = 1, 2, \ldots$. A *structural equation* of a model can be a behavioural equation, an accounting identity or an equilibrium condition. The set of equations (A1.2.1) is known as the *structural form* (and corresponds to (A1.1.1) and (A1.1.4) in appendix 1.1).

For a given vector of exogenous variables *x*, the solution of the equilibrium equations entails an equilibrium vector of the endogenous variables *y*. If we assume that the structural equations are differentiable in the neighbourhood of (y', x') and that the Jacobian determinant

$$\begin{vmatrix} \dfrac{\partial f_1}{\partial y_1} & \dfrac{\partial f_1}{\partial y_2} & \cdots & \dfrac{\partial f_1}{\partial y_n} \\[2mm] \dfrac{\partial f_2}{\partial y_1} & \dfrac{\partial f_2}{\partial y_2} & \cdots & \dfrac{\partial f_2}{\partial y_n} \\[2mm] \vdots & \vdots & & \vdots \\[2mm] \dfrac{\partial f_n}{\partial y_1} & \dfrac{\partial f_n}{\partial y_2} & \cdots & \dfrac{\partial f_n}{\partial y_n} \end{vmatrix}$$

is non-zero at (y', x'), then we can apply a mathematical result, the implicit function theorem, which asserts that each of the endogenous variables can be expressed as functions of the exogenous variables that are well behaved in the neighbourhood of (y', x'):

$$y_i = y_i(x_i, x_1, x_2, \ldots, x_m) \qquad i = 1, \ldots, n \qquad \text{(A1.2.2)}$$

Equations (A1.2.2) are referred to as the *reduced-form equations of the system*. If we can solve for (A1.2.2) directly then we can derive our comparative static results straightaway by calculating the matrix of the reduced-form partial derivatives:

$$\left[\frac{\partial y_i}{\partial x_j}\right], \qquad i=1, \ldots, n \qquad j=1, \ldots, m \qquad \text{(A1.2.3)}$$

and this we were able to do in our simple IS–LM example in appendix 1.1.

However, the implicit function theorem only tells us that (A1.2.2) exists, and the system may often in practice be difficult to solve. Moreover, economic theory is often postulated in terms of non-specific functional forms (and not the simpler *linear* equations of appendix 1.1).

Substituting (A1.2.1) into (A1.2.2):

$$f_i(y_1(x_1, \ldots, x_m), \ldots, y_n(x_1, \ldots, x_m), x_1, \ldots, x_m) = 0$$
$$i = 1, \ldots, n. \qquad \text{(A1.2.4)}$$

Applying the chain rule of differentiation:

$$\sum_{s=1}^{n} \frac{\partial f_i}{\partial y_s} \frac{\partial y_s}{\partial x_j} + \frac{\partial f_i}{\partial x_j} = 0, \qquad i=1, \ldots, n \qquad j=1, \ldots, m$$

or in a matrix notation:

$$\begin{bmatrix} \dfrac{\partial f_1}{\partial y_1} & \dfrac{\partial f_1}{\partial y_2} & \cdots & \dfrac{\partial f_1}{\partial y_n} & \dfrac{\partial y_1}{\partial x_j} \\[2ex] \dfrac{\partial f_2}{\partial y_1} & \dfrac{\partial f_2}{\partial y_2} & \cdots & \dfrac{\partial f_2}{\partial y_n} & \dfrac{\partial y_2}{\partial x_j} \\[1ex] \vdots & \vdots & & \vdots & \vdots \\[1ex] \dfrac{\partial f_n}{\partial y_1} & \dfrac{\partial f_n}{\partial y_2} & \cdots & \dfrac{\partial f_n}{\partial y_n} & \dfrac{\partial y_n}{\partial x_j} \end{bmatrix} \begin{bmatrix} \dfrac{\partial y_1}{\partial x_j} \\[2ex] \dfrac{\partial y_2}{\partial x_j} \\[1ex] \vdots \\[1ex] \dfrac{\partial y_n}{\partial x_j} \end{bmatrix} = \begin{bmatrix} -\dfrac{\partial f_1}{\partial x_j} \\[2ex] -\dfrac{\partial f_2}{\partial x_j} \\[1ex] \vdots \\[1ex] -\dfrac{\partial f_n}{\partial x_j} \end{bmatrix}, j=1, \ldots, m$$

More compactly:

$$\mathbf{A}B_j = \gamma_j \qquad j=1, \ldots, m \qquad \text{(A1.2.5)}$$

Define $\Delta \equiv |\mathbf{A}|$ and Δ_i^j as the determinant obtained by substituting γ_j into the *i*th column of Δ. Then by Cramer's rule (see, e.g., Chiang 1967)

$$\frac{\partial y_i}{\partial x_j} = \frac{\Delta_i^j}{\Delta} \qquad i=1, \ldots, n \qquad j=1, \ldots, m. \qquad \text{(A1.2.6)}$$

Note that by invoking the implicit function theorem we have assumed that Δ exists, which implies that (A1.2.5) is always soluble (i.e. $\mathbf{A}^{-1}$ exists).

Of course we are now left with the problem of determining the signs and relative sizes of Δ_i^j and Δ in order to determine the sign and size of the reduced-form partial derivatives. Samuelson postulates that there are basically three methods by which comparative static information can be deduced.

Firstly we may have qualitative information on the model that will allow us to deduce qualitative comparative static properties. For example, economic theory may suggest the signs of the first derivatives of all the endogenous variables and this may enable us to determine the signs of Δ_i^j and Δ.

Secondly, in many economic models some form of maximization or minimization is involved. For example, the structural form (A1.2.1) may be taken as describing the first-order conditions for an extremum. Characterization of an extremum problem involves determining the sign of the Hessian determinant (Chiang 1984). However, if (A1.2.1) describes the first-order conditions then the Hessian is nothing but our Jacobian determinant Δ. Hence, viewing the problem as, for example, the minimization of a government loss function (see chapter 6) may help determine the sign of Δ and perhaps that of Δ_i^j.

The third way in which 'meaningful theorems' may be derived is by considering the implicit dynamics of the system (the implicit dynamics of the IS–LM system are sometimes referred to as the 'pseudo-dynamics' – Chick 1977). Although comparative statics by definition is merely the comparison of different static equilibria, consideration of the implicit dynamics may often help us to deduce information about the reduced-form partial derivatives. Implicit in most economic models is the assumption that the system will converge upon a new equilibrium when the system is shocked. Indeed, models that do not display this property are in some sense meaningless since they can give no definite guide as to the eventual outcome of a change in circumstances. The use of implicit or explicit assumptions about the dynamic behaviour of a system in order to deduce comparative static results is the essence of what Samuelson termed the 'correspondence principle'.

We conclude this section by providing a recipe for comparative statics:

1 solve the system for its equilibrium (this may involve maximization or minimization);
2 differentiate with respect to each of the exogenous variables;
3 solve for the reduced-form partial derivatives of the endogenous variables making use of any relevant *a priori* qualitative (or indeed quantitative) information that is available, relevant information obtained by considering the model as an extremum problem or relevant information available by considering the implicit or explicit dynamics of the system.

By way of a simple example we now consider a general formulation of our IS–LM model where the behavioural equations are not assumed to be linear.

The Comparative Statics of the IS–LM Model   Consider the following simple macro model:

$$S = S(Y, \alpha) \qquad 0 < \frac{\partial S}{\partial Y} < 1 \qquad \frac{\partial S}{\partial \alpha} > 0 \qquad\qquad (A1.2.7)$$

$$I = I(r, \beta) \qquad \frac{\partial I}{\partial r} < 0 \qquad \frac{\partial I}{\partial \beta} > 0 \qquad\qquad (A1.2.8)$$

$$I = S \qquad\qquad (A1.2.9)$$

$$L = L(Y, r) \qquad \frac{\partial L}{\partial Y} > 0 \qquad \frac{\partial L}{\partial r} < 0 \qquad\qquad (A1.2.10)$$

$$L = M/P = \overline{m}. \qquad\qquad (A1.2.11)$$

Prices are assumed fixed. Equation (A1.2.7) describes savings as an increasing function of income and another exogenous variable ('thrift'); equation (A1.2.8) is the investment function, a decreasing function of the interest rate but on increasing function of the exogenous variable β (Keynes's 'animal spirits'); equation (A1.2.9) is the flow equilibrium condition for the goods market; equation (A1.2.10) describes the real demand for money, L, as an increasing function of income and a decreasing function of interest rates; finally (A1.2.11) is the stock equilibrium for the money market for an exogenously given level of the real money stock $\overline{m}$.

Solving for the equilibrium of the system we have the IS and LM functions:

$$I(r, \beta) - S(Y, \alpha) = 0 \qquad\qquad (A1.2.12)$$
$$L(Y, r) - \overline{m} = 0 \qquad\qquad (A1.2.13)$$

Since investment, saving and money demand have now effectively been solved out of the system, we have two equations in two endogenous variables, r and Y. Now, say we start at an initial equilibrium point, (y^*, r^*), and assume that the Jacobian of the system

$$\begin{bmatrix} \dfrac{\partial I}{\partial r} & -\dfrac{\partial S}{\partial Y} \\[2ex] \dfrac{\partial L}{\partial r} & \dfrac{\partial L}{\partial Y} \end{bmatrix} = \Delta$$

is non-vanishing at this point. Then we know that there exist functions

$$r = r(\alpha, \beta, \overline{m}) \qquad\qquad (A1.2.14)$$
$$Y = Y(\alpha, \beta, \overline{m}) \qquad\qquad (A1.2.15)$$

that can then be substituted into (A1.2.12) and (A1.2.13) and the chain rule of differentiation applied.

Suppose that we are concerned with the comparative static effects of an increase in the money supply. Applying the chain rule of differentiation to (A1.2.12) and (A1.2.13)

$$
\begin{bmatrix} \dfrac{\partial I}{\partial r} & -\dfrac{\partial S}{\partial Y} \\[3mm] \dfrac{\partial L}{\partial r} & \dfrac{\partial L}{\partial Y} \end{bmatrix} \begin{bmatrix} \dfrac{\partial r}{\partial \overline{m}} \\[3mm] \dfrac{\partial Y}{\partial \overline{m}} \end{bmatrix} = \begin{bmatrix} 0 \\[3mm] 1 \end{bmatrix}
$$

so we have

$$\partial r/\partial \overline{m} = (\partial S/\partial Y)/\Delta. \tag{A1.2.16}$$

Using the *a priori* qualitative information given in (A1.2.7) – (A1.2.11) concerning the signs of the partial derivatives of the system, we are easily able to determine the sign of (A1.2.16):

$$\partial r/\partial \overline{m} < 0. \tag{A1.2.17}$$

Similarly

$$\partial Y/\partial \overline{m} > 0. \tag{A1.2.18}$$

Now consider the effect of an autonomous change in investment. We have

$$
\begin{bmatrix} \dfrac{\partial I}{\partial r} & -\dfrac{\partial S}{\partial Y} \\[3mm] \dfrac{\partial L}{\partial r} & \dfrac{\partial L}{\partial Y} \end{bmatrix} \begin{bmatrix} \dfrac{\partial r}{\partial \beta} \\[3mm] \dfrac{\partial Y}{\partial \beta} \end{bmatrix} = \begin{bmatrix} -\dfrac{\partial I}{\partial \beta} \\[3mm] 0 \end{bmatrix}
$$

so we have

$$\frac{\partial r}{\partial \beta} = -\frac{(\partial I/\partial \beta)(\partial L/\partial Y)}{\Delta} > 0 \tag{A1.2.19}$$

$$\frac{\partial Y}{\partial \beta} = \frac{(\partial L/\partial r)(\partial I/\partial \beta)}{\Delta} > 0. \tag{A1.2.20}$$

Note that if we let the interest elasticity of the demand for money tend to infinity, the system reduces to the one-sector Keynesian model, in which case (A1.2.19) reduces to

$$\frac{\partial Y}{\partial \beta} = \frac{\partial I/\partial \beta}{\partial S/\partial Y} \tag{A1.2.21}$$

which is of course the familiar Keynesian multiplier.

By a similar analysis for changes in thrift we can deduce

$$\frac{\partial r}{\partial \alpha} = \frac{(\partial S/\partial \alpha)(\partial L/\partial Y)}{\Delta} < 0 \qquad\qquad\qquad (A1.2.22)$$

$$\frac{\partial Y}{\partial \alpha} = \frac{(\partial L/\partial r)(\partial S/\partial \alpha)}{\Delta} < 0. \qquad\qquad\qquad (A1.2.23)$$

The negative sign of (A1.2.23) is often referred to as the 'paradox of thrift'.

Finally, note that the reduced-form partial derivatives of S, I and L can be calculated from the above results by applying the chain rule of differentiation to (A1.2.7), (A1.2.8) and (A1.2.9) respectively.

The Comparative Statics of a Modified Keynesian Model: an Application of the Correspondence Principle   Suppose that we now extend the preceding model to allow for interest rate effects in saving and income effects in investment:

$$S = S(Y, r, \alpha) \qquad 0 < \frac{\partial S}{\partial Y} < 1 \qquad \frac{\partial S}{\partial r} > 0 \qquad \frac{\partial S}{\partial \alpha} > 0 \quad (A1.2.24)$$

$$I = I(Y, r, \beta) \qquad 0 < \frac{\partial I}{\partial Y} < 1 \qquad \frac{\partial I}{\partial r} < 0 \qquad \frac{\partial I}{\partial \beta} > 0 \quad (A1.2.25)$$

$$I = S \qquad\qquad\qquad\qquad\qquad\qquad\qquad\qquad\qquad (A1.2.26)$$

$$L = L(Y, r) \qquad\qquad \frac{\partial L}{\partial Y} > 0 \qquad \frac{\partial L}{\partial r} < 0 \qquad\qquad (A1.2.27)$$

$$L = M/P = \bar{m}. \qquad\qquad\qquad\qquad\qquad\qquad\qquad (A1.2.28)$$

The IS and LM functions now become

$$I(Y, r, \beta) - S(Y, r, \alpha) = 0 \qquad\qquad\qquad\qquad\qquad (A1.2.29)$$
$$L(Y, r) - \bar{m} = 0 \qquad\qquad\qquad\qquad\qquad\qquad (A1.2.30)$$

and we require a non-vanishing Jacobian determinant at equilibrium:

$$\begin{vmatrix} \left[\dfrac{\partial I}{\partial r} - \dfrac{\partial S}{\partial r}\right] & \left[\dfrac{\partial I}{\partial Y} - \dfrac{\partial S}{\partial Y}\right] \\[2ex] \dfrac{\partial L}{\partial r} & \dfrac{\partial L}{\partial Y} \end{vmatrix} = \Delta.$$

Now consider the comparative static effects of an increase in the money supply. We have

$$
\begin{bmatrix} \dfrac{\partial I}{\partial r} - \dfrac{\partial S}{\partial r} & \dfrac{\partial I}{\partial Y} - \dfrac{\partial S}{\partial Y} \\[2ex] \dfrac{\partial L}{\partial r} & \dfrac{\partial L}{\partial Y} \end{bmatrix}
\begin{bmatrix} \dfrac{\partial r}{\partial \overline{m}} \\[2ex] \dfrac{\partial Y}{\partial \overline{m}} \end{bmatrix}
=
\begin{bmatrix} 0 \\[2ex] 1 \end{bmatrix}
$$

so we have

$$
\frac{\partial Y}{\partial \overline{m}} = \frac{\partial S/\partial r - \partial I/\partial r}{\Delta} \tag{A1.2.31}
$$

$$
\frac{\partial r}{\partial \overline{m}} = \frac{\partial I/\partial Y - \partial S/\partial Y}{\Delta} \ . \tag{A1.2.32}
$$

Using qualitative information on the signs of the derivatives in (A1.2.24)–(A1.2.28) we are now only able to determine the sign of the numerator of (A1.2.31), which is positive, whilst the signs of Δ and the numerator of (A1.2.32) remain indeterminate. In order to be able to determine the comparative static properties we shall have to examine the implicit dynamics of the system.

Two implicit dynamic assumptions usually made in the context of the Keynesian model are that income rises in response to an excess of *ex ante* investment over *ex ante* saving and that interest rates rise in response to an excess demand for money. Letting a dot over a character denote a time derivative, these assumptions can be written formally:

$$
\dot{Y} = \phi_1(I(Y,r) - S(Y,r)) \qquad \phi_1' > 0 \qquad \phi_1(0) = 0 \tag{A1.2.33}
$$
$$
\dot{r} = \phi_2(L(Y,r) - \overline{m}) \qquad \phi_2' > 0 \qquad \phi_2(0) = 0. \tag{A1.2.34}
$$

Taking a Taylor series expansion of (A1.2.33) and (A1.2.34) around the equilibrium point (Y^*, r^*) (Chiang 1984):

$$
\dot{Y} = \phi_1'(0) \left(\frac{\partial I}{\partial Y} - \frac{\partial S}{\partial Y} \right) (Y - Y^*) + \phi_1'(0) \left(\frac{\partial I}{\partial r} - \frac{\partial S}{\partial r} \right) (r - r^*) + \ldots
$$

$$
\dot{r} = \phi_2'(0) \frac{\partial L}{\partial Y} (Y - Y^*) + \phi_2'(0) \frac{\partial L}{\partial r} (r - r^*) + \ldots .
$$

Ignoring higher-order terms, these can be written as

$$
\begin{bmatrix} \dot{Y} \\[3ex] \dot{r} \end{bmatrix}
=
\begin{bmatrix} c_1 \left(\dfrac{\partial I}{\partial Y} - \dfrac{\partial S}{\partial Y} \right) & c_1 \left(\dfrac{\partial I}{\partial r} - \dfrac{\partial S}{\partial r} \right) \\[3ex] c_2 \dfrac{\partial L}{\partial Y} & c_2 \dfrac{\partial L}{\partial r} \end{bmatrix}
\begin{bmatrix} (Y - Y^*) \\[3ex] (r - r^*) \end{bmatrix}
$$

$$
\tag{A1.2.35}
$$

where $c_1 = \phi_1'(0) > 0$ and $c_2 = \phi_2'(0) > 0$. Necessary and sufficient conditions for the system to exhibit stability about the equilibrium are that the coefficient matrix on the right-hand side of (A1.2.35) has negative trace and positive determinant (Chiang 1984); that is

$$c_1 \left(\frac{\partial I}{\partial Y} - \frac{\partial S}{\partial Y} \right) + c_2 \frac{\partial L}{\partial r} < 0$$

$$c_1 c_2 \Delta > 0 \Rightarrow \Delta > 0.$$

Using these conditions we can now determine that

$$\partial Y / \partial \overline{m} > 0. \qquad \qquad \text{(A1.2.36)}$$

The sign of (A1.2.32), however, remains indeterminate.

We have demonstrated how additional information about the dynamics of the model provides restrictions that can be useful in establishing the 'sign' of certain comparative static results. This is Samuelson's correspondence principle.

Appendix 1.3   Wealth Effects, Crowding Out and the Government Budget Constraint

In order to clarify some of the issues raised in chapter 1, consider the following simple model, which is based on the analysis of Blinder and Solow (1973). We assume that the price level is fixed and exogenous, so it need not be considered (we effectively set $P = 1$, so for example $M/P = M$). The government raises revenue either by printing money, issuing bonds or raising taxes. If the amount of bonds outstanding is B, let ΔB be the amount of bonds issued. Assume that these are perpetuities paying a coupon of £1 per year, and that the interest rate is r. The market price of the bond is $1/T$, the market value of the bond *issue* is therefore $\Delta B/r$ and each year the government has to pay out £B to the holders of bonds. If ΔM^s is the change in the money supply (amount of money printed) then the government budget constraint is

$$\Delta M^s + \Delta B/r + T(Y + B) = G + B. \qquad \qquad \text{(A1.3.1)}$$

Note that we have now amended the tax schedule so that income from bond holding is also taxed.

Now consider wealth effects in the money market. We assume that the demand for money is increasing with wealth, W, as well as a function of income and the interest rate:

$$M^d = M(Y, r, W) \qquad \qquad \text{(A1.3.2)}$$

where W is defined as the value of money and bonds held:

$$W = M + B/r. \tag{A1.3.3}$$

Given the stock equilibrium condition $M^s = M^d = M$, the LM curve is

$$M = M(Y, r, M + B/r). \tag{A1.3.4}$$

On the 'real' side, we assume that consumption is a function not only of disposable income (amended to take account of coupon payments to bond holders) but also of wealth. Ignoring imports and exports, aggregate demand is therefore given by

$$AD = C(Y + B - T(Y + B), W) + I(r) + G. \tag{A1.3.5}$$

Given the flow equilibrium condition $Y^s = AD = Y$, the IS curve is

$$Y = C(Y + B - T(Y + B), M + B/r) + I(r) + G. \tag{A1.3.6}$$

Now, in long-run equilibrium, wealth must be constant, since otherwise the IS and LM curves would be shifting about. Hence, in long-run equilibrium we can set

$$\Delta W = \Delta M + \Delta B/r = 0 \tag{A1.3.7}$$

so (A1.3.1) becomes

$$T(Y + B) = G + B.$$

Differentiating totally:

$$T' \, dY + T' \, dB = dG + dB$$

or

$$\frac{dY}{dG} = \frac{1 + (dB/dG)(1 - T')}{T'}. \tag{A1.3.8}$$

However, this is an expression for the long-run multiplier. Moreover, if government expenditure is financed purely by money, $dB/dG = 0$, so (A1.3.8) reduces to

$$dY/dG = 1/T' \tag{A1.3.9}$$

If $dB/dG \neq 0$ then expression (A1.3.8) must give a greater value for dY/dG than does (A1.3.9). Thus, a government deficit that is at least partly financed by issuing bonds will be more expansionary than one that is financed purely by money, the degree of effectiveness increasing with the proportion of bond financing. For example, if the marginal tax rate is 25 per cent ($T' = 0.25$) then the pure-money-finance long-run multiplier is four, whilst the pure-bond-finance ($dB/dG = 1$) long-run multiplier is seven.

The logic behind this result is quite intuitive. The more bond finance the government employs, the more debt service it has to pay out in the long run (i.e. the greater is B). Since the budget must be balanced in the long run, the equilibrium level of income must be higher in order to yield a higher tax revenue sufficient to service this extra debt.

However, the foregoing assumes that the long-run equilibrium under bond financing is *stable* – which is really rather begging the question.

Suppose we solved the above system to get Y and r (the endogenous variables) as a function of M, B and G (the exogenous variables) – i.e. obtained the reduced form (as per equation (A1.2.2) in appendix 1.2)

$$Y = F(M, B, G) \qquad\qquad (A1.3.10)$$
$$r = H(M, B, G). \qquad\qquad (A1.3.11)$$

Differentiating (A1.3.10) with respect to B gives the effect on aggregate output of issuing one extra bond:

$$\partial Y / \partial B = F_B. \qquad\qquad (A1.3.12)$$

Thus, if the government issues an amount of bonds ΔB, the increase in output will be

$$\Delta Y = F_B \Delta B \qquad\qquad (A1.3.13)$$

but tax must be paid at the rate T' both on this extra output and on the additional coupon payments, ΔB, so the increase in tax revenue is

$$\Delta T = T' (F_B + 1) \Delta B. \qquad\qquad (A1.3.14)$$

For long-run stability, the extra revenue raised in this way must be at least as great as the extra debt service paid out by the government, ΔB; that is,

$$T' (F_B + 1) \Delta B \geqslant \Delta B$$

which reduces to

$$F_B \geqslant (1 - T') / T' \qquad\qquad (A1.3.15)$$

which is the stability condition for long-run equilibrium. If the system satisfies this condition, some measure of bond finance will lead to a stable long-run equilibrium with a higher level of real output than would have been obtained under finance purely with money.

2 Quantity-constrained macroeconomics

2.1 Introduction

Keynes clearly believed that with the publication of his '*General Theory of Employment, Interest and Money*' (Keynes 1936) he was going to change fundamentally the nature of economic theory. In a letter to George Bernard Shaw he wrote

> To understand my state of mind, however, you have to know that I believe myself to be writing a book on economic theory which will largely revolutionize – not, I suppose at once but in the course of the next ten years – the way the world thinks about economic problems.

Yet within a year, Hicks (1937) had published an article that apparently formalized the ideas of Keynes's 'General Theory' into a system of simultaneous equations but that, it subsequently transpired, appeared to show that the Keynesian system was really a special case of the pre-Keynesian or 'neoclassical' orthodoxy – hence the term 'neoclassical synthesis'. The neoclassical synthesis, i.e. the IS–LM system, formed the basis of our analysis in the previous chapter. We showed there that if we preclude money illusion and price rigidity, the IS–LM system can only generate an unemployment solution in three very special circumstances – where there is a liquidity trap, interest-inelastic investment or rigid nominal wages. Moreover, once we allow the possibility of a wealth effect or 'Pigou effect' in consumption, only the last of these is sufficient to generate unemployment. Hence, the logical conclusion of the neoclassical synthesis is to minimize Keynes's contribution to economics. Hines (1971) writes

> It would not be overstating the position to say that the prevailing view was that so far as pure theory was concerned Keynes would have been well advised

not to have written the 'General Theory' at all. He should have written a note in the 'Economic Journal' (or perhaps more appropriately written a letter to 'The Times') making the rather obvious observation that in modern capitalist economies money wages are rigid in a downward direction.

However, beginning in the late sixties with the work of Clower (1965) and Leijonhufvud (1968), a school of thought began to emerge that fundamentally reinterprets Keynes's work outside the framework of the neoclassical synthesis. This literature of the 'Keynesian reappraisal' sought to reinterpret the economics of Keynes as essentially non-Walrasian equilibrium economics, where prices may not always adjust to clear markets continuously.

2.2   Non-Market-Clearing and the Dual Decision Hypothesis

Traditional general equilibrium theory goes to great lengths to make sure that prices clear markets. The most famous example of this is the Walrasian auctioneer who calls out various price vectors (presumably applying an adjustment rule such as 'reduce price where there is excess supply') until he shouts out the price vector at which *ex ante* supply is equal to *ex ante* demand in all markets. Moreover, an important assumption in this story is that no trade at all takes place until the market-clearing price vector is called out. Edgeworth suggested an alternative mechanism by which an economy could arrive at general market clearing. Imagine all the agents of the economy locked together in a large room or hall. Each transactor makes a set of agreements to trade with other agents but, should he or she subsequently discover a more advantageous agreement, he or she is free to annul the previous agreement. Eventually, such a system of 'recontracting' will converge on a market-clearing outcome. A third adjustment process was suggested by Marshall. He suggested that prices adjust with infinite speed to excess demand or supply, e.g. by means of an adjustment rule:

$$\dot{p}_i = \alpha(x_i^d - x_i^s)$$

where $\dot{p}_i$ is the rate of change of the price of the ith good, x_i^d and x_i^s are the *ex ante* demand and supply of the ith good respectively and α is a very large, positive number. If this is the case, and supply and demand curves have the usual slopes, then prices will tend to adjust in response to *incipient* rather than *actual* market disequilibria, with an eventual convergence on market clearing before any significant trading takes place.

Walras, Edgeworth and Marshall are three of the greatest names in the history of economic thought. Why were they apparently willing to go to such lengths to preclude trading at prices that may not clear markets?

If prices are exogenous, then the demand for the ith good in a market-clearing general equilibrium will be a function of the price vector:

$$c_i^d = c_i^d(p) \tag{2.1}$$

where $p = (p_1, p_2, \ldots, p_n)'$ is the market-clearing price vector (which may contain the wage rate). Now if we were to evaluate demand at a price vector other than p, say p^1, then (assuming uniqueness of equilibrium) there must be excess supply or demand in other markets, and agents on the 'long' side of these markets will face quantity constraints – for example workers may find they cannot sell all the labour services they would like to for the going set of wages and prices, or firms may not be able to sell as much output as they would wish to at the going price. In such circumstances it seems unlikely that, say, households rationed in the labour market will continue to demand the same value of goods as if they were fully employed. Similarly, firms finding that they cannot sell all their output are quite likely to reduce their demand for factors of production, including labour. The notion that demand conditions in the goods market may affect firms' behaviour in the labour market was discussed by Patinkin (1956), although the general point that non-clearing in one market will have spillover effects on other markets was explicitly analysed first by Clower (1965), who described this process as the 'dual decision hypothesis'. If a household cannot sell all the labour it wishes, the dual decision hypothesis implies that the household will recompute its demand for the ith good to take account of this fact, so (2.1) becomes

$$\bar{c}_i^{\mathrm{d}} = \bar{c}_i^{\mathrm{d}} (p, \bar{z}) \tag{2.2}$$

where $\bar{z}$ is the *realized* level of income from the labour market. $\bar{z}$ appears in (2.2) because it is effectively an extra exogenous variable, as far as the household is concerned. Since the household's behaviour is more circumscribed in (2.2) than in (2.1), we expect

$$\bar{c}_i^{\mathrm{d}} \leqslant c_i^{\mathrm{d}}$$

Equation (2.2) establishes our notational convention. Where a decision variable is computed on the basis of perceived rationing in another market, we shall place a bar over it and describe it as *rationed*. The rationing variable itself we shall also denote by placing a bar over it (e.g. $\bar{z}$). In (2.2) the rationing variable is in fact labour demand;

$$\bar{z} = w\bar{\ell}^{\mathrm{d}}$$

where w denotes the wage rate and ℓ^{d} labour demand. When a decision variable is not subject to any quantity constraints (e.g. (2.1)) we shall term it *notional*. The *actual* supply or demand that is transacted in a market we shall term *effective*. When effective and notional demands coincide, markets are clearing. The essence of the dual decision hypothesis is that notional and rationed demands and supplies are not the same. Walrasian economics deals only with notional plans; the economics of quantity rationing deals with effective demands and supplies, and in particular it is concerned with the case where effective and notional demands and supplies do not coincide, not all markets are clearing and there is 'false trading'.

Implicit in our discussion so far is the idea of some sort of rationing scheme operating more or less systematically in markets that do not clear – e.g. the total demand for labour is allocated in some way between workers.[1] Of course, constraints (i.e. rationing) in a market will have an impact on agents' behaviour in other markets (i.e. the dual decision hypothesis will operate) only when agents actually *perceive* them – although this is hardly likely to be a problem. When the supplies and demands of agents, the rationing schemes and agents' perceptions are mutually consistent, we shall say that the system is in equilibrium. However, we shall also refer to this situation as a (fix-price) *temporary* equilibrium since we shall treat wages and prices as fixed during the period under consideration. Thus, the unit time period we shall typically consider is just long enough for agents' behaviour to be mutually consistent, but not long enough for prices and wages to change.

The reader may at this point be forgiven for wondering whether we are about to serve up old wine in elegant new bottles – after all, doesn't traditional Keynesian economics rely on price rigidities? However, the motivation for making the fix-price assumption is just to get agents trading at 'false' (i.e. non-market-clearing) prices without, for example, Marshallian high-speed price adjustments coming into play. As we shall see, once the possibility of false trading is allowed, self-correcting adjustment of the economy towards Walrasian equilibrium may be sluggish or non-existent even where there are no institutional price or wage rigidities. The fix-price assumption also serves to highlight the importance of *quantity signals*. When markets fail to clear, relative prices may not disseminate all the appropriate information to an agent. For example, a firm will take into account its projected sales when planning its labour demand, rather than just looking at the current level of the real wage.

2.2.1   The Behaviour of the Household
Under Quantity Rationing

We shall now begin to develop a model to analyse more formally the economic significance of the dual decision hypothesis, drawing particularly on the work of Muellbauer and Portes (1978). In doing so we shall follow the literature and conduct our analysis in terms of a 'representative' household and firm. That is, we assume all firms and households are identical and that aggregate behaviour is just a scaled-up version of individual behaviour. Thus, we need only consider the behaviour of one of the (clone) households and one of the (clone) firms of our hypothetical economy.

We assume that the household's preferences may be represented by a well behaved quasi-concave utility function, which has current household consumption (c), labour supply (ℓ^s) and current money balances (m) as arguments:

$$U = u(c, \ell^{\text{s}}, m, \theta) \tag{2.3}$$

$$\frac{\partial u}{\partial c} > 0 \qquad \frac{\partial u}{\partial \ell} < 0 \qquad \frac{\partial u}{\partial m} > 0$$

$$\frac{\partial^2 u}{\partial c^2} < 0 \qquad \frac{\partial^2 u}{\partial \ell^2} < 0 \qquad \frac{\partial^2 u}{\partial m^2} < 0.$$

Setting aside motives of avarice or a desire to leave bequests, money balances are assumed to enter the utility function because of future uncertainties faced by the household. We assume that money is the only financial asset available, so there are no speculative money balances. A major element of the household's demand for money will therefore be precautionary. The household forms expectations concerning, amongst other things, future prices and wages, future supply-and-demand conditions in the goods and labour markets and, perhaps, future dividend payments and other non-labour income. These expectations will be conditioned at least partly by current levels of consumption, employment, prices, wages and dividend payments. The purpose of including the vector θ in (2.3) is to capture the influence of changes in these variables (besides c and ℓ), as well as exogenous shifts in expectations (e.g. households simply become more pessimistic) on the utility function; i.e. θ is a shift parameter. Intuitively, if households become more pessimistic and expect to be unemployed at some point in the future, they may wish to increase their money balances now in order to be better prepared for this possibility. Thus, an appropriate change in θ in this case may cause preferences to switch towards m – that is, the marginal rate of substitution of consumption for money balances will rise. We shall use this apparatus later to demonstrate so-called 'bootstraps' effects – the idea that agents' expectations may be largely self-fulfilling.

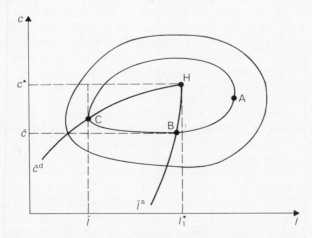

Figure 2.1   The Household's behaviour under rationing

For simplicity, we assume that consumption consists of only one good, so c is a scalar. The household's objective is to maximize (2.3) subject to a budget constraint. The budget constraint simply says that the sum of household consumption and saving must be equal to the sum of labour and non-labour income:

$$w\ell^s + \pi_{-1} = pc + (m - m_{-1}) \qquad (2.4)$$

where w is the wage rate, π_{-1} is profit earned last period by the firm and distributed at the beginning of this period, p is the price of the consumption good and m_{-1} is the money balance left over from last period.

Constrained maximization of (2.3) subject to (2.4) is equivalent to unconstrained maximization of the function obtained by substituting (2.4) into (2.3):

$$U = u(c, \ell^s, (m_{-1} + \pi_{-1} + w\ell^s - pc), \theta) \qquad (2.5)$$

Now, for given m_{-1}, π_-, w, p and θ, we can plot the values of c and ℓ that maximize (2.5) in (c, ℓ) space – this is represented in figure 2.1 by the point H. Holding all variables except c and ℓ constant, we can analyse how the household behaves under rationing by drawing a set of iso-utility curves around H. Clearly, since H maximizes (2.5), a point such as A will yield less utility. However, suppose we started at A and reduced ℓ a little. Although this would reduce utility by reducing end-of-period money balances, the initial utility of the extra leisure may be so large as to enable us to reduce consumption a little whilst keeping utility constant. However, because of diminishing marginal utility, we might soon have to start increasing consumption in order to keep utility intact, to a point such as C. Continuing in this fashion, we can easily see that there will be a continuous set of points around H, beginning and ending at A, that yield the same level of utility as A. Moreover, there will be a continuous family of such iso-utility contours around H, none of which can cross (without violating the axioms of consumer theory). For a given set of utility levels, this gives a diagram in (c, ℓ) space a somewhat onion-like appearance. Utility falls as we move to iso-utility contours further away from H.

How can we use this diagram to analyse behaviour under rationing? Remember that at H the household encounters no rationing, and consumes an amount c^* and supplies labour ℓ^*. Now suppose that the household perceived a labour constraint – e.g. could only sell $\bar{\ell} < \ell^*$ units of labour. The highest utility level it can achieve is that represented by a contour tangential to a vertical line at $\bar{\ell}$ – i.e. at point C. This indicates a level of consumption $\bar{c}^d(\bar{\ell};.) < c^*$. Clearly, if we consider the whole range of possible labour rations between ℓ^* and the origin, we can extend HC and trace out a labour-rationed consumption function $\bar{c}^d$ – in effect by joining up all the points that are tangential to a vertical line.

Similarly, we can consider the effect of rationing in the goods market on labour supply by considering the highest utility that can be attained for a given goods ration – e.g. $\bar{c}$. By joining up all the points at which the iso-utility curve is tangential to a horizontal line, we can derive a consumption-rationed labour supply function, $\bar{\ell}^s$.

To summarize, $\bar{c}^d$ represents the locus of labour-rationed consumption choices in (c, ℓ) space, whilst $\bar{\ell}^s$ represents the locus of consumption-rationed labour supply choices. H represents the point in (c, ℓ) space that the household would choose if it did not encounter rationing in either the goods or the labour market. One should also not lose sight of the fact that the analysis is essentially intertemporal – for example, a given change in expectations of the future may alter the household's optimal level of money holding which may in turn affect its optimal consumption–labour choices. This is a point we shall return to.

2.2.2 The Behaviour of the Firm Under Quantity Rationing

A point we stressed at the end of the last section is that the household's behaviour is essentially intertemporal. This is also true of the firm, which has to form expectations about future output demand and labour supply conditions, and so on. Analogously to the household's use of money balances, we can think of firms holding inventories largely as a proxy for future profits – e.g. if demand is expected to be particularly strong or labour particularly short in the future, the firm may wish to build up inventories during the current period. Thus, we can think of the firm as maximizing a utility function with current profit and inventory holdings as arguments:

$$V = v(\pi, i, \psi) \qquad \frac{\partial y}{\partial \pi} > 0 \qquad \frac{\partial y}{\partial i} > 0 \qquad (2.6)$$

$$\frac{\partial^2 v}{\partial \mu^2} < 0 \qquad \frac{\partial^2 v}{\partial i^2} < 0$$

where V represents firm utility, π is current-period profit and i is the level of inventory holdings. ψ is analogous to θ, and represents variables conditioning the firm's expectations of the future. The firm's objective is to maximize (2.6) subject to a given technology that translates labour employed into output, and to an identity that defines profit as equal to output sold less labour costs (for simplicity we ignore other inputs and costs of inventory holding):

$$y = f(\ell^d) \qquad f' > 0 \qquad f'' < 0 \qquad (2.7)$$
$$\pi \equiv px - w\ell^d \qquad (2.8)$$

where y represents output, x represents sales (so $y - x$ represents the change in inventories) and ℓ^d is labour demand.

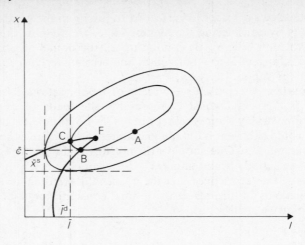

Figure 2.2   The Firm's behaviour under rationing

Substituting (2.8) into (2.6) we have

$$V = v((px - w\ell^d), i, \psi). \tag{2.9}$$

Analogously to our analysis of the values of x and ℓ that maximize (2.9) subject to a given p, w and ψ in (x, ℓ) space as in figure 2.2 at point F. Moreover, we can again consider a point away from the optimum F, such as A, and try and trace out an iso-utility contour for the firm. Reducing labour demand reduces the wage bill, so the firm can reduce sales a little and still obtain an inventory/profit mix yielding the same utility as at A at a point such as B. Reducing labour inputs any further reduces inventories and so sales must rise in order to bring about a compensating rise in current-period profits. Continuing in this fashion, we can see that there will be, like in the case of the consumer, an onion-like iso-utility map around F, with firm utility falling as we move outward.

Moreover, we again trace out, for example, the labour-rationed supply function of the firm by considering the family of points tangential to a vertical line that initially passes through F and then shifts continuously towards the origin. For example, the x-coordinate corresponding to point C is the amount of supply that would be forthcoming if the firm perceived that it could only purchase $\bar{\ell}$ units of labour, and $\bar{x}^s$ is in general the labour-rationed supply function. Similarly, the ℓ-coordinate of B tells us the amount of labour demanded by the firm when it perceives that it can only sell $\bar{x}$ units of output, and $\bar{\ell}^d$ is in general the sales-rationed labour demand function.

2.2.3 The Complete Model

We can now put together the preceding analysis and analyse the complete two-market model. We can also bring in at this stage a government sector in a simple way by assuming that government consumption, g, always takes precedence over household consumption; i.e. the government is never rationed. Hence, 'consumption supply', the amount offered to the household, is just the residual of sales less government consumption, $c^s = x - g$. We can then translate the firm's behavioural functions to (c, ℓ) space simply by shifting them vertically down by an amount g.

So far we have considered two types of rationing on each of our representative agents. Agents may be rationed in either the goods or the labour market. Hence, considering the firm and the household together, we shall see that there are four possible rationing combinations.

Underlying our analysis is the notion of the dual decision hypothesis, so the form a particular demand or supply function takes depends upon rationing conditions in the other market. Moreover, we assume that the short side of the market dominates so, for example, $c^d < c^s$ implies $c = c^d$; i.e. consumption demand being less than consumption supply implies that actual consumption is equal to *ex ante* consumption demand (note that $c^s = x - g$).

More generally, we can write

$$c^d = \begin{cases} c^d & \text{if } \ell = \ell^s \leqslant \ell^d \\ \bar{c}^d(\bar{\ell}; .) & \text{if } \ell = \ell^d < \ell^s \end{cases} \tag{2.10}$$

$$c^s = \begin{cases} x^s(.) - g & \text{if } \ell = \ell^d \leqslant \ell^s \\ \bar{x}^s(\bar{\ell}; .) - g & \text{if } \ell = \ell^s < \ell^d \end{cases} \tag{2.11}$$

$$c = \min(c^d, c^s). \tag{2.12}$$

Note that (2.10) and (2.11) formalize the dual decision hypothesis. For example, equation (2.10) says that consumption demand is equal to notional consumption unless households perceive a labour ration, in which case consumption demand becomes labour-rationed consumption. Similarly, consumption supply is equal to notional supply less government consumption, unless firms perceive rationing in the labour market, in which case it becomes labour-rationed supply less government consumption. Equation (2.12) is the celebrated 'min condition' which simply says that the actual amount transacted will be the lesser of demand and supply, i.e. that the short side dominates.

Precisely analogously, for the labour market we can write

$$\ell^d = \begin{cases} \ell^d(.) & \text{if } c=c^s \leqslant c^d \\ \bar{\ell}^d(\bar{c};.) & \text{if } c=c^d < c^s \end{cases} \tag{2.13}$$

$$\ell^s = \begin{cases} \ell^s(.) & \text{if } c=c^d \leqslant c^s \\ \bar{\ell}^s(\bar{c};.) & \text{if } c=c^s < c^d \end{cases} \tag{2.14}$$

$$\ell = \min(\ell^d, \ell^s). \tag{2.15}$$

Examining (2.10)–(2.12) and (2.13)–(2.15) together, we can begin to see the two markets interact. For example, if the firm perceives that it cannot sell all the output it wishes, it will switch to its sales-rationed labour demand function which, through the min condition, may then determine the amount of labour actually transacted. This may then cause households to perceive a labour ration (they cannot sell all the labour they would wish to), and so consumption demand switches to its labour-rationed form. This may cause effective consumption to fall, via the min condition, which again has an impact on firms if consumption demand is even less than firms initially anticipated. In fact, as we shall see, this is just the multiplier process in action.

Let us now put together the foregoing diagrams in (c, ℓ) space to see how they can aid our analysis.

In figure 2.3 we have drawn the behavioural functions of the firm and the household such that they intersect at their end-points: $F = H = W$. Clearly all plans are mutually consistent and everyone is optimizing fully with no perceived constraints in any market, at point W, which therefore represents the point of Walrasian equilibrium.[2]

Starting from a position of Walrasian equilibrium, imagine what would happen if there were an autonomous reduction in demand, say due to a fall

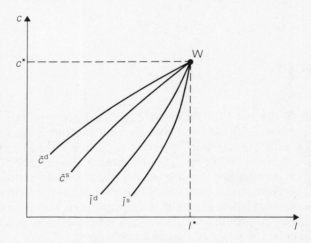

Figure 2.3   The complete model

in government spending by an amount dg. Clearly, the effect of this is to shift the firm's behavioural functions upward by the amount dg, as in figure 2.4 (intuitively there is now an extra amount dg available to households, so $\bar{c}^s$ shifts up by an amount dg). The initial effect is for the firm to experience a ration in the goods market. It therefore reduces its demand for labour as the dual decision hypothesis comes into play. Via the dual decision hypothesis again, households then reduce their consumption demand because they now experience a labour ration. This again impacts on the firm and the negative multiplier process continues until a new temporary equilibrium is established at point K, where the plans of the firm and of the household are again mutually consistent. Note that throughout we have assumed that prices and wages are fixed. At point K, we see that the min condition (2.12) determines effective consumption as equal to consumption demand, $c = c^d < c^s$. Hence there is *ex ante* excess supply in the goods market of $c^s - c^d$. Similarly, min condition (2.15) determines effective employment as equal to labour demand, $\ell = \ell^d < \ell^s$. Hence there is *ex ante* excess supply in the labour market, i.e. unemployment of $\ell^s - \ell^d$. This combination of unemployment and excess goods supply is usually termed *Keynesian unemployment*, since it is exactly the regime that confronted Keynes in the thirties, and that the 'General Theory' was an attempt to explain.

To analyse the movement from Walrasian equilibrium to Keynesian unemployment more fully, we can write down the consumption demand and labour demand functions explicitly. Labour demand is a function of the sales ration

$$\ell = \bar{\ell}^d(\bar{x};.) \tag{2.16}$$

whilst consumption is a function of the labour ration

$$c = \bar{c}^d(\bar{\ell};.). \tag{2.17}$$

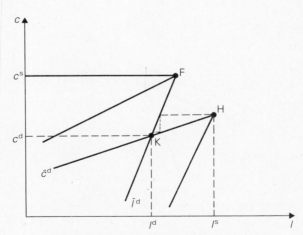

Figure 2.4 Keynesian unemployment

Combining (2.16) and (2.17):

$$c = \bar{c}^d(\bar{\ell}^d(\bar{x}); .).$$ (2.18)

Substituting $c = x - g$ into (2.18) and totally differentiating:

$$dx - dg = \frac{\partial \bar{c}^d}{\partial \ell} \frac{\partial \bar{\ell}^d}{\partial x} \, dx.$$

Hence,

$$\frac{dx}{dg} = \frac{1}{1 - (\partial \bar{c}^d / \partial \ell)(\partial \bar{\ell}^d / \partial x)}.$$ (2.19)

However, equation (2.19) is just the familiar Keynesian demand side multiplier, since the denominator on the right-hand side is just one minus the marginal propensity to consume (MPC). The MPC is the marginal increase in consumption due to increased labour demand as a result of increased output demand. This provides a strong clue that we have established a rigorous microfoundation for traditional Keynesian analysis. In particular, since reducing government expenditure shifted the economy into Keynesian unemployment, it is clear that the traditional Keynesian prescription of increased government expenditure will get us out of it. Using (2.19) and $dc = dx - dg$, we have

$$\frac{dc}{dg} = \frac{(\partial \bar{c}^d / \partial \ell)(\partial \bar{\ell}^d / \partial x)}{1 - (\partial \bar{c}^d / \partial \ell)(\partial \bar{\ell}^d / \partial x)} > 0.$$ (2.20)

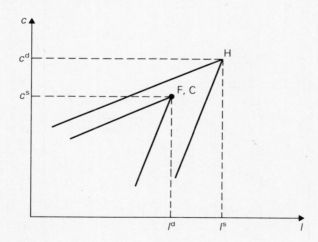

Figure 2.5   Classical unemployment

Now suppose that we drew our 'double-wedge' diagram as in figure 2.5. The firm has achieved its optimum point in both the goods and labour markets before the household. Hence, the min conditions imply that there is *ex ante* excess goods demand of $c^d - c^s$ combined with unemployment of $\ell^s - \ell^d$. This situation is usually termed *classical unemployment*, or 'stagflation'. The adjective 'classical' refers to the interpretation that this is the case implicitly analysed by those whom Keynes termed the 'classical economists'. To see this, consider the effect of a cut in the nominal wage (i.e., holding prices constant, a cut in the real wage) on the firm and household behavioural functions.

Reducing the wage will reduce the household's willingness to supply labour (leisure becomes cheaper) and ability to consume. The net effect is a movement of the point H (the end-point of the labour supply and consumption functions) down to the left in (c, ℓ) space. Conversely, a reduction in the wage has the effect of making the firm wish to employ more labour and hence produce and sell more output, shifting point F (the end-point of the consumption supply and labour demand functions) up and to the right in (c, ℓ) space. From examining figure 2.5, this clearly suggests that a careful application of wage cutting will shift the economy out of classical unemployment towards Walrasian equilibrium. On the other hand, examination of figure 2.4 reveals that cutting the wage in Keynesian unemployment will actually make things worse by increasing both unemployment and excess goods supply.

What happens to the multiplier in classical unemployment? From (2.11) we have

$$c = x^s - g.$$

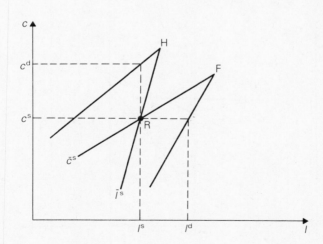

Figure 2.6 Repressed inflation

Hence,

$$\mathrm{d}c/\mathrm{d}g = -1. \tag{2.21}$$

That is, there is perfect crowding out of household consumption by government consumption – Keynesian pump priming just makes things worse.

Now consider the situation as depicted in figure 2.6 where F is down and to the right of H. Applying the min condition implies that households are rationed in the goods market, with excess goods demand $c^d - c^s$, and firms are rationed in the labour market, with excess labour demand $\ell^d - \ell^s$. This regime is usually termed *repressed inflation*. The name in fact suggests its cause and cure. Allowing prices (but not wages) to rise causes the firm to wish to employ more labour (real wage is lower) and produce and sell more output – F moves up and to the left. Since goods are dearer, the household will tend to reduce its consumption. However, although the real wage is now lower, the rise in prices will have eroded the value of the household's money balances. Hence, the household will tend to supply more labour in order to increase its saving. Thus, H moves down and to the right. Rising prices thus tend to push H and F together to a Walrasian equilibrium.

The Keynesian multiplier under repressed inflation also turns out to be quite interesting. Combining (2.11) and (2.13) and applying the min conditions:

$$c = \bar{x}^s(\bar{\ell}^s; .) - g$$

Hence

$$\frac{\mathrm{d}c}{\mathrm{d}g} = \frac{-1}{1 - (\partial \bar{x}^s/\partial \ell)(\partial \bar{\ell}^s/\partial c)} < 0. \tag{2.22}$$

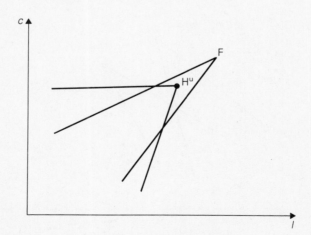

Figure 2.7   Underconsumption

The denominator of the right-hand side of (2.22) is one minus the 'marginal propensity to supply'. The marginal propensity to supply measures the marginal change in supply as a result of the labour supply response to a change in the amount of goods available. Note in particular that the 'supply side' multiplier is negative: increased government consumption crowds out private consumption, reducing labour supply, which further reduces the amount available for consumption.

The final possible combination of goods–labour market rationing is depicted in figure 2.7 where the household has achieved its optimal point independently of the firm in both the goods and labour markets. The firm is rationed in both markets, with excess labour demand $\ell^d - \ell^s$ and excess goods supply $c^s - c^d$. This might be thought of as something of a curiosity since, although firms cannot sell all they would like to, they still try to take on more labour to produce more. However, such a situation might occur if the real wage was so low that firms wanted to produce more for inventory. This regime is normally termed *underconsumption*.

2.3 Further Analysis of Keynesian Unemployment

We can gain some further insight into the nature of Keynesian unemployment at the expense of making one or two additional assumptions. Note firstly that Keynesian unemployment is determined by the interaction of the labour-rationed consumption function, $\bar{c}^d(\bar{\ell};.)$ and the sales-rationed labour demand function, $\bar{\ell}^d(\bar{x};.)$. In fact, figure 2.8, which depicts the Keynesian unemployment case, is really the familiar 45° Keynes cross diagram, represented in (c, ℓ) space rather than the more usual income–expenditure space. Moreover, for given wages and prices, the labour ration $\bar{\ell}$

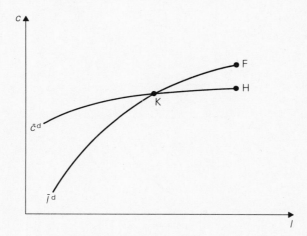

Figure 2.8 The Keynesian cross in (c, ℓ) space

determines household income uniquely. Thus, the labour-rationed consumption function could alternatively be expressed as a function of household income. This therefore provides a micro-theoretic basis for Keynes's 'fundamental psychological law' that consumption is a function of income. Before the Keynesian reappraisal this had always been thought of as rather *ad hoc*, since (market-clearing) price theory suggests that demand should be a function of relative prices.

Let us now make the assumption that the household's utility function (2.3) is of a special form. More specifically, suppose that it is additively separable in labour supply and in consumption and money balances. Basically, this means that it can be written as the sum of two separate functions:

$$U = u_1(\ell^s, \ldots) + u_2(c, m, \ldots). \tag{2.23}$$

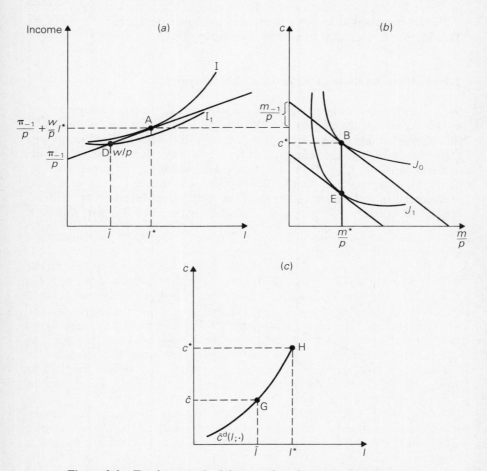

Figure 2.9 Tracing out the labour-rationed consumption function

If this is the case, the maximizing U is equivalent to maximizing u_1 and u_2 separately. This allows us to draw indifference maps in labour–income space and consumption–money space in order to analyse the household's behaviour.

Panel (*a*) of figure 2.9 shows the household's behaviour in income–labour space. The household receives the real profits of the firm's last period, π_{-1}/p, distributed as a dividend payment at the beginning of the current period. It can then add to this by selling labour at the rate w/p, i.e. the real wage, along a line with slope w/p and intercept π_{-1}/p. Since the household's indifference curves will be convex and upward-sloping in income–labour space, the optimal income–labour choice for the household in figure 2.9(*a*) is the tangency solution at point A, with optimal labour supply ℓ^*. The total of earned income plus non-earned income is then transmitted to the vertical axis of figure 2.9(*b*), where it is then added to real money balances held over from last period, m_{-1}/p. This gives the total amount available for real consumption and holding as real money balances, since by rearranging the budget constraint (2.4) we have

$$\frac{\pi_{-1}}{p} + \frac{m_{-1}}{p} + \frac{w}{p}\,\ell^s = c + \frac{m}{p}\,.$$

The budget line in figure 2.9(*b*) is therefore a 45° negatively sloped line with intercept

$$\pi_{-1}/p + m_{-1}/p + w\ell^s/p.$$

Standard indifference curve analysis then yields the optimal consumption–money choice at point B, with real money balances m^*/p and real consumption c^*. In figure 2.9(*c*), point H is simply the point in (c,ℓ) space with coordinates (c^*,ℓ^*) and, as in parts (*a*) and (*b*), represents the household's unconstrained consumption–labour choice.

Now consider what happens if the household perceives a labour ration $\bar{\ell}$. In figure 2.9(*a*), the highest indifference curve it can now achieve is I_1, instead of I, at point D. Transmitting the income corresponding to point D onto the vertical axis of figure 2.9(*b*) and adding m_{-1}/p to it then has the effect of shifting the budget line in figure 2.9(*b*) inwards. Utility maximizing then yields an optimal consumption choice $\bar{c}$. Point G in (c,ℓ) space has coordinates $(\bar{c},\bar{\ell})$, and clearly must lie on the labour-rationed consumption function. In fact, repeating this exercise for the range of possible labour rations between ℓ^* and the origin will trace out the labour-rationed consumption function, $\bar{c}^d(\bar{\ell};.)$.

Now consider what would happen if, starting from a position of Keynesian unemployment, the real wage were cut. This would have the effect of making the budget line in figure 2.9(*a*) flatter. Since effective labour supply is constrained at $\bar{\ell}$, total income would then fall. This would then have the effect of shifting the budget constraint in figure 2.9(*b*) inwards. If consumption is a normal good, then the effect of this pure income effect would then be to reduce consumption. This means that for any given level of $\bar{\ell}$, consumption would be lower – i.e. the consumption function in figure 2.9(c) would shift downwards. As pointed out in the previous section, this would have the effect of deepening the recession by inducing firms to reduce labour demand even further.

What would be the effect of a pure expansionary monetary policy on an economy in Keynesian unemployment? Pure monetary policy amounts to changing the amount of money available to households at the beginning of the period (e.g. by a 'helicopter drop'). This would have the effect of shifting the budget line in figure 2.9(b) outwards. For any given level of ℓ, this income effect would then increase the chosen level of consumption. Therefore, the labour-rationed consumption function would shift upwards, moving the economy out of recession.

Finally, imagine starting from an initial Walrasian equilibrium, and then increasing prices, p, and wages, w, in the same proportion, so that the real wage, w/p, remains constant. The main effect this will have on the household will be to reduce the real value of its wealth – i.e. π_{-1}/p and m_{-1}/p both fall as p rises. Although the slope of the budget line in figure 2.9(a) remains constant at w/p, it will shift downwards by the amount of the reduction in π_{-1}/p. This may lead to an increase in the amount of labour that the household wishes to offer for a given real wage. However, it will almost certainly reduce the amount of income available for consumption. Moreover, the real value of the money balance, m_{-1}/p, has been eroded, so the budget line in figure 2.9(b) will almost certainly move inwards. The net effect on the labour-constrained consumption function it to move it downwards, and perhaps to the right, but this is exactly the case depicted in figure 2.8 which shows that the economy will shift into Keynesian unemployment.

Of course, starting from a position of Keynesian unemployment, an equiproportionate decline in wages and prices will tend to shift the economy towards Walrasian equilibrium – this is what is normally termed the 'wealth effect', 'real balance effect' or 'Pigou effect', as we saw in chapter 1.

When we started to set up the microeconomic basis of our model, in §2.2, we were careful to point out the intertemporal nature of the analysis and the role played by expectations. Up until now, however, we have implicitly assumed that agents' expectations are unaffected by changes in variables such as prices, wages, money balances and government expenditure. The impact of expectations is the topic of the next section.

2.4 'Bootstraps' Effects

In previous sections we have mentioned that agents' expectations, by affecting their demand for current-period money balances (or inventories), would actually be self-fulfilling. As we noted above, the demand for money in this model is really a precautionary demand. Imagine, therefore, what might happen if agents for some reason became more pessimistic about the future – e.g. households started to expect to be rationed in the labour market. This would have the effect of raising the demand for money balances as agents try and build up a buffer against future adversity. In micro terms, this amounts to an increase in the marginal rate of substitution of consumption for money. In figure 2.9(b), the indifference curves would become steeper as larger increases in consumption would now be needed to compensate for a marginal reduction in the money balances. This is illustrated in figure 2.10, which shows that the effect would be to reduce consumption, for any given level of effective labour supply. This means that the labour-rationed consumption function would shift down in (c, ℓ) space and, starting from an initial Walrasian equilibrium, the economy would shift into Keynesian unemployment. Households' expectations would be self-fulfilling, like people lifting themselves into the air by their own bootstraps. In fact, this is really a rather well known phenomenon in a new guise, and is normally termed the 'paradox of thrift', although the explicit expectations-based cause of the shift in saving is not normally stressed.

We can also examine what would happen if firms expected to be rationed in the goods market in the future – i.e. that there will be a situation of excess goods supply. Clearly, this would cause them to want to run down inventories, produce less and sell more in the current period. Thus, the sales-rationed labour demand function would shift up and to the left in (c, ℓ) space, the economy would tend to shift into Keynesian unemployment, and producers' expectations would be self-fulfilling – they would indeed face a situation of excess goods supply.

Although we can no longer use our three-quadrant diagram, figure 2.9, a similar analysis can be applied to the case where the household expects

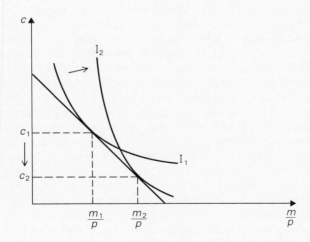

Figure 2.10   The effect of increased pessimism on the consumption-saving choice

to be rationed in the goods market in the future. If the goods won't be available to consume, it would be pointless to run up large money balances. Hence, as agents attempt to run down money balances, they tend to consume more goods and supply less labour in the current period. Thus, the consumption-rationed labour supply function shifts up and to the left in (c, ℓ) space. The economy would move from Walrasian equilibrium into repressed inflation (figure 2.6) and the household would indeed encounter rationing in the goods market. The reader should verify that repressed inflation would also ensue if, starting from Walrasian equilibrium, the firm anticipated a future labour market constraint and therefore attempted to build up inventories in the current period.

2.5   The Model in a Simple Open Economy

Throughout the foregoing analysis we have implicitly assumed that the economy is closed to foreign trade. In this section, following Dixit (1978), we relax this assumption in a very simple way by assuming that all goods are tradeable, that the economy is 'small' in the sense that it faces perfectly elastic supply and demand for the tradeable in world markets, and that the exchange rate is fixed.

The major impact of these assumptions is that there cannot now be excess supply or demand in the goods market – any gap between effective domestic demand and supply of goods has its counterpart in increased imports or exports. Since neither households nor firms now experience quantity rationing, there can be no feedback from the goods market to the labour market. The dual decision hypothesis can only operate by labour market constraints spilling over to affect behaviour in the goods market. This means that we can ignore the sales-constrained labour demand function and the consumption-constrained labour supply function in our analysis. Given the assumed relative slopes of the labour-constrained consumption demand function and the labour-constrained consumption supply function, the four possible combinations of unemployment/unfilled vacancies and balance-of-trade surplus/deficit are depicted in figure 2.11.

Note that the household is always at point H, since it cannot be rationed in the goods market. If H is below the consumption supply function, there is a balance-of-trade surplus; if it is above, there is a balance-of-trade deficit. If H is to the right of F, then households wish to supply more labour than firms find profitable to employ, even given perfectly elastic goods demand, so there is unemployment. If H is to the left of F, then households supply less labour than firms wish to employ and there is excess demand for labour – i.e. unfilled vacancies.

There are two points worthy of note. Firstly, since there are no spillover effects from the goods market to the labour market, any excess supply or demand for labour must be due to its price – i.e. the real wage. Thus, any unemployment that does occur is purely because the real wage is too high to clear the market – i.e. it is of the classical variety. Secondly, since consumption supply is the residual of what firms wish to sell less government consumption, any change in government spending simply moves the end-point of the consumption supply function, F, vertically up or down. Since unemployment is measured as the *horizontal* distance between F and H, it is therefore unaffected by government expenditure.

Finally, it should be noted that a far richer analysis is provided if we allow nontradeables or intermediate inputs into the model, and/or relax the small-country assumption – see, for example, Neary 1980, Kennally 1983, Taylor 1984.

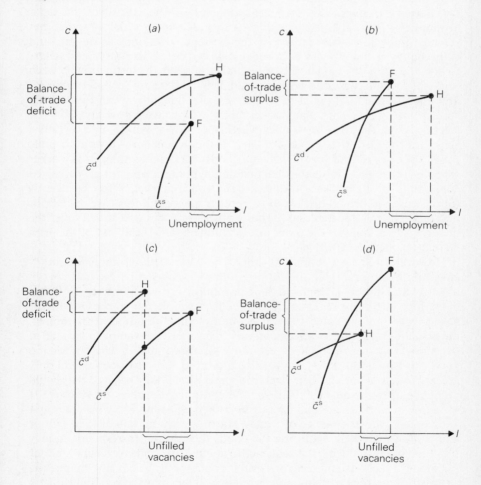

Figure 2.11 The model in a simple open economy

2.6   The Role of Money and Assets in Quantity-Constrained Macroeconomics

It is sometimes argued that money plays a crucial role in quantity-constrained models because, acting as a medium of exchange, it effectively drives a wedge between offers to supply and offers to demand. Consider, for example, a moneyless economy where firms produced only, say, corn and workers were paid in corn. If an unemployed worker offered to work for his or her marginal physical product of, say, fifty bushels of corn per week, the offer of labour is simultaneously a demand for output. The worker would then be taken on since the firm would not have to worry about being constrained in the market for output. In fact, this is a central tenet of the so-called 'classical' economics – i.e. that 'supply creates its own demand', which is sometimes referred to as Say's law. However, the existence of money as the medium of exchange essentially drives a wedge between offers to supply and offers to demand, or looked at another way, makes possible the distinction between *notional* demand (what the worker would demand if he or she were employed) and *effective* demand (what he or she actually demands, given the existing state of unemployment). The worker might offer to work for, say, £100 per week, leaving the firm to wonder whether or not it will be able to find a buyer for the extra fifty bushels of corn. If the firm believes it won't be able to sell the extra output (i.e. perceives a goods market constraint), the worker won't be taken on. This is the dual decision hypothesis operating – perceived constraints in one market (in this case the goods market) affect an agent's (in this case the firm's) behaviour in another market (in this case the labour market). Thus, it appears that money, rather than acting as 'a veil' over the underlying workings of the economy, actually impairs the ability of the price system to operate effectively.

However, upon reflection, it should be clear that although quantity-constrained temporary equilibrium requires a wedge to be driven between effective and notional demands, there is nothing intrinsic in money itself that does this. The more realistic alternative to a simple one-good, one-factor economy is not the same type of economy with the addition of money, but a multi-good, multi-factor economy. Consider for example a variant of the moneyless, corn-producing economy discussed above, where a second good ('consumer durables', say) is also produced. Corn workers would only accept bushels of corn as their weekly remuneration if they believed they could exchange at least some of them for the consumer durables they desire. If we allow even more goods into our hypothetical economy, workers might anticipate a whole sequence of trades, starting with the sale of their labour and ending with them acquiring the goods they desire. Introducing money simplifies life by reducing this sequence to at most two trades (exchange labour for money, exchange money for desired goods), but it does not change the nature of the problem in any significant way. Thus, it is the very multiplicity of goods in real-world economies, rather than the existence of money, that allows a wedge to be driven between offers to supply and offers to demand or, equivalently, allows the distinction between notional and effective demands to be drawn.

At least one part of the foregoing analysis does, however, rely on the existence of money (or some other non-produced asset) – that concerning the 'bootstraps' effects we discussed in §2.4, which rely upon the role of money not as a medium of exchange, but as a store of value. For example, as workers become less optimistic about their prospects in the labour market for some future period, they may wish to transfer some consumption from the present to the future by saving, i.e. reducing current consumption. If this took the form of hoarding extra consumption goods, there would not be a fall in current aggregate (effective) demand and the (negative) multiplier process would not come into operation. If, however, saving takes the form of increasing holdings of non-produced assets such as money at the expense of current consumption, the negative multiplier *does* come into operation and agents' expectations become self-fulfilling.

2.7 Endogenous Prices in Quantity-Constrained Models

Throughout the chapter we have implicitly treated prices and wages as parametric, or 'given'. There are two possible ways to interpret this 'fix-price' methodology. One is to argue that the fix-price temporary 'equilibria' discussed above are not equilibria at all, but in fact describe the kinds of trade that would occur during the transition (made up of many temporary 'equilibria') to the full, market-clearing equilibrium. However, this interpretation is very close to the spirit of the neoclassical synthesis whereby Keynesian economics is seen as a special case of the neoclassical orthodoxy when the frictions and imperfections of real-world economies are stressed (note that Friedman (1969) defines the natural rate of employment as that rate ground out by a Walrasian general equilibrium system with friction).

Another interpretation is that these temporary equilibria are in fact true states of rest of the system. As an empirical matter, prices for a wide variety of goods appear to be set by firms independently of short-run fluctuations in demand or supply conditions (see, e.g., Carlton 1986). However, one would clearly like to incorporate a *theory* of price formation into a model of fix-price temporary equilibria in order to close the model in a satisfactory way. In other words, if non-Walrasian equilibria are to be taken seriously as a foundation for real-world policy analysis, one has to explain *why* prices are not perfectly flexible, as for example in the New Classical paradigm.

The literature on quantity-constrained models with endogenous price setting is technically quite difficult, and our remarks here are therefore intended to dispel any suspicions the reader may have had that it is the exogeneity of prices itself that is the cause of 'market failure', rather than to spell out an explicit model.

Perhaps an obvious way to introduce price setting whilst retaining the non-market-clearing possibility is by assuming imperfect (or monopolistic) competition in the goods and/or labour markets. This is the approach taken, *inter alia*, by Grandmont and Laroque (1976) and Hart (1983a). In the Grandmont–Laroque paper, for example, firms choose levels of output consistent with their forecast of the price at which they will be able to sell the output. Bootstraps effects are present in their model, since if firms are pessimistic with respect to future aggregate demand, there may be excess supply of labour (i.e. unemployment) at all positive wage rates.

Another way of introducing endogenous price setting into quantity-constrained models is through 'conjectural equilibria' (Hahn 1977, Gale 1978). Every agent in the economy is endowed with a 'conjecture function' which relates, for a given set of observed price and quantity signals, the price vector that the agent conjectures he or she must offer to trade in excess of his or her other constraints). A conjectural equilibrium is one where the conjectured price vector for the equilibrium set of trades coincides with the actual price vector. Hahn (1977) shows that, under fairly weak assumptions, at least one conjectural equilibrium will exist that is non-Walrasian (i.e. non-market-clearing).

A third possibility is to introduce explicit or implicit contracting into the model – it may be optimal under certain circumstances for firms and workers to agree on a degree of price and wage inflexibility. The microeconomics of implicit labour contracts are dealt with in chapter 4.

2.8   Summary and Conclusion

The inexorable logic of the fully specified neoclassical synthesis (i.e. with output price flexibility and wealth effects) is that the 'automatic route' to full employment can only be blocked by downwardly rigid nominal wages. Although quantity-constrained economics has now taken on an intellectual life of its own (see, e.g., Drazen 1980 for a survey), it was originally developed largely as an antidote to the 'rigid-nominal-wage' interpretation of Keynes's contribution to macroeconomics (see particularly Leijonhufvud 1968). If markets do not clear and there is 'false trading' (i.e. at non-market-clearing prices), prices may fail to reflect adequately the underlying (*ex ante*) pattern of supply and demand in the economy. In part, this arises because in a multi-good economy it is impossible to synchronize fully offers to supply and offers to demand, so it is possible to draw a distinction between notional and effective demands. Although money, *per se* does not force this denial of Say's law, an aggregative model with one kind of output and money will generate similar results.

We introduced the idea of the dual decision hypothesis in §2.2, where it was formalized as a switching condition in the behavioural functions of firms and households ((equations 2.10)–(2.12) and (2.13)–(2.15)). Using fairly standard neoclassical analysis, we were then able to build up a model in which Walrasian general equilibrium was a special case, but quantity-constrained temporary equilibrium was more likely to occur. Although a number of quantity–constraint combinations are possible, we focused particularly on the case of 'Keynesian unemployment' – where households encounter rationing in the labour market (i.e. are unemployed) and firms encounter rationing in the goods market (i.e. cannot sell all the output they would wish at the going price). In this case we were able to derive formally the Keynesian consumption function (consumption as a function of income rather than relative prices), the Keynesian multiplier ($dx/dg = 1 - \text{MPC})^{-1}$), and familiar Keynesian fiscal and monetary policy prescriptions. Moreover, reducing wages in Keynesian unemployment actually deepens the recession by setting a negative multiplier effect into operation.

In §2.5 we examined 'bootstraps effects' in the context of a quantity-constrained macromodel (the idea that agents' expectations can be largely self-fulfilling – e.g. the paradox of thrift), while in §2.6 we looked at the consequences of opening the model to foreign trade in a simple way. In §2.7 we discussed the role of money and assets in quantity-constrained macromodels, while in §2.8 we made some remarks concerning the endogeneity of prices and the fix-price assumption.

Notes

1 The only explicit stipulation we shall make concerning the rationing scheme is that the government is never rationed – it simply takes whatever it wants of aggregate output leaving the rest to be rationed amongst households. We are, however, assuming that the rationing scheme is non-manipulable. A manipulable rationing scheme is one where the amount an agent receives is proportional to his or her excess demand (this is often the type of scheme used to allocated oversubscribed issues of new shares on the stock exchange, for example). A problem with manipulable rationing schemes is that agents have a strong incentive to overbid in an attempt to achieve their desired transactions (see, e.g., Benassy 1977).

2 Note that figure 2.3 is drawn very carefully so that the household's 'wedge' fully encloses the firm's 'wedge'. This is deliberate, since the slopes of the various supply and demand functions that this implies are necessary for stability of the model (existence and stability of equilibrium are assumed). To verify this, the reader should attempt to try and work through the negative multiplier process following a reduction in government expenditure (as outlined below) when the labour-rationed consumption function has a steeper slope than the sales-rationed labour demand function (or indeed any of the exercises below with qualitatively different function slopes).

3 Rational expectations and the New Classical view

3.1 Introduction

Expectations play an important role in many aspects of macroeconomics. For example in Keynes's speculative demand for money and Tobin's (1958) risk-aversion model the demand for money depends on expected holding-period yields. In an intertemporal framework, consumption depends on expected (or permanent) income while for firms the desired capital stock depends on expected future profits. The Phillips curve has current (wage or price) inflation determined by expected inflation. Until the 1970s most applied research into the above relationships invoked the first-order adaptive expectations hypothesis (AEH) which provided a method of modelling these 'unobservable expectations'.

An implication of the AEH is that the expected value of say the price level is a geometrically declining weighted average of past values of the price level. Critics of the hypothesis have noted two problems. First, except under rather special circumstances §3.9 systematic forecast errors are made: agents do not fully correct for their past mistakes. For example, if actual prices rise *continuously*, expected prices always understate the actual price level. Second, predictions made using the AEH are unlikely to be *consistent* with the *predictions* of the complete macromodel in which the adaptive expectations equation forms a part: the behaviour of agents in one section of the model does not conform to their behaviour as expressed in the *whole* model. Thus the AEH attracted the pejorative term 'ad hoc'.

Whether one alters one's forecasting formula in the face of systematic errors depends, of course, on the 'real costs' of such errors relative to the costs involved in obtaining the information required to produce better forecasts. For example, at low rates of price inflation the cost in terms of a loss in *real* wages, when using first-order adaptive expectations to predict the price level when setting nominal wage claims, may not be large and may not therefore warrant the search for new information and forecasting methods. Alternative 'adaptive' expectations mechanisms might include taking account of the rate of growth in the price level (i.e. 'change of gear', Flemming 1976, or higher-order partial adjustment) or special factors (such as the devaluation of sterling in the UK in 1967). These *ad hoc* modifications can be used to make the AEH fit the data reasonably well (Carlson and Parkin 1975, Holden and Peel 1977, Turnovsky 1970). However, from a theoretical point of view there is still the consistency problem of the AEH. The desire for a theory of expectations that produces forecasts that are compatible with the underlying model assumed provided part of the impetus towards the development of the rational-expectations hypothesis REH).

3.2   Basic Tenets of the Rational-Expectations Hypothesis

To the uninitiated the basic postulates of the REH seem innocuous enough. In forming their expectations, agents are assumed to 'do the best they can', given the constraints that they face; this is the familiar constrained maximization approach of neoclassical economics. However it is in the interpretation of 'do the best they can' and in delineating the constraints that 'full' or 'Muth–RE' agents face, that fuels the criticism of RE, that it is 'unrealistic'.

Muth (1961) suggested that individuals form their assessment of future events, *as if* they used the correct economic model characterizing these events. The predictions from the economic model provide their 'rational expectation' of economic variables. In forming their expectations about the future, individuals use all relevant information available at the time at which they make their prediction. Since their prediction is formed using the 'true' model of the process generating the data, the *expected value* of a variable differs from the actual outcome only by a random error. If there were no random element in behaviour the prediction would equal the actual outcome and RE would reduce to perfect foresight. Since expectations are consistent with model predictions a more accurate description of this kind of expectations formation is that of 'consistent expectations' but the term 'rational expectations' has pervaded the literature and we shall use it here. In RE, the individuals' *subjective* probability distributions concerning future events are the same as the *actual* probability distributions, conditional on the information available to them. In principle the REH considers all moments of the probability distribution but in most RE models one only considers the mean or expected value of the distribution and ignores higher-order moments, such as the variance (the latter make the analysis much more difficult but see Walshe 1984 on this aspect).

Critics of RE argue that the informational and computational requirements of Muth–RE appear to be severe if all agents actually have to know the true model and solve it to obtain their predictions. However, this requirement is weakened if agents merely act *as if* they used the 'true' model. Some informed agents may use the true model and other agents obtain the information relatively costlessly, for example via government or research publications. However, if information is useful, presumably it is not always provided without cost and some information gathering and processing costs are inevitable.

A second major criticism of RE is that it provides no scope for learning since agents are always using the 'correct' model to produce their 'optimal' predictions. If there is a switch from fixed to flexible exchange rates, agents are assumed to know the 'true' model immediately even though no data on the new regime are yet available. Clearly, while agents are learning, RE may not be a useful characterization of how people form expectations. The greater the frequency of rather fundamental changes the less useful RE is, since it relies on an unchanging underlying structure. Under such uncertainty it may be that rather simple rules of thumb are used to forecast economic variables. To make RE more operational Feige and Pearce (1976) propose that agents use *economically rational expectations*: agents acquire information up to the point where the expected marginal benefit from additional information just equals the expected marginal cost of acquiring and processing such information. This approach still leaves open the question of how wide the information set actually used in forming expectations might be, but suggests that it is often less than the 'complete economic model' of the variables under study.

Recently there has been some interesting work done on how agents learn about the economic environment and whether agents who initially do not use RE, and hence make systematic mistakes, might eventually adopt the RE approach. However it appears that there is no general theoretical presumption that agents modify their forecasts to approximate rational expectations (De Canio 1979) although conclusions in this area are still of a very preliminary nature (see Blume et al. 1982).

When moving from the individual to the aggregate level we have the problem that not all individuals may form their expectations using the *same* model of the economy. If each agent forms RE based on a different model, what will the outcome be for an aggregate variable that arises from the behaviour of individuals using different expectations mechanisms? However, the assumption of similar behaviour for all agents is usually made in all branches of macroeconomics, and it should not be seen as too exceptional when this assumption is applied to RE.

In what follows we shall refer to both 'Muth' and 'full' RE simply as RE. The REH may in principle be applied to any type of model for which we require expectations to be consistent with the forecasts of the model. However in the 1970s the REH was predominantly analysed using market-clearing macromodels and these quickly became known as *New Classical* (NC) models. NC ideas were initially developed by US economists such as Robert E. Lucas, Robert Barro, Thomas Sargent and Neil Wallace although, as noted above, Muth had expounded the basic ideas as early as 1961 (Muth 1961). The NC view has a strong neoclassical basis: agents maximize some objective function (e.g. utility, profits) subject to constraints, and base their decisions largely on relative prices. Thus, for example, the NC economists would accept the neoclassical view of the labour market (§1.5.3). Markets are assumed to 'clear' very quickly and hence we are always very close to general equilibrium. The 'new' element in the NC approach is that in forming their expectations of economic variables agents do not make systematic forecasting errors because they use the 'true' model of the economy. Thus NC models are based on two key assumptions: (i) all markets have perfectly flexible prices and are in equilibrium (i.e. clear) in all periods; (ii) agents use RE when forecasting the future course of economic variables. However, it is worth emphasizing at the outset that the RE hypothesis is logically distinct from the market-clearing assumption and indeed RE has been applied to non-market-clearing models, as we shall see below. Nevertheless, it is the conclusions from the NC market-clearing RE models that provide startling policy prescriptions, some of which it could reasonably be argued have influenced actual policy decisions, in particular in the US post-1980 and in the UK post-1979.

The 'consensus view' of macroeconomists of the 1950s and 1960s could be said to embrace the notion that discretionary fiscal (and in the US, monetary) policy could mitigate cycles in output and move the economy towards a 'desired' level of output without excessive inflation. The stagflation of the 1970s tempered the views of economists, particularly as regards the notion that the authorities could, by altering aggregate demand, *permanently* alter the level of output (and unemployment) without causing accelerating inflation. As noted in the previous chapter, the latter argument was reflected in debates about the vertical long-run Phillips curve. However, in the first half of the 1970s it was probably still widely accepted that the authorities could *speed up* the move to a 'full-employment' level of output as well as mitigate cycles in output, particularly if the economy had entered a deep and prolonged recession (or inflationary boom). It may be said, without exaggeration, that initially NC models completely undermined even this mildly interventionist approach to demand management. NC models assert that known *systematic* government policy rules cannot *in principle* influence movements of the level of output around its 'natural' or equilibrium rate and hence cannot reduce the variance of output: counter-cyclical aggregate demand policy is at best superfluous. The key distinction is between systematic (or anticipated) policy changes and unanticipated (or non-systematic) ones. According to one version of the NC model, cycles in output around the natural rate are caused *solely* by forecast errors, e.g. about the price level. Forecast errors would arise, for example, if the authorities caused a sudden *unanticipated* change in the money supply. The corollary to the above is that NC models imply that systematic known policy rules do not influence real variables such as output and unemployment and the latter only respond to surprises or unanticipated changes in policy. This is the policy ineffectiveness proposition. In choosing between a simple (non-feedback) known rule (e.g. a *constant* rate of growth in the money supply) or a 'complex' feedback rule, the authorities must choose that rule that is likely to be most easily understood and correctly monitored by the private sector. Unanticipated (or unsystematic) changes in the money supply will then be kept to a minimum ensuring that the variance of output is minimized. The economy is basically 'self-correcting' (i.e. all markets clear) and the authorities can at best seek to minimize uncertainty about their own policy actions.

The reader may be wondering precisely what the role is of the money supply and fiscal policy in NC models. NC models frequently incorporate a monetarist or neoclassical structure and we have seen (§1.5.4) that in such models money is neutral *in the long run* and fiscal policy working via changes in aggregate demand is fully 'crowded out'. Money affects only nominal variables such as the price level in the long run; output changes (if at all) only in the short run. In many NC models announced (expected) changes in the money supply, if believed by agents (i.e. if the policy is credible), are immediately reflected in price expectations and, because prices are assumed to be perfectly flexible, in actual price changes. Hence there is a direct link between the money supply and inflation, and money is neutral *in the short run*. A counter-inflationary monetary policy (if credible) may therefore reduce inflation at little or no cost in 'transitory' unemployment: the addition of RE to conventional monetarist models may therefore 'collapse' the time-lags of the response of the economy to announced policy changes. Again, it is important to note that these monetarist results are due to the underlying 'monetarist model'; RE merely accentuates the speed of response.

The choice between alternative discretionary policies is often based on the predictions from macroeconomic models. Lucas (1976) in his *policy evaluation proposition* suggested that when agents use RE, policy simulations on conventional (i.e. non-RE) models will give incorrect and therefore misleading results, the reason being that RE agents change their method of forecasting (of, say, inflation) when the authorities announce alternative policies (e.g. a move from fixed to floating exchange rates). Hence the advent of RE again severely weakens the theoretical basis for the analysis of alternative discretionary policies. If correct, the 'Lucas critique' would at a minimum render many government macroeconomic advisers redundant or, alternatively, would require many more in order to tackle the very difficult economic and econometric problems raised.

Since the REH is concerned with the way in which agents form expectations and the relation between these forecasts and the out-turns, we begin with a discussion of the basic axioms or postulates of RE. Survey data on expectations of inflation, output, sales, interest rates etc. are available in either qualitative or quantitative terms for a number of years. Published forecasts of economic variables also provide a time series of 'expectations' of forecasters. These expectations data may be compared with actual values (or out-turn values) to see if agents' forecasts are 'correct on average' and use all available relevant information: this provides *direct tests* of the REH.

In a number of NC models it is assumed that the supply of output (above the 'normal' or natural rate) is determined by considerations of short-run profitability that arise unexpectedly. For example, in the Sargent–Wallace 'surprise' supply function an unanticipated increase in prices leads to an increase in the supply of output as firms take advantage of this (unexpectedly) profitable market environment. There are a number of variants of 'surprise' supply functions and the policy implications of NC models may differ depending on the particular supply function incorporated into the model. In §3.4 we therefore discuss their theoretical pedigree and their relationship to the Phillips curve of §1.7.

In §3.5 we present a very simple 'monetarist' NC model, which allows us to analyse the policy ineffectiveness, and policy evaluation propositions. The conditions under which both market-clearing (NC) and non-market-clearing models, which embody RE, lead to policy ineffectiveness are explored. We find that the assumption that all markets clear is as important in producing policy ineffectiveness as is the assumption of RE. In the final section of the chapter we discuss the ability of RE models to explain the business cycle and 'persistence' in the level of real variables such as output. In this context the Blanchard (1981) model has the attractive property that agents in asset markets have Muth–RE whilst goods and labour markets may not clear in the short run and may exhibit 'sluggish' behaviour. The Blanchard 'partly rational' model provides an introduction to RE models with 'sticky' variables in which the distinction between anticipated and unanticipated policy changes is found to be crucial. The model also allows the authorities to influence the mean level of output, which also exhibits persistence as the supply function is of the Keynesian fix-price variety.

Our analysis in this chapter centres on the macroeconomic 'systems' implications of the REH and NC view. Technical problems (e.g. multiple solutions and instability) are relegated to the appendix. In the text we use as simple a model as possible to demonstrate the points at issue and concentrate on the economics behind the results. We do not discuss the application of RE to behavioural equations (e.g. the consumption function) or to the efficient markets hypothesis. (On the former see Begg 1982a or Holden et al. 1985; on the latter see also Brooks et al. 1986 or MacDonald and Taylor 1988.)

3.3   Axioms of RE

The REH has several implications concerning the relationship between an agent's subjective expectation and the *ex post* (out-turn) value of the forecast variable. First, on average, expectations are correct; this is the *unbiasedness* property. Second, 'rational' agents must use all the relevant information available at the time at which they form their expectations: when the relevant information set is assumed to consist only of past values of the variable being forecast, this property is known as *efficiency*. When the information set assumed known to the agent includes a wider set of variables (than their own lagged values) the efficient use of information is known as the *orthogonality* condition. Third, when 'rational' agents form expectations (at time t) over successive time horizons (e.g. one year, two years ahead) then they must utilize the information available at t in a logically consistent manner; this is the so-called *consistency* property of RE.

We must make a clear distinction between mathematical and subjective expectations and survey data on expectations. An individual's subjective expectation of a variable is what influences his behaviour in some way. A conditional mathematical expectation is a relationship obtained by using the conditional expectations operator on an economic model. The expectations of 'Muth–RE' are *assumed* to be identical to conditional mathematical expectations. This assumption allows one to make the concept of subjective expectations an operational one, since if we can correctly estimate the 'true' model we obtain an estimate of the unobservable subjective expectations. It may be shown (although we do not prove it here) that conditional mathematical expectations, *by definition*, obey certain axioms, which we list below. A question then arises as to whether individuals' *actual* subjective expectations are the same as conditional mathematical expectations and therefore obey the same axioms. A *direct* test of this proposition is not possible since we do not know agents' subjective expectations. However, if we assume that *survey data* on expectations measure an individual's 'true' subjective expectations we can *test* the former to see if they obey the axioms (of conditional mathematical or rational expectations). Below, we therefore state the axioms that are implied by conditional mathematical expectations, outline possible tests using survey data and briefly discuss some of the results of these direct tests of RE. We assume that 'S' is the variable about which expectations are being formed: for example, S might represent income, the rate of inflation, the exchange rate or the price of bonds, all of which appear as expectational variables in a number of macroeconomic models.

In forming RE the individual is concerned with three elements: the horizon over which expectations are being formed, the time at which expectations are formed and the 'information set' available to them. For example, expectations of a variable S formed at time $t-1$, about time period t, conditional on information Ω available at time $t-2$ may be written $E_{t-1}(S_t|\Omega_{t-2})$. With RE it is not the time at which expectations are formed that is important but the *dating of the information set* available to individuals. However, we shall assume these two dates are the same and unless otherwise stated we shall assume a one-period forecast horizon. Thus, for example, we shall write $E_{t-1}(S_t|\Omega_{t-1})$ as S_t^e, ES_t, or ES; and $E_t(S_{t+1}|\Omega_t)$ as S_{t+1}^e or ES_{t+1}. Where any ambiguity might arise we shall explicitly use the expectations operator $E_{t\pm j}$ with the implicit assumption that Ω is also dated $t\pm j$.

3.3.1 Axioms of Rational Expectations

Unbiasedness On average, RE *individuals* forecast correctly; they neither systematically underestimate nor overestimate the *actual* future value, S_{t+1}, so that

$$S_{t+1} = E_t S_{t+1} + u_{t+1} \equiv S_{t+1}^e + u_{t+1} \tag{3.1}$$

where u_{t+1} is the 'forecast error' $(S_{t+1} - S^e_{t+1})$, which *by assumption* must be zero 'on average' (i.e. its expected value is zero, $E_t u_{t+1} = E(S_{t+1} - S^e_{t+1}) = 0$). The forecast error in each period, u_{t+1}, will generally be non-zero, but it will be zero on average over a number of predictions: over-prediction and under-prediction cancel out over time. When dealing with *aggregate* expectations, the forecast error u_{t+1}, averaged over *all* individuals for a number of predictions, will also be zero. Under RE, expectations can be wrong but they cannot be systematically wrong. Since prediction errors, u_{t+1}, are by definition random and unpredictable, they represent new information arriving between the time at which the forecast is made (or the date of the information set Ω), and the time at which the actual value is realized. The RE forecasting error is therefore sometimes referred to as being due to 'news'. A typical 'news' item might be, for example, an unexpected change in government policy.

An additional property is required for the definition of 'unbiasedness': the forecast error should be serially uncorrelated (i.e. uncorrelated with its own future and past values). If u_{t+1} is a zero-mean, serially uncorrelated error and if u_{t+1} has a constant variance, then u_{t+1} is said to be a 'white noise' error. If we have survey data on S^e_{t+1} a *test of unbiasedness* is that $\alpha = 0$, $\beta = 1$ and u_{t+1} is 'white noise' in the regression:[1]

$$S_{t+1} = \alpha + \beta S^e_{t+1} + u_{t+1}. \tag{3.2}$$

The unbiasedness property $\alpha = 0$, $\beta = 1$ implies that the expected value of the forecast error (given the information available) is zero[2]

$$E(u_{t+1}/I_t) = E(S_{t+1} - S^e_{t+1}) = 0. \tag{3.3}$$

Information: the Orthogonality and Efficiency Properties   RE speculators use all the relevant information available at time t, or earlier (Ω_t) to form a view about S^e_{t+1}. If X_t is any *subset* of the information set actually used by agents, then the forecast error, u_{t+1}, must be independent of (orthogonal to) any information in X_t. The forecast error u_{t+1} is due to unpredictable shocks and will be unrelated to any relevant information available at time t. Thus if X is a vector of variables, the orthogonality property of RE implies that all the $\beta_i = 0$ in the regression

$$S_{t+1} - S^e_{t+1} = \alpha_0 + \sum_{i=0}^{N} \beta_i X_{t-i} + \epsilon_{t+1}. \tag{3.4}$$

A special case of the orthogonality property occurs when the information subset X_t includes information on *previous* forecast errors $S_t - S^e_t = u_t$, only. 'Current' forecast errors $u_{t+1} = S_{t+1} - S^e_{t+1}$ must be independent of previous forecast errors, $u_t = S_t - S^e_t$, which are known at the time at which the current forecast is made. Hence if $X_t = S_t - S^e_t$ in equation (4.4), its coefficient must be zero. Also forecast errors u_{t+1} must be serially uncorrelated if the orthogonality property is to hold.[3]

The orthogonality property is often expressed more generally in terms of conditional expectations rather than in the terminology of regression equations (although the two are equivalent for linear structures). The correlation (covariance) between the forecast error u_{t+1} and the information set used in making the forecast Ω_t is denoted by $E_t(u'_{t+1}\Omega_t)$. Given Ω_t, this correlation is zero; hence, the orthogonality property is succinctly expressed as $E_t(u'_{t+1}\Omega_t | \Omega_t) = 0$. We present this alternative formulation here to prevent confusion should the reader consult other texts in this area; we do not use this expression in our analysis.

If the information set is assumed to consist only of past values of S then the orthogonality condition is known as the *efficiency* property.

The orthogonality (efficiency) property is also *implied* by the RE assumption that agents use the true (reduced-form) model of the economy when forming their expectations. To demonstrate this, assume that actual values S_{t+1} are determined by the *set* of variables Ω_t (known at time t) and hence the 'true' (reduced-form) equation, where a_1 is a coefficient vector:

$$S_{t+1} = a_0 + a_1 \cdot \Omega_t + u_{t+1}. \tag{3.5}$$

Suppose the agent forms expectations according to

$$S^e_{t+1} = b_0 + b_1 \cdot \Omega_t \tag{3.6}$$

The forecast error is (3.5) minus (3.6):

$$S_{t+1} - S^e_{t+1} = (a_0 - b_0) + (a_1 - b_1) \cdot \Omega_t + u_{t+1} \tag{3.7}$$

but if agents use the true model in forming S^e_{t+1} then $a_i = b_i$ in (3.7). Hence only when agents use the 'true' model is the forecast error in (3.7) independent of all known information at time t; but the latter is also the orthogonality (efficiency) property.

In view of the use of the term 'efficiency' in widely different contexts in economics and econometrics we shall refer to this property of RE as the orthogonality property, to avoid confusion.

Revision of Expectations: 'Consistency' We shall not be directly concerned very much with this aspect, but for completeness we note that this property of REH simply states that it is impossible to know in advance how one will change one's expectations. For example if individuals knew in January that in three months' time they would alter their expectation of the price level for July, then they should use that information *today* to alter their view of the price level for six months hence, formed in January. To ignore such information would (by definition) be irrational. In testing survey data against actual outcomes this property is often referred to as consistency. Another way of stating the consistency property is that it is only *new* information that leads one to alter one's expectations. Formally, consistency requires that

$a_i = c_i$ for all i in the following regressions, where the agent forecasts S at time t first using information at $t-2$ and then using information at $t-1$;

$$_{t-2}S_t^e = c_0 + c_1 \,_{t-2}S_{t-1}^e + c_2 S_{t-2} + c_3 S_{t-3} + \ldots + u_t \tag{3.8}$$

$$_{t-1}S_t^e = a_0 + a_1 S_{t-1} + a_2 S_{t-2} + \ldots + v_t \tag{3.9}$$

where S^e is the (known) *survey data* on expectations of the variable S. To see how the restrictions on the coefficients are needed to ensure that only *new* information leads to *a revision* of expectations, subtract (3.8) from (3.9) and rearrange, to obtain

$$_{t-1}S_t^e - _{t-2}S_t^e = (a_0 - c_0) + a_1(S_{t-1} - _{t-2}S_{t-1}^e) + (a_1 - c_1)_{t-2}S_{t-1}^e$$
$$+ \sum_{i=2}^{\infty} (a_i - c_i) S_{t-i} + (u_t - v_t). \tag{3.10}$$

The second term in brackets on the RHS is new information (or 'news') that arrives between $t-2$ and $t-1$ and is the only variable to cause a revision of expectations if $a_i = c_i$ for all i.

The Chain Rule of Forecasting   This final property of RE occurs only in *linear* models (and is not unique to RE). The chain rule allows all future values of a variable to be expressed as a function only of information known at the time the forecast is made. For example, suppose y_t is generated by the AR(2) process

$$y_t = a_1 y_{t-1} + a_2 y_{t-2} + \epsilon_t \tag{3.11}$$

where $E_{t-1}\epsilon_t = 0$ and ϵ_t is white noise. Then it follows that, with information at $t-1$ and earlier,

$$_{t-1}y_t^e = a_1 y_{t-1} + a_2 y_{t-2} \tag{3.12}$$

and

$$_{t-1}y_{t+1}^e = a_1 \,_{t-1}y_t^e + a_2 y_{t-1}. \tag{3.13}$$

Substituting (3.12) in (3.13)

$$_{t-1}y_{t+1}^e = (a_1^2 + a_2)y_{t-1} + a_1 a_2 y_{t-2}. \tag{3.14}$$

By repeated substitution we find that a 'chain' is established whereby $_{t-1}y_{t+i}^e$ ($i \geq 0$) depends only on the known values y_{t-1}, y_{t-2}. The method can be generalized when the RHS of (3.11) contains variables other than lagged ys: to determine $_{t-1}y_{t+i}$ then requires a further set of forecasting equations for these variables (e.g. vector autoregressive (VAR) models).

Direct Tests of the Axioms of RE   It is worth noting that all of the above properties are (automatically) satisfied by conditional mathematical expectations but may not be satisfied by *survey* data on expectations. Also the REH assumes that people's *subjective* expectations are equated with conditional mathematical expectations and therefore obey the basic postulates. If survey data give an accurate indication of agents' subjective expectations then such data should also obey the basic postulates. Hence *direct tests* of the REH use regression analysis on survey data to test the above axioms.

The literature here is voluminous and most tests have used survey data on inflation, interest rates and sales. In the main, the tests use data on expectations aggregated over all respondents to the survey although there are a few studies that use data on individuals' expectations (e.g. Figlewski and Wachtel 1981). The results can only be described as mixed (Sheffrin 1983, Holden et al. 1985) and perhaps on balance could not be said to lend support to the hypothesis. At this point the reader may well feel that it is not worth proceeding any further. If expectations are not rational why go on to discuss macromodels that assume rationality? There are several answers to this. First and perhaps most importantly RE macromodels may yield *indirect* tests of the REH that are supported by the data, thus complementing our results obtained using the survey data, which are far from definitive. Second, tests using the expectations data are open to criticism. The survey data may not reflect agents' true subjective expectations, since individuals have little to lose if they give answers that reflect little thought; when faced with real-world decisions that may be costly if expectations turn out to be incorrect, they may give very different answers. The aggregate data reflect average expectations and it may be that a few well informed sophisticated agents are responsible for markets behaving according to the REH. If the true stochastic processes governing the behaviour of variables of interest undergo frequent changes and the investigator either fails to take account of such changes when splitting the data sample into sub-periods or does not allow a sufficient 'learning period', the rationality tests on the survey data are bound to fail – see Taylor 1987a,b. In short, to be somewhat cynical, if a vital hypothesis fails some crucial tests, it is generally possible to think of reasons for the tests and not the hypotheses being incorrect.

3.4   Surprise Supply Functions and the Phillips Curve

In chapter 2, the Phillips curve was derived by assuming that workers and firms have different information at their disposal In much of the RE literature the supply of output is determined by 'surprises', usually price surprises. For example in the Sargent–Wallace, SW, supply function the movement in output around its 'normal' or expected level, y^*, depends positively on surprises in the aggregate price level:

$$y - y^* = d(p - Ep) \tag{3.15}$$

where Ep is the price level expected in period t based on information available at $t-1$ or earlier (i.e. $Ep = E_{t-1}p_t$). The horizon over which expectations are formed and the information set assumed may vary and we discuss some of these alternative surprise supply functions below. It is often asserted that equation (3.15) above is merely a rearrangement of the Phillips curve, with output replacing unemployment as a measure of the pressure of demand and (3.15) is sometimes explicitly referred to as a 'Phillips curve'. However, as we point out below the relationship between surprise supply functions and the Phillips curve is by no means straightforward and we need to differentiate clearly between the two concepts to avoid confusion. Surprise supply functions of various types frequently appear as *crucial* elements in RE models. We therefore investigate their theoretical pedigree in some detail, below, as well as commenting on their relationship to the Phillips curve of §1.7. We begin with an account of *direct methods* of deriving 'surprise' supply functions that utilize the supply curve only. The SW supply function (Sargent and Wallace 1975) is based on expectational errors whilst the Lucas supply function is based on intertemporal substitution. After presenting some criticisms of this direct approach we discuss whether it is possible to derive a 'surprise' supply function indirectly, as a 'quasi-reduced form' of a complete RE model. Finally we discuss the relationship between the surprise supply function and the Phillips curve.

Lucas (1972) provides a theoretical model of the SW supply function based on a competitive market-clearing model, in which all unemployment is voluntary and decisions about real variables are based on relative prices, as in the neoclassical framework. Unlike in the Phillips curve story of the previous chapter, movements in real variables are not caused by informational *asymmetries* between workers and firms but by possession of less than complete information by *both* sets of agents. Information about local prices (and wages) is given but *all* agents lack information about the *general* price level. First, consider the behaviour of firms. In the Lucas model firms alter their supply y_z, around its normal level, y_z^*, because they become confused between changes in aggregate and relative prices. Firms have information about the price for the homogeneous single 'good' in their local market, z, and expand output if the local price, p_z, is above the expected economy-wide price, p, based on information available in market z, $E_z p$:

$$y_z - y_z^* = \gamma(p_z - E_z p). \tag{3.16}$$

At the outset, therefore, Lucas assumes that firms respond to price surprises in *local* markets: there is no 'maximizing' theory put forward to support this supposition – Lucas merely asserts that suppliers will produce more in the current period to reap the benefit of locally higher perceived prices and hence profits. (We return below to the question of the role of profits in the supply curve.) The problem firms face is to determine the 'expected' or normal price, which is an average of prices for the good in *all* markets. The firm has definite information on the price in its local market p_z and it can form an expectation of the average price in *all* other markets based on information at time $t-1$, that is, $E_z p$ where p is the (aggregate) price over all markets. Note that information in market z is greater than information in the 'general' information set, since p_z is known. Lucas assumes that the price in market z is equal to the average price of the good in all markets plus a random error term that depends only on events in the local market:

$$p_z = p + u_z. \tag{3.17}$$

u_z therefore picks up changes in the *relative* price of the good in market z (i.e. $u_z = p_z - p$). Now the economy-wide or average price, p, will differ from its 'average' expectation, Ep, by a forecasting error, u_p say:

$$p = Ep + u_p. \tag{3.18a}$$

Hence, using (3.17) we have

$$p_z = Ep + u_p + u_z. \tag{3.18b}$$

Hence, the price in market z is equal to the sum of the economy-wide expectations of the average price, Ep, plus the economy-wide surprise u_p, plus the surprise peculiar to market z, u_z. Now, agents in market z want to form their best prediction of p, based on 'z-information', i.e. $E_z p$. This must differ from the economy-wide expectation, Ep, because of the extra information available in market z because p_z is known. Thus, if Ep_z is the economy-wide expectation of p_z, then $p_z - Ep_z$ is the extra information. Thus, $E_z p$ will be the sum of Ep plus that part of the forecast error, $p - Ep$, that could be avoided by using the extra information about market z:

$$E_z p = Ep + E[(p - Ep) | (p_z - Ep_z)]. \tag{3.18c}$$

Now, from (3.18a),

$$p - Ep = u_p.$$

Taking expectations of (3.18b) with respect to economy-wide market information:

$$Ep_z = Ep + E(u_p + u_z) = Ep. \tag{3.18d}$$

Since u_p is the economy-wide forecast error for p and u_z is the market z shock, and both have an expected value of zero, i.e. substituting (3.18d) in (3.18b),

$$p_z - Ep_z = u_p + u_z. \tag{3.18a}$$

Now, it turns out that the 'best' (i.e. minimum-variance linear unbiased) estimate of $p - Ep$ based on knowledge of $p_z - Ep_z$ is

$$E[(p - Ep)|(p_z - Ep_z)] = \theta(p_z - Ep_z) \qquad (3.18f)$$

where

$$\theta = \sigma_p^2/(\sigma_p^2 + \sigma_u^2) \qquad (3.18g)$$

and σ_p^2 and σ_u^2 are the (conditional) variances of u_p and u_z respectively. In fact, assuming the covariance of u_p and u_z to be zero, θ is just the ordinary least-squares coefficient from a regression of $p - Ep = u_p$ on $p_z - Ep_z = u_p + u_z$.

Substituting (3.18f) into (3.18c) we have

$$E_z p = Ep + \theta(p_z - Ep_z)$$

and, using (3.18d),

$$E_z p = \theta p_z + (1 - \theta)Ep. \qquad (3.18h)$$

Expression (3.18h) says that the expected value of p given market-z information is a weighted average of p_z and the economy-wide expectation of p, Ep, with the weights depending on the relative variances of the economy-wide and market-z price shocks according to (4.18g). If, for example, market-z shocks are particularly volatile (i.e. σ_u^2 is large), then not much will be gained from information on p_z when forecasting p, so $E_z p$ and Ep will be close – i.e. θ will be small. The converse will hold if market z is stable relative to a 'noisy' economy (i.e. σ_p^2 is much bigger than σ_u^2) – in this case p_z will be a better indicator of p, and $E_z p$ and p_z will be close (θ will be near unity).

Substituting (4.18h) into (4.16) we have

$$y_z - y_z^* = \gamma(1 - \theta)(p_z - Ep) \qquad (3.18i)$$

and aggregating over all markets, so that we can drop the subscripts z this yields

$$y - y^* = \gamma(1 - \theta)(p - Ep). \qquad (3.19)$$

Firms in the Lucas model face a 'signal extraction problem'. When faced with a change in their local price they have to decide whether this reflects an increase relative to the price in all other markets. From (3.18a), the greater the variance in the general price level, σ_p^2, relative to the variance of local prices, σ_u^2 (i.e. the more 'noise' there is in the signal), the smaller θ is, and the more the firms perceive this as a rise in the general price level (equations (3.18)). $E_z p$ therefore increases as much as p_z and (local) supply does not change from its normal level (equation (3.16)). Note also that y^* in equation (3.16) is the level of output that ensues when there are no expectational errors and it is not clear that this is equivalent to the 'natural rate' of output given by equilibrium in the labour market (together with the production function).

In countries that have had a stable general price level, a 'boom' engineered by the authorities, if it leads to a rise in prices, will lead to a substantial rise in output in the short run as firms perceive this as an increase in their 'local' relative price. However, if the policy is repeated, the variance of the general price level increases and the supply response becomes muted. Thus the Lucas model accounts for the supposed lack of response of output to policy changes as inflation (and its variability) increased in the 1970s. It also explains why countries with highly variable inflation (e.g. Argentina) have an output response to a demand stimulus that is smaller than that for countries with low variability in inflation (e.g. West Germany). Unfortunately the latter assertion does not always hold for countries where the variability in inflation differs only moderately (Lucas 1973) and the theory clearly needs more rigorous empirical testing.

Another direct method of obtaining a 'surprise' supply function is based on *intertemporal* substitution of production. If prices are higher today than one expects them to be tomorrow, $E_t p_{t+1}$ (based on information available at t), then it pays to produce and sell in 'today's' profitable market. There is an added complication in that this return must exceed the time preference rate or interest rate, r, at which firms discount future profits. Hence the *intertemporal supply hypothesis* is

$$y_t - y' = a(p_t - E_t p_{t+1} + r) \tag{3.20}$$

y' is the level of output produced when there is no incentive to switch production between different time periods.

It is worth noting that Lucas and Rapping (1969) have also applied the intertemporal model to the determination of labour supply. If wages are expected to be temporarily high, labour supply increases markedly. On the other hand if a wage increase is expected to be permanent there will be no large switch to consuming leisure tomorrow rather than today and labour supply will be sluggish. Unemployment is seen as voluntary in this model, being an intertemporal rearrangement of leisure time.

Minford and Peel (1982) have criticized these two direct routes to obtaining a 'surprise' supply function on the grounds that they consider revenues but not costs. In the SW supply function, agents react positively to prices that are higher than expected, but it seems reasonable to assume that they also curtail output when costs are higher than expected – assuming, that is, that firms know their current costs. The Minford–Peel version of the SW supply function is therefore

$$y_t = y^{*'} + a\left[(p-c) - (E_{t-1}p - E_{t-1}c)\right] \tag{3.21}$$

so output responds to a *profit* margin ($p-c$) over costs that is higher than expected (all variables are in logarithms). The 'Lucas' supply function (3.20) can be similarly amended to include costs, and output then depends on the relative profit in different periods:

$$y_t = y'' + a\,[(p-c)-(E_t p_{t+1} - E_t c_{t+1} - r)]. \tag{3.22}$$

Minford and Peel seek to augment the above supply relationships by adding a theory about the determination of costs, thus producing a more complete model of supply. They succeed in generating a SW-type supply function as a 'pseudo-reduced form' of a rather complex model. Their model has: desired supply determined as in (3.21); a full intertemporal model of the supply of labour; a demand curve for labour depending on output (i.e. the inverse of the production function); conventional IS and LM curves; and all markets clearing. It must be noted that the SW supply function is not a structural equation (based on maximizing behaviour) but is merely a *partial* relationship in the complete model between the endogenous variables $y-y^{*\prime}$ and $p-E_{t-1}p$ (in much the same way as the IS curve is a partial relationship between endogenous variables (y and r) in that particular model). However, they note that the SW supply function derived from their model is unsatisfactory since it requires rather unrealistic assumptions about the asymmetry of information on costs and prices. Firms are assumed to know both their local wage costs and their local prices whereas workers know their current nominal wages but not the *general* price level. A slight change in this informational assumption can destroy the SW supply relationship. For example, if firms know their input costs but not their output prices then an unanticipated inflation (in all nominal variables) would lead to a fall in output according to the Minford–Peel intertemporal profit supply function (3.21). Thus the Minford–Peel clearing-markets model in which there is no labour search (unlike in the usual derivation of the Phillips curve – §1.7) fails to provide an acceptable underpinning for the SW supply function. However, Minford and Peel are able to rescue the SW supply relationships by positing a variant of the above model, in which wages are set one period ahead by contract while prices are perfectly flexible and clear the goods market. In this model with mixed contract–flexible prices the supply curve of labour is replaced by a wage-setting (contract) equation in which nominal wages are based on the *expected* market-clearing *real* wage and the expected price level. Unexpected events can influence flexible prices but not wages, thus causing real-wage (cost) surprises and a change in intertemporal supply via equation (3.22).

3.4.1 *The Contract Model and the Phillips Curve*

At the risk of confusing the reader we wish to note the implications of the above Minford–Peel 'contract models' as regards the Phillips curve relationship, that is, a relationship between the rate of change of nominal wages, price expectations and some measure of the *level* of (excess) demand (i.e. the PEAPC). The contract model differs from the normal Phillips curve derivation in that wages are determined by expectations of the future *market-clearing* level of employment and therefore agents consider *quantity* as well as price information. Minford and Peel demonstrate that a model in which both wages *and* prices are set by contract does not produce the 'normal' PEAPC since the rate of change of nominal wages in their model depends on *changes* in both the level of output and past expectational errors for the price level (e.g. $E_{t-1}p_t - E_{t-2}p_{t-1}$) rather than the expected change in prices, $E_{t-1}p_t - p_{t-1}$, which appears in the PEAPC. Even if the model is amended so that wages are set by contract but prices are flexible, it is still not possible to derive an identical relationship to the Phillips curve since other variables such as interest rates enter the relationship. Thus a model that is capable of reproducing a SW supply function may not be consistent with the 'normal' PEAPC, thus emphasizing the difference between the two concepts. This should not be too surprising since the SW supply curve deals with the determination of output and the PEAPC with the determination of unemployment and these are clearly distinct (if interrelated) phenomena.

To summarize, we have noted the criticism of the direct derivation of the SW and 'Lucas' surprise supply functions that they ignore costs. Attempts to rationalize these supply functions using an indirect derivation involving, *inter alia*, the Minford–Peel intertemporal profit supply function are possible, providing one assumes wages are fixed by contract for one or more periods ahead while prices are flexible. However, the SW supply function that ensues is not a structural behaviour equation but a 'pseudo-reduced form' of the complete model. Although the SW supply function is widely used in RE models, its theoretical underpinnings are therefore not completely satisfactory.

3.5   Policy Ineffectiveness

3.5.1   *Theoretical Considerations*

In a wide variety of RE models it is possible to demonstrate that counter-cyclical monetary policy is futile: the known *systematic* part of a policy rule does not influence the variance of output around its natural (or equilibrium) rate. However, in implementing a systematic policy the authorities may make (non-systematic) mistakes and these 'surprises' may affect the variance of output. As 'simple' policy rules *may* involve smaller 'mistakes' than 'complex' rules, the policy ineffectiveness idea has implications for the rules-versus-discretion debate. Below, we consider the money supply as our policy instrument.

To avoid confusion it is worth noting that 'systematic' has a rather precise meaning here, namely that the authorities set the money supply based on parameters (g_i) that are held constant over the 'policy period'. For example, a counter-cyclical monetary policy rule might be

$$m_t = g_0 + g_1(y_n - y_{t-1}) + w_t \qquad g_1 > 0 \tag{3.23}$$

where w_t is ('white noise') random error representing the non-systematic part of the policy, and $g_0 + g_1 y_{t-1}$ represents the systematic element of the policy. The authorities increase the money supply when the previous period's output y_{t-1} is 'low' relative to the equilibrium or natural rate y_n – the precise amount being determined by the authorities' choice of the 'constants' g_0 and g_1. If $g_1 \neq 0$ then the rule is said to be a 'closed-loop' (feedback or contingent) rule. If $g_1 = 0$ and $g_0 \neq 0$ then the money supply is not altered according to the state of the economy but is held fixed at a value g_0; this is an open-loop (or non-contingent) policy rule.[4] Note that a feedback or contingent *rule* is often referred to as a 'discretionary policy'. Here 'discretionary policy' implies that g_0 and g_1 are held constant over a 'reasonable' time period. Thus the definition excludes the possibility that the authorities alter the strength of their policy response from period to period even though the latter may be more akin to the commonly accepted notion of discretionary action. The non-contingent rule is often just referred to as a (simple fixed) 'rule'.

The basic assumptions needed to produce policy ineffectiveness are: (i) the supply function is of SW type; (ii) all agents have access to the same information set; (iii) agents form Muth–RE and therefore know the systematic part of the authorities' policy reaction function; (iv) prices are perfectly flexible and markets clear in all periods.

On the demand side our illustrative model may be represented by the reduced-form solution of the 'normal' IS–LM model (in log–linear form) and may be written (appendix 1.1) as

$$y_t^d = b(m - p)_t + k + u_t. \tag{3.24}$$

The real money supply affects aggregate demand while for algebraic simplicity we assume that fiscal policy (government expenditure and tax rates) is held constant and is subsumed in the constant k. Aggregate supply is determined by the SW 'surprise' supply function

$$y^s = y_n + d(p_t - Ep_t) \tag{3.25}$$

with expectations for time t based on information available at $t-1$, or earlier $(Ep_t = E_{t-1} p_t)$. u_t is a white noise structural disturbance term (which without loss of generality is suppressed in the supply function).

For given expectations about the price level, the supply of output (equation (3.25)) is positively related to the current price level (as in figure 3.1). Given an increase in the money supply the AD curve shifts to the right; excess demand leads to a rise in the price level and *for given expectations* this leads to an increase in supply and the equilibrium level of output (A to B). In the usual fixed-wage Keynesian model of §1.6.1 this is the end of the matter. However in NC models systematic forecast errors are not allowed: Ep_t is endogenous and must *immediately* be brought into equality with the actual price level (except for a random error). When this occurs the SW supply function indicates that output will be at its natural rate (point C) given by the long-run AS curve, ASL. The assumption that output supplied depends on (price) 'surprises', and that RE does not allow the *systematic* element of policy to embody surprises for the private sector, ensures the policy invariance result: the AD relationship is rather superfluous here.

To understand fully the working of this simple model and to gain an insight into one method of solving RE models we proceed as follows. First we solve for the reduced form of the model in the normal way treating expectations as exogenous; next we take expectations Ep_t and solve for the latter in terms of the exogenous variables (i.e. m, y_n, k); and finally we substitute this expression for the expectations variable Ep_t back into the 'solution' of the model obtained in the first stage. Our 'final' equation has p_t (or y_t) depending only on the exogenous variables (and not on Ep_t). An example will make this clearer, where y_t, p_t and Ep_t are endogenous and y_n and (for the moment) m_t are exogenous.

Solving the model by equating supply and demand (assuming expectations are exogenous) gives

$$p_t = \frac{1}{d+b}\,(bm_t - y_n + k) + \frac{d}{d+b}\,Ep_t + \frac{u_t}{d+b}\,. \tag{3.26}$$

Taking expectations of (3.26) and rearranging we find that the expected price

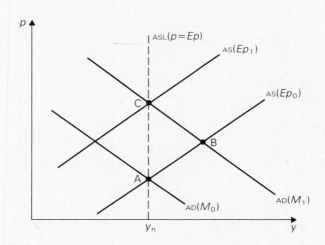

Figure 3.1 A simple RE model: policy ineffectiveness

level depends on the expected money supply (and the other exogenous variables, y_n and k):

$$Ep_t = Em_t - \frac{1}{b} y_n + \frac{1}{b} k. \tag{3.27}$$

Substituting (3.27) back into (3.26) we obtain the solution for p_t in terms of the exogenous variables (with the endogenous Ep_t term excluded):

$$p_t = \left(Em_t - \frac{1}{b} y_n + \frac{1}{b} k \right) + \frac{b}{d+b}(m_t - Em_t) + \frac{u_t}{d+b}. \tag{3.28}$$

Note that the first term in brackets is Ep_t and that substituting for $(p - Ep)_t$ from (3.27) and (3.28) into the SW supply gives the reduced-form solution for the actual path of output:

$$y_t = y_n + \frac{db}{d+b}(m_t - Em_t) + \frac{du_t}{d+b}. \tag{3.29}$$

Thus the actual path of prices depends on the expected money supply, Em_t, surprises in the money supply, $m_t - Em_t$, and the structural disturbance u_t. Output fluctuations around the natural rate $(y_t - y_n)$ depend only upon the unanticipated component of the money supply (and u_t). A systematic monetary policy rule allows RE agents to predict the expected component of the money supply Em_t and hence for the authorities to influence the actual price level (equation (3.28)) but it does not allow the authorities to influence real output. Known systematic changes in the money supply are *neutral* in the short run. Let us now append a monetary feedback rule to the model – for example, the counter-cyclical policy rule:

$$m_t = g_0 + g_1(y_n - y_{t-1}) + w_t \qquad g_1 > 0 \tag{3.30}$$

where w_t is a white noise random error. Taking expectations of (3.30) with information available at time $t - 1$ we see that

$$Em_t = g_0 + g_1(y_n - y_{t-1})$$

and that

$$w_t = m_t - Em_t$$

is the monetary surprise. Substituting the latter expression in equations (3.29) and (3.28) for output and the price level we obtain:

$$p_t = Ep_t + \frac{1}{d+b}(bw_t + u_t) \tag{3.31}$$

$$y_t = y_n + \frac{d}{d+b}(bw_t + u_t). \tag{3.32}$$

Therefore

$$\text{var}(p_t) = \frac{b^2 \sigma_w^2 + \sigma_u^2}{(d+b)^2} \tag{3.31a}$$

$$\text{var}(y_t) = \frac{d^2 b^2 \sigma_w^2 + d^2 \sigma_u^2}{(d+b)^2} \tag{3.32a}$$

where we have assumed $\text{cov}(u, v) = 0$. Clearly the deviation of output around the natural rate consists of a zero-mean serially uncorrelated random element and is *unaffected by the (systematic) policy parameters*, g_i of the authorities' reaction function. The authorities could have a 'closed-loop' feedback policy (i.e. g_1 non-zero) or an 'open-loop' rule, whereby the money supply has a constant value g_0 (i.e. $g_1 = 0$) and in both cases the mean level of output would be unaffected. The variance of output around its natural rate and of the price level around its expected value are given in (3.31a) and (3.32a). Under a non-contingent (simple) rule such as a constant growth rate for the money supply we might expect the variance of the forecast error of the money supply, σ_w^2, made by private agents to be less than under a complex feedback (contingent) rule. If so the variance of output will be less under a simple open-loop rule than under a 'closed-loop' policy. However, this appears to be a rather weak rationale for the superiority of non-contingent over contingent rules. If the latter have been in operation for some time both g_0 *and* g_1 will be known and under both types of rule σ_w^2 will be determined by the authorities' ability to *control* precisely the money supply. The degree of successful control in both 'regimes' is likely to be the same for both types of 'rule'.

What about fiscal policy in this NC model? Government expenditure, G, may be introduced into our IS–LM reduced form for y^d by replacing k in equation (3.24) by kG_t (assuming that crowding out is less than complete). However, if G is set by a systematic rule (like equation (3.30)) then only terms in unanticipated government expenditure enter the reduced form for output. Hence policy ineffectiveness applies to G as well as to monetary policy. However, if we introduce direct taxes into the y^d equation the parameter k depends on 'τ', the direct marginal tax *rate*. It is then easy to show (and this is left as an exercise for the reader) that the reduced-form equation for output also depends on τ (McCallum and Whittaker 1979, Holden et al. 1985), provided we do not introduce the Ricardian proposition that anticipated changes in tax rates are offset by changes in expected wealth (Barro 1974). Thus systematic (anticipated) changes in tax rates do affect the variance of output around its natural rate.

3.5.2 *Robustness of the Policy Ineffectiveness Proposition*

If we relax some of the assumptions of the above simple model but still retain the assumption of RE then it becomes possible for the authorities to influence real output. However, the scope for policy in certain cases is severely circumscribed as compared with that in non-RE models. In Keynesian fix-price models the authorities may influence the (mean) level of output, while in non-RE models incorporating a neoclassical labour market or a vertical PEAPC the authorities may exploit adjustment or expectations lags (e.g. in the AEH) to influence the speed of convergence to the equilibrium rate and hence the variability in output. It turns out that the authorities' ability to reduce cyclical movements in output when agents use RE depends on the precise model assumed. Variations in the form of the supply function used, in the informational assumptions used and particularly as to whether all markets are assumed to clear continuously may all negate the policy ineffectiveness proposition.

The Information Sets   If some agents have access to less information than others then the ineffectiveness proposition may not hold. To see the intuitive reasoning behind this result, suppose that the government has information on the *current* price level but private agents do not. The authorities are aware of how private agents determine Ep_t and, knowing the current price level, they can calculate the private sector's forecast error $(p - Ep)_t$. If the authorities do nothing then the forecast error in prices leads private sector firms to change y_t from its natural rate. However, if the current-period money supply has an impact on current-period prices, the authorities can alter it to offset $(p_t - Ep)_t$ and maintain y_t at the natural rate. Even here it must be admitted that the government would have to react rather quickly. The policy instrument would have to have immediate effect and the information would not have to be subject to statistical error: rather a difficult set of conditions to achieve.

Muth–RE agents cannot foresee the policy change, at time t, by the authorities since they base their expectations on information available at time $t-1$. The authorities cannot of course hold output above the natural rate for any length of time by having a permanently higher money supply since the RE agents would then incorporate this into their expectations. It turns out that an informational advantage held by a subset of the private sector rather than the authorities can also negate the invariance proposition (Weiss 1980a and King 1982) and McCallum (1980) demonstrates that this is also the case if agents have access to some *global* information such as the economy-wide interest rate.

While it may be considered implausible to assume that in highly sophisticated markets where continuous trading takes place (e.g. the stock market and foreign exchange and certain commodity markets) the government has superior information to the private sector, this may not be the case for, say, certain manufacturing firms when they consider the overall prospects for domestic and world demand, for example. However, as compared with the pre-RE arguments of sticky prices and 'disequilibrium trades' as a basis for government stabilization policy the above informational asymmetries provide a relatively unconvincing reason for implementing a vigorous discretionary policy.

Other Supply Functions The policy ineffectiveness proposition in *equilibrium* RE models is extremely sensitive to slight changes in the supply function. With a Lucas-type supply function (where $y*$ is the normal level of supply)

$$y - y* = a(p_t - E_{t-1}p_{t+1}) \tag{3.33}$$

so profit-orientated firms increase current output if current prices are higher than prices expected for the next period, $E_{t-1}p_{t+1}$; this is a form of intertemporal substitution. Here monetary policy does influence the variance of output (Barro 1976, Barro and Fischer 1976). However, if future prices are (appropriately) discounted using an interest rate r_t the supply function becomes

$$y - y* = a(p - E_{t-1}p_{t+1} + E_{t-1}r_t) \tag{3.34}$$

and the previous conclusion is reversed (McCallum 1978). Further variations on this theme include adding wealth effects (assuming bonds are net wealth) into the expenditure function, which restores the effectiveness of systematic monetary policy in the McCallum model (Minford and Peel 1981) while fiscal policy is also effective (even without wealth effects). With a *non-linear* SW supply function, stabilization policy becomes feasible (Dickinson et al. 1982). However, all of these cases provide a rather tenuous rationale for policy to be 'feasible' and certainly do not establish that policy feedback rules are beneficial (in a welfare sense). However, overlapping-contracts models provide an alternative supply function that is perhaps more realistic than those discussed above and do allow systematic monetary (and fiscal) policy to affect the variance of output.

Wage-Contract Models In the simplest form of these models (Phelps and Taylor 1977, Fischer 1977) there are two groups of workers who set nominal wage contracts for a two-period (year) horizon in order to clear their particular labour market. The first group settles in years t, $t+2$ etc. while the second group settles in periods $t+1$, $t+3$ etc. and both groups base their nominal wage claims on their (RE) view of expected prices in the subsequent two periods (years) of their respective contracts. In this model the authorities have a '*timing advantage*' over the private sector in that they can alter policy every period (year), whereas the private sector is 'locked in' for two periods. Half-way through their wage contract period private agents may note any shocks to the economy (i.e. there are no informational asymmetries between the private sector and the authorities) but they cannot alter the nominal wage level in response to these shocks: they have entered into non-contingent contracts.

The essential element in overlapping-wage-contract models is the replacement of the SW supply function. Nominal wages, w, are set two periods ahead to maintain *expected* real wages constant at their 'normal' (equilibrium) level (Fischer 1977). In logarithms we have

$$_{t-i}w_t = E_{t-i}p_t \qquad (3.35)$$

(where for simplicity we assume the logarithm of 'normal' real wages is set at zero). Aggregate current nominal wages are

$$w_t = 0.5(_{t-2}w_t + _{t-1}w_t) = 0.5(E_{t-2}p_t + E_{t-1}p_t). \qquad (3.36)$$

A neoclassical 'clearing' labour market (together with the production function) implies that the supply of output y_t^s around the normal (natural) rate is a negative function of the real wage:

$$y_t = -\alpha(w-p)_t + y_n. \qquad (3.37)$$

Substitution for w_t from (4.36) we obtain our overlapping-contracts supply function:

$$y_t = 0.5\alpha[(p_t - E_{t-2}p_t) + (p_t - E_{t-1}p_t)] + y_n. \qquad (3.38)$$

The difference between (3.38) and the SW supply function rests on the additional term $p_t - E_{t-2}p_t$ and it is this that allows the variance of output around the natural rate to depend on the (systematic) feedback policy parameter g_1 and hence the policy ineffectiveness proposition to be negated (see the 'sticky price' model of Buiter's 1980 in appendix 3.1).

That counter-cyclical policy may be 'effective' in this model may be easily demonstrated at an intuitive level. For example, if there is an adverse supply shock at the end of the first year the authorities can increase the money supply thus raising prices, lowering the real wage so that firms hire more labour: the variability in output (and employment) is reduced, providing a role for stabilization policy. Clearly, the longer the period for which wage contracts are set the more beneficial is government stabilization policy. Note that the authorities cannot alter the *mean* level of output since a permanently higher money supply would lead 'rational' wage setters to anticipate higher prices and therefore request higher nominal wages at the beginning of each wage contract period.

This type of model has its critics (Barro 1977a). Workers and firms allow a greater variability in *real* wages in return for less variability in employment and this may not be rational ('efficient'). Why don't firms make shorter wage contracts or negotiate contracts that allow for all probable contingencies? In general terms the answer would seem to be that it is because of the cost of writing, monitoring, enforcing and continually changing such contracts. There have been a small number of formal models that seek to provide rational (i.e. maximizing) reasons for 'inflexible' contracts whereby low-skilled homogeneous labour willingly accepts high overtime payments in booms and layoffs in slumps (see Blanchard 1979 and Hall and Lilien 1979, and chapter 4).

Non-Market-Clearing RE Models Hitherto we have considered only equilibrium RE models but RE is not inconsistent with models that allow involuntary unemployment and in such models stabilization policy becomes feasible. Thus whether stabilization policy is useful becomes as much a question of whether markets clear as of the nature of expectations formation. Market clearing is a characteristic of the neoclassical view which we contrasted with the Keynesian disequilibrium view in previous chapters. In RE models the assumption of market clearing is again crucial to the issue of the desirability and effectiveness of stabilization policy.

Begg (1982b) presents a two-period overlapping-contracts model that allows involuntary unemployment in an RE framework. In this model prices are more flexible than wages, the demand for labour (and output supplied) is determined by marginal productivity conditions and aggregate demand responds to real wages (income) and real money balances. Starting from equilibrium, a *permanent* downward shock to aggregate demand at time *t* leads to a fall in the price level. Workers, A, settling at time *t* can (if they wish) immediately adjust their nominal wages downwards by the *full* amount of the price fall and maintain their real wages and employment constant. The second group of workers, B, are 'locked in' to their nominal wage and hence their real wage rises and they experience unemployment at *t*. In period *t* + 1, group B adjusts its nominal wage downwards to ensure its full employment. Is there any reason why the first group to settle (at time *t*) should immediately reduce its wage by the *full* amount of the fall in prices? The answer is no. The first group, A, being rational, realize that the second group, B, is locked in to a high real wage: hence group A can obtain some of group B's market share by cutting its wages at *t* but by less than the full amount of the price rise. Similarly when group B settles at *t* + 1 it too can obtain an increase in its market share from group A who are 'locked in' in period *t* + 1. Wages, prices and output approach equilibrium only gradually – that is, output persists below its natural rate for several periods. Eventually the lower price level increases real balances and aggregate demand, which counterbalances the effects of the permanent shock to output.

The temporary increase in market share and higher real wages that occur if workers adjust slowly involves a cost in terms of involuntary unemployment every other period, which is perfectly foreseen: as we noted at the outset, workers could choose to reach full equilibrium in two periods. Hence the speed with which full equilibrium is reached depends on workers' intertemporal preferences between lower real wages in the short run and unemployment in the future. However, once the relative wage of one group gets out of line this will persist for some time unless the other group is willing to make a large cut in its real wage in the short run. In a world of uncertainty and collective bargaining it is unlikely that such sacrifices will be made. The scope for active stabilization policy should be obvious. A permanent increase in government expenditure (or the money supply) at time *t* can be used to offset the permanent adverse shock to aggregate demand so that full employment prevails at unchanged nominal wages and prices. Begg demonstrates that stabilization policy can return output to its full-employment level more quickly than the free market even when there is a lag in the implementation of policy.

The model requires an assumption of sticky wages – that is, wages are only altered every other period and workers do not adjust wages immediately to the full equilibrium. One argument for the latter is provided by models of adverse selection in the labour market. If skilled unemployed workers offer themselves for work at a lower wage, this may be taken as a signal by the prospective employer that the workers are really unskilled since they are prepared to work for 'low' wages. Hence skilled workers may be reluctant to undercut the going wage rate (see also chapter 4).

Quantity-Constrained Models and RE   In §2.4 of chapter 2 we discussed the notion of 'bootstraps' effects in quantity-constrained models. For example, agents expecting to find the economy in Keynesian unemployment (i.e. excess goods and labour supply) *next* period will reduce their consumption today in order to build up precautionary money balances – thereby setting into play negative multipliers which actually shift the economy into Keynesian unemployment *today*. In fact, there is nothing new about the notion of bootstraps effects, as demonstrated by the more familiar notion of the 'paradox of thrift', which is essentially a bootstrap effect.

We said nothing in chapter 2, however, about the nature of expectations, and in particular whether or not they are 'rational'. The implications of rational expectations in quantity-constrained macromodels have been examined by Neary and Stiglitz (1983), who introduced the notion of 'rational constraint expectations' – agents correctly perceive next period's (aggregate) constraints, subject only to surprises. Neary and Stiglitz show that an unemployment equilibrium is compatible with rational constraint expectations. More interestingly, they show that the expansionary effects of systematic government policy are actually *enhanced* by the rationality of expectations. The intuition is straightforward: the announcement of an expansionary policy to come into effect next period reduces agents' anxiety concerning employment prospects. They therefore run down precautionary money balances, i.e. spend more in the current period. If the economy is initially in Keynesian unemployment, the consequent positive multipliers will start shifting the economy towards Walrasian equilibrium even *before* the expansionary policy comes into force.

3.5.3   *Policy Ineffectiveness – Observational Equivalence and Tests of the Policy Ineffectiveness Proposition*

The two essential elements in the policy ineffectiveness proposition are that (i) unanticipated policy actions influence the variability of real variables such as output and unemployment around their natural rates and (ii) anticipated policy changes do not. The latter is often referred to as the (structural) neutrality proposition. To test these propositions we need an operational theory of the behaviour of the natural-rate variables, a measure of anticipated and unanticipated policy changes and a model of the working of the economy. Most tests of the policy ineffectiveness proposition do not involve an elaborate *full* structural RE model of the economy but a small set of reduced-form equations that assume market clearing. For example, to test the policy ineffectiveness proposition for output, y_t, the following equations have been investigated:

$$y_t = y_n + \beta(L)(X_t - E_{t-1} X_t) + \delta(L)(E_{t-1} X_t) + v_t \tag{3.39}$$
$$X_t = Z\gamma + w_t \tag{3.40}$$

where $\beta(L)$ and $\delta(L)$ are scalar polynomials in the lag operator, L. In the reduced-form equation for output (3.39) the natural rate y_n is often (rather crudely) modelled by past levels of actual output or a time trend (although other variables such as the benefit–earnings ('replacement') ratio could be included, for example. Surprise variables $(X_t - E_{t-1} X_t)$ are assumed to influence output and therefore we expect $\beta(L) \neq 0$ (and $\beta(0) > 0$) whereas anticipated variables do not, and we expect $\delta(L) = 0$. Although in principle the X-vector can include many different variables, often only the money supply is considered. We expect v_t to be a white noise error term which picks up the effect of any omitted current 'surprises' on current output. The second equation (3.40) is used to generate *expected* values of the X-variable(s). Any current-period value of X is assumed to be generated by a reduced-form equation of the complete (but unspecified) model, which has a *set* of exogenous variables Z, known to the agent; these are usually (but not always) dated at time $t-1$ or earlier. For example in the model of Barro (1977b), X is the *rate of growth* in the money supply and expectations are formed primarily on the basis of past money supply growth and past movements in unemployment (the counter-cyclical element in the money supply rule). The expected value of the growth in the money supply $(E_{t-1} X_t)$ then consists of the one-step-ahead predictions from the estimate of equation (3.40).

Two-Step Estimates Early empirical studies of the ineffectiveness proposition use a 'two-step' method. Equation (3.40) is estimated by OLS and the predictions $\hat{X}_t$ are used to form a series for the unanticipated variable, $X_t - \hat{X}_t$. The latter variables (plus those determining y_n) allow estimation of (3.39) by OLS and a test of the joint hypothesis $\beta(L) \neq 0$, $\delta(L) = 0$ using conventional likelihood ratio (LR) tests or F-tests is then possible.

Using two-step methods, Barro (1977b, 1978) and Barro and Rush (1980) find support for the policy ineffectiveness proposition for US unemployment. However, as we demonstrate below, these two-step procedures test the policy ineffectiveness proposition, while *imposing the assumption that agents use* RE. To test the latter assumption we need to estimate equations (3.39) and (3.40) jointly.

Joint Estimation: Cross-Equation RE Restrictions   To simplify the algebra, assume there are no lags in equation (3.39), that the money supply X is the only variable that influences y_t, and that the money supply is set by the authorities according to the single variable Z (e.g. lagged output) known to agents at time $t-1$. Also we impose the assumption of structural neutrality: $\delta(L) = 0$. The policy ineffectiveness hypothesis plus the assumption of RE, namely our 'maintained hypothesis', is therefore

$$y_t = \beta(X_t - Z\gamma) + v_t \qquad (3.41)$$
$$X_t = Z\gamma + w_t \qquad (3.42)$$

where v_t and w_t are independent white noise errors. Consider the following *unrestricted* version of the above two equations:

$$y_t = \pi_0 X_t + \pi_1 Z + v_t \qquad (3.43)$$
$$X_t = Z\pi_2 + w_t. \qquad (3.44)$$

Comparing (3.43) and (3.44) with (3.41) and (3.42), if policy ineffectiveness *and* RE hold we expect

$$\pi_0 = \beta \qquad \pi_1 = -\beta\gamma \qquad \pi_2 = \gamma. \qquad (3.45)$$

We have two parameters, β and γ, in our maintained hypothesis (equations (3.41) and (3.42)) and in the unrestricted model (equations (3.43) and (3.44)) we estimate three coefficients, π_0, π_1 and π_2. If our maintained hypothesis is true we expect the unrestricted regressions to yield estimates π_i such that $\pi_1/\pi_2 = -\beta = -\pi_0$ – that is, that there are non-linear cross-equation restrictions between the parameters π_1. The latter is a hallmark of RE models. If the maintained hypothesis is true then (3.43) and (3.44), which do not impose any restrictions, should 'fit' the data as well as (3.41) and (3.42), which automatically impose the cross-equation RE restrictions: this provides a test of the assumption of RE (conditional on the structural model which imposes neutrality: $\delta(L) = 0$).[5] If we find the RE restrictions hold we may then test the second part of our hypothesis, namely $\beta > 0$ (using for the latter a conventional t-statistic). In this RE model the structural parameters are 'over-identified'. The estimate of π_0 from equation (3.43) and of π_2 from equation (3.44) directly provide estimates of β and γ. If the RE hypothesis is correct we can then use the estimate of π_1 to obtain another estimate for β or γ – hence the term 'over-identified'. The latter also implies one or more (cross-equation) restrictions between the parameters.

Observational Equivalence   Equation (3.43) looks very much like a *non*-RE model of output determination: the money supply (X) *whether anticipated or unanticipated* influences output (with a distributed lag since Z = lagged output). However, if the RE policy ineffectiveness model is correct, then the non-linear restrictions between the parameters π_i of equations (3.43) *and*

(3.44) hold and this distinguishes it from the non-RE interpretation. This argument suggests that situations may arise where RE policy ineffectiveness models are indistinguishable from non-RE models. This may be demonstrated in the following simple model where the Z-variable (lagged output) enters equation (3.39) determining current output (a reasonable *a priori* assumption). Our policy ineffectiveness RE model is now

$$y_t = \beta_0(X_t - Z\gamma) + \beta_1 Z + u_t = \pi_0 X_t + \pi_1 Z + u_t \tag{3.46}$$
$$X_t = Z\gamma + v_t = Z\pi_2 + v_t \tag{3.47}$$

where

$$\pi_0 = \beta_0 \qquad \pi_1 = \beta_1 - \beta_0 \gamma \qquad \pi_2 = \gamma. \tag{3.48}$$

If we run the unrestricted regressions and obtain estimates of the three coefficients π_i we can solve for ('identify') the three parameters of our RE model $\beta_0 = \pi_0$, $\gamma = \pi_2$, $\beta_1 = \pi_1 + \pi_0 \pi_2$. We have just enough equations to determine β, γ and β_1: the system is 'exactly identified'. However, there are no cross-equation restrictions between the π_i implied by this RE model and hence equations (3.46) and (3.47) are observationally equivalent to a *non-RE* model for y_t and a feedback rule for the money supply, respectively. Thus even if the RE parameters are (exactly) identified we may still have the problem of observational equivalence.

The reader might at this stage ask the question 'How can we be sure that the true model in reality is not capable of being interpreted as two (or more) very different models: does the real world always yield observational equivalence?' The answer is that we do not know. We can always (usually somewhat arbitrarily) omit some variables from an equation for an RE model in order to (artificially) produce over-identification and hence remove the observational equivalence problem. This problem also applies to non-RE models where 'economic theory' supposedly suggests variables for inclusion or exclusion in particular equations. The problem looks severe enough as it is, but RE models probably pose greater problems of identification and observational equivalence than do non-RE models. In a simultaneous model the reduced form for an endogenous variable if it is determined by expectations of other (non-policy) endogenous variables will usually depend on all the exogenous and lagged variables in the *whole* model. So, for example, in a 'complete' RE model (if all the structural equations are explicitly written down) the reduced form for output (equation (3.39)) would depend on all the exogenous and lagged variables. It would therefore most likely contain all variables that could possibly appear in a policy reaction function such as equation (3.40) and in this case as we noted above the RE model becomes observationally equivalent to non-RE models. (In the econometrics jargon there are said to be too few exclusion restrictions.)

Sargent (1976) and Buiter (1983) provide other examples of observational equivalence and the seminal article by Pesaran (1981) is extremely pessimistic on the prospects for identifying and hence testing the RE assumption in macromodels. However, economists have to try to interpret events and 'near impossibility' hardly ever deters the intrepid applied RE economist. By sidestepping this particular 'black hole' of the RE paradigm we therefore briefly note some tests of the RE cross-equation restrictions and policy ineffectiveness (including the neutrality) proposition. Of course, the authors' concerned make sure that their *a priori* restrictions preclude the observational equivalence problem.

Joint Tests of RE, and Neutrality   Attfield et al. (1981a,b) test the RE cross-equation restrictions using real output as the variable of interest. Output is determined by the natural rate (measured by a time trend and the variance of inflation, which captures the effect of resource misallocation due to 'noisy' relative price signals), and current and lagged unanticipated monetary growth. Monetary growth (equation 3.40)) is determined by lagged monetary growth, the real borrowing requirement and the real current account payments surplus. For both annual data 1946–77 and quarterly data 1963–78, Attfield and co-workers find that both the cross-equation RE restrictions and the neutrality proposition may (just) be supported by the data.

There have been a number of studies that basically use Barro's US data but extend the range of tests considered. Leiderman (1980), for example, finds the joint test of 'rationality' and neutrality is accepted. However, when Mishkin (1982a,b, 1983) extends the lag lengths on anticipated and unanticipated money up to 24 quarters he finds (for US data) that 'neutrality' is definitely not accepted by the data and the validity of the RE restrictions varies with slight specification changes in the model.

Pesaran (1982) criticizes Barro (1977) for assuming that the *current-period* fiscal variable that influences monetary growth is known to agents at time *t*. Pesaran reworks the Barro 'unemployment model' assuming agents have to forecast the fiscal variable and also sets up a rival 'Keynesian' model where unemployment is determined by monetary growth (whether anticipated or unanticipated), government expenditure and variables that are assumed to influence the natural rate of unemployment. He then tests the statistical performance of the Barro unanticipated-money model *relative to* the Keynesian model and finds that the latter conforms 'more closely' to the data than does the Barro model.[6]

There are a large number of studies of the above type which it would be too tedious to mention. The evidence goes against the hypothesis of neutrality but the rationality assumption probably has a little more empirical content. However a 'dark shadow' looms over all these tests, namely the possibility that in the real world we have 'observational equivalence'. Tests of the RE hypothesis involving *individual* behavioural equations (e.g. the consumption function, Hall (1978), Bilson (1980), Muellbauer (1983), Wickens and Molana (1984)), rather than reduced-form equations, may give some indirect evidence on the validity of the RE and neutrality propositions but space constraints preclude discussion of these.

3.6 Policy Evaluation: the Lucas Critique

Lucas (1976) asserts that it is probably impossible to use existing econometric models to evaluate the consequences of alternative policy scenarios. This arises because the parameters of the model are likely to change under alternative policy regimes and it may not be possible to ascertain the new 'correct' values of the parameters at the time of the policy change. It also follows that the Lucas critique provides an explanation for the observed instability in coefficients of econometric models: different policy regimes give rise to 'shifts' in parameters. The Lucas critique, if empirically important, is rather devastating. To see this, consider the way in which existing econometric models are used. After the model has been constructed on a particular data set the model builder then uses it to predict the consequences of say an increase in the money supply, on the assumption that the parameters of the model remain unchanged in the new environment. The model user then makes pronouncements that policy A rather than policy B will product a 'better' outcome. Optimal control techniques (see chapter 6) provide a method of obtaining the optimal setting for the money supply given the preferences of the policy maker and has been fairly extensively used in policy analysis at least at an informal level. This technique also requires an assumption that parameters are constant (or their probability distribution is known). It is worth noting that it is the *empirical* importance of the Lucas critique that is the crucial issue. The idea that econometric models may not give useful answers under certain policy simulations is not a new one. Model-builders have always recognized that the model may only be valid if the variation in the data set in the simulation is similar to that used in estimating the equations. (This is not just a matter of non-linearities in responses by agents.) For example, it would be accepted by most model-builders that a simulation involving a high rate of growth in the money supply, and hence possible high inflation, may not provide sensible results if the Phillips curve in the model has been estimated for a period of low inflation. If expectations are formed on the basis of past inflation one might expect the coefficient of current prices in the price expectations equation to increase at high rates of inflation. Model-builders would make judgemental adjustments or give results under different assumptions about the expectations coefficients, if no data for a high-inflation period were available. Judgemental adjustments might be made on the basis of results from other high-inflation countries and as data became available the model might be re-estimated with increased weight being given to the more recent 'high-inflation data' (e.g. the technique of discounted least squares, Harvey 1981).

To demonstrate the Lucas critique consider the model of §3.5.1, and substitute for Em_t from the monetary feedback rule (3.30) into the 'reduced form' for output, equation (3.29):

$$y = \left(1 - \frac{g_1 db}{d+b}\right) y_n - \frac{db}{d+b} g_0 + \frac{db}{d+b} m_t + \frac{g_1 db}{d+b} y_{t-1} + \frac{d}{d+b} u_t.$$

$$(3.49)$$

Although equation (3.49) is derived from an RE model, viewed as a single equation it appears to be a reasonable representation of the reduced form of a conventional (non-RE) fix-price IS–LM model with a vertical LM curve, and a lag effect of monetary policy on output (i.e. the term in y_{t-1}) – observational equivalence again. Interpreted as such, the *long-run* effect on output of a once-and-for-all *announced* step change in the money supply (i.e. set $y_{t-1} = y_t = y$ and differentiate) is

$$\frac{\partial y}{\partial m} = \frac{db}{d+b-g_1 db} .$$

$$(3.50)$$

However, given our assumption that agents use RE, the effect of an anticipated change in the money supply is zero (to see this put $m_t = g_0 = m$ and $g_1 = 0$, which represents a constant level for the money supply, in equation (3.49), or note equation 3.29). Hence a 'conventional policy' simulation (which disregards RE), using equation (3.49) gives incorrect results under the new policy regime. This arises because the estimated coefficients in (3.49) are a convolution of structural parameters b, d and expectations parameters g_0, g_1 and the latter alter under alternative policy regimes if agents use RE. It is also worth noting that if there have been several regime changes over the period of estimation of the reduced-form equation (3.49), the estimated coefficients (e.g. of y_{t-1}) which contain the expectations parameters may appear to be unstable even though the true structural (or 'deep') parameters (b, d) are not.

Although we have demonstrated the Lucas critique using *rational* expectations a similar argument applies to any expectations scheme whose parameters alter with the policy regime, as for example in the AEH when there is a 'change of gear' (Flemming 1976).

Can we make any assessment of alternative policies in RE models? The answer would appear to be a qualified 'yes' provided we can obtain separate estimates of the structural parameters b, d and the expectations parameters g_0, g_1 (rather than the composite terms in the reduced form (3.49)) – that is, if the model is identified. A rather trivial example would be if the authorities had a once-and-for-all unanticipated change in the level of the money supply from g_0 to $g_0^* \neq (= \overline{m})$ but retained the feedback rule thereafter. By inserting the new known value of g_0 in (3.49) the effect on y could be determined. However, cases may occur where separate estimates of the parameters cannot be obtained and hence we cannot evaluate the behaviour of the economy under RE in the new regime. Thus when agents change their method of forming expectations, instabilities in estimated coefficients may occur and it may be difficult to assess policy changes correctly. Under RE, changes in the policy regime *must* cause changes in the parameters of the reduced form and unless the new policy regime is a (nested) variant of the old regime and the parameters of the model can be identified then the behaviour of the economy cannot be predicted using the old model. Of course with a completely 'new' policy we have no information on which to base our estimates of the policy parameters g_i and presumably individuals will go through a learning process before they discover the new rule. RE has little to say about the behaviour of the economy during this learning period (but see DeCanio 1979, Bray and Savin 1986, for example).

Lucas's view of the supply curve relationship provides another example of the policy evaluation problem. A change in policy from a low rate of growth to a high rate of growth in the money supply may lead to general inflation rather than a change in relative prices and hence that the slope of the short-run aggregate supply curve becomes steeper.

Models that circumvent the Lucas critique and allow meaningful policy evaluation and simulation exercises are currently being investigated (see, e.g., Cuthbertson & Taylor 1987a,b). We have shown above that it is possible to obtain the model of the economy under the new policy regime if the parameters are identified. An alternative approach to solving the policy evaluation problem seeks to obtain the 'underlying' parameters of preferences and technology that are thought to be invariant to policy changes. At a more practical level if existing models 'track' the economy reasonably accurately over the past when there have been different policy regimes in operation, then we may have some faith that such models may yield meaningful simulation results for policies that are close to those pursued in the past. This applies *a fortiori* if the 'tracking performance' is good when the model is used to forecast outside its sample period of estimation (although see Hendry 1983 for a critique of the use of tracking performance to evaluate models). All models are approximations to reality. The importance of the Lucas critique therefore turns on whether one feels that the parameters of a model are stable under the policy change under consideration. This has always been a central question for model-users. If agents form Muth–RE, policy evaluation is more problematic but even then may not be impossible.

3.7   Cyclical or Persistence Effects

It is accepted by most economists that output (and employment) exhibits cycles around a trend growth path (i.e. that there is a business cycle). A high level of output in a particular year is often followed by high values in subsequent years and similarly for periods of low output. Put another way, output is serially correlated and exhibits 'persistence'. Early *equilibrium* (or market-clearing) RE models had difficulty in explaining this phenomenon since output deviates randomly around the natural rate as can be seen from equation (3.32):

$$y_t - y_n = v_t \tag{3.51}$$

where $v_t = d(bw_t + u_t)/(d + b)$ and is a white noise error. If we allow the forecast error for the money supply, w_t, to be serially correlated, then output would also be serially correlated. To see this let $v_t = \varrho v_{t-1} + \epsilon_t$, or $v_t = (1 - \varrho L)^{-1} \epsilon_t$ where ϵ_t is a white noise error and L is the lag operator (i.e. $L\epsilon_t = \epsilon_{t-1}$). Substituting for v_t in (3.51) and multiplying through by $(1 - \varrho L)$ we obtain persistence effects:

$$y - y_n = \varrho(y_{t-1} - y_{n,t-1}) + \epsilon_t.$$

However, serially correlated forecast errors for the money supply violate a basic postulate of RE and therefore cannot be invoked to explain persistence. Nevertheless there are several methods of obtaining serially correlated movements in output and unemployment while still retaining the RE assumption of serially uncorrelated forecast errors. We deal first with equilibrium RE models and then explanations involving RE in disequilibrium models.

3.7.1　Equilibrium Explanations

Lucas (1975) suggests that agents do not become aware of their forecast errors for several periods and this leads to persistent positive or negative values for $p - Ep$ hence $y - y_n$. However, this is an unlikely explanation for business cycles of several years' duration and sits uneasily in a model that places great emphasis on agents' willingness to correct quickly any systematic errors by investing time and money to discover the true model. Some RE equilibrium models suggest that cyclical variations in the *natural* rate of output (around its trend rate of growth) account for the cyclical behaviour of *actual* output. For example Blinder and Fischer (1981) show that the behaviour of inventories can produce cycles in an equilibrium model. If there is an unanticipated price surprise, production expands but there is also unanticipated destocking as some goods are sold from 'finished stocks'. When producers realize that the price increase is not an increase in the relative price of their output but only a rise in the general price level, they wish to return to normal levels of production. However, they cannot do so immediately because the stock output ratio would then be below its 'normal' (desired) level. Therefore, output continues above its normal level for several periods while stocks are replenished and the stock output ratio rises to its normal level.

A different approach is adopted by Sargent (1979) who demonstrates that if the firm chooses its level of employment to maximize (the discounted present value of) future profits and it is costly to alter employment then the desired short-run level of employment depends on lagged employment. (This model is explained in appendix 3.1.) If one then adds a neoclassical labour supply function one obtains *equilibrium* output depending on lagged output. The *equilibrium* RE explanation for 'persistence' in unemployment is perhaps not as convincing as in the case of employment and output. Since unemployment is assumed to be an equilibrium phenomenon, persistent unemployment must be due to voluntary search behaviour. In search models the individual only accepts a job offer when the wage offered exceeds his or her reservation wage. Although the latter is on average equal to the market-clearing wage (i.e. there are no systematic forecast errors by workers), there is a finite probability that the wage offer is below the reservation wage for a particular prospective employee because of the random element in forming expectations. Hence unemployment may persist. However, it remains to be demonstrated that this qualitative conclusion matches the actual duration of unemployment for the average unemployed worker.

3.8   Partly Rational Models

It may be reasonable to consider some markets to involve RE agents and also clear instantaneously and others to involve agents who do not use RE. *Asset* markets where homogeneous 'goods' are continuously sold in markets with low information and transactions costs might provide good candidates for the assumption of Muth–RE. On the other hand the labour market (and to a lesser extent the goods market), which consists of largely heterogeneous 'units' with firm-specific skills that are traded relatively infrequently, may not conform to the RE hypothesis. It seems natural to ask whether our previous results concerning the impotence of systematic monetary and fiscal policy still hold in models that are partly rational. There are now numerous models that embody the RE assumption in asset markets but not in the labour or goods market. We concentrate on two such models. The open-economy model of Dornbusch (1976) we discuss in § 5.4.1 while here we analyse the Blanchard (1979) closed-economy model. Three characteristics of these types of model stand out. First, overshooting in the instantaneous market-clearing variables may take place: the short-run response exceeds the long-run response. Second, and more important, the effects of anticipated and unanticipated changes in (policy) variables are very different over the path to the long-run equilibrium. Third, output rises only slowly and hence exhibits 'persistence'.

Blanchard's model has a Keynesian aggregate supply curve and output is determined by demand: there is no RE behaviour by goods and labour market participants and both markets react sluggishly to external shocks. Stock market participants form Muth–RE in determining the current stock market valuation of equities. The model is a variant of the simple fix-price IS–LM model. Consumption, c, is determined by wealth, namely, the market valuation of equities, q. The capital stock is fixed and therefore changes in the price of an equity are proportional to changes in the *total* stock market valuation of equity. Output adjusts sluggishly to changes in demand and rises when consumption demand $c(q)$ plus government expenditure, g, exceeds supply:

$$\dot{y} = a(c(q) + g - y) \qquad c_q > 0. \tag{3.52}$$

There are three assets. Money, which earns no interest, has a conventional demand function with the independent variables output and the interest rate, r, on capital safe liquid assets. The other two assets, namely, equities and liquid assets are perfect substitutes, there is no risk aversión and agents equalize expected (one-period) yields on the two assets. (The assumption of perfect substitutability is as important here as that of Muth–RE and this also applies to the Dornbusch model of §5.4.1.) The expected (one-period) yield on shares is made up of the running yield or profit (T) per share T/q and the expected capital gain which under the assumption of perfect foresight is equal to the *actual* proportional capital gain, $\dot{q} = \Delta q/q$.

Equilibrium in the three financial markets is maintained continuously and is given by the liquid-assets–equity relationship (3.53) and equilibrium in the money market ($M = M^d = m_y y - m_r r$):

$$r = T/q + \dot{q} \tag{3.53}$$

and

$$r = (m_y/m_r)y - (1/m_r)M = b_0 y - b_1 M \tag{3.54}$$

where M is the money supply. The share price at any time period t is given by the discounted present value of future profits with r as the discount rate (as may be seen by integrating equation (3.53) forward through time). In long-run equilibrium $\dot{q} = 0$ by definition; hence, from (3.53),

$$r = T/q. \tag{3.55}$$

Profits are assumed to be positively related to y:

$$T = a_0 + a_1 y. \tag{3.56}$$

3.8.1   Long-Run Equilibrium

The model is very similar to the simple fix-price IS–LM model but the link between the goods and money markets is provided by the interest rate acting on equity prices. In the simple IS–LM model an increase in the money supply leads to a fall in interest rates and a rise in interest-elastic (investment) expenditures. In the Blanchard model an initial fall in the interest rate (at an unchanged level of output and hence profits – equation (3.56)) requires a *rise in q* for equilibrium between liquid asset and equity holdings (equation (3.55)) and the latter triggers a rise in consumers' expenditure and demand. There is a *permanent* rise in output in the long run because we have a Keynesian rather than say a Sargent–Wallace supply function. However it is not the long-run result that is unusual but the path to long-run equilibrium where q acts as a 'jump' variable to clear the asset market in *all* periods.

Below we present the solution of the model in terms of phase diagrams and this will also prove useful in analysing the Dornbusch model. Before doing so, however, it is worth discussing the economic aspects of the model.

3.8.2   *Unanticipated Increase in the Money Supply*

The long-run equilibrium after a rise in the money supply involves a higher level of output and stock market valuation q as discussed above, but changes in output are sluggish and in the short-run output remains (virtually) constant. Muth–RE agents with perfect foresight recognize that because output will increase *in the future* the interest rate will have to rise *in the future* to maintain money market equilibrium (equation (3.54).

To maintain the arbitrage relation (3.53), equity yields T/q will be expected to rise in the future and if profits, T, are not very sensitive to output (see below) this implies a fall in q *in the future*. (Also r must take a value that offsets any capital loss due to this fall in q.) Since q must fall *in the future*, but has a higher level in long-run equilibrium, it must *initially* 'overshoot' its long-run equilibrium value. Equity prices act as a 'jump' variable to allow equilibrium instantaneously in the demand for liquid assets and equities. Along the path to equilibrium the arbitrage condition holds continuously: the return on liquid assets, r, is matched by (expected) capital losses ($\dot{q} < 0$) plus the rise in T/q as q falls and rising output leads to higher profits, T.

3.8.3   *Anticipated Increase in the Money Supply*

In this case the long-run equilibrium is the same as above but the path to equilibrium is very different. Output and equity prices change *before the actual change in the money supply*, which casts doubt on studies that attempt to test monetarist propositions by analysing leads and lags between the money supply and income and prices (Sims 1972, Goodhart et al. 1976).

When it is announced at time t that the money supply is to be increased at time $t+j$, RE agents (who we assume believe the announcement) know that output and profits will be higher and interest rates lower in the future. The discounted present value of profits will therefore be higher and RE agents immediately 'mark up' the price of equities. The latter leads to a rise in consumption and output at time t, *before* the actual increase in the money supply. Stock market 'speculators' purchase or 'mark up' prices immediately because otherwise they would forego profitable opportunities. It is really the *threat* of large purchases that causes prices to change: no 'trades' need actually take place. The model demonstrates that volatile changes in equity prices may be due to (Muth-) rational behavioural rather than caprice.

3.8.4   *Qualitative Solution Using Phase Diagrams*

There are numerous methods of solving RE models (see appendix 3.1) and the phase diagram approach which is widely used allows qualitative solutions to be determined without analytically solving the full differential equation system. *Goods market equilibrium* in the Blanchard model is given by $\dot{y} = 0$ in equation (3.52) and this yields a positive relationship between q and y (the yy locus in figure 3.2). A higher level of q leads to a higher demand for consumption goods and hence a higher level of output supplied, y, is needed to achieve equilibrium. A higher level of government expenditure leads to a higher level of (government) output (at any level of q) and the yy locus shifts to the right. At a point like A demand exceeds output and via (3.52) output must be increasing as indicated by the arrows. (The converse applies at A'.)

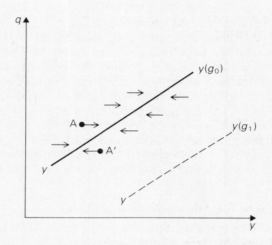

Figure 3.2   The Blanchard model – goods market equilibrium

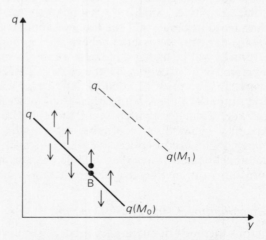

Figure 3.3   Asset market equilibrium

Asset market (static long-run) *equilibrium* is given by $\dot{q} = 0$ and from (3.53), (3.54) and (3.56) this gives an ambiguous relationship between y and q (for given M). However, if profits are only weakly related to output in (3.56) ($a_1 \rightarrow 0$), the relationship will be negative (the qq locus in figure 3.3). When $\dot{q} = 0$, asset market equilibrium requires $r = T/q$ and therefore, above the qq locus (i.e. q higher), r must exceed T/q and short-run equilibrium requires a capital gain – equation (3.53). Hence, at a point like B (figure 3.3), q is increasing as indicated by the arrows.

An increase in the money supply leads to a shift to the right (up) in the qq locus: at any given level of output, equilibrium in the *money* market requires a lower interest rate but long-run equilibrium in the equity market then requires a higher level of equity prices (equation (3.55)).

Long-run equilibrium in both goods and asset markets is at point E_0 in figure 3.4. Except along the *saddle path* AB which we have drawn in, the arrows of motion indicate that the system is unstable: either q or y moves off to infinity. Somewhat paradoxically this instability in RE models provides us with a unique solution (i.e. path to equilibrium). For any arbitrary starting value y_0 for output there is only one starting value q_0 for equity prices that allows that equilibrium point E_0 to be attained. After a 'shock' or unanticipated change in policy, it is assumed that RE agents quickly (instantaneously) learn about their new environment and, for example, q instantaneously 'jumps' onto the new stable path to equilibrium. Some economists have found this assumption of 'instantaneous acquisition of knowledge' rather hard to accept. If agents are initially confused and are then hit by other 'shocks' they may never attain the unique equilibrium path and the economy will not proceed as predicted by the RE model. Advocates of RE point to the absence of 'speculative bubbles' and variables moving off to infinity in the real world and infer from this that agents may quickly move

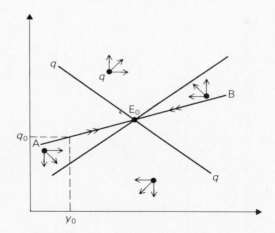

Figure 3.4   The saddle path AB

onto the new equilibrium RE path. There is clearly a problem with RE here in that at a minimum it does not explain the path of the economy over a finite 'learning period'; unfortunately we cannot develop these arguments further here. (Incidentally some RE models produce only unstable paths and others provide multiple stable paths. One may wish to rule out the former as useful descriptions of the real world and there are reasonably sensible ways of choosing one out of a multiplicity of stable paths – McCallum 1983.)

We are now in a position to analyse monetary and fiscal policy in the model. Consider again an *unanticipated* increase in the money supply. The qq locus shifts to the right and the new long-run equilibrium is at E_1 in figure 3.5.

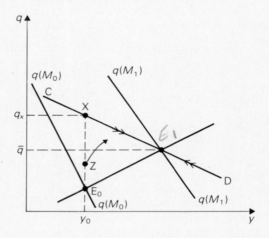

Figure 3.5   Anticipated (Z) and unanticipated expansionary monetary policy

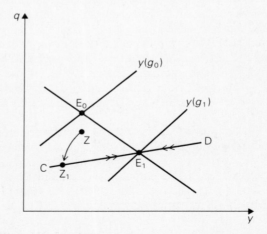

Figure 3.6   Anticipated expansionary fiscal policy

In the short run, output is fixed at y_0, and we jump to point X, so q overshoots its long-run equilibrium value, $\bar{q}$. In moving towards equilibrium along CD, output rises and equity prices fall.

With an *anticipated* increase in the money supply the qq locus does not move at time t, but at time $t+j$ when the actual money supply increases. At time $t+j$ we must be on the new stable saddle-path line, CD. However at time t with output fixed, stock prices must 'jump' to a point like Z in order to maintain equilibrium in the equity market after the fall in interest rates. Between t and $t+j$, y and q move towards CD as indicated by the arrow from Z in figure 3.5.

An *anticipated* increase in government spending also has interesting short-run implications for output. The long-run equilibrium is given by E_1 in figure 3.6 with higher output and lower stock prices. The latter occurs because the higher output requires a higher interest rate for money market equilibrium and if profits are only weakly related to output this implies lower equity prices (equation (3.55)). At the *time of the announcement* of the proposed increase in expenditure, Muth–RE agents realize that with marginally higher future profits being more than offset by higher interest rates, the discounted present value of future profits is low and hence they 'mark down' stock prices today. However, lower equity prices imply lower consumption and lower output at time t. After the initial jump in stock prices to Z in figure 3.6 output (and stock prices) follow the path to Z_1 which is reached at time $t+j$; output then *rises* along the new stable saddle path CD, finally reaching E_1. Thus for an announced *increase* in government expenditure output *falls* between the time of the announcement and the actual increase in government expenditure, and rises thereafter.

There is nothing particularly remarkable about the overshooting results described above, which tend to occur in any model where a subset of the variables are 'sticky'. What is interesting in RE models is the *discontinuous* jump in the 'free' variables and the markedly different short-run response to anticipated and unanticipated events.

The importance of the assumption of 'sluggish output' can be seen by noting that if output changes are instantaneous then an increase in the money supply (whether anticipated or unanticipated) results in r, q and y immediately attaining their long-run equilibrium values and there is no overshooting. This 'sluggishness' is also crucial in the open-economy Dornbusch overshooting model of §5.4.1.

It should now be clear to the reader that the information assumptions for Muth–RE are substantial. If an analytic solution of the model is not possible agents act 'as if' they work out the path of the future course of the economy (given an expected path for the exogenous variables) and use this to calculate current equity prices. Agents then calculate whether the future course of the economy implied by this equity price assumption equals that used to calculate it: agents proceed by trial and error (i.e. 'iterate') until the two are consistent.

Most macroeconometric models do not incorporate Muth–RE agents operating in any markets and do not formally (although they may informally) make any distinction between anticipated and unanticipated policy changes. If some agents in the economy do apply Muth–RE then these models are clearly deficient.

One of the few people to incorporate an element of Muth–RE into a large model is Fair (1979) who assumes participants in the government bond and in the equity markets are Muth-rational. The model incorporates a term structure relationship between long rates and expected short-term interest rates while expenditures depend on stock market wealth. These two relationships provide the main money market transmission mechanism. The results from Fair's model are similar in spirit to those of the Blanchard model where anticipated and unanticipated policy effects are markedly different, although the mechanism involved in Fair's model is primarily via the bond yield. For example an announced increase in government expenditure to take effect in period $t + j$ leads to an *immediate* rise in bond yields as RE agents realize that the consequences of the policy will be higher short-term interest rates *in the future* (the simple IS–LM result). Hence 'crowding out' of private expenditure occurs and output *falls* in the short run. Only when government expenditure rises at $t + j$ does output begin to rise. This is in sharp contrast to the 'normal' Keynesian model where crowding out only begins to take effect *after* the increase in government expenditure. Fair finds that the difference in the path of output between the rational case and the 'normal' (or non-rational) case can be substantial. Consistent solutions of some macroeconomic models containing 'future variables' are discussed in chapter 6.

3.9   Adaptive and Rational Expectations

By now the reader must have noted that the informational requirements of Muth-rational agents are substantial, particularly in an uncertain world where history tends not to repeat itself exactly. Agents' views of the workings of the economy may change over time as they (slowly) learn about their new environment (Friedman 1979). In the real world therefore, where information and learning are costly, agents may use fairly simple rules of thumb when forecasting. When a particular 'rule' produces large systematic errors agents may then search for a 'better', alternative, yet simple rule. It follows from this that simple rules like first-order adaptive expectations may actually be used by agents:

$$y^e_{t+1} - y^e_t = \lambda(y_t - y^e_t).$$

True, such a rule is unlikely to be consistent with the predictions of a complete model of the economy that one might care to write down, but the rule may not lead one into errors that are too costly. For example at low rates of inflation systematic errors in forecasting prices using adaptive expectations may be relatively 'inexpensive' for firms or persons compared with the other economic 'problems' facing them (e.g. restrictive practices and job choice).

The above speculations prompt the question of whether there are any circumstances in which first-order adaptive expectations are 'optimal' in some sense. The answer is that there are. Many economic time series, y_t, may be shown (to a good approximation) to evolve according to

$$y_{t+1} = y_t + \pi_0 \epsilon_{t+1} + \pi_1 \epsilon_t \qquad (3.57)$$

where ϵ_t is white noise. Equation (3.57) is known as 'integrated moving-average one–one' IMA(1, 1) (Granger and Newbold 1977). The growth in y i.e. $(y_{t+1} - y_t)$ is a weighted average of white noise errors $\epsilon_{t+1}, \epsilon_t$. If (3.57) is a good description of the data then first-order adaptive expectations are 'optimal' (i.e. produce minimum mean square forecast errors; see Muth 1960, Harvey 1981). To see this, note first from (3.57),

$$E_t y_{t+1} = y_t + \pi_1 \epsilon_t. \qquad (3.58)$$

To obtain ϵ_t in terms of y_t and expectations we have from (3.57)

$$y_{t+1} - y_t = (\pi_0 + \pi_1 L)\epsilon_{t+1} \qquad (3.59)$$

where L is the lag operator, that is $L\epsilon_{t+1} = \epsilon_t$. Hence,

$$L\epsilon_{t+1} = \epsilon_t = (y_t - y_{t-1})/(\pi_0 + \pi_1 L). \qquad (3.60)$$

Substituting (3.60) in (3.58) and rearranging:

$$E_t y_{t+1} - E_{t-1} y_t = \frac{\pi_0 + \pi_1}{\pi_0}(y_t - E_{t-1} y_t)$$

which may be written in the more familiar form of the first-order adaptive expectations hypothesis:

$$y^e_{t+1} - y^e_t = \lambda(y_t - y^e_t)$$

where $y^e_{t+j} \equiv E_{t+j-1}(y_{t+j})$, and 'adaptive agents' must choose the value of λ to equal $(\pi_0 + \pi_1)/\pi_0$.

If we take y_t to be the price level, then if inflation (the *growth* in the price level) is MA(1) (i.e. has no positive trend) then first-order adaptive expectations for the price *level* constitute an optimal forecasting scheme and do not produce systematic errors. However if *inflation* has an upward trend then first-order adaptive expectations applied to the inflation *rate* may be required to avoid systematic errors. This is a 'change-of-gear' process of learning by agents (Fleming 1976). Patterson (1985) has investigated autoregressive equations for prices that do not allow systematic errors to emerge while Lawson (1980) and Cuthbertson and Taylor (1987c,d), for example, have allowed the partial adjustment parameter λ to vary over time as agents 'optimally' learn about the stochastic process of the variable they are trying to forecast. Thus progress is being made on how agents might learn about their changing environment, an aspect neglected (at least until recently) by the RE paradigm.

Another 'simple' forecasting rule is that of regressive expectations:

$$y_t^e - y_{t-1}^e = \theta(\bar{y} - y_{t-1}) \qquad 0 < \theta < 1$$

where $\bar{y}$ is the (static) long-run equilibrium value of y usually given by a 'complete' model of the system. Here agents revise their expectations upwards if the actual value of y (in the previous period) is below its equilibrium value. Now this expectations scheme will not in general be *consistent* with the predictions of y using the complete model. In certain (special) circumstances, however, regressive expectations are also 'rational' (consistent) and an example of this is found in §5.4.1 where in the Dornbusch overshooting model exchange rate expectations follow such a scheme (in continuous time).

In conclusion it is worth the reader reflecting on the possible defects of RE in part as an antidote to the plethora of literature that take it as almost axiomatic that RE is the *only* form of expectations mechanism that it is sensible for economists to attribute to agents. Although (Muth–) RE are (by definition) *consistent* with the predictions of the *assumed* model, other expectations schemes may be 'optimal' (i.e. maximize welfare) given uncertainty and an ever-changing economic environment. While the neoclassical model assumes an omnipotent Walrasian auctioneer (chapter 2) the NC school has the equally tenuous assumption of instantaneous learning and knowledge, obtained by agents, of the working of the economy. Neither proposition seems more than a somewhat unrealistic working assumption whose main advantage is analytic tractability. Hence *radical* policy conclusions from NC (and indeed other rival views) should be viewed circumspectly.

3.10   Summary

That the REH has had a powerful impact on macroeconomic theory there can be no doubt; however, its impact on macroeconomic policy, particularly outside the US, has been less marked. In this chapter we have emphasized the implications of the REH for macroeconomic policy analysis and briefly outlined some tests of the hypothesis. On balance we found that direct tests using survey data do not tend to support the hypothesis. However, supporters of RE argue that survey data do not measure individuals' 'true' subjective expectations.

Economists have always been aware of the difficulties in evaluating alternative policy scenarios. The REH provides no guide to the 'learning process' involved when new policies are implemented but does suggest ways in which coefficients may change once the new policy rule is understood by the private sector (see, e.g. Walshe 1984). Ultimately, whether the Lucas policy evaluation proposition destroys the credibility of the results of 'conventional' policy analysis is an empirical one. For most policy changes it may be that the 'new' policy is a close variant of the 'old' policy and the parameters of the model may be reasonably invariant to such changes. A further discussion of the Lucas critique is given in chapter 6.

The inability of the authorities to affect (the probability distribution of) output by monetary and fiscal policy in RE models depends on several rather restrictive assumptions – notably, the presence of a Sargent–Wallace supply function. We noted that the theoretical basis of the latter and its relationship to the Phillips curve of §1.7 is, as yet, not well established. In any case the policy ineffectiveness proposition may be overturned by numerous minor changes in RE models. For example, if we assume different information sets or use a different supply function but still utilize an equilibrium model, then the authorities may influence the *variance* of output. When we allow disequilibrium in the labour market with overlapping contracts, the authorities can also influence the mean level of output. Tests of the policy ineffectiveness proposition use highly simplified aggregate models and results here are far from definitive: the observational equivalence problem also lurks uneasily in the background. In short, the policy ineffectiveness proposition does not necessarily hold in market-clearing RE models, and is unlikely to hold when non-market-clearing of labour or goods markets is assumed, and its empirical validity is open to doubt. None of the above implies that government stabilization policy is beneficial – only that it is feasible.

Equilibrium RE models are capable of explaining the stylized facts of the business cycle but complete RE models have not yet been constructed to ascertain how well they explain *quantitative* movements over the business cycle. An interesting development is the use of partly rational models in which anticipated and unanticipated policy changes imply very different time paths for output, even though the long-run response is the same for both types of policy. While the very controversial results of the REH do not hold in general, the additional insights provided by the REH into possible mechanisms at work in the macroeconomy are substantial.

Notes

1 If u_{t+1} is serially correlated, for example, exhibits first order autocorrelation, then $u_{t+1} = \varrho u_t + \epsilon_{t+1}$ – (i), where ϵ_{t+1} is 'white noise' (by assumption). Multiplying (3.2) by ϱ and lagging one period, we have $\varrho S_t = \varrho \alpha + \beta \varrho S_t^e + \varrho u_t \ldots$ (ii). Subtracting (ii), from (3.2) and using (i) we have

$$S_{t+1} = \varrho S_t + \alpha(1 - \varrho) + \beta S_{t+1}^e - \beta \varrho \ S_t^e + \epsilon_{t+1}$$

Thus even if $\alpha = 0$, $\beta = 1$ then S_{t+1}^e is not an unbiased predictor of S_{t+1} since then

$$S_{t+1} = S_{t+1}^e + \varrho S_t - \varrho S_t^e + \epsilon_{t+1}$$

We also require $\varrho = 0$ for unbiasedness.

2   This follows directly from the fact that the forecast *is* the conditional expectation for a Muth RE agent hence $E(u_{t+1}|\Omega_t) = E_t[S_{t+1} - E(S_{t+1}|\Omega_t)] = E(S_{t+1}|\Omega_t) - E(S_{t+1}|\Omega_t) = 0$.

3   From footnote 1 we see that u_{t+1} must be serially uncorrelated for unbiasedness. By a similar reasoning ϵ_{t+1} in the orthogonality equation (3.4) must also be serially uncorrelated (and with zero mean) otherwise $(S_{t+1} - S_{t+1}^e)$ would depend upon previous forecast errors.

4   This is the static equivalent of Friedman's (1968) view that the money supply should be set at a constant growth rate and not altered in response to other economic variables.

5   The variance–covariance matrix of the restricted system (3.31) and (3.32) is $E(v_t \, w_t)' \, (v_t \, w_t) = \Sigma$, where Σ is a 2×2 matrix of variance σ_u^2, σ_w^2 and covariance, σ_{uw}. If the variance–covariance matrix of the unrestricted system is denoted Ω the likelihood ratio statistic, $\text{LR} = -2(\ln\det\Sigma - \ln\det\Omega)$ is asymptotically distributed as central χ^2 under the null, that the restrictions hold.

6   So called non-nested tests are used (Davidson and MacKinnon 1982). For example in the non-nested J-test we run a regression of the form: $y = X\beta + \alpha\hat{y}_k + u$ where $y = $ output/unemployment, $X = $ set of variables in the NC model, $\beta = $ vector of NC parameters, and $\hat{y}_k$ are the *predictions* of output from the Keynesian model. If $\hat{y}_k$ provides no additional statistical explanation of y (i.e. $\hat{\alpha} = 0$) then the NC model is not rejected by the Keynesian model. One can reverse the procedure and each model can in principle reject the other.

Appendix 3.1   Solution of RE Models

In the text we demonstrated how phase diagrams may be used to obtain qualitative insights into the solution of (continuous-time) RE models using the Blanchard (1979) model as an example. In chapter 5 we repeat this solution method for the open-economy Dornbusch (1976) overshooting model. However, many RE models use discrete time intervals as this allows relatively complex lag structures to be handled. We deal only with solutions of *linear* RE models. If large-scale non-linear RE macromodels can be satisfactorily linearized then our solution methods could in principle be applied here. However, large non-linear models are usually solved by non-linear iterative techniques and we do not discuss these solutions (see, for example, Hall 1985, Fisher et al. 1985).

Our aim in this appendix is to present various RE solution methods so that the reader will be able to begin to solve RE models that appear in the literature. We use very parsimonious (and therefore somewhat 'incomplete') models so the *method* of obtaining the RE 'solutions' does not disappear behind a mass of algebra.

We discuss three methods of solving RE models: 'expectations of the reduced form' and the Muth and Sargent methods. In general we shall be interested in whether a solution exists, if so whether it is a unique solution and whether the solution is a dynamically stable one. We gradually move from simple models to more complex models. We begin with models with no forward-expectations terms, add forward expectations and finally also include lagged variables.

Models with No Forward Expectations, No Lagged Variables   The model discussed in the main text in § 3.5.1 is of this type because it contains terms in $E_{t-1}p_t$ and *not* forward-expectations terms of the form $E_{t-1}p_{t+j}$, $j \geqslant 1$, for example.

The 'expectations of the reduced form' solution method   To illustrate this solution method we take a model that allows 'sticky prices' (Buiter 1980) as this has the added advantage of formally demonstrating that 'sticky prices' allow monetary policy to be 'effective'. A SW-type 'surprise' supply function determines 'desired' prices p_t^* but actual prices p_t adjust with a (partial-adjustment) lag:

$$p_t^* = \alpha(y - y_n) + {}_{t-1}p_t^e \qquad\qquad\qquad\qquad\qquad (A3.1.1)$$
$$p_t - p_{t-1} = \beta(p_t^* - p_{t-1}) \qquad 0 < \beta < 1. \qquad\qquad (A3.1.2)$$

If $\beta = 1$ we have the normal SW flexible-price model. For algebraic simplicity we put $y_n = 0$; aggregate demand is determined by a vertical LM curve:

$$y^d = \gamma(m - p)_t + \epsilon_t^d. \qquad\qquad\qquad\qquad\qquad (A3.1.3)$$

The variables y, p, p^e (and p^*) are endogenous, while p_{t-1}, m_t (and ${}_{t-1}m_t^e$) are exogenous (predetermined). Substituting (A3.1.1) into (A3.1.2) and equating supply and demand for output we obtain the pseudo-reduced-form equation for p_t ('pseudo' because it contains the endogenous variable ${}_{t-1}p_t^e$)

$$p_t = \alpha\beta\gamma(m - p)_t + (1 - \beta)p_{t-1} + \beta\ {}_{t-1}p_t^e + \alpha\beta\epsilon_t^d. \qquad (A3.1.4)$$

To 'solve' for the endogenous variable ${}_{t-1}p_t^e$ we take expectations of (A3.1.4) with information at $t - 1$ and noting that $E_{t-1}p_{t-1} = p_{t-1}$ and $E_{t-1}\epsilon_t^d = 0$, and rearranging, we obtain the reduced-form equation for ${}_{t-1}p_t^e$:

$$
{}_{t-1}p_t^e = \frac{\alpha\beta\gamma}{1 + \alpha\beta\gamma - \beta}\ {}_{t-1}m_t^e + \frac{(1 - \beta)}{1 + \alpha\beta\gamma - \beta}\ p_{t-1}. \qquad (A3.1.5)
$$

When $0 < \beta < 1$ the past price level carries direct information about the current price level, and perhaps indirectly, via ${}_{t-1}m_t^e$, and as we see below this has a bearing on 'policy ineffectiveness'. However if $\beta = 1$, then ${}_{t-1}p_t^e = {}_{t-1}m_t^e$ and the past price level has no effect on ${}_{t-1}p_t^e$.

Having obtained the reduced form for $_{t-1}p_t^e$ this may be substituted into the supply–demand relation (A3.1.4) to obtain the reduced form for p_t:

$$p_t = \frac{1-\beta}{\theta_0} p_{t-1} + \frac{\alpha\beta\gamma}{\theta_1} m_t + \frac{\alpha\beta^2\gamma}{\theta_1\theta_0} {}_{t-1}m_t^e + \frac{\alpha\beta}{\theta_1} \epsilon_t^d \qquad (A3.1.6)$$

where

$$\theta_0 = 1 - \beta + \alpha\beta\gamma \qquad \theta_1 = 1 + \alpha\beta\gamma.$$

Substituting (A3.1.6) in the demand equation (A3.1.6) yields the reduced form for output

$$y_t = \frac{\gamma}{\theta_1} m_t - \frac{\alpha\beta^2\gamma^2}{\theta_1\theta_0} {}_{t-1}m_t^e - \frac{(1-\beta)\gamma}{\theta_0} p_{t-1} + \frac{1}{\theta_1} \epsilon_t^d. \qquad (A3.1.7)$$

Unless prices are perfectly flexible (i.e. $\beta = 1$) then the expected money supply $_{t-1}m_t^e$ influences output: policy ineffectiveness does *not* apply. If $\beta = 1$ then only unanticipated money affects output and (using (A3.1.5)) $_{t-1}p_t^e = {}_{t-1}m_t^e$.

To summarize, this method of solution has three main steps:

1   from the equilibrium relationship ($y = y^d$) solve for the pseudo-reduced form for *actual* prices $p_t = f({}_{t-1}p_t^e$, exogenous variables);
2   take expectations of the pseudo-reduced form to obtain the reduced form for *expected* prices $_{t-1}p_t^e$ as a function only of exogenous variables;
3   substitute the solution in (2) for $_{t-1}p_t^e$ back into the pseudo-reduced form in (1) to obtain actual prices as a function only of exogenous (predetermined variables).

Steps (1) and (2) form part of the solution provided by the Muth approach and a further extension discussed below where we solve a difference equation on the expectations variables.

Muthian solution method (no forward expectations)   Let us take a very simple Keynesian model where *current* consumption is determined by $_{t-1}y_t^e$. Goods market equilibrium with exogenous government expenditure G (assumed constant) is

$$y = a + b\,{}_{t-1}y_t^e + G + \epsilon_t \qquad 0 < b < 1 \qquad (A3.1.8)$$

where ϵ_t is a white noise random-error term. The Muth (1960) method relies on the Wold decomposition theorem, namely that the solution of any linear stochastic model may be written as the sum of a deterministic component $\bar{y}_t$ and an infinite moving-average term

$$\sum_0^\infty \pi_i \epsilon_{t-i}$$

where ϵ_t are white noise errors (Hannan 1970). The solution for y_t therefore has the general form

$$y_t = \bar{y} + \sum_{i=0}^{\infty} \pi_i \epsilon_{t-i} \tag{A3.1.9}$$

where the π_i are for the moment unknown. Muth's solution method equates the unknown coefficients π_i with the 'known' parameters a and b, thus obtaining a solution for y_t in terms of a and b (and the exogenous variables G_t, ϵ_t). To utilize the method, note that

$$\begin{aligned} E_{t-1}y_t \equiv {}_{t-1}y_t^e &= E_{t-1}(\bar{y} + \pi_0\epsilon_t + \pi_1\epsilon_{t-1} + \ldots) \\ &= \bar{y} + \pi_1\epsilon_{t-1} + \pi_2\epsilon_{t-2}. \end{aligned} \tag{A3.1.10}$$

$E_{t-1}\epsilon_t = 0$ as ϵ_t is unknown at $t-1$ and its expected value is zero by assumption, while $\bar{y}$ is *deterministic*; hence $E_{t-1}\bar{y} = \bar{y}$. Using (A3.1.9) and (A3.1.10) in (A3.1.8) we have

$$\bar{y} + \pi_0\epsilon_t + \pi_1\epsilon_{t-1} + \ldots = a + b(\bar{y} + \pi_1\epsilon_{t-1} + \pi_2\epsilon_{t-2} + \ldots) + G + \epsilon_t. \tag{A3.1.11}$$

Equating coefficients, equation (A3.1.11) can only hold if

$$\bar{y} = a + b\bar{y} + G \tag{A3.1.12a}$$
$$\pi_0\epsilon_t = \epsilon_t \tag{A3.1.12b}$$
$$\pi_i\epsilon_{t-i} = b\pi_i\epsilon_{t-i} \qquad i \geqslant 1. \tag{A3.1.12c}$$

Since ϵ_{t-i} $(i = 0, \ldots, \infty)$ can take on any values, the conditions in (A3.1.12) can only hold if

$$\bar{y} = (a + G)/(1 - b)$$
$$\pi_0 = 1$$
$$\pi_i = 0 \qquad i \geqslant 1.$$

Hence the solution to the model is

$$y_t = \frac{a + G}{1 - b} + \epsilon_t. \tag{A3.1.13}$$

Models with Forward Expectations, No Lagged Variables In our previous model (A2) we obtained a single (unique) solution and as there are no dynamics the solution is a stable one. When forward expectations enter the model there is a likelihood of both instability and non-uniqueness (and possibly a solution may not exist). Our simple Keynesian model where G_t is allowed to vary now becomes

$$y_t = a + b \,_t y_{t+1}^e + G_t + \epsilon_t \qquad 0 < b < 1. \tag{A3.1.14}$$

It turns out that this model cannot be solved using the reduced-form method of A1. However, it is instructive to proceed initially as if this were *not* the case. Moving (A3.1.14) one period ahead but retaining the assumption that information is available only at time t or earlier, and taking expectations, yields

$$_t y_{t+1}^e = a + b\,_t y_{t+2}^e +\,_t G_{t+1}^e. \qquad (A3.1.15)$$

The problem in this pseudo-reduced form for expectations is that $_t y_{t+1}^e$ depends upon the unknown $_t y_{t+2}^e$. If we knew $_t y_{t+2}^e$ we could solve the model backwards, obtain $_t y_{t+1}^e$ and, using (A3.1.14), y_t. (Our RE model assumes we can make forecasts of the exogenous variable $_t G_{t+1}^e$ outside of the model, for example using the chain rule of forecasting when $G_{t+1} = g(L)G_t$ where $g(L)$ is a scalar polynomial in the lag operator.) Thus, whatever value we choose for $_t y_{t+i}^e$ $(i = 1, \ldots, \infty)$, we can solve the model backwards. However, our choice of a terminal value at time $t + N$, that is, $_t y_{t+N}^e$ appears to be arbitrary in that the structure of the model gives us no indication of the 'correct' value. It appears as if the model may have an infinite number of possible solutions based on arbitrary choices of $_t y_{t+N}^e$. Expectations are self-fulfilling but arbitrary. (In the 'usual textbook' difference equations we have *initial* conditions (at $t = 0$), which help us to pin down the unique solution (Chiang 1984), but in this RE model we need a terminal or transversality condition at $t + N$, which is unavoidable.)

Note that (A3.1.15) appears to be a first-order difference equation in *expectations*: this will help us to find a unique solution but, for the moment, try successive substitutions in (A3.1.15):

$$_t y_{t+1}^e = a + b(a + b\,_t y_{t+3}^e +\,_t G_{t+2}^e) +\,_t G_{t+1}^e \text{ etc.}$$

and then substitute the resulting expression for $_t y_{t+1}^e$ in (A3.1.14) to obtain

$$y_t = a(1 + b + \ldots + b^{N-1}) + \sum_{i=0}^{N-1} b^i\,_t G_{t+i}^e + b^N\,_t y_{t+N}^e \qquad (A3.1.16)$$

We still have the problem that y_t depends on an arbitrary value for the endogenous variable $_t y_{t+N}^e$. Over a finite time horizon (i.e. N small), b^N $(0 < b < 1)$ may not be small enough to ignore and therefore the arbitrary choice $_t y_{t+N}^e$ will influence y_t. The latter occurs in large-scale 'short-term' forecasting models with consistent (rational) expectations and there does not yet appear to be a wholly satisfactory solution to the problem. The non-uniqueness problem may still be severe even if N is large since there is nothing *in the model* to ensure $_t y_{t+N}^e$ is not 'large' and hence that $b^N\,_t y_{t+N}^e$ is relatively unimportant.

There are a number of somewhat artificial and ad hoc ways around this problem of non-uniqueness, which come under the heading of terminal or transversality conditions. Minford et al. (1979) propose a *Deus ex machina* in the form of the authorities who convince agents that (in this static model) output will be stabilized (constant) at some finite time $t+N$ in the future. Alternatively, if N is large $b^N {}_t y^e_{t+N}$ may become negligible and, for example, the solution as $N \to \infty$ is

$$y_t = \frac{a}{1-b} + \sum_0^\infty b^i {}_t G^e_{t+i} + \epsilon_t \qquad (A3.1.17)$$

which if ${}_t \overline{G}^e_{t+i} = \overline{G}$ (a constant) yields

$$y_t = \frac{a+\overline{G}}{1-b} + \epsilon_t. \qquad (A3.1.18)$$

Hence the somewhat arbitrary terminal condition provides us with a unique stable solution. The solution method we have used here is (a 'longhand' version of) the Sargent (1979) 'forward-operator' method (see below).

Solution of the implicit expectations difference equation   In terms of expectations and for simplicity taking $G_t = \overline{G}$, equation (A3.1.15) yields

$$_t y^e_{t+1} = a + b {}_t y^e_{t+2} + \overline{G}. \qquad (A3.1.19)$$

if we let $x_i = {}_t y^e_{t+i+1}$ this can be written as a first-order difference equation in x_i:

$$x_{i+1} = \frac{1}{b} x_i - \frac{a+\overline{G}}{b}$$

which has the solution (Chiang 1984)

$$x_i = \left(x_0 - \frac{a+\overline{G}}{1-b} \right) \left(\frac{1}{b} \right)^i + \frac{a+\overline{G}}{1-b}. \qquad (A3.1.20)$$

The solution is not unique since we have no way of pinning down the arbitrary value of $x_0 = {}_t y^e_{t+1}$. One arbitrary method of obtaining a unique solution is suggested by (A3.1.20). If $0 < b < 1$ and hence $(1/b)^i \to \infty$ as $i \to \infty$ the solution (A3.1.20) is unstable. If we *assume* that RE agents do not choose to 'set off' along an explosive path (i.e. we rule out bubbles) then the *only stable* solution is $x_0 = {}_t y^e_{t+1} = (a+\overline{G})/(1-b)$. Hence by *assuming stability* we impose uniqueness. Of course if $|1/b| < 1$, which may occur in some models, this course is not open to us: we then have an infinite set of stable RE solutions (Taylor 1977). Substituting the stable solution for y_t in (A3.1.14) the solution for y is

$$y_t = \frac{a+\overline{G}}{1-b} + \epsilon_t. \qquad (A3.1.21)$$

The Muthian solution   This essentially results in the same kind of difference equation as above. Equating both sides of (A3.1.14) using our Wold decomposition formula (A3.1.9) we have

$$\bar{y} + \pi_0 \epsilon_t + \pi_1 \epsilon_{t-1} + \ldots = a + b(\bar{y} + \pi_1 \epsilon_t + \pi_2 \epsilon_{t-1} + \ldots) + \bar{G} + \epsilon_t.$$
(A3.1.22)

Equating coefficients:

$$\bar{y} = a + b\bar{y} + \bar{G} \qquad\qquad\qquad\qquad\qquad\qquad\text{(A3.1.22a)}$$
$$\pi_0 = b\pi_1 + 1 \qquad\qquad\qquad\qquad\qquad\qquad\text{(A3.1.22b)}$$
$$\pi_i = b\pi_{i+1} \qquad\qquad i \geqslant 1. \qquad\qquad\qquad\text{(A3.1.22c)}$$

Equation (A3.1.22c) is a first-order difference equation in π_i with the solution

$$\pi_i = A\,(1/b)^i \qquad i \geqslant 1 \qquad\qquad\qquad\qquad\text{(A3.1.23)}$$

where A is an unknown constant. Equation (A3.1.23) mirrors equation (A3.1.20) and is unstable if $1/b > 1$. Ruling out the unstable root implies putting $A = 0$ and hence $\pi_i = 0$ for $i \geqslant 1$. Substituting $\pi_1 = 0$ in (A3.1.22b) yields $\pi_0 = 1$ and a stable unique solution

$$y_t = \frac{a + \bar{G}}{1 - b} + \epsilon_t$$

(the same as in (A3.1.21) above).

Sargent's method using the forward-lag operator   In the text we discussed how some RE models incorporate persistence effects. Sargent (1979) has shown that 'persistence' in the form of a lagged dependent variable, as well as (future-) expectations terms will appear in behavioural equations if agents minimize a quadratic cost function that is forward-looking. In examining this widely used model (used particularly in empirical work) we are also able to demonstrate another solution method for a particular type of RE model. Suppose that agents have quadratic costs of being away from their long-run equilibrium value y_t^* but also incur quadratic costs of adjustment, and these costs are discounted by a constant factor, $0 < D < 1$. We assume the agent chooses a current 'short-run' value of y_t in order to minimize expected costs C with information available at $t - 1$:

$$\min\ C = E_{t-1} \sum_{i=0}^{\infty} \tfrac{1}{2} D^i a_0 (y - y^*)_{t+i}^2 + a_1 (y_{t+i} - y_{t+i-1})^2. \qquad\text{(A3.1.24)}$$

E_{t-1} is the expectations operator. The above equation is just a multi-period generalization of the 'theory' behind the well known first-order partial adjustment equation.

To make the example more concrete, y might be any real variable such as employment or the capital stock, which are 'costly' to adjust. The quadratic form for the loss function (A3.1.24) was not chosen arbitrarily. Since the solution to a quadratic optimization problem is *linear* in expectations (because the first-order conditions, or 'Euler equations', are linear) and therefore does not involve, say, the *variance* of forecast errors, the problem is simplified somewhat. The simplification is that we can solve the optimization problem as if agents *knew* all the future y-values (i.e. had perfect foresight) and then, once we have obtained the solution, substitute in 'expected' for 'actual' future values. This property is usually termed 'certainty equivalence' or the 'separation principle'.

The first-order condition from (A3.1.24) assuming agents have information at $t-1$ is

$$\left(1 - \frac{1+D+a}{D} L + \frac{1}{D}L^2\right)y_t = - \frac{a}{D} y_{t-1}^* \tag{A3.1.25}$$

where $a = a_0/a_1$ and L is the backward-lag operator. Equation (A3.1.25) is often referred to as the Euler equation. The quadratic equation (A3.1.25) in L may be written as

$$(1 - \lambda_1 L)(1 - \lambda_2 L)y_t = (-a/D)y_{t-1}^* \tag{A3.1.26}$$

where

$$\lambda_1 \lambda_2 = D^{-1} \qquad \lambda_1 + \lambda_2 = (1+D+a)/D \tag{A3.1.27a}$$

and

$$(1 - \lambda_1)(1 - \lambda_2) = -a/D \tag{A3.1.27b}$$

It is easy to see from $\lambda_1 \lambda_2 = D^{-1}$ that the roots λ_1 and λ_2 lie on either side of unity (for $0 < D < 1$). We now need a short digression to explain Sargent's use of the forward-lag operator. Sargent (1979) demonstrates that, if $|\lambda| > 1$, then

$$\frac{1}{1 - \lambda L} y_t^* = - \frac{1}{\lambda} y_{t+1}^* - \frac{1}{\lambda^2} y_{t+2}^* - \ldots \tag{A3.1.28}$$

To prove (A3.1.28) note first that

$$\frac{1}{1 - \lambda L} = \frac{1}{(-\lambda L)[1 - (\lambda L)^{-1}]} = -(\lambda L)^{-1}[1 + (\lambda L)^{-1} + (\lambda L)^{-2} + \ldots] \tag{A3.1.29}$$

where we have used the result $(1-x)^{-1} = 1 + x + x^2 + \ldots, |x| < 1$, with $x = (\lambda L)^{-1}$ and $|1/\lambda| < 1$. Substituting (A3.1.29) in (A3.1.28) we have

$$\frac{1}{1-\lambda L}y_t^* = [-(\lambda L)^{-1} - (\lambda L)^{-2} - \ldots]y_t^*$$

$$= -\frac{1}{\lambda}y_{t+1}^* - \frac{1}{\lambda^2}y^*_{t+2} - \ldots$$

where we have used the forward operator given by $L^{-j}y_t^* = y_{t+j}^*$.

Using Sargent's forward-operator result and (A3.1.27b), equation (A3.1.26) becomes

$$(1-\lambda_1 L)y_t = \frac{(1-\lambda_1)[1-(\lambda_1 D)^{-1}]}{1-\lambda_2 L}y_{t-1}^*$$

$$= (1-\lambda_1)[1-(\lambda_1 D)^{-1}][-(\lambda_1 D)y_t - (\lambda_1 D)^2 y_{t+1} - \ldots]$$

$$(1-\lambda_1 L)y_t = (1-\lambda_1)(1-\lambda_1 D)\sum_{i=0}^{\infty}(\lambda_1 D)^i {}_{t-1}y_{t+i}^{*e} \qquad (A3.1.30)$$

where we have replaced future values of y by their expectation based on information at $t-1$ (using the separation principle). If our static equilibrium theory suggests y_t^* depends on a vector of variables e.g. $y_t = kx_t$ then our behavioural equation in a suitable form for estimation and testing is

$$y_t = \lambda_1 y_{t-1} + (1-\lambda_1)(1-\lambda_1 D)k\sum_{i=0}^{\infty}(\lambda_1 D)^i {}_{t-1}x_{t+i}^e + u_t$$
$$\qquad (A3.1.31a)$$
$${}_{t-1}x_t^e = \Phi(L)x_{t-1} + v_t \qquad (A3.1.31b)$$

where we have added a (vector autoregressive) expectations scheme to generate the variables ${}_{t-1}x_t^e$. There are a number of different ways of estimating (A3.1.31a) and (A3.1.31b) and studies on employment (Sargent 1978, Kennan 1979), stockbuilding (Hall et al. 1986) and the demand for money (Cuthbertson and Taylor 1987a) provide practical examples of this. We do not dwell on the econometric issues here but merely note that the above equation imposes testable restrictions on the parameters. First, the weights in the forward variables decline geometrically; expectations formed for the 'distant future' carry less weight than expectations held about the near future and this appears plausible on *a priori* grounds. Second, the weight on the forward variables contains λ_1 and this is the coefficient that appears in the lagged dependent variable y_{t-1}. Of course, RE provides additional *cross-equation* restrictions in that the $\Phi(L)$ appear in the expectations generation equation (A3.1.31b) and in the structural equation for y_t (in the guise of ${}_{t-1}x_{t+i}^e$). However, tests of these cross-equation restrictions are rather complex (Hansen and Sargent 1980). For the interested reader the relationships between solely backward-looking models and forward-looking models like (A3.1.31) are dealt with by Cuthbertson (1986), Kelly (1985), Nickell (1985) and Taylor (1987c). Also, model B is amenable to solution using the Sargent forward-operator method and this is left as a simple exercise.

Models with Forward Expectations and Lagged Variables Assume the model has current consumption determined by $_ty^e_{t+1}$ and G is determined by a feedback rule $G_t = gy_{t-1}$, we then have

$$y_t = a + b \, _ty^e_{t+1} + g \, y_{t-1} + \epsilon_t \qquad 0 < b, g < 1. \tag{A3.1.32}$$

As we move the equation forward through time and take expectations, the lagged variable y_{t-1} will be projected into the future and we obtain a difference equation solely in terms of expectations of y:

$$_ty^e_{t+2} = a + b \, _ty^e_{t+3} + g \, _ty^e_{t+1}. \tag{A3.1.33}$$

We could now use the solution for a second-order difference equation and immediately solve for y_t as in the method used in §B1 above. However, for illustrative purposes consider the following.

The Muth solution method

$$y_t = \sum_{i=0}^{\infty} \pi_i u_{t-i} + \bar{y} \tag{A3.1.34}$$

$$_ty^e_{t+1} = \sum_{i=1}^{\infty} \pi_i u_{t+1-i} + \bar{y}. \tag{A3.1.35}$$

Substitute these expressions in (A3.1.32):

$$\begin{aligned}
\pi_0 u_t + \pi_1 u_{t-1} + \ldots + \bar{y} &= a + b(\pi_1 u_t + \pi_2 u_{t-1} + \ldots + \bar{y}) \\
&\quad + g(\pi_0 u_{t-1} + \pi_1 u_{t-2} + \ldots + \bar{y}) + u_t.
\end{aligned} \tag{A3.1.36}$$

Equating coefficients of $\bar{y}$, u_t, u_{t-1}, u_{t-2} we obtain

$$\begin{aligned}
\bar{y} &= a/(1-b-g) & \text{(A3.1.37}a\text{)} \\
\pi_0 &= 1 + b\pi_1 & \text{(A3.1.37}b\text{)} \\
\pi_1 &= b\pi_2 + g\pi_0 & \text{(A3.1.37}c\text{)} \\
\pi_2 &= b\pi_3 + g\pi_1 & \text{(A3.1.37}d\text{)}
\end{aligned}$$

etc. A *second-order* difference equation emerges from (A3.1.37c) and (A3.1.37d):

$$\pi_i = \frac{1}{b} \, \pi_{i-1} - \frac{g}{b} \, \pi_{i-2} \tag{A3.1.38}$$

has a solution

$$\pi_i = A \mu_1^i + B \mu_2^i \tag{A3.1.39}$$

where

$$\mu_i = \frac{1 \pm (1 - 4bg)^{\frac{1}{2}}}{2b} \qquad i = 1, 2. \tag{A3.1.40}$$

If the two roots are stable we have a non-uniqueness problem. If we have two unstable roots the model explodes. Hence, to obtain a stable unique solution it is usual to assume one stable and one unstable root and put the latter to zero. Assuming μ_1 is the stable root the solution is

$$\pi_i = A \mu_1^i \qquad\qquad\qquad (A3.1.41a)$$

which implies $\pi_0 = A$. Substituting $\pi_1 = \pi_0 \mu_1$ into (A3.1.37b) we obtain $\pi_0 = 1/(1 - b\mu)$. From (A3.1.41) we have by repeated substitution

$$\pi_i = \pi_0 \mu_1^i. \qquad\qquad\qquad (A3.1.41b)$$

One form of solution is then given by substituting (A3.1.41a) and (A3.1.37a) in (A3.1.34):

$$y_t = \frac{a}{1-b-g} + \pi_0 \sum_0^\infty \mu^i u_{t-i} \qquad\qquad (A3.1.42)$$

The solution (A3.1.42) contains only the structural parameters, since μ and the π_i depend on b and g. It is worth noting that the solution for y_t depends on the feedback parameter g and hence, in this model, systematic fiscal policy influences output.

Summary   The aim in this appendix has been to introduce the reader to alternative methods of solving RE models that are fairly commonplace in the literature. Very simple examples have been used to highlight the principles involved. The reader will not have to look far to put these methods into operation in more complex models and at a later stage should consult Whiteman 1985 or Blanchard and Khan 1980. In appendix 6.1 we present a further method of solving RE models using a matrix approach to solve the Dornbusch exchange rate overshooting model.

4 New theories of employment: implicit contracts and adverse selection

4.1 Introduction

Traditional neoclassical economics predicts that competitive firms will vary both employment and the real wage over the business cycle in response to fluctuations in product demand. However, the observed normal practice in most Western economies is to lay off workers as product demand falls, paying the rest of the workers a fairly unchanged wage. Laid-off workers may even be later re-hired by the same firm at the same wage as before the layoff.

This is an example of an empirical anomaly. Where the empirical evidence is clearly contrary to the positive predictions of a theory or paradigm, there is pressure to alter the theory in order to explain the facts of observation. One such change in the theory, or paradigm shift, was discussed in chapter 1 in the context of the Keynesian revolution. The phenomenon of sticky wages and layoffs is not unrelated. One response has been to abandon the idea of market clearing altogether and to take sticky wages and prices as parametric. This was the basis of the temporary-equilibrium analysis of chapter 2. However, some economists would argue that fix-price models really beg the question as to why prices and wages should be fixed. Indeed, it could be argued that since supply-and-demand schedules are the outcome of optimizing behaviour, non-market-clearing situations are inefficient in the welfare sense. This implies that, collectively, agents are in some sense acting irrationally if they do not adjust prices towards their market-clearing levels.

Nevertheless, it remains true that the evidence appears at odds with competitive wage theory. The theories discussed in this chapter take a different approach and try to show that, under certain plausible assumptions, the existence of sticky wages, layoffs and job queues may in fact be the outcome of optimizing behaviour on the part of agents.

We shall illustrate two major approaches that have been brought to bear on this issue: implicit contract theory and theories of adverse selection applied to the labour market. The basic assumption of implicit contract theory is that there is an asymmetry in the degree of risk aversion between employers and workers, workers being the more risk-averse. If this is the case then it may be Pareto-optimal to shift the risk of wage variation from the employee to the employer, so that firms pay out a fixed wage irrespective of demand conditions. The bulk of this chapter is devoted to a discussion of implicit contract theory.

Adverse-selection theories of employment start with the assumption that the workforce is heterogeneous. Further, a good indicator of the quality of a worker is the wage he or she is willing to work for. This has two implications. Firstly, in a recession, if the firm cuts wages the best workers may quit: it might be better to keep wages constant and lay off workers randomly. Secondly, if unemployed workers offer to undercut the going wage, they automatically signal that they are of poor quality and so reduce their chances of being taken on. In contrast to implicit contract theory, however, the adverse-selection explanation of sticky wages and layoffs in general represents an example of market failure.

4.2   Implicit Contracts[1]

The belief that wages should vary (counter-cyclically) over the business cycle is implicitly based on a view of the labour market as a spot auction. The insight of implicit contract models (see, e.g., Baily 1974, Azariadis 1975) is that labour is not in fact auctioned off at each point in time in quite the same way as, say, fresh fruit or vegetables are, but is rather more complex. In particular, the wage for a particular job will generally be only one element of an overall package that a job offers. Other factors that the worker might consider are, for example, whether there is a staff canteen, how sociable the hours are, how congenial the working environment is, and so on (you can make your own list). A chief item that most workers will be looking for in a job is job security – whether or not there is a risk of redundancy or layoff at some point, and how regular the wages are. The theory of implicit labour contracts models the labour market not as a spot auction but as one where employers and workers enter into mutually advantageous, unwritten, long-term contracts. Such contracts will indicate the wage that will be paid and the probability of being laid off at various phases over the business cycle (as well as other factors in the job package which we can ignore for a first approximation).

The starting point for most implicit contract models is that employers are less risk-averse than workers. In fact, we shall temporarily assume that employers are risk-neutral. By this we mean that employers stand ready to accept (actuarially) fair bets in unlimited quantities. By a fair bet we mean a gamble where the stake is just equal to the expected payoff. For example, if I tossed a fair coin and offered to pay you £2 if it came down heads and nothing if it came down tails, then the expected payoff would be £1. If I offered you this gamble for a stake of £1 (i.e. 'double or quits') this would be a fair bet. On the other hand, workers, since they are assumed to be risk-averse, will *never* accept a fair bet. However, risk-averse workers will generally accept some, but not all, favourable bets – for example if I offered the above gamble for a stake of only 50p perhaps.

One way in which this might be rationalized is to argue that entrepreneurs, as a self-selecting group, are inherently less risk-averse than workers. Probably a more convincing argument is based on the observation that shareholders rather than entrepreneurs are in fact the ultimate owners of most modern firms. The majority of shareholders are either wealthy individuals or large institutions such as pension funds or insurance companies. These agents are able to hold large, diversified portfolios and to employ or take advice from financial experts. On the other hand a typical worker's assets might consist of durable goods, a small cash balance, and human capital – the worker may even have outstanding consumer credit liabilities. He or she cannot diversify his or her 'portfolio' by holding several jobs simultaneously, and is also far less likely to have a good knowledge of the capital markets or to be able to employ someone else who does. Hence, by utilizing their greater wealth and financial expertise, shareholders are much more able to bear risk than workers. This difference in characteristics suggests that there may be gains from trade.

By agreeing to accept some of the risk of wage variations, employers implicitly offer an insurance service to workers. This is relatively costless to the firm because of its risk neutrality. Workers find this service attractive because of their risk aversion, and so a risk-reducing employment policy is a relatively cheap way of attracting a given work force.

4.2.1 *The Variability of Wages with Full-Employment Contracts*

Initially, we assume that the firm holds employment constant over the business cycle but may or may not vary wages. In the next section we relax this assumption and allow the firm to vary or hold constant both real wages and employment.

We assume a competitive firm that can sell all of its output at a given price. At any point in time, one of two states of nature will prevail – state one ('boom') or state two ('slump'). The known probability of state one occurring is ϱ_1 and of state two $1 - \varrho_1$. Both workers and employers are able to observe which state of the world is prevailing.

Corresponding to the state of nature there will be a certain output price, p_1 (for state one) or p_2 (for state two), that the firm faces and that reflects industry demand conditions ($p_2 < p_1$). An important assumption we make is that the firm and industry are small in the sense that variations in the product price do not affect the overall, exogenous price level, which is fixed. Thus, variations in product price affect the *real* value of output that can be produced with a given level of inputs. Another interpretation that could therefore be given to the states of nature is the incidence of technology shocks with a fixed product price. That is, occurrence of state two can be interpreted as a decline in technological efficiency such as might result from a 'supply side' shock.

Before the state of nature is actually observed, the firm chooses a wage and employment level for each state – w_i and n_i respectively, $i = 1,2$, where the subscript denotes the relevant state. This composes the labour contract. Formally, we can define a contract as an ordered list, or vector, (w_1, n_1, w_2, n_2), which specifies what the wage and employment prospects are for the worker for any given state of nature.

Technology is described by an increasing, monotone, strictly concave function through the origin (i.e. a standard production function):

$$y_i = f(n_i) \qquad f' > 0, f'' < 0, f(0) = 0 \tag{4.1}$$

where y_i and n_i denote output and employment respectively in state i, $i = 1,2$. In this section and throughout we assume that there is full employment in state one. In this section only we set $n_2 = n_1$.

Since we assume the firm is risk-neutral, it is indifferent to the expected value of profit and the certainty equivalent of that expected profit. The firm's objective is therefore to maximize its expected real profit:

$$\Pi = \varrho_1(p_1 y_1 - w_1 n_1) + (1 - \varrho_1)(p_2 y_2 - w_2 n_1). \tag{4.2}$$

At first sight this may appear to be expected nominal rather than real profit. Recall, however, that the overall price level is fixed and independent of the output price of the firm, so changes in the firm's product price therefore reflect changes in the real value of output.

Now consider the typical worker, who is endowed with a von Neumann–Morgenstern utility function with real wage income and leisure as arguments. We shall assume that each worker supplies labour in an indivisible unit, so wage income is strictly proportional to the wage rate. It makes no difference therefore if we treat the utility function as a function of the wage rate rather than wage income. Further, since we initially assume full employment in boom and slump, the amount of leisure enjoyed is the same over the business cycle. Thus, utility can only vary in the wage dimension. We can therefore think of the worker's utility in state i as an increasing, strictly concave, monotone function of w_i:

$$u = u(w_i) \qquad u' > 0, u'' < 0. \tag{4.3}$$

The concavity of the utility function is of course due to the worker's risk aversion. The worker maximizes his or her expected utility:

$$U = \varrho_1 u(w_1) + (1 - \varrho_1) u(w_2). \tag{4.4}$$

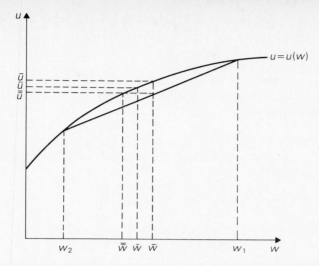

Figure 4.1   The optimality of state-invariant wages under full employment

We assume that the firm cannot drive down both w_1 and w_2 indefinitely without losing its work force. There will be a certain level of expected utility, $\tilde{U}$, say, which is determined by market forces and which workers could get by working for other firms. Hence, the firm's problem is to choose w_1 and w_2 to maximize (4.2) subject to

$$\varrho_1 u(w_1) + (1 - \varrho_1)u(w_2) \geqslant \tilde{U}. \tag{4.5}$$

A contract that satisfies (4.5) is termed feasible (Azariadis 1975). We should expect a profit-maximizing firm (knowing $u(.)$ and $\tilde{U}$) to force (4.5) to an equality. A contract that is feasible and yields a higher level of expected profit than any other feasible contract will be termed optimal (Azariadis 1975).

Since state one is 'boom', let us assume the firm is considering paying $w_1 > w_2$.[2] The worker's utility function will then look something like figure 4.1. The expected utility obtained by the worker is $\bar{\bar{U}} = \varrho_1 u(w_1) + (1 - \varrho_1)u(w_2)$. Clearly, the worker would prefer to receive a constant real wage of $\bar{w} = \varrho_1 w_1 + (1 - \varrho_1)w_2$ which confers a level of expected utility of $\bar{U} > \bar{\bar{U}}$. This is a consequence of the concavity of u which itself reflects the risk aversion of the worker.

However, the worker would in fact be content with a fixed wage of $\tilde{w}$, which yields a level of expect utility, $\tilde{U}$, just sufficient to retain him or her. If we had $\tilde{U} < \bar{\bar{U}}$, the fixed wage could be further reduced to $\bar{\bar{w}}$ before the worker would prefer variable to fixed wages. It is clear, therefore, that the firm will in general be able to make the worker better off by paying him or her a state-invariant real wage that is slightly less than the expected value of the state-variable wage. Say this fixed wage is in fact $\tilde{w}$, the minimum wage the worker will accept, or the 'acceptance wage'.

Now, because the firm is risk-neutral, it is indifferent to paying out a constant wage of

$$\bar{w} = \varrho_1 w_1 + (1 - \varrho_1)w_2$$

or w_1 with probability ϱ_1 and w_2 with probability $1 - \varrho_1$. To see this, simply rearrange equation (4.2):

$$\begin{aligned}
\varrho_1(p_1 y_1 - w_1 n_1) + (1 - \varrho_1)(p_2 y_1 - w_2 n_1) \\
= [\varrho_1 p_1 + (1 - \varrho_1)p_2]y_1 - [\varrho_1 w_1 + (1 - \varrho_1)w_2]n_1 \\
= [\varrho_1 p_1 + (1 - \varrho_1)p_2]y_1 - \bar{w}n_1.
\end{aligned} \tag{4.6}$$

Moreover, since $\tilde{w} < \bar{w}$, equation (4.6) implies

$$\begin{aligned}
\varrho_1(p_1 y_1 - \tilde{w}n_1) + (1 - \varrho_1)(p_2 y_1 - \tilde{w}n_1) > \varrho_1(p_1 y_1 - w_1 n_1) \\
+ (1 - \varrho_1)(p_2 y_1 - w_2 n_1)
\end{aligned} \tag{4.7}$$

i.e. it is more profitable on average to pay a fixed wage of $\tilde{w}$ than to vary it. Since $\tilde{w}$ is the lowest wage that can be paid before workers quit to find employment elsewhere, the solution to the firm's maximization problem is clearly

$$w_1 = w_2 = \tilde{w} \tag{4.8}$$

Thus the profit-maximizing, feasible, full-employment contract is $(\tilde{w}, n_1, \tilde{w}, n_1)$. Indeed, it is clear that this contract is Pareto-optimal (in this partial-equilibrium context). From figure 4.1 we can see that $w_1 - \tilde{w}$ is the maximum insurance premium that the worker would be willing to pay in order to have their wage made up to w_1 (i.e. receive indemnity of $w_1 - w_2$ should state two occur). Note that this is less than $w_1 - \bar{w}$, which is the maximum premium the worker would pay in the absence of expected utility opportunities of $\bar{U}$ elsewhere. Hence we can see that the firm is in effect offering insurance to the worker against variations in the real wage. The firm is happy to do this because it is less risk-averse than the worker. Put slightly differently, the risk is transferred from wages to profits and hence to the capital market, and so the firm implicitly acts as a financial intermediary. Given the attitudes toward risk of the worker and the firm, this is an optimal risk-sharing equilibrium.

4.2.2   The Existence of Layoffs

So far we have been able to gain some insight into why real wages may be sticky by examining the nature of the full-employment contract, but we have yet to provide an explanation for the existence of layoffs. We now relax the assumption of constant (full) employment and allow the firm to choose what levels of employment to offer simultaneously with wages.

We shall in fact continue to assume that everyone is employed during state one ('boom'), but there may now be layoffs during state two ('slump'). Hence, n_1 still denotes full employment but $n_1 - n_2$ workers will be randomly laid off should state two occur. Thus, if state one occurs, workers are certain of finding employment. If state two occurs, workers will find employment with conditional probability n_2/n_1 and will be laid off with the conditional probability $1 - n_2/n_1$.

In the discussion in §4.2.1 workers were never laid off, so we did not have to consider leisure explicitly as an argument in the utility function. Now suppose that if workers are employed they have leisure ℓ_e whilst if they are laid off they have leisure ℓ_u, $\ell_u > \ell_e$. We now have to redefine the utility function to take explicit account of leisure, ℓ:

$$u = v(w,\ell) \qquad \partial v/\partial w > 0, \ \partial^2 v/\partial w^2 < 0,$$
$$\partial v/\partial \ell > 0, \ \partial^2 v/\partial \ell^2 < 0. \tag{4.9}$$

In fact, the discussion in §4.2.1 can be made consistent with (4.9) by defining $u(.)$ appropriately:

$$u(w) = v(w,\ell_e). \tag{4.10}$$

Now suppose that when the worker is unemployed he or she receives real unemployment benefit of b paid from an economy-wide fund. Further, let c be the value that the worker attaches to having leisure ℓ_u rather than ℓ_e, i.e. c is just enough to compensate for the loss of leisure $\ell_u - \ell_e{}^3$. Then if we define r as

$$r = c + b \tag{4.11}$$

r is the real wage that will make the worker indifferent between working (and receiving r) and not working (and receiving b):

$$v(b, \ \ell_u) = v(r, \ \ell_e) = u(r). \tag{4.12}$$

In the light of (4.12) we can continue to use $u(.)$ as before, so long as we take care regarding its interpretation.

Now workers know that there is probability ϱ_1 of a boom occurring, in which case they derive utility of $u(w_1)$. There is probability of $1 - \varrho_1$ of a slump occurring. Given that a slump occurs, with a homogeneous workforce there is a probability of n_2/n_1 of finding employment and deriving utility $u(w_2)$, and a probability of $1 - n_2/n_1$ of being laid off and deriving utility $u(r)$. Hence, the expected utility for the worker is

$$U = \varrho_1 u(w_1) + (1 - \varrho_1)[(n_2/n_1)u(w_2) + (1 - n_2/n_1)u(r)]. \tag{4.13}$$

We again assume that there is some market-determined level of expected utility $\tilde{U}$ that the worker could obtain by accepting a contract elsewhere.

The firm's expected real profit is similar to (4.2) except that output and employment can now vary between states:

$$\Pi = \varrho_1(p_1 f(n_1) - w_1 n_1) + (1 - \varrho_1)(p_2 f(n_2) - w_2 n_2). \tag{4.14}$$

As before, the firm maximizes expected real profit, now with respect to n_2 as well as w_1 and w_2, subject to the worker achieving a level of expected utility of at least $\bar{U}$. This is equivalent to unconstrained maximization of the Lagrangean:

$$\mathcal{L} = \varrho_1(p_1 f(n_1) - w_1 n_1) + (1 - \varrho_1)(p_2 f(n_2) - w_2 n_2) + \lambda[\varrho_1 u(w_1) \\ + (1 - \varrho_1)(n_2/n_1)u(w_2) + (1 - \varrho_1)(1 - n_2/n_1)u(r) - \bar{U}] \tag{4.15}$$

where λ is a Lagrange multiplier. The necessary first-order conditions for maximization of (4.15) are

$$\partial\mathcal{L}/\partial n_2 = (1 - \varrho_1)(p_2 f'(n_2) - w_2) \\ + \lambda(1 - \varrho_1)(1/n_1)(u(w_2) - u(r)) = 0 \tag{4.16}$$

$$\partial\mathcal{L}/\partial w_1 = -\varrho_1 n_1 + \lambda\varrho_1 u'(w_1) = 0 \tag{4.17}$$

$$\partial\mathcal{L}/\partial w_2 = -(1 - \varrho_1)n_2 + \lambda(1 - \varrho_1)(n_2/n_1)u'(w_2) = 0 \tag{4.18}$$

$$\partial\mathcal{L}/\partial\lambda = \varrho_1 u(w_1) + (1 - \varrho_1)(n_2/n_1)u(w_2) \\ + (1 - \varrho_1)(1 - n_2/n_1)u(r) - \bar{U} = 0. \tag{4.19}$$

Equation (4.17) can be written as

$$-\varrho_1 n_1 = -\lambda\varrho_1 u'(w_1) \tag{4.20}$$

and equation (4.18) can be written as

$$-(1 - \varrho_1)n_2 = -\lambda(1 - \varrho_1)(n_2/n_1)u'(w_2). \tag{4.21}$$

Dividing (4.20) by (4.21) gives

$$\frac{-\varrho_1 n_1}{-(1 - \varrho_1)n_2} = \frac{\varrho_1 u'(w_1)}{(1 - \varrho_1)(n_2/n_1)u'(w_2)}. \tag{4.22}$$

Now $-\varrho_1 n_1$ is the marginal expected profit accruing to the firm from an increase in w_1 – i.e. total expected profits would fall by $-\varrho_1 n_1$ if w_1 rose one unit. Similarly, $-(1 - \varrho_1)n_2$ is the marginal expected profit of wages in state two. Hence, the left-hand side of (4.22) is the firm's marginal rate of substitution between real wages in different states of nature, or (minus) the slope of an iso-profit line in (w_1, w_2) space, holding n_1 and n_2 constant. (To prove that the left-hand side of (4.22) is a marginal rate of substitution for the firm, totally differentiate (4.14), set $d\Pi = 0$, $dn_1 = 0$, $dn_2 = 0$ and solve for dw_2/dw_1).

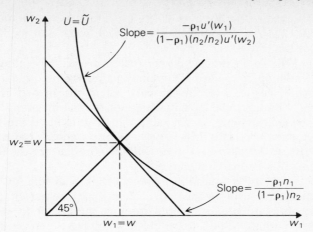

Figure 4.2   The optimal risk-sharing wage is state-invariant

Similarly, $\varrho_1 u'(w_1)$ is the marginal expected utility to the worker of an increase in w_1 and $(1 - \varrho_1)(n_2/n_1)u'(w_2)$ is the marginal expected utility of an increase in w_2. This implies that the right-hand side of (4.22) is the worker's marginal rate of substitution of income in state two for income in state one, or (minus) the slope of an indifference curve in (w_1, w_2) space, holding n_1 and n_2 constant. (To prove that this is so, totally differentiate (4.13), set $dU = 0$, $dn_1 = 0$, $dn_2 = 0$ and solve for dw_2/dw_1.)

Thus, equation (4.22) simply says that real wages in boom and slump should be chosen so as to equalize marginal rates of substitution between incomes in different states for the firm and the worker. This condition for optimal risk-sharing is a special case of a result due to Borch (1962) and Arrow (1971).

However, equation (4.22) can be written, after cancelling common factors and rearranging, as

$$u'(w_1) = u'(w_2) \tag{4.23}$$

i.e. the slope of the worker's utility curve at w_1 is the same as at w_2. But we assumed that u is a strictly concave function – i.e. its slope is continuously falling, $u'' < 0$. This implies that it cannot have the same slope at two points, i.e. equation (4.23) cannot be satisfied for $w_1 \neq w_2$. Thus, we must have

$$w_1 = w_2 = w \tag{4.24}$$

that is, the optimal risk-sharing wage is state-invariant.

We can view this diagrammatically. Note that the preceding discussion implies that the firm's iso-profit curves will be straight lines in (w_1, w_2) space for given n_1, n_2, whilst the worker's indifference curves will be convex. Thus as figure 4.2 illustrates, maximizing expected profit Π, for a given level of the worker's expected utility $\tilde{U}$, will result in a tangency solution. However, as equation (4.22) implies, tangencies only occur when $w_1 = w_2$, i.e. on a 45° ray through the origin.

Therefore, the result derived earlier that firms will be willing to absorb the risk of variation in wages, by essentially acting as a financial intermediary to the worker, carries over to the case where the firm is free to vary employment. Although relaxing the assumption of state-invariant employment apparently complicates matters, the same arguments as in the previous section go through as before. The firm is still willing to absorb the risk of wage variation, since it is risk-neutral – but will it be optimal for the firm to vary employment over booms and slumps?

In order to answer this question we pose it slightly differently. Given that the optimal contract will be one with a fixed wage, the question is whether or not it is optimal to reduce employment in slumps, or to maintain full employment (perhaps with a lower fixed wage). In other words, are full-employment contracts optimal?

Firstly, we examine how, starting from a position of state-invariant full employment ($n_2 = n_1$) changes in n_2/n_1 below unity affect the firm. We have already shown that it is optimal for the firm to set a state-invariant wage, regardless of whether employment is state-invariant or not. From the previous section, we know that, in a full-employment contract, this wage will be $\tilde{w}$, the worker's acceptance wage.

Taking the expression for the firm's expected real profit, equation (4.14), and differentiating totally:

$$d\Pi = - [\varrho_1 n_1 + (1 - \varrho_1)n_2]\, dw + \varrho_1(p_1 f'(n_1) - \tilde{w})\, dn_1$$
$$+ (1 - \varrho_1)(p_2 f'(n_2) - \tilde{w})\, dn_2. \qquad (4.25)$$

Since we are starting from a position of state-invariant employment ($n_2 = n_1$), and are only interested in variations in n_2, we can set $n_2 = n_1$, $dn_1 = 0$:

$$d\Pi = - n_1\, dw + (1 - \varrho_1)(p_2 f'(n_1) - \tilde{w})\, dn_2. \qquad (4.26)$$

Now the firm will be indifferent to changes in w and n_2 that leave its expected real profit constant, i.e. such that $d\Pi = 0$ in (4.26), which implies

$$\frac{dw}{dn_2} = \frac{1 - \varrho_1}{n_1}\,(p_2 f'(n_1) - \tilde{w})$$

or

$$\frac{dw}{d(n_2/n_1)} = (1 - \varrho_1)(p_2 f'(n_1) - \tilde{w}) \qquad (4.27)$$

since $d(n_2/n_1) = (1/n_1)\, dn_2$ when $dn_1 = 0$. Since $p_2 < p_1$ and $\tilde{w}$ is state-invariant, we might suspect that (4.27) is negative. That this is in fact the case can be seen by noting that (4.17) can be written as

$$\lambda = n_1/u'(\tilde{w}) \tag{4.28}$$

which, when substituted into (4.16), yields, after rearrangement,

$$p_2 f'(n_1) - \tilde{w} = -\frac{u(\tilde{w}) - u(r)}{u'(\tilde{w})} < 0. \tag{4.29}$$

Thus the firm pays a real wage greater than the value of the marginal product in state two at full employment. Therefore it would like to reduce employment in that state.

Now the probability that a worker will be unemployed is $(1 - \varrho_1)$ $(1 - n_2/n_1) = \phi$, say. Since $(1 - \varrho_1)$ is fixed, $d\phi = -(1 - \varrho_1)d(n_2/n_1)$, so (4.27) may be alternatively expressed as

$$\left.\frac{dw}{d\phi}\right|^{F}_{n_2 = n_1} = \tilde{w} - p_2 f'(n_1) \qquad (>0). \tag{4.30}$$

Equation (4.30) says that the marginal increment to the state-invariant wage that the firm is willing to pay to the worker in return for a tiny reduction in the probability of employing him or her, is just equal to the excess of the real wage over the slump value of the full-employment marginal product – i.e. the amount real profit would rise if one worker were laid off in state two. The vertical bar is to remind us that this expression is computed at full employment and the 'F' shows that it relates to the firm's behaviour.

How will changes in the level of slump employment and the state-invariant real wage affect workers? To answer this, we start by totally differentiating the expression for the worker's expected utility, equation (4.13), setting $n_2 = n_1$ and $w_2 = w_1 = \tilde{w}$:

$$dU = u'(\tilde{w})\, dw + (1 - \varrho_1)(u(\tilde{w}) - u(r))\, d(n_2/n_1). \tag{4.31}$$

If the firm wishes to lay off workers during the slump (state two) it will have to increase the state-invariant real wage in order to compensate the worker for an increase in the probability of unemployment, i.e. it will have to pay an 'under-employment premium' (Azariadis 1975). Otherwise, expected utility would fall below $\tilde{U}$ and workers would quit (the contract ceases to be feasible).

In order to find the marginal under-employment premium demanded for a marginal increase in the probability of unemployment in slump, evaluated at the full-employment contract, we set $dU = 0$ in (4.31) and solve for $dw/d(n_2/n_1)$:

$$\frac{\mathrm{d}w}{\mathrm{d}(n_2/n_1)} = -(1-\varrho_1)\frac{u(\tilde{w})-u(r)}{u'(\tilde{w})}$$

$$\frac{\mathrm{d}w}{\mathrm{d}\phi}\bigg|_{n_2=n_1}^{W} = \frac{u(\tilde{w})-u(r)}{u'(\tilde{w})} \qquad (>0) \qquad (4.32)$$

where the vertical bar is to remind us that this expression is computed at the full-employment contract and the W reminds us that we are concerned with the behaviour of the worker. The right-hand side of (4.32) is the marginal under-employment premium, $z(\tilde{w},r)$ say,

$$z(\tilde{w},r) = \frac{u(\tilde{w})-u(r)}{u'(\tilde{w})}. \qquad (4.33)$$

This is the amount the worker would have to be paid in order to compensate for an infinitesimally small probability of unemployment. If the worker stands to lose a lot by being unemployed (i.e. $u(\tilde{w})-u(r)$ is large), then this will be reflected in the size of $z(\tilde{w},r)$. If marginal utility is low ($u'(\tilde{w})$ is small), then a larger increase in the wage is necessary in order to compensate for the risk of unemployment. Given that there is diminishing marginal utility ($u''<0$), z will clearly be increasing in w and decreasing in r:

$$\frac{\partial z(\tilde{w},r)}{\partial w} = 1 - \frac{(u(\tilde{w})-u(r))u''(\tilde{w})}{(u'(\tilde{w}))^2} > 0 \qquad (4.34)$$

$$\frac{\partial z(\tilde{w},r)}{\partial r} = -\frac{u'(r)}{u'(\tilde{w})} < 0. \qquad (4.35)$$

The question that remains is whether, by reducing n_2/n_1 below unity and increasing the state-invariant wage above $\tilde{w}$, the firm can increase its expected profit whilst keeping the worker's expected utility constant (i.e. keeping the contract feasible). This will clearly be the case if expression (4.30) is greater than expression (4.32):

$$\tilde{w} - p_2 f'(n_1) > z(\tilde{w},r)$$

that is

$$p_2 f'(n_1) < \tilde{w} - z(\tilde{w},r) \qquad (4.36)$$

for then the marginal increase in the wage that the firm is willing to concede for a marginal increase in ϕ is actually greater than the marginal under-employment premium demanded by the worker. This means that, for a tiny increase in ϕ, the firm can pay an increase in the wage that will increase rather than merely hold constant its expected profit, whilst keeping the contract feasible. Viewed slightly differently, $p_2 f'(n_1)$ is the marginal cost of laying off one worker in state two (the value of the worker's marginal product), whilst $\tilde{w} - z(\tilde{w}, r)$ is the marginal benefit to the firm of such an action (the wage saving of $\tilde{w}$ less the marginal under-employment premium that has to be paid to keep contracts feasible). Clearly, the firm will wish to lay off workers in state two so long as marginal benefit exceeds marginal cost.

Inequality (4.36) is a necessary and sufficient condition for the sub-optimality of full-employment contracts.

Under what conditions is (4.36) more likely to hold? From (4.35) we can see that the right-hand side of (4.36) will be bigger the bigger r is; but r, the wage that would have to be paid in order to make the worker indifferent between working and not working, is an increasing function of the level of unemployment compensation and the worker's valuation of extra leisure (see (4.11)). Hence, layoffs will be more likely to occur for levels of unemployment benefit. This makes intuitive sense, since unemployment benefit serves to cushion the impact of being laid off. The Arrow–Pratt measure of (absolute) risk aversion is

$$Q(w) = -u''(w)/u'(w).$$

To see how Q relates to (4.36), expand $u(r)$ in a Taylor series about $\tilde{w}$ (Chiang 1984):

$$u(r) = u(\tilde{w}) + (r - w)u'(\tilde{w}) + \tfrac{1}{2}(r - \tilde{w})^2 u''(\tilde{w}) + \ldots .$$

Ignoring terms in derivatives of u higher than the second (assuming r is fairly close to $\tilde{w}$), this gives us

$$\frac{u(\tilde{w}) - u(r)}{u'(\tilde{w})} = (\tilde{w} - r) + \tfrac{1}{2}(r - \tilde{w})^2 Q(\tilde{w}) = z(\tilde{w}, r) \tag{4.37}$$

so the marginal under-employment premium is an increasing function of Q, for given $\tilde{w}$. This makes sense intuitively since the more risk-averse the worker is the more they will have to be compensated for the probability of unemployment; but (4.37) implies

$$\tilde{w} - z(\tilde{w}, r) = r - \tfrac{1}{2}(r - \tilde{w})^2 Q(\tilde{w}) \tag{4.38}$$

so the right-hand side of (4.36) is a decreasing function of the worker's risk aversion. Hence, layoffs, are less likely to occur the more risk-averse workers are.

The left-hand side of (4.36) will obviously be smaller for lower p_2. Therefore the inequality is more likely to hold the more volatile industry demand shifts over the business cycle are and the more inelastic that demand is. Recall from (4.29) that the firm pays a real wage in excess of the value of marginal product in a slump. This excess increases as p_2 falls, making the firm more anxious to lay workers off.

Having derived the necessary and sufficient condition for layoffs to occur and the conditions under which this condition is likely to hold, we can now characterize the optimal level of employment in slump, n_2. Recall that the probability a worker will be unemployed is $(1 - \varrho_1)(1 - n_2/n_1) = \phi$. Given that $\phi \neq 0$, i.e. that there are layoffs, we can compute the marginal increase in the wage that the worker would require to compensate for a tiny increase in ϕ. Going through the same steps as in the derivation of (4.32) but with $n_2 \neq n_1$, we can derive

$$\frac{\mathrm{d}w}{\mathrm{d}\phi}\bigg|_{n_2 \neq n_1}^{\mathrm{W}} = \frac{u(\tilde{w}) - u(r)}{\varrho_1 + (1 - \varrho_1)(n_2/n_1)]u'(\tilde{w})}. \tag{4.39}$$

Similarly, we can derive the marginal increase in the wage that the firm is willing to pay for a tiny increase in ϕ, given that $n_2 \neq n_1$. This will be the analogue of (4.30):

$$\frac{\mathrm{d}w}{\mathrm{d}\phi}\bigg|_{n_2 \neq n_1}^{\mathrm{F}} = \frac{\tilde{w} - p_2 f'(n_2)}{\varrho_1 + (1 - \varrho_1)(n_2/n_1)}. \tag{4.40}$$

It will be in the firm's interest to keep refashioning the contract with w higher and n_2 lower so long as (4.40) exceeds (4.39), i.e.

$$\frac{\tilde{w} - p_2 f'(n_2)}{\varrho_1 + (1 - \varrho_1)(n_2/n_1)} > \frac{u(\tilde{w}) - u(r)}{[\varrho_1 + (1 - \varrho_1)(n_2/n_1)]u'(\tilde{w})}$$

or equivalently

$$p_2 f'(n_2) < \tilde{w} - z(\tilde{w}, r). \tag{4.41}$$

However, as n_2 falls, the left-hand side of (4.41) rises because of diminishing returns. As $\tilde{w}$ rises, the right-hand side falls (see (4.34)). This implies that an 'equilibrium' level of layoffs will be reached, and at this point

$$p_2 f'(n_2) = \tilde{w} - z(\tilde{w}, r). \tag{4.42}$$

Of course, the firm could run out of workers to lay off before (4.42) could be satisfied–i.e. equation (4.41) may hold with $n_2 = 0$. This situation could be avoided by assuming that the marginal product of labour becomes infinite as the production function approaches the origin, that is

$$\lim_{n \to 0} f'(n) = \infty.$$

To summarize the results developed so far, implicit contract theory develops the observation that labour is not generally sold in a spot auction but will be traded subject to implicit long-term commitments by the firm and workers. The firm, being less risk-averse than workers, will in effect insure workers against real-wage variation. This implies that the equilibrium real wage is no longer equal to the marginal product of labour at each point in time, but will instead differ from this value by a premium paid to the firm in favourable states of nature and by an indemnity received by the worker in adverse states of nature. Moreover, even though workers are assumed to be risk-averse, it turns out that it may be optimal for firms to pay a slightly higher fixed wage and to lay off workers over the cycle. Layoffs are more likely to occur in an industry when more of the following conditions hold: output demand shifts are volatile and/or demand is inelastic, unemployment compensation is high, workers are only 'slightly' risk-averse, there is a competitive demand for labour.

Thus, the empirically observed phenomenon of sticky real wages and layoffs may in fact be the outcome of jointly optimizing behaviour on the part of workers and firms who enter into long-term, unwritten agreements. This is the invisible handshake at work!

4.2.3 The Nature of Unemployment under Implicit Contracts

Is the unemployment generated under implicit labour contracts involuntary? (By 'involuntary' we normally mean that unemployed workers would be willing to work at the going wage but are unable to do so.) Clearly, unemployment in a slump is voluntary at the time at which the contract is negotiated, since it is freely agreed to, but this is before the true state of nature materializes, so unemployment might be said to be voluntary in an '*ex ante*' sense. However, after the state of nature, say slump, materializes, laid-off workers would presumably envy their working colleagues and would wish to work at the going rate. Does this constitute involuntary unemployment, in an '*ex post*' sense perhaps?

> The fact that laid-off workers would gladly exchange places with their employed colleagues is not in itself sufficient to establish a misallocation of resources. After all, accident victims may very well envy more fortunate individuals without any implication that the insurance industry works poorly. *(Azariadis and Stiglitz 1983, p 8)*

Implicit in this quotation is the idea that the existence of involuntary unemployment constitutes a market failure. We know that if labour was auctioned off by the Walrasian auctioneer at each point in time then this market would by definition clear, i.e. Walrasian unemployment is purely voluntary. Therefore, one way of judging whether contractual unemployment is voluntary is to compare its magnitude with that predicted by a Walrasian spot auction.

We shall return to this idea presently. For the moment, we can show that even the '*ex post*' notion of involuntary unemployment can be precluded if we allow the firm to pay unemployment compensation directly to the worker. In the above discussion we were careful to point out that any unemployment compensation was paid out of an economy-wide fund, which did not directly affect the firm's behaviour. Now assume that the firm can make a payment to laid-off workers without affecting their entitlement to dole from the central fund[5]. Alternatively, let the economy-wide dole payment be zero (b = 0 in (4.11)). To simplify matters, we shall assume that consumption and leisure are perfect substitutes. Since there is no saving and labour is supplied in an indivisible unit, this is equivalent to saying that wages and leisure are perfect substitutes. We can do this by letting the utility function v take the form

$$u = v(w + R\ell) \qquad v' > 0, \ v'' < 0 \tag{4.43}$$

where ℓ is leisure as before. R is a scale factor that puts w and $R\ell$ into the same units of measurement. Recall that leisure for the laid-off worker is ℓ_u and leisure is ℓ_e otherwise. Also, r is the wage payment that makes the worker indifferent between working and not working, so:[6]

$$b + R\ell_u = r + R\ell_e$$

or, setting $b = 0$ for simplicity

$$R\ell_u = r + R\ell_e. \tag{4.44}$$

Now suppose the firm is free to pay the worker an amount w_3 if he or she is laid off during slump. Adding this to both sides of (4.44):

$$w_3 + R\ell_u = w_3 + r + R\ell_e. \tag{4.45}$$

Now recall the definition of our equivalent utility function, u:

$$u(w) = v(w, \ell_e)$$

or

$$u(w) = v(w + R\ell_e). \tag{4.46}$$

From (4.45) we have

$$v(w_3 + R\ell_u) = v(w_3 + r + R\ell_e) = u(w_3 + r). \tag{4.47}$$

So, if the firm pays w_3 to laid-off workers, they derive utility of $u(w_3 + r)$, where r is the wage payment that makes the worker indifferent between working and not working.

The firm now designs a contract (w_1, n_1, w_2, n_2, w_3) by maximizing the following Lagrangean:

$$\mathcal{L} = \varrho_1(p_1 f(n_1) - w_1 n_1) + (1 - \varrho_1)[p_2 f(n_2) - w_2 n_2 - w_3(n_1 - n_2)]$$
$$+ \lambda[\varrho_1 u(w_1) + (1 - \varrho_1)(n_2/n_1)u(w_2)$$
$$+ (1 - \varrho_1)(1 - n_2/n_1)u(w_3 + r) - \bar{U}]. \tag{4.48}$$

The only difference between (4.48) and (4.15) is that the firm's profits in state two are now reduced by the total amount of the payment to laid off workers, $w_3(n_1 - n_2)$, and that the utility of a laid-off worker is $u(w_3 + r)$ rather than $u(r)$.

The first-order conditions with respect to w_1 and w_2 are identical to (4.17) and (4.18):

$$- \varrho_1 n_1 + \lambda \varrho_1 u'(w_1) = 0. \tag{4.49}$$

$$- (1 - \varrho_1)n_2 + \lambda(1 - \varrho_1)(n_2/n_1)u'(w_2) = 0. \tag{4.50}$$

The first-order condition with respect to w_3 is

$$- (1 - \varrho_1)(n_1 - n_2) + \lambda(1 - \varrho_1)(1 - n_2/n_1)u'(w_3 + r) = 0. \tag{4.51}$$

Equations (4.49), (4.50) and (4.51) can be written respectively as

$$n_1 = \lambda u'(w_1) \tag{4.52}$$

$$n_1 = \lambda u'(w_2) \tag{4.53}$$

$$n_1 = \lambda u'(w_3 + r) \tag{4.54}$$

which imply

$$w_1 = w_2 = w_3 + r \tag{4.55}$$

by the concavity of u. Therefore, if the firm is allowed to pay unemployment compensation, the workers bear no risk whatsoever. They receive state-invariant wages when they are working and, when they are laid off, the firm pays them just enough money (w_3) to make them indifferent between working at the going wage (w_2) and being laid off. In this case, involuntary unemployment in the '*ex post*' sense discussed above would be precluded.

A similar result would follow if unemployment compensation from the firm was not allowed but work sharing was. In the above analysis, each worker's leisure is ℓ_e when employed and ℓ_u when unemployed. Therefore, the worker supplies labour in an indivisible unit of $\ell_u - \ell_e$. Suppose that hours of work could vary so that instead of having to supply either zero or eight hours per day, the worker could supply anywhere between zero and eight hours. If the wage was paid at an hourly rate and w_3 was constrained to

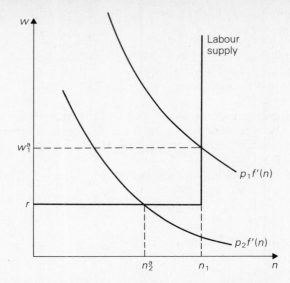

Figure 4.3 The occurrence of Walrasian unemployment

zero, an analysis similar to that in §4.2.2 would lead to the following contract. The hourly wage rate would be state-invariant with each worker supplying $\ell_u - \ell_e$ units of labour in state one and $\beta(\ell_u - \ell_e)$ units of labour in state two where β (<1) is such that total wage income for the worker in state two, plus the value of the extra leisure, is just equal to the total wage income in state one. As in the case of discrete labour and unemployment compensation, each worker would be just as well off in both states in both the '*ex ante*' and '*ex post*' sense – all risk would be traded to the firm.[7]

Let us now return to the discussion of whether contractual employment is more variable than 'Walrasian' employment (Akerlof and Miyazaki 1980). In a Walrasian spot auction, the labour market clears with the real wage set equal to the value of the marginal product of labour. We have assumed that labour is supplied inelastically at n_1 above a wage of r, but workers would prefer to be unemployed if the going wage in the auction was below r (i.e. supply is perfectly elastic at r). In state one, the firm's labour demand schedule is its marginal product schedule, $p_1 f'(n)$, and in state two it is $p_2 f'(n)$.

This situation is depicted in figure 4.3. A Walrasian auction in state one would determine full employment at a wage of w_1^a (where the superscript is to denote the auction variable). An auction in state two would determine employment of n_2^a at a wage equal to r. Note that unemployment in the Walrasian model, $n_2^a < n_1$, can only occur if the full-employment value of the marginal product in state two is less than r. If this was not the case then the $p_2 f'(n)$ schedule would intersect the vertical part of the labour supply schedule and there would be full employment at a wage at or above r. Hence, a necessary and sufficient condition for Walrasian unemployment is

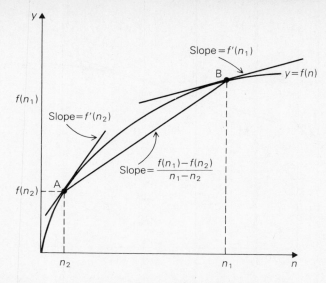

Figure 4.4   The sub-optimality of full employment contracts

$$P_2 f'(n_1) < r. \tag{4.56}$$

Now consider unemployment under an implicit contract. Initially, constrain w_3 to be zero – the firm pays no unemployment compensation. Suppose the fixed-wage optimal contract is (w, n_1, w, n_2) with $n_2 < n_1$, so if state one occurs the worker derives utility of $u(w)$. If state two occurs, the worker derives utility of $u(w)$ with probability n_2/n_1 and utility of $u(r)$ with probability $1 - n_2/n_1$. Hence, *given* that state two occurs, the expected utility of the worker is

$$(n_2/n_1)u(w) + (1 - n_2/n_1)u(r).$$

Given that the worker is risk-averse, he or she would in fact prefer to be employed in state two and paid a lower wage of

$$w^o = (n_2/n_1)w + (1 - n_2/n_1)r.$$

This contract will only be blocked if it reduces the firm's expected profit – i.e. if

$$\varrho_1(p_1 f(n_1) - wn_1) + (1 - \varrho_1)(p_2 f(n_2) - wn_2) > \varrho_1(p_1 f(n_1) - wn_1)$$
$$+ (1 - \varrho_1)p_2 f(n_1) - [(n_2/n_1)w + (1 - n_2/n_1)r]n_1. \tag{4.57}$$

However, after rearrangement and cancelling, equation (4.57) reduces to

$$\frac{f(n_1) - f(n_2)}{n_1 - n_2} < \frac{r}{p_2}. \tag{4.58}$$

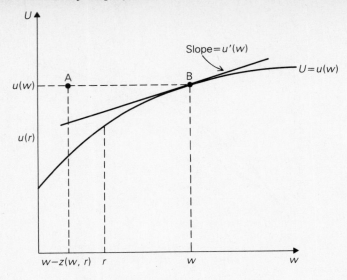

Figure 4.5 $w - z\,(w,r) \leqslant r$ for $w \geqslant r$

If (4.58) holds then a full-employment contract, even with a varying wage, will not be optimal. Consider figure 4.4, which is a graph of the production function. The left-hand side of (4.58) is the slope of a chord joining A and B. This is clearly greater than the slope of a tangent at B, i.e. $f'(n_1)$. Therefore

$$f'(n_1) < \frac{f(n_1) - f(n_2)}{n_1 - n_2}. \tag{4.59}$$

This is due to the concavity of f. Expressions (4.58) and (4.59) jointly imply

$$p_2 f(n_1) < r. \tag{4.60}$$

If (4.60) holds then full-employment contracts are never optimal and some contractual unemployment will occur over the business cycle; but (4.60) is identical to (4.56), the necessary and sufficient condition for Walrasian unemployment. Therefore, we have the result that unemployment will never occur under an implicit contract unless it would also occur under the corresponding Walrasian spot auction.

We can in fact go further than this. Recall from §4.2.2 that the equilibrium condition for layoffs in state two is

$$p_2 f'(n_2) = w - z(w,r) \tag{4.61}$$

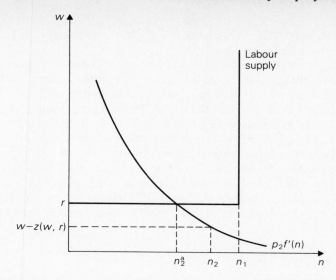

Figure 4.6 Unemployment under an implicit contract cannot exceed the Walrasian level

so employment in state two under the optimal contract, n_2, can be found by solving (4.61). From the definition of z

$$z(w,r) = \frac{u(w) - u(r)}{u'(w)} \tag{4.62}$$

where w is the optimal state-invariant wage. In figure 4.5, using (4.62), $z(w,r)$ is easily seen to be equal to the horizontal distance AB so, clearly

$$w - z(w,r) \leqslant r \qquad \text{for } w \geqslant r. \tag{4.63}$$

Using (4.63), we can see from figure 4.6 that the contractual level of state two employment, n_2, will generally be greater than the Walrasian level, n_2^a. This gives us the interesting result that, provided that r, p_1 and p_2 are the same for each regime and the firm cannot pay unemployment compensation, unemployment under an implicit contract regime cannot exceed the corresponding level of unemployment under a standard neoclassical regime of Walrasian labour auctions:

$$n_1 - n_2 \leqslant n_1 - n_2^a. \tag{4.64}$$

This is to say, compared with the spot auction regime, implicit labour contracts tend to stabilize both the level of wages *and* employment. As is well known, Walrasian outcomes generally define the social optimum at each point in time under fairly weak (Pareto-) criteria. In this sense, implicit labour contracts may lead to 'socially excessive' volumes of employment in some states of the world.

Would this result be changed if firms were allowed to pay unemployment compensation (Grossman and Hart 1981)? We showed above that such an institution would lead to workers obtaining complete insurance – they derive the same utility in all states of the world. The worker is indifferent between working for a fixed wage w or being laid off with compensation w_3, where $w_3 = w - r$. Now, if the firm lays off a worker at the margin in state two, it loses the value of that worker's marginal product and has to pay him or her unemployment compensation. The total marginal cost is therefore $p_2 f'(n_2) + w_3$. On the other hand, there is a marginal saving equal to the worker's (employed) wage, w. The equilibrium level of employment is therefore given by solving the condition that marginal benefit equals marginal cost:

$$w = p_2 f'(n_2) + w_3 \tag{4.65}$$

but, since $w = r + w_3$, equation (4.65) implies

$$p_2 f'(n_2) = r. \tag{4.66}$$

Now, the value of n_2 that solves (4.66) is precisely the level of employment that would transpire in a Walrasian spot auction, n_2^2 in figures 4.3 and 4.6. This means that, if the firm is allowed to pay unemployment compensation, the same amount of employment would occur in each state of the world regardless of whether the prevailing regime was one of implicit contracts or Walrasian spot auctions – i.e. any contractual unemployment is 'Walrasian' and in that sense is not involuntary.

4.2.4   Risk-Averse Firms

A central assumption of the preceding analysis is that the firm is risk-neutral. We consider the consequences of relaxing this assumption in this section. The assumption of firm risk aversion can be motivated in a number of ways. For example, if the returns to shareholders from all firms in their portfolios are positively correlated, then they cannot 'diversify away' the income risk from any one firm in particular. Intuitively, portfolio diversification makes shareholders less risk-averse with respect to the income from any one firm because any loss is likely to be offset elsewhere in the portfolio (a little like 'putting eggs into more than one basket'). If there is a positive correlation between firms' incomes, however, losses from one firm are in fact likely to be accompanied by losses from other firms (a little like knowing that all the baskets are tied together). This will generally induce risk-averse behaviour on the part of shareholders and hence of 'firms'.

A second reason for which risk aversion of firms might arise is the fact that even if shareholders are risk-neutral, they generally have to rely upon a manager or managers to run the firm on a day-to-day basis. Assume that there is in fact a single manager. It seems reasonable to suppose that, other things equal, the profits of the firm will depend upon how hard the manager works – but how hard the manager works is only observable to that manager. The owners of the firm and the manager are therefore in what is sometimes termed a 'principal–agent' relationship – the manager is a more informed 'agent' acting on behalf of a less informed 'principal' (the shareholders) – see, e.g., Arrow 1985, Rees 1985a, 1985b. In order to induce the manager to work hard the owners may therefore wish to make the manager's salary an increasing function of the firm's profit (e.g. operate a bonus scheme). Since the manager is an individual he or she is likely to be risk-averse. An interesting but equivalent way of viewing the owner–manager relationship is as a problem of 'moral hazard'. Moral hazard normally arises in insurance markets where the risks borne by the insurer are a function of the care taken by the insured party and the level of care cannot be directly observed by the insurer. For example, if my bicycle is fully insured I have little incentive to lock it up at night since, if it is stolen, I know the insurance firm will fully compensate me. Assuming that they are loath to charge very high premiums, the insurance company will find it better to offer me less than full coverage – i.e. I would have to pay the first fifty pounds or so of a replacement. Having a deductible policy, i.e. less than full coverage, then induces me to take better care of my property. In the same way, even where shareholders are risk-neutral and the manager is risk-averse, the shareholders will not in general wish to insure the manager fully against variations in profit because the level of profit is itself a function of, amongst other things, the unobservable level of manager effort – i.e. there is moral hazard.

Let us assume therefore that the firm is run by a single manager who is endowed with a von Neumann–Morgenstern utility function with profit as argument:

$$V = v(\pi_i) \qquad v' > 0, \; v'' < 0 \tag{4.67}$$

where π_i denotes the *ex post*, level of profit in state i, e.g.

$$\pi_1 = p_1 f(n_1) - w_1 n_1.$$

What difference does this change in our assumptions make? Let us assume that the firm pays unemployment compensation. Then we know from above that if the firm is risk-neutral, the optimal contract will dictate a state-invariant wage to be paid to employed workers and a level of unemployment compensation that, when combined with the utility of additional labour, makes workers indifferent to being laid off. Further, this contract predicts exactly the same amount of employment as a Walrasian spot auction.

If the firm is risk-averse, the Lagrangran (4.48) must be modified slightly, so the optimal contract maximizes:

$$\mathcal{L} = \varrho_1 v(p_1 f(n_1) - w_1 n_1) + (1 - \varrho_1)v\,[p_2 f(n_2) - w_2 n_2 - w_3(n_1 - n_2)]$$
$$+ \lambda[\varrho_1 u(w_1) + (1 - \varrho_1)(n_2/n_1)u(w_2)$$
$$+ (1 - \varrho_1)(1 - n_2/n_1)u(w_3 + r) - \bar{U}]. \tag{4.68}$$

The first-order conditions with respect to w_1, w_2 and w_3 are respectively

$$-\varrho_1 v'(\pi_1)n_1 + \lambda\varrho_1 u'(w_1) = 0$$
$$-(1 - \varrho_1)v'(\pi_2)n_2 + \lambda(1 - \varrho_1)(n_2/n_1)u'(w_2) = 0$$
$$-(1 - \varrho_1)v'(\pi_2)(n_1 - n_2) + \lambda(1 - p_1)(1 - n_2/n_1)u'(w_3 + r) = 0$$

or, equivalently,

$$v'(\pi_1)n_1 = \lambda u'(w_1) \tag{4.69}$$

$$v'(\pi_2)n_1 = \lambda u'(w_2) \tag{4.70}$$

$$v'(\pi_2)n_1 = \lambda u'(w_3 + r). \tag{4.71}$$

From (4.70) and (4.71) we have

$$w_2 = w_3 + r \tag{4.72}$$

by the concavity of u, as before; but (4.69) and (4.70) imply

$$\frac{v'(\pi_1)}{v'(\pi_2)} = \frac{u'(w_1)}{u'(w_2)}. \tag{4.73}$$

Equation (4.73) is now the optimal risk-sharing condition. It states that the marginal rates of substitution between incomes in different states are equalized for the firm and the worker. Since $v'' \neq 0$, equation (4.73) implies that the optimal wage is now variable – less risk is traded to the firm because it is now risk-averse. Clearly, the less risk-averse the firm is, i.e. the smaller v'' is in absolute terms for any given level of profit, the closer the left-hand side of (4.73) will be to unity, and so the closer w_2 and w_1 will be. In general though, the worker obtains less than full insurance from wage variation over the business cycle because this insurance is now costly to the firm due to its risk aversion.

Equation (4.72), however, implies that, *within states*, workers obtain full insurance. That is to say, all workers are equally well off for any given state of the world. In state one all workers receive w_1. In state two, employed workers receive w_2 and derive utility $u(w_2)$ whilst laid-off workers receive w_3 and derive utility $u(w_3 + r) = u(w_2)$. The firm is willing to provide full insurance *within* states (and notably in state two) because, although it is risk-averse with respect to the overall size of the wage bill (and hence profits) it is indifferent as to how the wage bill is divided between employed and laid-off workers.

Another point worth noticing about (4.73) is that, because both the firm and the worker experience diminishing marginal utility ($v'' < 0$, $u'' < 0$), $\pi_1 > \pi_2$ implies $w_1 > w_2$ (since $v'(\pi_1) < v'(\pi_2)$ implies $u'(w_1) < u'(w_2)$ by (4.73)) or, more generally,

$$\pi_i > \pi_j \Rightarrow w_i > w_j \qquad i,j = 1,2. \tag{4.74}$$

So the firm pays higher wages in states where profit is correspondingly high. This result is sometimes termed co-insurance.

Now consider the optimal level of layoffs. Since workers are fully compensated for being laid off, the firm can continue reducing n_2 until the marginal utility of doing so becomes zero. That is:

$$v'(\pi_2)(p_2 f'(n_2) - w_2 + w_3) = 0. \tag{4.75}$$

This is just the derivative of the utility of state two profits, with respect to n, set equal to zero; but since $w_2 = w_3 + r$ and $v'(\pi_2) \neq 0$, equation (4.75) implies

$$p_2 f'(n_2) = r. \tag{4.76}$$

However, as we saw in §4.2.3, the level $p_2 f'(n_2)$ that solves (4.76) is precisely the level of employment that would occur in state two under a Walrasian spot auction (recall figure 4.3). Thus, even under the assumption of firm risk aversion, workers are never involuntarily unemployed either in the '*ex post*' sense of envying their working colleagues or in the sense of unemployment differing from the Walrasian level.

4.2.5 *Summary, Conclusion and Extension for Implicit Labour Contracts*

The theory of implicit contracts was developed largely as an antidote to the empirical anomaly that cyclical output fluctuations tend to be associated with high employment variability and low real-wage variability, in defiance of competitive wage theory. The central insight of the theory is that it may be optimal for less risk-averse employers effectively to insure more risk-averse employees against real-wage variability. Real wages are shown to differ from the marginal product of labour by an insurance indemnity paid to the worker in adverse states of nature and by a premium paid by the worker in favourable states. Given this optimal risk-sharing agreement concerning wage payments, it is natural to wonder why the firm does not offer the worker insurance against employment variation also. It turns out that, if the firm is allowed to pay the worker unemployment compensation (redundancy pay), this is exactly what happens. Given their unemployment compensation, laid-off workers are just as well off as their working colleagues – all risks are traded to the firm. In this sense, contractual unemployment is not involuntary. Moreover, implicit contracts tend to stabilize the level of employment in the sense that unemployment under an implicit contract cannot be greater than it would have been under a Walrasian spot auction, so any unemployment that does occur is Walrasian.[8]

If we abandon the idea that firms are completely risk-neutral, then the optimal risk-sharing condition (i.e. that the marginal rate of substitution between income in different states of nature should be the same for the firm and worker) no longer dictates a state-invariant wage. However, so long as the firm is less risk-averse than the worker, optimal risk-sharing will still impart some degree of stickiness to the wage, the less so the more risk-averse the firm is – the firm absorbs some but not all of the risks. Thus, the real wage paid will be lower in adverse states of nature, but not as low as it would be under a Walrasian spot auction.

Implicit in the foregoing analysis is the assumption of symmetric information – both the firm and the worker are able to observe which state of the world is prevailing. This may be a somewhat strong assumption. For example, the firm may be a producer of intermedate goods or other specialized equipment that may not appear directly in the high-street shops. In such cases, the worker may very well have to take the firm's word for it that times are either good or bad – information is asymmetric. So long as firms are risk-neutral, informational asymmetry does not make very much difference (that is, as long as the firm does not pretend to be risk-averse). However, as argued above, wages will tend to be state-contingent when firms are risk-averse. Calvo and Phelps (1977) were the first to point out that if wages are state-contingent and information is asymmetric it may be in the firm's interest to lie about the state of nature – for example by claiming that times are bad when in fact they are good and thereby reducing the wage bill. Azariadis (1982) and Grossman and Hart (1981, 1983) have shown that the implicit contracts in models displaying informational asymmetry and firm risk aversion will generate levels of unemployment greater than those that would prevail under a corresponding Walrasian spot auction. This is because the firm has to convince workers that times really are bad before they will agree to a wage cut in adverse states. It can do this by reducing employment as well as wages when times are bad. Thus, employment will be more variable 'simply because this is the only way the firm can get wages down' (Hart 1983, p.3). (See appendix 4.1 for a discussion of implicit contracts under asymmetric information.)

Finally, given the wage stickiness generated within implicit contract models of the employment process, it is natural to ponder whether they can be used as a rationalization of Keynesian macroeconomics, as opposed to monetarist or new classical macroeconomics which assumes flexible wages and prices. The first point to note is that Keynesian economics of the traditional variety, once wealth effects are allowed, requires stickiness of *nominal rather than* real wages, and it is the stickiness of the latter that implicit contract theory seeks to explain.[9] Moreover, as the discussion of the nature of contractual unemployment above makes clear, contract theory cannot be used to explain 'involuntary' unemployment – the apparent rigidities engendered by contractual agreements do not necessarily signal market failure. Staggered nominal-wage contract models of the kind discussed for example by Fischer (1977) are rather different from those discussed in this chapter and do not appear to have a microeconomic foundation more rigorous than a rather vague appeal to the costs of wage setting and the difficulties of contract writing.

4.3   Adverse Selection in the Labour Market

In our discussion of implicit contracts we mostly assumed that all workers were alike – i.e. labour was homogeneous. We did indicate how labour heterogeneity and also asymmetric information might be introduced but the central plank of the analysis was the idea that workers are more risk-averse than firms. Adverse selection theories of the labour market start from the idea that labour is heterogeneous but is in many ways *observationally* homogeneous to the firm – i.e. there is an informational asymmetry. For example, there may be observable signals that allow the firm to sort its potential workforce into broad categories – e.g. whether or not they are graduates or how many years of education they have undergone. Beyond that there may be differences between people who look the same on paper that make some workers more productive than others – for example manual dexterity. This situation is another example of the principal–agent problem, which we encountered in our discussion of firm risk aversion in §4.2. An adverse-selection problem is a case where the principal is attempting to control a more informed agent, and the principal has no way of checking whether the agent has used his or her superior information in a way that best serves the principal's interests. In this case the worker (the agent) knows his or her own capabilities and the employer (the principal) has to attempt to control his or her behaviour without this knowledge.

In such a situation, one way of judging how good a worker is over and above his or her observable characteristics is to examine the lowest wage he or she is willing to work for, or 'acceptance wage'. It could be argued that the better a worker is, the higher the remuneration he or she could command by working for other firms or going self-employed. Hence, it seems reasonable to believe that 'productivity' of a worker will be a positive function of his or her acceptance wage.

Once it is realized that labour is not homogeneous in terms of productivity, we can no longer think of output as a simple function of the number of workers employed. If we think of more productive workers possessing more 'efficiency units' of labour, then output will be a function of the total efficiency units of the workforce. Of course, the firm will not know for sure

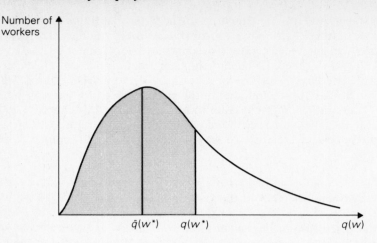

Figure 4.7   The conditional mean of the labour endowment distribution, given w = w*

how many efficiency units its workforce possesses at any point since, if it offers a certain wage, it will get a few workers with an acceptance wage equal to that amount but a lot of workers with a lower acceptance wage (who are therefore extracting an economic rent). However, if the distribution of labour endowment (i.e. efficiency units) across the workforce is known, along with the relationships between labour endowment and acceptance wage, then the firm can form the mathematical expectation of the labour endowment of a worker hired when a certain wage is offered. Under such conditions, it turns out that the profit-maximizing firm will offer a wage that minimizes the average cost per efficiency unit of labour. Further, the firm will continue to offer this wage even in the presence of excess supply of labour, i.e. job queues. If someone in the queue offers to work for a lower wage, he or she automatically signals to the firm that he or she is of a poorer quality, i.e. has fewer efficiency units. If this is the case then, although he or she is willing to work for a lower wage, the expected cost per efficiency unit of hiring him or her will be greater than the firm is willing to pay. Thus, undercutting the going wage will actually reduce the worker's chances of being taken on.

Assume that the observed characteristics of all members of the workforce are identical. (See Weiss 1980 for an extension to the case of where the workforce can be sorted into broad categories.) The production function is now taken to be a function of the total number of efficiency units hired. Thus, if n is the number of workers taken on:

$$y = f(\sum_{i=1}^{n} \theta_i) \qquad f' > 0, f'' < 0 \qquad (4.77)$$

where θ_i is the labour endowment of the ith worker in efficiency units. We assume that the acceptance wage, w, is positively related to the labour endowment of the workers; hence

$$\theta_i = q(w) \qquad q' > 0. \tag{4.78}$$

We assume that the function q is the same for all workers.

Now suppose that the firm knows how θ is distributed over the workforce (e.g. log–normally). Then, having offered a wage of, say, w^*, the firm can form the conditional expectation of the labour endowment of the average worker given that w^* is offered:

$$E(\theta|w = w^*) = \bar{\theta}(w^*) = \bar{q}(w^*) \text{ say.} \tag{4.79}$$

This is illustrated in figure 4.7 where the hump-shaped curve depicts the distribution of labour endowment θ over the workforce. If a wage of w^* is offered, the firm might expect to take on all workers with a labour endowment less than or equal to $\theta^* = q(w^*)$. Thus, the total labour endowment hired will be the shaded area under the curve. The mean of this shaded area is $\bar{q}(w^*)$.

Given that n workers have been taken on at a wage of w^*, the total expected labour endowment is therefore

$$E(\sum_{i=1}^{n} \theta_i) = nE(\theta|w = w^*) = n\bar{q}(w^*). \tag{4.80}$$

If output price is given at p, using (4.77) and (4.80), expected profit is approximately[10]

$$\Pi = pf(n\bar{q}(w^*)) - w^*n. \tag{4.81}$$

Now we postulate that maximizing expected profit, equation (4.81), is tantamount to minimizing the cost per expected efficiency unit of labour; i.e. profit-maximizing firms will pay a wage $\tilde{w}$ that minimizes $w/\bar{q}(w)$ (the cost per expected efficiency unit), even if there is excess supply of labour at this wage.

To see this, suppose that $\tilde{w}$ is in fact the unique wage that minimizes $\tilde{w}/\bar{q}(\tilde{w})$. Consider any other wage, $\hat{w}$ say, and an associated employment level, $\hat{n}$. Expected profit will be approximately

$$\hat{\Pi} = pf(\hat{n}\bar{q}(\hat{w})) - \hat{w}\hat{n}. \tag{4.82}$$

Now define $n^0 = \hat{w}\hat{n}/\tilde{w}$. Then consider expected profit if n^0 workers are taken on at a wage of $\tilde{w}$:

$$\tilde{\Pi} = pf(n^0\bar{q}(\tilde{w})) - \tilde{w}n^0 = pf\left(\frac{\hat{w}\hat{n}}{\tilde{w}}\bar{q}(\tilde{w})\right) - \tilde{w}\frac{\hat{w}\hat{n}}{\tilde{w}}$$

$$= pf\left(\frac{\hat{w}\hat{n}}{\tilde{w}}\bar{q}(\tilde{w})\right) - \hat{w}\hat{n}. \tag{4.83}$$

However, since $\tilde{w}$ minimizes $w/\bar{q}(w)$, we have

$$\frac{\tilde{w}}{\bar{q}(\tilde{w})} < \frac{\hat{w}}{\bar{q}(\hat{w})} \qquad \text{for all } \hat{w} \neq \tilde{w}. \tag{4.84}$$

Rearranging (4.84) and multiplying by $\hat{n}$:

$$\frac{\hat{w}\hat{n}}{\tilde{w}} \bar{q}(\tilde{w}) > \hat{n}\tilde{q}(\hat{w}). \tag{4.85}$$

Since f is an increasing, monotone function, equation (4.85) implies

$$f\left(\frac{\hat{w}\hat{n}}{\tilde{w}} \bar{q}(\tilde{w}) \right) > f(\hat{n}\bar{q}(\hat{w})) \tag{4.86}$$

Subtracting (4.82) from (4.83):

$$\tilde{\Pi} - \hat{\Pi} = f\left(\frac{\hat{w}\hat{n}}{\tilde{w}} \bar{q}(\tilde{w}) \right) - f(\hat{n}\bar{q}(\hat{w})) \tag{4.87}$$

which, by (4.86) is positive. This means that $\tilde{w}$ is the profit-maximizing wage for the firm to pay, since given any wage and employment configuration $\hat{w}$, $\hat{n}$, it is always more profitable to employ n^0 at $\tilde{w}$. This does not mean, however, that n^0 is the profit-maximizing level of employment. To find that we differentiate the expression for expected profit, equation (4.81), with respect to n to find the usual first-order condition:

$$\frac{\partial \Pi}{\partial n} = pf'(n\bar{q}(w))\bar{q}(w) - w = 0$$

that is

$$f'(n\bar{q}(w))\bar{q}(w) = w/p. \tag{4.88}$$

Equation (4.88) is just the usual profit-maximizing condition that the real wage should be set equal to the marginal product. Since $\tilde{w}$ is the profit-maximizing wage level, if the firm can find all the labour it wants at this wage, it will choose the employment level, $\tilde{n}$, to solve

$$f'(\tilde{n}\bar{q}(\tilde{w}))\bar{q}(\tilde{w}) = \tilde{w}/p. \tag{4.89}$$

Note that we have derived the (expected) profit-maximizing wage and employment level with virtually no reference to labour supply. In particular, it is quite possible that at a wage $\tilde{w}$ labour supply exceeds labour demand. In that case there will be unemployment, or job queuing.

The next question is that of why unemployed workers do not offer to undercut the going wage. Suppose, for example, that an unemployed worker offers to work for slightly less than $\tilde{w}$, for say $\tilde{w} - \Delta w$. In offering to work for this lower wage, the worker implicitly signals an upper bound to his or her acceptance wage – i.e. his or her true acceptance wage must lie somewhere between zero and $\tilde{w} - \Delta w$. The firm then infers his or her expected labour endowment to be

$$\bar{q}(\tilde{w} - \Delta w) = E(\theta | w = \tilde{w} - \Delta w).$$

By definition of $\tilde{w}$ we have

$$\frac{\tilde{w} - \Delta w}{\bar{q}(\tilde{w} - \Delta w)} > \frac{\tilde{w}}{\bar{q}(\tilde{w})} \qquad \text{for } \Delta w \neq 0$$

so, although the worker is willing to work for less than the going wage, the actual cost per expected efficiency unit of employing him or her would be greater than the profit maximizing level of $\tilde{w}/\bar{q}(\tilde{w})$. Hence, undercutting the going wage will actually reduce the worker's chances of being taken on.

If labour demand, determined by (4.89), exceeds labour supply at wage $\tilde{w}$, then competition for workers will drive the wage paid above $\tilde{w}$. Given the labour supply schedule, w and n will then be determined simultaneously to satisfy the marginality condition (4.88).

Now suppose we are in fact in a job queuing equilibrium as described above – i.e. there is excess supply of labour at a wage of $\tilde{w}$, and there is a fall in demand for output. This translates into a fall in output price, p. Assuming that fluctuations in output demand do not affect workers' reservation wages, $\tilde{w}$ will still minimize the cost per expected labour input. Recall the marginality condition (4.89):

$$f'(\bar{n}\bar{q}(\tilde{w}))\bar{q}(\tilde{w}) = \tilde{w}/p.$$

A fall in p means the right-hand side of (4.89) increases, since $\tilde{w}$ remains constant. In order to increase the left-hand side to maintain the equality, the firm must alter $\bar{n}$, the employment level. Since f is a concave production function, $f'' < 0$, so f' increases as $\bar{n}$ falls (i.e. there are diminishing marginal returns). Hence, the firm will respond to a fall in demand by reducing employment and keeping wages constant. This is an alternative explanation of the sticky-wages – layoffs phenomenon.

Why exactly does the firm not cut wages during recession? Say the firm was to cut wages from $\tilde{w}$ to $\bar{w} < \tilde{w}$. Then everyone working for the firm with a reservation wage between $\bar{w}$ and $\tilde{w}$ would immediately leave. Workers remaining with the firm would have to have a reservation wage between zero and $\bar{w}$. However, since the productivity of the workers (i.e. how many 'efficiency units' they have) is related positively to the acceptance wage, this means that *all* the very best workers would leave. If, however, the firm randomly lays off a proportion of the work force, it will probably lose only a percentage of the best workers. This phenomenon reveals the adverse-selection nature of the problem – by cutting the wage the firm would inadvertently select the worst workers to remain in the workforce. It is in order to avoid the adverse-selection implications of a wage cut that the firm will prefer to lay workers off randomly.

The simple adverse selection model presented above therefore provides an alternative explanation for the coexistence of sticky wages and layoffs, in addition to that provided by implicit contract theory. However, note that implicit contract theory generates the sticky-real-wage-layoffs phenomenon as the outcome of jointly optimizing behaviour on the part of workers and firms. In the model outlined in this section, the preferences of workers were not even considered, and will clearly not in general generate a Pareto-optimal outcome. To that extent, therefore, adverse selection in the labour market represents an example of market failure.

Notes

1   Some of the material on implicit contracts in this chapter drawn from Taylor 1987d and Taylor 1987e. Taylor 1987e contains a number of extensions to the basic model outlined below – notably the assumption of a heterogeneous labour force and its implications for preferential layoffs.

2   Since $p_1 > p_2$ implies a higher marginal product for the firm, wages vary pro-cyclically at the firm level.

3   Note that c will itself generally be a positive function of b. However, the results below require only that r be an increasing function of b. At a less general level, we could assume perfect substitution between income and leisure (see §4.2.3 and note 6).

4   We assume that the firm forces the worker's expected utility to its lowest feasible level, U, and that an interior solution is obtained to (4.15).

5   Since the model we are using is essentially timeless (compare Baily 1974), firm-paid unemployment compensation can be interpreted as redundancy pay or 'severance pay'.

6   In terms of equation (4.11), the perfect substitutability assumption implies $c = R(\ell_u - \ell_e)$.

7   The proof of this assertion is left as an exercise.

8   This is only true of the simple, symmetric information contracts considered so far – see the appendix 4.1.

9   Sargent (1979) appears to say that implicit contract theory can be used to bolster nominal wage rigidities. However, his analysis is misleading in this respect, since he makes the workers' utility a function of the *nominal* wage – i.e. it is *money illusion* rather than contracting that is driving the nominal-wage rigidity in his model. Sutton (1979) argues that nominal-wage rigidities may arise if workers and employers fail to agree on a common price index.

10 The approximation arises because in general the mathematical expectation of a non-linear function of a random variable is not equal to the function

of the mathematical expectation of that variable, i.e. if $g(.)$ is a non-linear function and x a random variable

$$E(g(x)) \neq g(E(x)).$$

However, we assume that the equality will hold to a close approximation.

Appendix 4.1 Implicit Contracts under Asymmetric Information

This appendix extends the analysis in the text by examining the case where only the firm can examine the true state of nature. If firms are risk-averse, implying that the optimal wage is state-contingent, this gives firms an incentive to pretend times are bad when in fact they are not, in order to cut wages. Let π_{ij} be the *ex post* level of profit that accrues to the firm if state i materializes but the firm announces to the worker that state j has in fact occurred, i.e.

$$\pi_{11} = p_1 f(n_1) - w_1 n_1 \tag{A4.1.1}$$

$$\pi_{12} = p_1 f(n_2) - w_2 n_2 - w_3(n_1 - n_2) \tag{A4.1.2}$$

$$\pi_{22} = p_2 f(n_2) - w_2 n_2 - w_3(n_1 - n_2) \tag{A4.1.3}$$

$$\pi_{21} = p_2 f(n_1) - w_1 n_1. \tag{A4.1.4}$$

Assuming that a contract has been agreed to, $(w_1, n_1, w_2, n_2, w_3)$, then (A4.1.1) defines π_{11} as the level of profit if state one occurs (the price is p_1) and the firm announces the truth (i.e. employs n_1 people at a wage of w_1). Expression (A4.1.2) defines π_{12} as the level of profit if state one occurs (the price is p_1), but the firm lies and announces state two to the workers (i.e. employs n_2 people at wage w_2 and pays w_3 to those laid off). Expressions (A4.1.3) and (A4.1.4) define π_{22} and π_{21} similarly.

We assume that the worker will not enter into a contract in which the firm has an incentive to lie. In other words, the contract must satisfy the following inequalities:

$$\pi_{11} \geqslant \pi_{12} \tag{A4.1.5}$$

$$\pi_{22} \geqslant \pi_{21} \tag{A4.1.6}$$

If a contract satisfies both (A4.1.5) and (A4.1.6) then the incentives of the firm (i.e. whether to tell the truth or to lie) are compatible with the interests of the workers. Accordingly, inequalities such as (A4.1.5) and (A4.1.6) are termed incentive-compatibility constraints and contracts that satisfy them are termed incentive-compatible.

Our assumption that workers will not enter into a contract that is not incentive-compatible is unrestrictive since any non-incentive-compatible contract can be shown to be equivalent to one that is incentive-compatible. For example, consider the contract $(w_1, n_1, w_2, n_1, 0)$, where w_2 is much less than w_1. Since the contract is for full employment ($n_2 = n_1$), firms have an incentive always to claim that they are in a slump since this allows them to keep the wage bill down without affecting the level of output. However, since workers know that the firm will lie, this is just as if they had been offered the fixed-wage, full-employment contract $(w_2 n_1, w_2, n_1, 0)$, which is quite obviously incentive-compatible. Moreover, the firm will clearly be indifferent between offering this contract and always telling the truth, and offering $(w_1, n_1, w_2, n_1, 0)$ and always claiming that times are bad, since each strategy yields the same actual levels of employment and wages. This result is sometimes term the revelation principle and is due to Myerson (1979).

For any given level of p_1 and p_2 and distribution of states of nature (i.e. value of ϱ_1), we shall term a contract that is optimal under symmetric information the first-best contract. A contract that is optimal under exactly the same conditions except that the state of nature is not directly observable by workers (i.e. information is asymmetric) we shall term the second-best contract (Azariadis and Stiglitz 1983). If the optimal, symmetric-information contract satisfies the incentive-compatibility constraints (A4.1.5) and (A4.1.6) then the first-best and second-best coincide.

Before we write down the maximization problem that determines the second-best contract, we make a simplification. As we showed above, the firm is risk-averse to the overall size of the wage bill but indifferent to its composition. This means that it is willing to offer full insurance to workers within states and, in particular, sets $w_2 = w_3 + r$. This allows us to substitute out for w_3 and maximize with respect to one less variable. Specifically, instead of writing the state two wage bill as

$$w_2 n_2 + w_3 (n_1 - n_2)$$

we shall write it as

$$w_2 n_1 - r(n_1 - n_2).$$

Also, instead of writing the typical worker's expected utility as

$$\varrho_1 u(w_1) + (1 - \varrho_1)(n_2/n_1) u(w_2) + (1 - \varrho_1)(1 - n_2/n_1) u(w_3 + r)$$

it can be written as

$$\varrho_1 u(w_1) + (1 - \varrho_1) u(w_2).$$

Since w_3 need not be specified, contracts may now be designated by a vector excluding this term – e.g. (w_1, n_1, w_2, n_2).

The maximization problem facing the firm can now be explicitly written down: maximize

$$\varrho_1 v(p_1 f(n_1) - w_1 n_1) + (1 - \varrho_1)v\,[p_2 f(n_2) - w_2 n_1 + r(n_1 - n_2)]$$

subject to

$$\varrho_1 u(w_1) + (1 - \varrho_1)u(w_2) \geqslant \tilde{U}$$

$$p_1 f(n_1) - w_1 n_1 \geqslant p_1 f(n_2) - w_2 n_1 + r(n_1 - n_2)$$

$$p_2 f(n_2) - w_2 n_1 - r(n_1 - n_2) \geqslant p_2 f(n_1) - w_1 n_1.$$

Note that the last two inequalities are just the incentive-compatibility constraints (A4.1.5) and (A4.1.6), where we have substituted for the π_{ij} using (A4.1.1)–(A4.1.4) and the fact that $w_2 = w_3 + r$.

The second-best contract then defines a saddle-point of the Lagrangean:

$$
\begin{aligned}
\mathcal{L} = {}& \varrho_1 v(p_1 f(n_1) - w_1 n_1) + (1 - \varrho_1)v\,[p_2 f(n_2) - w_2 n_1 + r(n_1 - n_2)] \\
& + \lambda\,[\varrho_1 u(w_1) + (1 - \varrho_1)u(w_2) - U] + \gamma_1\,[p_1 f(n_1) - w_1 n_1 - p_1 f(n_2) \\
& + w_2 n_1 - r(n_1 - n_2)] + \gamma_2\,[p_2 f(n_2) - w_2 n_1 + r(n_1 - n_2) - p_2 f(n_1) \\
& + w_1 n_1]
\end{aligned}
$$

$$\text{(A4.1.7)}$$

where λ, γ_1 and γ_2 are non-negative Lagrange mutlipliers. The necessary Kuhn–Tucker conditions for this optimization problem are, assuming an interior solution (i.e. $w_1, w_2, n_1, n_2 > 0$) (see, e.g. Chiang 1984, Baumol 1977)

$$\frac{\partial \mathcal{L}}{\partial w_1} = \varrho_1 v'(\pi_{11})n_1 + \lambda \varrho_1 u'(w_1) - \gamma_1 n_1 + \gamma_2 n_1 = 0 \qquad \text{(A4.1.8)}$$

$$\frac{\partial \mathcal{L}}{\partial w_2} = -(1 - \varrho_1)v'(\pi_{22})n_1 + \lambda(1 - \varrho_1)u'(w_2)$$
$$+ \gamma_1 n_1 - \gamma_2 n_1 = 0 \qquad \text{(A4.1.9)}$$

$$\frac{\partial \mathcal{L}}{\partial n_2} = (1 - \varrho_1)v'(\pi_{22})(p_2 f'(n_2) - r) - \gamma_1(p_1 f'(n_2) - r)$$
$$+ \gamma_2(p_2 f'(n_2) - r) = 0 \qquad \text{(A4.1.10)}$$

$$\lambda\,[\varrho_1 u(w_1) + (1 - \varrho_1)u(w_2) - \tilde{U}] = 0 \qquad \lambda \geqslant 0 \qquad \text{(A4.1.11)}$$

$$\gamma_1(\pi_{11} - \pi_{12}) = 0 \qquad \gamma_1 \geqslant 0 \qquad \text{(A4.1.12)}$$

$$\gamma_2(\pi_{22} - \pi_{21}) = 0 \qquad \gamma_2 \geqslant 0 \qquad \text{(A4.1.13)}$$

where we have used (A4.1.1)–(A4.1.4) to simplify as much as possible. We have also again imposed full employment in state one, so n_1 is not a choice variable.

Will a second-best contract generally predict levels any different from those that would prevail under a neoclassical Walrasian auction regime? In order to make this answer interesting, we shall assume that a Walrasian auction would predict full employment in state one and unemployment in state two. As we saw above, this implies

$$p_1 f'(n_1) > r \qquad\qquad\qquad\qquad\text{(A4.1.14)}$$

$$p_2 f'(n_1) < r \qquad\qquad\qquad\qquad\text{(A4.1.15)}$$

(recall figure 4.3). The level of Walrasian employment in state two then solves

$$p_2 f'(n_2^s) = r. \qquad\qquad\qquad\qquad\text{(A4.1.16)}$$

We can distinguish between four cases concerning whether or not the incentive-compatibility constraints (A4.1.5) and (A4.1.6) are binding. They can either both be slack (i.e. (A4.1.5) and (A4.1.6) are satisfied for strict inequality), both be binding (equations (A4.1.5) and (A4.1.6) are satisfied for equality) or any one of them can be binding.

If both of the incentive-compatibility constraints are slack, then the first-best contract is incentive-compatible. Intuitively, if we do not have to impose the constraint that firms tell the truth then they become irrelevant, as in the symmetric-information case. Formally, if both (A4.1.5) and (A4.1.6) are slack, then from (A4.1.12) and (A4.1.13) we must have $\gamma_1 = 0$ and $\gamma_2 = 0$, so the Lagrangean (A4.1.7) is formally identical to (4.68). In this case, therefore, the second-best coincides with the first-best, and since we have already characterized the first-best, this is an uninteresting case.

What if both of the incentive-compatibility constraints are binding, i.e. $\pi_{11} = \pi_{12}$ and $\pi_{22} = \pi_{21}$? In that case we have

$$p_1 f(n_1) - w_1 n_1 = p_1 f(n_2) - w_2 n_1 + r(n_1 - n_2) \qquad\text{(A4.1.17)}$$

and

$$p_2 f(n_2) - w_2 n_1 + r(n_1 - n_2) = p_2 f(n_1) - w_1 n_1. \qquad\text{(A4.1.18)}$$

After rearrangement, equations (A4.1.17) and (A4.1.18) become respectively

$$p_1(f(n_1) - f(n_2)) = n_1(w_1 - w_2) + r(n_1 - n_2)$$
$$p_2(f(n_1) - f(n_2)) = n_1(w_1 - w_2) + r(n_1 - n_2)$$

which imply

$$p_1(f(n_1) - f(n_2)) = p_2(f(n_1) - f(n_2)). \qquad\text{(A4.1.19)}$$

Since $p_1 > p_2$, equation (A4.1.19) can only be satisfied if $n_2 = n_1$. Substituting this into the first-order condition (A4.1.10) and rearranging:

$$(1-\varrho_1)v'(\pi_{22})+\gamma_2=\gamma_1\ \frac{p_1f'(n_1)-r}{p_2f'(n_1)-r}. \tag{A4.1.20}$$

Now, in general, γ_1 and γ_2 will be positive for binding incentive-compatibility constraints (see (A4.1.12) and (A4.1.13)). Therefore the left-hand side of (A4.1.20) is positive. However, using (A4.1.14) and (A4.1.15), the right-hand side of (A4.1.20) will be negative, so (A4.1.12) cannot be satisfied. This means that, if a Walrasian auction regime would result in full employment in state one and unemployment in state two, both of the incentive-compatibility contracts cannot be binding simultaneously for the second-best contract.

A third possibility is that (A4.1.6) is binding but (A4.1.5) is slack, i.e. $\pi_{22}=\pi_{21}$ and $\pi_{11}>\pi_{12}$. This means that, in the absence of the incentive-compatibility constraints, the firm would announce the correct state only if state one occurred – i.e. it would generally claim that times were good even if they were bad. One might suspect that this will not generally be the case. This possibility can be ruled out formally quite straightforwardly. Firstly, $\pi_{11}>\pi_{12}$ implies $\gamma_1=0$, by the Kuhn–Tucker condition (A4.1.12), whilst γ_2 will in general be positive. Substituting $\gamma_1=0$ into (A4.1.10) and rearranging slightly:

$$(1-\varrho_1)v'(\pi_{22})(p_2f'(n_2)-r)=-\gamma_2(p_2f'(n_2)-r). \tag{A4.1.21}$$

Now since $(1-\varrho_1)v'(\pi_{22})>0$ whilst $-\gamma_2\leqslant0$, equation (A4.1.21) can only be satisfied for $p_2f'(n_2)-r=0$, i.e.

$$r=p_2f'(n_2). \tag{A4.1.22}$$

Now

$$f'(n_2)>\frac{f(n_1)-f(n_2)}{n_1-n_2} \tag{A4.1.23}$$

by the concavity of f (recall figure 4.4). Combining (A4.1.22) and (A4.1.23):

$$r(n_1-n_2)>p_2(f(n_1)-f(n_2)) \tag{A4.1.24}$$

Since $\pi_{22}=\pi_{21}$,

$$p_2f(n_2)-w_2n_1+r(n_1-n_2)=p_2f(n_1)-w_1n_1$$

or

$$r(n_1-n_2)=p_2(f(n_1)-f(n_2))+(w_2-w_1)n_1. \tag{A4.1.25}$$

Expressions (A4.1.24) and (A4.1.25) are only compatible if $(w_2 - w_1)n_1 > 0$, i.e.

$$w_1 < w_2. \tag{A4.1.26}$$

Intuitively, firms only have an incentive to claim times are good when in fact they are bad if the wage is lower in the best state of the world.

However, $\pi_{11} > \pi_{21}$ (clearly,

$$p_1 f(n_1) - w_1 n_1 > p_2 f(n_1) - w_1 n_1$$

since $p_1 > p_2$), so if $\pi_{22} = \pi_{21}$, then $\pi_{11} > \pi_{22}$ – i.e. profits are higher in state one than state two when the firm tells the truth. The co-insurance result discussed earlier would therefore suggest that w_1 should be greater than w_2. This is easily seen to be the case since: setting $\gamma_1 = 0$ and letting $\gamma_2 \geqslant 0$ in (A4.1.8) implies

$$v'(\pi_{11})n_1 \geqslant \lambda u'(w_1) \tag{A4.1.27}$$

and similarly, from (A4.1.9)

$$v'(\pi_{22})n_1 \leqslant \lambda u'(w_2). \tag{A4.1.28}$$

Hence,

$$\frac{v'(\pi_{11})}{v'(\pi_{22})} \geqslant \frac{u'(w_1)}{u'(w_2)}. \tag{A4.1.29}$$

By diminishing marginal utility ($v'' < 0$), $\pi_{11} > \pi_{22}$ implies that the left-hand side (and hence the right-hand side) of (A4.1.29) is less than unity, i.e.

$$u'(w_1) < u'(w_2). \tag{A4.1.30}$$

However, given diminishing marginal utility ($u'' < 0$), inequality (A4.1.30) implies

$$w_1 > w_2 \tag{A4.1.31}$$

which contradicts (A4.1.26). This contradiction rules out the possibility that $\pi_{11} > \pi_{12}$ and $\pi_{22} = \pi_{21}$ for the second-best contract.

The only remaining possibility is $\pi_{11} = \pi_{12}$ and $\pi_{22} > \pi_{21}$. This seems the most intuitively plausible case since one can easily imagine a situation where the firm would find it profitable to claim that times are bad when in fact they are good, but not vice versa. From the Kuhn–Tucker conditions (A4.1.12), (A4.1.13) we have in this case $\gamma_2 = 0$ and $\gamma_1 \geqslant 0$. Substituting into condition (A4.1.10) yields

$$(1 - \varrho_1) v'(\pi_{22})(p_2 f'(n_2) - r) = \gamma_1(p_1 f'(n_2) - r). \qquad \text{(A4.1.32)}$$

Now, since we assumed state one Walrasian full employment, $p_1 f'(n_1) > r$ (equation (A4.1.14)), and since $f'(n_2) > f'(n_1)$ for $n_1 > n_2$ by diminishing returns, we have $p_1 f'(n_2) > r$. Therefore, the right-hand side of (A4.1.32) is non-negative; but the left-hand side will only be non-negative if $p_2 f'(n_2) - r$ is, i.e.

$$p_2 f'(n_2) \geqslant r. \qquad \text{(A4.1.33)}$$

Except under very special circumstances, the Lagrange multiplier γ_1 will in fact be strictly greater than zero, so (A4.1.33) can in general be strengthened to a strict inequality:

$$p_2 f'(n_2) > r. \qquad \text{(A4.1.34)}$$

Comparing (A4.1.34) with (A4.1.16) (which gives the level of Walrasian state two employment), we can see that a second-best contract will generate a lower level of employment in a slump than would occur under a Walrasian regime (or indeed under a first-best contract – see (4.76)). This means that implicit labour contracts under asymmetric information will in general create socially deficient levels of employment in some states of nature (Azariadis 1983, Grossman and Hart 1981, 1983).

What is the intuition underlying this under-employment result? Since workers do not trust firms to report the state of nature truthfully, they will not enter into a contract in which the wage is purely a function of which state prevails. Instead, wages will effectively be made to depend on variables that the worker can observe, such as the level of employment. Thus, reductions in the wage will only be allowed in the contract if the firm also reduces the level of employment enough to convince the workers that times actually are bad and this is not just a ploy to cut the wage bill. Thus, in adverse states of nature, the firm may have to reduce employment below the socially efficient level purely because this is the only way it can get wages down.

Will optimal risk sharing occur under asymmetric information? Substituting $\gamma_2 = 0$ and assuming γ_1 strictly positive in (A4.1.8) yields, after rearrangement:

$$v'(\pi_{11}) n_1 - \lambda u'(w_1) = -\gamma n_1 / \varrho_1 < 0$$

which implies

$$v'(\pi_{11}) n_1 < \lambda u'(w_1). \qquad \text{(A4.1.35)}$$

Similarly, from (A4.1.9),

$$v'(\pi_{22}) n_1 > \lambda u'(w_2). \qquad \text{(A4.1.36)}$$

Expressions (A4.1.35) and (A4.1.36) imply

$$\frac{v'(\pi_{11})}{v'(\pi_{22})} < \frac{u'(w_1)}{u'(w_2)}. \qquad\qquad (A4.1.37)$$

Since (A4.1.37) is an inequality, the optimal risk-sharing condition is violated – marginal rates of substitution between incomes in different states are not equalized for the firm and the worker. However, optimal risk sharing could be achieved by reducing w_2 a little and increasing w_1, holding n_1 and n_2 constant. This would have the effect of reducing π_{11} and increasing π_{22}. Given diminishing marginal utility for the firm and the worker, juggling with w_1 and w_2 in this way could clearly turn (A4.1.37) into an equality. What is precluding this result? Again, the firm would have to reduce employment further in state two if it were to cut w_2, in order to convince the worker that its intentions are honourable. Given that output would fall in state two (and total unemployment compensation rise), π_{22} would not rise enough to prevent (A4.1.37) holding as an inequality (indeed, π_{22} may even fall).

5 Open-economy models

5.1 Introduction

In this chapter we analyse a number of models of a small open economy. 'Small' means that changes in the domestic economy under study are assumed to have no feedback effects on the world economy and the latter is exogenous to the domestic economy. In open-economy models we have to deal with the determinants of current and capital account flows on the balance of payments, and hence on the behaviour of the exchange rate in a floating regime. The return in domestic currency to investing in foreign securities depends, inter alia, on movements in the exchange rate and agents engaged in foreign portfolio investment may have to form a view about the *expected* level of the exchange rate. Hence, in analysing the open economy, expectations should be explicitly modelled and here the rational-expectations hypothesis tends to play a key role. Exporters and importers are also affected by changes in the exchange rate since this alters price competitiveness (or profitability) in the traded goods sector, and has repercussions on aggregate demand as well as the balance of payments.

Changes in the current account and the exchange rate alter the wealth of domestic residents. A current account surplus implies that domestic residents have increased claims on foreign residents which may for example result (at least initially) in an increase in foreign bank deposits held by domestic residents. In addition, changes in the exchange rate lead to valuation changes in terms of domestic currency of any foreign assets held by domestic residents. Clearly a current account surplus (with income constant) implies a *continuously* rising wealth-to-income ratio for domestic residents and our discussion in §1.4.1 suggests that this is likely to cause changes in aggregate demand and, via the Phillips curve, changes in the rate of inflation. In addition there may be a more direct effect on domestic prices as exchange rate changes lead to changes in the domestic price of importables (e.g. raw materials). An analysis of the interaction between fiscal and monetary policy and the exchange rate has clear implications for an understanding of inflation in small open economies.

To present immediately a 'complete' macromodel that embodied the closed-economy elements discussed in earlier chapters and the above open-economy aspects would be difficult and confusing and would result in an analytically intractable model. Our approach therefore is to extend a 'basic' closed-economy model in a rather piecemeal fashion, examining the implications of relaxing various restrictive assumptions one at a time. This allows expositional clarity but suffers from the drawback that one may end up with a rather disparate (non-overlapping) set of open-economy models. To some extent, this is unavoidable but in mitigation we compare the different models at various points.

In the 1950s, and 1960s the Bretton–Woods adjustable-peg (or fixed-exchange-rate) system held centre-stage. Short-term 'portfolio' capital flows were severely restricted by government legislation and policy emphasis was placed on the behaviour of the current account. Whether a country could alter its payments position by a step change in the exchange rate depended in part on the degree of expenditure switching between imports and domestically produced goods and in the response of exports to a change in competitiveness. This analysis leads to the Marshall–Lerner condition which we investigate in the next section. In the late 1960s and early 1970s the money supply and monetarism became of increasing importance in policy debates. The so-called Mundell–Fleming (MF) model (Mundell (1963) Fleming (1962)) which neatly augmented the closed-economy IS–LM analysis, could be used to analyse the effect on the exchange rate and output of a change in the money supply or government expenditure in a fix-price small open economy. We discuss this in §5.2 for fixed- and flexible-exchange-rate regimes. This is followed by a brief discussion of possible wealth effects working via current account surpluses and deficits in the fix-price MF model. As in the closed-economy case, the monetary and fiscal multipliers are altered when wealth effects are added to the model.

A major defect of the basic Mundell–Fleming model is the assumption of fixed prices, particularly given the likely feedback from the exchange rate, via import prices to domestic prices. One solution, which one might dub 'eclectic monetarist', is to add a PEAPC for wages to the MF model and a cost mark-up equation with prices depending on unit labour costs and import prices. This approach is also examined in §5.2. It produces neoclassical 'neutrality results' in the long run if we incorporate the vertical PEAPC (or aggregate supply curve); however, in the short run (which could involve a time span of five to ten years), changes in output may also occur. To represent the short-run response of the economy analytically is quite difficult and we are only able to sketch out the process.

In the 1970s, along with the increasing importance of the money supply in economic debates, a view emerged that control of the money supply was sufficient for control of the domestic price level *and* the exchange rate (under floating rates). The current account monetarist (CAM) model was able to explain why in the fixed-exchange-rate era devaluation had often been unsuccessful in altering the payments position. The CAM model concentrates on the current rather than the capital account and deals with the long run where prices are flexible and output is exogenously determined by the supply side of the economy. Under floating rates the CAM model predicts a close relationship between rapid monetary growth and a depreciating exchange rate (and vice versa) – which is broadly consistent with events in Italy, the United Kingdom, Germany and Japan in the first half of the 1970s, for example. In terms of its predictions we are able to show in §5.3 that the MF model under the assumption of a full-employment level of output yields similar results to the CAM model.

Unfortunately, the CAM model failed to explain adequately the large swings in the *real* exchange rate (or competitiveness) that occurred in a number of small open economies, such as those of the UK, the Netherlands and Italy in the second half of the 1970s, and continue to date. The CAM model takes 'money' as the only asset of importance and hence ignores the capital account of the balance of payments. It also has no explicit model of price adjustment: prices are (usually) simply *assumed* to be flexible. Once we recognize the importance of capital flows that have obviously increased due to the recycling of OPEC balances and the gradual dismantling of exchange controls, we have to address the question of expectations. Speculative short-term capital flows respond to relative interest rates between the domestic and foreign country but also depend upon expectations about exchange rate movements. Capital account monetary (KAM) models, discussed in §5.4, invoke the rational-expectations hypothesis (REH) to deal with exchange rate expectations and often assume that capital account flows are perfectly mobile. Price adjustment is slow and is determined by excess demand working via a (long-run vertical) PEAPC. The combination of sticky prices (or sluggish output response) and high capital mobility results in changes in monetary and fiscal policy causing 'large' swings in the nominal and real exchange rate – that is, exchange rate overshooting. In addition, KAM models allow one to analyse why a resource discovery in a small open economy (e.g. North Sea Oil in the UK) might lead to a loss of competitiveness and a recession in the traded goods sector.

A recurring theme in the exchange rate literature concerns the response of the exchange rate to a change in domestic interest rates. The CAM model predicts that a depreciation ensues after a *rise* in domestic interest rates, while the KAM model yields the opposite conclusion. The model of Frankel (1979) involving the real interest rate and the contributions of Dornbusch (1976, 1980) clarify this exchange-rate – interest-rate nexus and also yield insights into why exchange rate movements appear to be 'excessively' volatile. These matters are discussed in §5.5.

A defect in the KAM model is its implicit assumption of the perfect substitutability of domestic and foreign assets and failure to analyse explicitly the stock flow interactions arising from current account imbalances. This is remedied in the portfolio balance model of exchange rates (PBM) which we discuss in §5.6.

We end with a brief summary and discuss the explicit solution of open-economy RE models in the appendices.

5.2   The Mundell–Fleming Model

In this section we begin with an analysis of the conditions under which a devaluation leads to an improvement in the balance of *trade* (i.e. exports of goods and services less imports) purely via expenditure switching: this is the Marshall–Lerner condition. We then discuss the determinants of trade and capital flows and derive a condition for balance-of-payments equilibrium which we term the BB locus. The latter, when added to the closed-economy IS–LM diagram, yields the basic Mundell–Fleming model which allows us to analyse the impact of monetary and fiscal policy under fixed and flexible exchange rates. We then further augment our open-economy Mundell–Fleming model by introducing wealth effects and end this section with a discussion of how one might incorporate price changes into the Mundell–Fleming model.

5.2.1   The Marshall–Lerner (ML) Condition

After a depreciation of the exchange rate the balance of trade improves only under certain restrictive assumptions, and perhaps the simplest of these deals purely with expenditure switching and is known as the Marshall–Lerner (ML) condition. Make the simplifying assumptions (i) domestic prices P are unaffected by the exchange rate S (ii) domestic output is held constant (say, by altering fiscal or monetary policy), (iii) exports X and import volumes Z are determined by real competitiveness (the terms of trade) with imports also influenced by domestic output Y, (iv) the domestic economy is 'small'; hence it does not have a major influence on the world economy and (v) there is no model of independent 'supply' decisions: supply reacts passively to demand at the fixed price level. The balance of trade N in domestic currency (sterling) may be written as

$$N = PX - (P^*S)Z \tag{5.1}$$

where $X = X(P^*S/P)$ and $Z = Z[(P^*S/P), Y]$ where P^* is the foreign price level and S is measured in units of the domestic currency per unit of foreign currency. Hence (P^*S) is the *domestic* (sterling) price of imported (world) goods and P^*S/P is the *relative* price of traded goods (i.e. 'competitiveness', or the terms of trade or the real exchange rate). Note that a devaluation is represented by an *increase* in S.

Assumptions (i) and (ii) imply $\partial P/\partial S = \partial Y/\partial S = 0$. To determine the impact of a change in S on N we have

$$\frac{\partial N}{\partial S} = \frac{P \partial X}{\partial S} - P^*S \frac{\partial Z}{\partial S} - P^*Z \tag{5.2}$$

$$= \frac{PX}{S} \left(\frac{S}{X} \frac{\partial X}{\partial S} - \frac{P^*S^2}{PX} \frac{\partial Z}{\partial S} - \frac{SP^*Z}{PX} \right). \tag{5.3}$$

If we assume initial payments equilibrium $PX = (P^*S)Z$, then

$$\frac{\partial N}{\partial S} = \frac{PX}{S} (|\eta_X| + |\eta_Z| - 1) \tag{5.4}$$

where η_X and η_Z are the exchange rate (competitiveness) elasticities of exports and imports. Given the definition of S, a rise (fall) indicates a depreciation (appreciation) of the domestic currency. For a depreciation to lead to an improvement in the trade balance due to expenditure switching we require $\partial N / \partial S > 0$ and hence

$$|\eta_X| + |\eta_Z| - 1 > 0. \tag{5.5}$$

Equation (5.5) is the ML condition. (Since we have assumed domestic and foreign prices are constant, the ML condition is also applicable when there are changes in the *real* exchange rate.)

In practice, the ML condition does not hold in the short run (say over one to two years) since export and import volumes take time to react to changes in relative prices. Hence the balance of payments deteriorates in the short run and only improves in the long run, after a depreciation. (This is often referred to as the J-curve effect.)

There are several other changes that ensue after a step devaluation. As long as $\eta_X > 0$, $\eta_Z < 0$ a depreciation (with domestic prices constant) will have a net expansionary effect. This sucks in imports ($\partial Z / \partial Y > 0$) and partially offsets an improvement in the payments position because of expenditure switching (the ML condition is derived under the assumption of a fixed level of output). Secondly, a depreciation raises the domestic (sterling) price of imported goods (e.g. raw materials) and this is likely to put upward pressure on domestic prices. In fact, if the percentage rise in domestic prices equals the change in the exchange rate in the long run, then competitiveness remains unchanged and the balance of trade does not improve since there is no expenditure switching. (We discuss this case in §5.2.11.) Hence, it must be remembered that the ML condition applies under rather restrictive assumptions.

5.2.2 The BB Locus

The MF model augments the basic closed-economy fix-price model of §1.3 with a balance-of-payments equilibrium condition (the BB locus) showing those combinations of the interest rate and income (output) that yield payments equilibrium. The impact of monetary and fiscal policy in this three-sector 'demand side' model may then be compared with its closed-economy counterpart. Broadly speaking the balance of payments consists of the balance of *trade* in goods and services and portfolio and real (or direct) capital flows (e.g. a purchase of UK firms by foreigners). Below we deal only with the determinants of trade and portfolio capital flows.

The Balance of Trade   If the ML conditions hold then $\partial N/\partial C > 0$ (where $C = (P*S/P)$ is the *real* exchange rate). Import volumes increase as domestic output rises and export volumes rise with world trade. If we assume domestic prices P are constant then the nominal trade balance N and the real trade balance $N' = N/P$ change in the same direction. Hence, as a linear approximation we can write

$$N/P = N' = \delta(s + p* - p) - \gamma y + q \tag{5.6}$$

where q represents the influence of world trade (and any other exogenous factors) on exports and the trade balance, δ and γ are positive constants and lower-case letters denote logarithms.

Capital Flows   Net capital flows *into* the domestic economy, ΔK, are assumed to depend positively on the domestic interest rate on bonds, r, relative to the world rate, $r*$ (which, given our small-country assumption, we assume is exogenously given and unaffected by changes in the domestic economy). Thus

$$\Delta K = \alpha(r - \overset{*}{r}) \qquad \alpha > 0. \tag{5.7}$$

The above equation is known as the *flow* theory of the capital account since a step increase in r above $r*$ leads to a *permanent* inflow of capital. This is in contrast to the *portfolio theories* of the demand for assets where the *stock* of assets depends on the interest differential. Note that we are implicitly assuming that *expected* changes in the exchange rate are either zero (i.e. 'static' expectations), or are ignored when deciding on portfolio allocation between domestic and foreign bonds. Relaxing this assumption may yield very different results from those discussed below as we see later when discussing the Dornbusch–KAM model.

In the portfolio theory a step increase in the interest rate leads to a capital inflow in the short run but when the new asset stock equilibrium is reached, inflows return to zero. Thus a *permanent* inflow requires an ever-increasing relative interest rate. Since r influences the real economy (through the slope of the IS curve) it appears that these two approaches could give very different conclusions about the efficacy of monetary and fiscal policy in an open economy. However we can, up to a point, reconcile the two approaches.

First, *ignoring expectations* and assuming perfect capital mobility (i.e. domestic and foreign assets are perfect substitutes, and adjustment to equilibrium is instantaneous) both approaches give the same results. Domestic interest rates are always equal to foreign rates. An (unexpected) rise in domestic rates leads to a potential or actual large capital inflow. This tends to cause bond prices to be 'marked up' and hence domestic interest rates fall back to the world level. Second, if portfolios are *growing*, a greater proportion of additional wealth may be placed in domestic assets at a constant but higher relative rate of return,[1] thus giving a permanent capital inflow for a given interest differential. The latter assumption introduces a continuous growth in wealth which can considerably complicate the analysis. For the moment we either assume away the problem by assuming perfect capital mobility or (more tenuously) assume our analysis is of a short-run nature so that the flow equilibrium theory is valid. In either case we ignore exchange rate expectations.

If the balance of *payments* (i.e. current plus capital account) is in surplus under fixed exchange rates, there will be an increase in foreign exchange reserves ΔR; thus, ignoring foreign income and interest rates, we have

$$\Delta R = N(SP^*/P, Y) + \Delta K(r) \tag{5.8}$$
$$\Delta R = N + \Delta K = \delta(s + p^* - p) - \gamma y + q + \alpha(r - r^*). \tag{5.9}$$

For balance-of-payments equilibrium $\Delta R = 0$, and equation (5.9) then gives a relationship between y and r (for given S) to maintain payments equilibrium.

For a given S, higher domestic output leads to higher imports and a higher domestic interest rate is therefore required to induce a capital inflow, to maintain payments equilibrium. This gives us the BB line in figure 5.1. If capital mobility is high (low) it takes a small (large) rise in r to offset the trade deficit as y rises, and BB is flat (steep). Hence the slope of the BB line varies for different degrees of capital mobility.

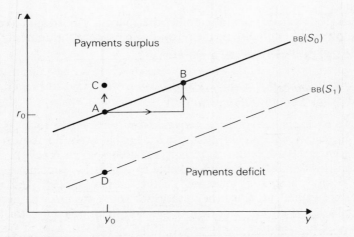

Figure 5.1 The payments equilibrium locus (BB)

Above any BB line (e.g. point C in figure 5.1) we have a payments surplus. At any level of output and hence imports, the interest rate is higher at C, thus inducing a capital inflow and a payments surplus. Under a floating exchange rate the surplus would cause the exchange rate to appreciate. The converse also applies.

For any given combination of r and y on the payments equilibrium locus BB (say r_0, y_0 in figure 5.1) a depreciation of the domestic currency will (given that the ML condition holds and domestic prices are fixed) lead to an improvement in the trade balance at *any given level of output* (expenditure switching) and hence allow a lower interest rate to maintain payments equilibrium (A to D). Thus the BB line shifts down if the exchange rate depreciates (i.e. S is higher). Under perfect capital mobility the balance of payments is always in equilibrium as long as $r = r^*$ regardless of the level of output and the exchange rate. Hence for perfect capital mobility the payments equilibrium locus is horizontal and does not shift as the exchange rate changes.[2]

To recapitulate, the assumptions that lie behind the normal upward-sloping payments equilibrium BB locus are as listed below.

1   Capital mobility is finite ($0 < \alpha < \infty$) and the trade balance depends negatively on domestic output.
2   A change in the exchange rate does not affect domestic prices and therefore leads to a change in competitiveness (or the 'terms of trade'). The latter leads to a change in the nominal (and real) trade balance (the ML condition holds). Under these conditions a change in S shifts the 'normal' BB line: for example, a depreciation shifts the BB locus down (to the right).
3   For completeness note that an increase in world trade or a fall in foreign interest rates will shift the BB locus to the right, allowing payments equilibrium at a lower domestic interest rate or higher level of domestic output.
4   Under perfect (zero) capital mobility the BB locus is horizontal (vertical). We now move on to discuss the relationship between the domestic money supply and the balance of payments.

5.2.3   The Balance of Payments and the Money Supply: Sterilization

Under fixed exchange rates a *payments* surplus leads to a 'sale' of foreign currency (perhaps held initially in foreign banks) by domestic residents to the Central Bank,[3] and a receipt of domestic currency (a cheque drawn on the Central Bank and payable to domestic residents). There is therefore an 'automatic' increase in the money supply. Under less-than-perfect capital mobility the authorities could sterilize this monetary inflow by sales of government debt to the non-bank private sector (NBPS). However, it is generally acknowledged that sterilization of a persistent payments surplus requires the NBPS to hold an ever-increasing ratio of bonds to money and it is unlikely that this could be maintained in a (static) economy with unchanged interest rates. Thus in the medium term the money supply will probably tend to increase.

With perfect capital mobility, sterilization is impossible. An attempt by the authorities to sell bonds to the NBPS leads to a *potential* rise in interest rates and this encourages a capital inflow. All the bonds are purchased by foreigners and there is merely an increase in foreign exchange reserves with an unchanged money supply and interest rates.

Charges in the money supply may therefore be thought of as being determined by the payments surplus (or changes in the foreign exchange reserves) as well as by changes induced by domestic factors ΔD. Some of the 'domestic factors' are more or less under the control of the authorities (e.g. open-market operations with less-than-perfect capital mobility and via the budget deficit) and others (e.g. bank advances) are not directly controllable. However, under fixed exchange rates with less-than-perfect sterilization, the money supply becomes endogenous because the balance-of-payments position has a direct effect on the total money supply:

$$\Delta M^s = \Delta D + \Delta R. \tag{5.10}$$

With floating exchange rates the exchange rate adjusts to produce payments equilibrium and the money supply is therefore insulated from the foreign sector ($\Delta R = 0$ at all times) and providing the authorities can control, ΔD, they can pursue an independent monetary policy.

We have spent some considerable time in developing the building blocks of the Mundell–Fleming model of the balance of payments as it provides a useful baseline in a number of models that follow. At the moment, the main results we wish to analyse within the MF framework are (i) *under perfect capital mobility* fiscal policy is potent under fixed exchange rates but impotent under flexible exchange rates and the converse applies for monetary policy; (ii) with low capital mobility the aforementioned results are largely reversed. We therefore add our BB locus to the 'normal' IS–LM model of the goods and money market, assuming a fix-price framework. The results from this three-market model are summarized in table 5.1. We deal first with fiscal and monetary policy under perfect capital mobility and then briefly summarize the results for the low-capital-mobility case for completeness.

Table 5.1 The open-economy fix-price Mundell–Fleming model

Policy	Exchange rate	High (perfect) capital mobility		Low capital mobility	
		Fixed	Flexible	Fixed	Flexible
Fiscal, $\Delta G > 0$		Full Keynesian multiplier	Complete crowding out	$\geqslant 0$	> 0
Monetary, $\Delta M^s > 0$		0	Full money multiplier	0	> 0

5.2.4　*Perfect Capital Mobility in the MF Model*

Fiscal Policy　Under fixed exchange rates an increase in government expenditure puts upwards pressure on domestic interest rates (A to B in figure 5.2) which leads to a capital inflow and an increase in the money supply. The final equilibrium level of output is at C which is larger than at B for the closed-economy IS–LM model. The capital inflow keeps the interest rate constant and allows the 'full' Keynesian goods market multiplier.

With flexible exchange rates, the large capital inflow exceeds the trade deficit at B and a *potential* payments surplus leads to an appreciation of the exchange rate. The latter leads to a fall in real net trade (IS to the left) which exactly counteracts the increase in *G*, on real output. Fiscal policy is impotent and completely 'crowded out' under flexible exchange rates and perfect capital mobility. Crowding out takes place via net trade flows rather than a fall in investment as in the closed-economy case of §1.3.3. Thus under perfect capital mobility the effect of fiscal policy under flexible exchange rates is in sharp contrast to the expansionary effect in the fixed-rate case (see table 5.1).

Monetary Policy　Under fixed exchange rates and increase in the *domestic* component of the money supply, by an open-market purchase of bonds, tends to lower interest rates and thus encourage a capital outflow (B in figure 5.3). The NBPS then purchase foreign currency from the Central Bank to buy foreign 'bonds'; hence the domestic money supply tends to fall back to its *original* level. (Alternatively, one might think of foreigners selling their foreign 'bonds' directly to the domestic monetary authorities in exchange for the domestic currency (sterling), but sterling held by foreign residents is not

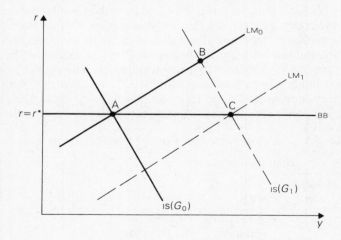

Figure 5.2　Fiscal policy: perfect capital mobility C, fixed exchange rate; A flexible exchange rate

counted as part of the UK money supply, which therefore remains constant.) Hence foreign exchange reserves fall and the total money stock is unchanged as are output and interest rates. The money supply is endogenous and monetary policy is impotent. The rate of growth in the money supply determines the *change* in foreign exchange reserves and hence the short-run balance-of-payments position (this is also a prediction of the CAM model; see § 5.3).

With *flexible exchange rates* the potential payments deficit at B (figure 5.3) leads to a depreciation of the exchange rate and an expansion of net trade and output (the IS curve shifts to the right). The final equilibrium position is at C where the level of output is higher than the 'normal' IS–LM equilibrium (at B).

5.2.5 Low Capital Mobility in the MF Model

For completeness we briefly present the results for the efficacy of fiscal and monetary policy when there is low capital mobility (table 5.1). We define the latter as when the BB curve is steeper than the LM curve. This is more likely to be the case when (domestic) money and domestic bonds are closer substitutes than are domestic bonds and foreign bonds.

Fiscal Policy   Under *fixed exchange rates* the higher level of output and interest rate consequent on a fiscal expansion leads to a trade deficit and a capital account surplus, but because of low capital mobility the overall balance of payments is in deficit (point B in figure 5.4). The money supply therefore falls as foreign exchange is purchased by NBPS to finance the deficit. The fall in the money supply puts upward pressure on interest rates, crowding

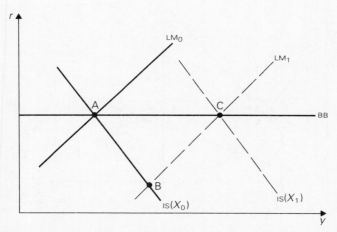

Figure 5.3 Monetary policy: perfect capital mobility. A, fixed exchange rate; C, flexible; (X = export volume)

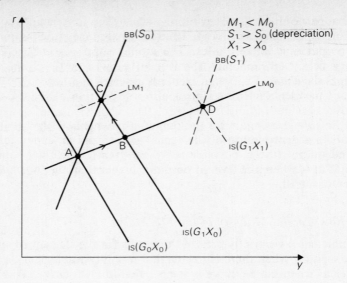

Figure 5.4 Fiscal policy: low capital mobility. C, fixed exchange rate; D, flexible exchange rate

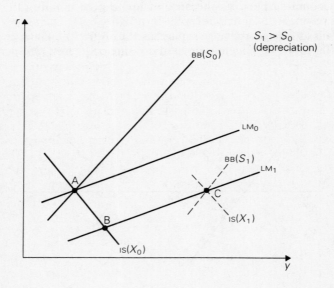

Figure 5.5 Monetary policy: low capital mobility, A, fixed exchange rate; C, flexible exchange rate

out private investment, so the final equilibrium is at C, with some rise in output. If there is *zero* capital mobility (BB vertical) the final level of output is unchanged at y_0 and there is complete 'crowding out'.[4] Under *flexible exchange rates* the payments deficit at B in figure 5.4 leads to a depreciation in the exchange rate. This stimulates real net trade and shifts the BB and IS curves to the right, the final equilibrium being at D: a higher level of output than in the closed-economy IS–LM case. This result is also in sharp contrast to the perfect-capital-mobility case where full crowding out occurs under flexible exchange rates (table 5.1).

Monetary Policy   Under fixed exchange rates the money supply is endogenous and there is no monetary policy effect on output. Under flexible exchange rates the situation is also qualitatively similar to that for the perfect-capital-mobility case. The increase in the money supply unambiguously leads to a payments deficit at B (figure 5.5). The exchange rate depreciates, net trade increases and the IS (and BB) curves shift to the right, the final equilibrium being at C. This qualitative result is unaffected when there is *zero* capital mobility.

5.2.6   A Summary of the Basic MF Model

What are the main conclusions to emerge from adding the MF model of the balance of payments to the 'normal' (closed-economy) IS–LM analysis? Referring to table 5.1 we note the following main conclusions.

Monetary Policy   Whereas in the closed-economy model, monetary policy influenced the level of output, in the open economy, the money supply is endogenous under *fixed exchange rates*. Changes in the domestic component of the money supply (by open-market operations) do not influence the level of output but determine the level of foreign exchange reserves, that is, the balance-of-payments position. The above outcome assumes that sterilization is not undertaken by the authorities, or is not possible (e.g. under the assumption of perfect capital mobility). If partial sterilization is possible the money supply will have some effect on output. Under *flexible exchange rates* with any degree of capital mobility, monetary policy is more potent than in the closed-economy case. This arises because the increase in the money supply initially leads to a fall in the interest rate and a rise in output, both of which lead to a payments deficit and a depreciation of the exchange rate. The latter causes an additional expansionary effect as the real net trade balance increases.

Fiscal Policy   Under *fixed exchange rates* the impact of fiscal policy on output depends crucially on the degree of capital mobility. With high capital mobility the 'full' Keynesian multiplier applies but with zero capital mobility a fiscal stimulus is completely 'crowded out' as the incipient trade deficit leads to a fall in the money supply, a rise in interest rates and a fall in private investment. Under *flexible exchange rates*, and a low degree of capital mobility fiscal policy is more potent than in the closed-economy case but with perfect capital mobility complete 'crowding out' occurs, due to a fall in net trade.

The limitations of the analysis so far must be noted. We have used a fix-price model where output is demand-determined. We have not considered expectations and the impact of 'wealth' effects on the goods and money markets.

5.2.7   Wealth Effects in the Open-Economy Fix-Price Model

Before describing the detailed results of fiscal and monetary policy in an open economy with wealth effects, it may be worthwhile repeating some general conclusions from the closed-economy case that also hold in our open-economy model.

1   Although it is possible in some cases for wealth effects to lead to crowding out of a fiscal stimulus, this can always be avoided by a suitable combination of monetary and fiscal policy instruments. Crowding out therefore results from an inappropriate method of finance.
2   The effects on output of *balanced-budget* fiscal changes are usually markedly different from bond- or money-financed fiscal deficits.
3   The relative size of the wealth effects on expenditure and the demand for money can substantially alter the time profile and final equilibrium value of output, after monetary and fiscal policy changes. The strength of the wealth effect on the demand for money influences the stability properties of the system under pure bond or mixed money–bond financing.

We have discussed how a budget deficit gives rise to an increase in financial wealth of the private sector but it may not be entirely clear why a *current* account surplus on the balance of payments has the same effect. If there is a current account surplus foreigners make *net* payments to domestic residents either in the form of foreign assets or domestic assets held by foreigners. On the other hand, changes in the *capital* account do not alter the net wealth of domestic (or foreign) residents.[5] If a domestic resident purchases an asset from a foreigner he or she must give up an equivalent amount of domestic assets (ultimately domestic money) in order to purchase the foreign exchange. The domestic resident merely exchanges a domestic asset for a foreign asset and there is no change in financial wealth. Thus it is only current account transactions, in which goods are exchanged for *additional* financial assets, that lead to changes in wealth. To make the analysis more tractable we deal exclusively with the case of perfect capital mobility, a not unreasonable assumption for the 1980s.

5.2.8 *Fixed Exchange Rates, Perfect Capital Mobility*

The output effects for monetary policy and an *unbalanced budget* fiscal expansion are qualitatively similar to those in the Mundell–Fleming approach (and the 'closed-economy wealth effects' model of §1.4). Thus monetary policy is impotent and unbalanced budget fiscal policy is potent (table 5.2).

Table 5.2 Wealth effects in the fix-price open-economy

Policy ＼ Exchange rate	Perfect capital mobility	
	Fixed	Flexible
Fiscal (i) $\Delta G>0$	Full Keynesian multiplier	Complete crowding out
(ii) balanced budget	Impotent	Small output effect
Monetary, $\partial M^s>0$	0	>0 but less than 'full' money multiplier

Monetary policy (if bonds are considered as net wealth) has *no* wealth effect and therefore under fixed exchange rates the money supply is endogenous and determined by the balance of payments. Thus the results and analysis for monetary policy are the same as in the basic MF model.

An unbalanced fiscal expansion (if stable) must lead to a rise in output and thus taxes ($T=t_y Y$) and imports, Z, until the trade deficit equals the budget deficit and wealth is constant at a new higher value. The multiplier is therefore given by

$$dG - t_y\, dY = dN = -z_y\, dY \tag{5.11}$$
$$dY/dG = 1/(t_y+z_y) \tag{5.12}$$

where z_y is the marginal propensity to import out of income. Initially, we reach MF equilibrium at C (figure 5.6) because the upward pressure on interest rates at B leads to a capital inflow and an expansion of the money supply (LM'). Since $r=r^*$ at C, the full Keynesian multiplier applies. However, this is not the end of the story since at C there is a budget deficit that is not fully offset by the trade deficit.[6] Hence, wealth increases and the IS curve shifts further to the right, raising output and interest rates (point D). The shift to the left of the LM curve due to the above increase in wealth is reversed by the capital inflow and consequent increase in the money supply, and the final equilibrium is at E.

For a *balanced-budget* fiscal expansion the MF result is reversed: fiscal policy is impotent.[7] There are no direct wealth effects from the *fiscal* stimulus ($dG=dT$) but the rise in output leads to a *trade deficit* and a fall in wealth. The IS curve returns to A due to the wealth effects on expenditures and output is unchanged (figure 5.6). The LM curve initially shifts to the left, but the upward pressure on interest rates and the subsequent capital inflow increases the money supply and allows r to fall to r^*, forcing the final position of the LM curve to pass through A.

The above analysis is easily extended to the case of imperfect capital mobility (i.e. an upward-sloping BB$'$ schedule). For an unbalanced-budget fiscal expansion the final equilibrium is at point F (figure 5.6).

5.2.9 *Flexible Exchange Rates, Perfect Capital Mobility*

In general, the MF result that a bond-financed fiscal expansion (i.e. an unbalanced-budget expansion) is impotent and monetary policy is very potent in influencing output, in a flexible-exchange-rate model with perfect capital mobility, is upheld when wealth effects are added to the model. In a rather 'special case', namely a *balanced-budget* expansion, the MF result is reversed and output increases (but not by much).

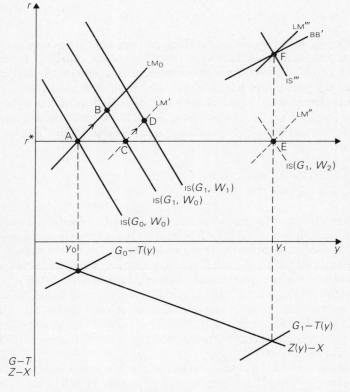

Figure 5.6 Unbalanced-budget fiscal expansion: fixed exchange rate. BB – perfect capital mobility; BB$'$ less-than-perfect capital mobility. Wealth equilibrium; $Z - X = G - T$

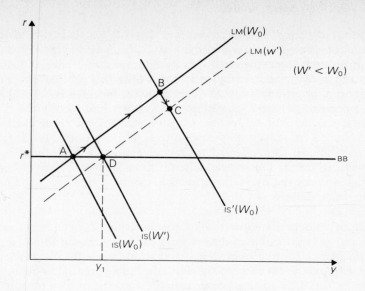

Figure 5.7 Balanced-budget fiscal expansion: flexible exchange rates, perfect capital mobility

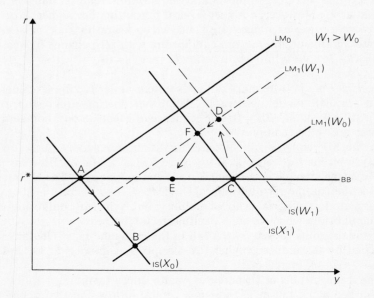

Figure 5.8 Monetary policy, flexible exchange rates

Unbalanced-Budget Fiscal Expansion   The MF result is that government
expenditure is completely crowded out as rising interest rates, a capital inflow
and an appreciation in the exchange rate reduce real net trade. All that remains
is to enquire whether A (figure 5.7) is a long-run equilibrium. Since r is
unchanged, investment is unchanged, as are the income-determined elements
of expenditure, namely, consumption, imports and income taxes. $\Delta Y = 0$
implies, via the national income identity, that $dG = dN$, the change in net
trade being a consequence of expenditure switching due to the appreciation
in the exchange rate referred to above. Hence at A no ensuing wealth
adjustments occur. The budget deficit is financed by the issue of bonds that
are taken up by the overseas sector (i.e. capital inflow) as the counterpart
to the trade deficit.

Balanced Budget Expansion   The mechanisms at work here are rather
intricate. Under flexible exchange rates the initial expansion in output (to
B figure 5.7) leads to a *trade* deficit and a fall in wealth. The IS curve shifts
to the left and the LM curve to the right: the latter is crucial to obtain positive
output effects. The upward pressure on the domestic interest rate (at C) leads
to a capital inflow, a rise in the exchange rate (as in the MF analysis) and
a fall in net trade and the IS curve shifts further to the left. As output falls
the trade balance improves and the wealth effects attenuate. The final
equilibrium is at D: the money supply and interest rate are unchanged, W
is lower, and therefore money market equilibrium requires a higher level of
output at y_1. However, a higher level of output implies higher imports and
therefore a *lower* exchange rate is needed to keep the trade balance equal
to zero and maintain long-run equilibrium with zero change in wealth (i.e.
$\Delta W = G - T - N = 0$ implies, for $G = T$, that $N = 0$).

Monetary Policy   Monetary policy is potent under flexible exchange rates
as in the MF model, except in the rather special circumstance where
$\partial M^d / \partial W \neq 0$ and $\partial C / \partial W = 0$. The sequence of events in our monetary policy
variant are rather complex.

In the MF analysis, an increase in the money supply puts downward
pressure on interest rates (at B in figure 5.8) a capital outflow ensues and
the exchange rate falls, boosting net trade and output to C. The MF multiplier
at C is the full money multiplier $dY = dM^s / m_y$ as r is constant because of
the assumption of perfect capital mobility; but is the MF equilibrium a long-
run equilibrium when we have wealth effects? The answer is no. At C there
is a trade surplus caused by the fall in the exchange rate. The latter is not
matched by the induced higher tax receipts and imports at C, and hence
$\partial W = G - T - N$ increases.[8]

The trade surplus at C increases wealth and a temporary equilibrium is
established at D; but at D there is a capital inflow and the exchange rate
appreciates pushing the IS curve to the left. The story becomes even more
complex here. Net trade falls due to the appreciation and wealth falls along
with output. As long as r is above r^*, the exchange rate appreciates and wealth

and output continue to fall. The final equilibrium is at E (which is less than the MF equilibrium level of output at C but still expansionary). As the final equilibrium involves a fall in wealth (compared with that at A) and an unchanged interest rate, the level of output must be higher to preserve money market equilibrium with the higher money supply. The 'IS curve' passively adapts to this 'LM-determined' equilibrium by changes in net trade caused by an appreciating exchange rate brought about by capital inflows (not shown in figure 5.8).

If there are wealth effects in the demand-for-money function but not in the expenditure function, then wealth effects at the MF equilibrium C shift the LM curve initially through E. However, the increase in wealth persists, and shifts the LM curve further to the left, putting upward pressure on interest rates (for a temporary fixed IS curve), giving rise to an appreciation in the exchange rate and a net trade-induced fall in output, until IS returns to its original position through A. In these rather special circumstances monetary policy is impotent under flexible exchange rates.

5.2.10 Summary: Wealth Effects

From tables 5.1 and 5.2 we see that the effect of monetary policy and an *unbalanced*-budget change in fiscal policy on output in an open-economy model with wealth effects are qualitatively similar to those obtained in the open-economy MF model (which has no wealth effects). Under fixed exchange rates the money supply is endogenous and has no effect on output but has a strong effect under flexible exchange rates when there is a high degree of capital mobility. For fiscal policy the converse applies. With a high degree of capital mobility, fiscal policy is potent under fixed exchange rates but impotent under flexible rates. The importance of the degree of substitutability between domestic and foreign assets (including money) and the strength of any wealth effects on the demand for money are clearly important in establishing the strength of monetary and fiscal policy effects.

It is probably widely accepted that the 'wealth effects' discussed above working via the budget and balance of payments surplus take considerable time to influence expenditures (and indeed are rather difficult to determine empirically). Thus for short-to-medium-term projections it may be the case that these wealth effects are *relatively* unimportant in influencing the time path of output. In the next section, however, we find that 'wealth effects' working via revaluation changes due to changes in prices (or interest rates and exchange rates) can be substantial and probably have a powerful influence on expenditures. Note that these revaluation effects are analytically distinct from those discussed above.

5.2.11 Mundell–Fleming Model with Flexible Prices

Our open-economy model has already become rather complex, with a large number of interdependencies between the variables. Nevertheless it is possible to outline ways in which we might incorporate price changes in the model. Because the MF model (in general) allows changes in output there is a link via a Phillips curve relationship with *wage* inflation, $\dot{w}$, and price inflation, $\dot{p}$, responding directly to excess demand $(y - \bar{y})$. However, it is often assumed that prices are determined by a mark-up on unit wage costs and domestic (sterling) import prices of raw materials; hence our wage–price model is[9]

$$\dot{w} = \dot{\chi}_w + a_1\dot{p} + a_2(y - \bar{y}) + f \tag{5.13}$$
$$\dot{p} = b_1(\dot{w} - \dot{\chi}_p) + b_2\dot{p}_m \tag{5.14}$$

where

$$\dot{p}_m = \dot{p}^* + \dot{s}$$

A dot over a variable indicates a time derivative, $\dot{\chi}_w$ is the trend growth in real wages, $\dot{\chi}_p$ is the trend growth in labour productivity and f represents 'wage-push' factors (e.g. trade union militancy). Substituting (5.13) into (5.14) we obtain

$$\dot{p} = (1 - a_1 b_1)^{-1}[b_1(\dot{\chi}_w - \dot{\chi}_p) + b_2\dot{p}_m + a_2 b_1(y - \bar{y}) + b_1 f]. \tag{5.15}$$

If we make the reasonable assumptions that in the long run $\dot{\chi}_w = \dot{\chi}_p$, there is no money illusion $(a_1 = 1)$ and there is homogeneity with respect to total costs $(b_1 + b_2 = 1)$, then (5.15) becomes

$$\dot{p} = \frac{b_1}{1 - b_1}[f + a_2(y - \bar{y})] + (\dot{p}^* + \dot{s}). \tag{5.16}$$

If we ignore the predominantly cyclical factors in equation (5.16), namely $(y - \bar{y})$ and f[10], then the long-run secular influences on domestic prices are p^* and s. Hence, under fixed exchange rates, this wage–price sub-model explains why domestic inflation is linked directly with foreign inflation $(\dot{p}^*)$. In addition, a step devaluation (i.e. an increase in s) leads to an equal increase in domestic prices; hence, in the long run a devaluation does not lead to expenditure switching since competitiveness remains unaltered. Now, given this result, how can we account for the improvement in say the UK payments position after the 1967 devaluation of sterling? Several answers are possible. One explanation is that world trade happens to have grown faster over the period; but the more important reason is that the induced price rise was deflationary: real after-tax incomes fell (as less-than-full indexation of tax allowances and welfare benefits caused 'fiscal drag') (Ball et al. 1977). Note also that the above wage–price sub-model also explains why a small open economy would have a relatively large change in inflation after the oil price rises of 1973 and 1979, and their fall in 1985–6. Abstracting from cyclical factors our sub-model predicts

$$\dot{p} = \dot{p}^* + \dot{s}$$

that is, that domestic prices rise at the same rate as foreign prices expressed in domestic currency ($\dot{p}^* + \dot{s}$); or equivalently that the real exchange rate is constant in the long run (or varies according to secular productivity trends if $\chi_w \neq \chi_p$). This is known as the (weak) *purchasing power parity* (PPP) condition which we reintroduce below, with a somewhat different interpretation. Under floating exchange rates, for equilibrium in the goods market ($y = \bar{y}$) and with constant push factors 'f', our sub-model predicts that PPP will hold in the long run. Note however that in this 'floating world' the model says nothing about the direction of causation between s and p (remember p^* is exogenous). Here, PPP is an *equilibrium* relationship, and does not uniquely determine changes in the exchange rate.

The Short-Run Impact on Output and Prices   How might the above sub-model alter the short-run impact of monetary and fiscal policy in the MF model under floating exchange rates, with 'high' but less-than-perfect capital mobility? Monetary and fiscal policy are expansionary and this is likely to put upward pressure on prices, more so in the case of monetary policy since this also causes a depreciation of the domestic currency (§5.24). An increase in the rate of inflation then has feedback effects on aggregate demand in a number of ways. First, an increase in the expected rate of inflation that is not fully reflected in higher nominal interest rates leads to a fall in real interest rates and this may increase real investment. Second, there may be a 'revaluation wealth effect' working via the 'inflation loss' on financial assets and this may reduce expenditure as individuals attempt to rebuild the real value of their financial assets. To see this, note that the change in real wealth RW is given by

$$\Delta \text{RW} = [\, W_{t-1}(1+r)/P_t\,] - (W/P)_{t-1} \tag{5.17}$$

where W is nominal wealth, r is the current period interest rate and P is the price level. If we now substitute in the identity $P_t = (1+\dot{p})P_{t-1}$ where $\dot{p}$ is the (proportionate) rate of inflation we obtain

$$\Delta \text{RW} = \frac{r-\dot{p}}{1+\dot{p}}\left(\frac{W}{P}\right)_{t-1} \tag{5.18}$$

Therefore the real value of the outstanding stock of wealth falls if the rate of inflation exceeds the nominal interest rate paid on the outstanding stock – that is, if *real* interest rates are negative. Of course if one is a net debtor then negative real interest rates confer an inflation gain. The personal sector is usually a net creditor and has positive net worth. For substantial periods of time the real rate of interest may be negative and the real value of personal sector net financial wealth falls. There is a great deal of evidence to suggest that this revaluation effect caused by inflation may lead to more saving and less consumption (Davidson et al. 1978, Hendry and von Ungern Sternberg 1979). For non-interest-bearing assets such as cash and sight deposits a higher rate of inflation always leads to an increase in the inflation loss on these assets. Assets held by the personal sector that are liabilities of the company sector yield no inflation gains or losses for the *private* sector as a whole; inflation merely alters the distribution of wealth. If the liabilities of the authorities (i.e. high-powered money and government bonds) are considered as net wealth by the private sector, then the inflation loss effect will operate on these assets. Individuals may alter their spending plans on the basis of past 'inflation losses' or future expected losses and empirical work appears to show that these effects are substantial.

The effect of inflation on the market value of a company and hence on equity prices may lead to an inflation gain and clearly this concept may be applied to real as well as financial assets. The personal sector, for example, has substantial wealth in the form of the housing stock and if house prices rise faster than the general level of consumer prices an inflation gain accrues (Cuthbertson 1982, Kennally 1985). However, it is debatable whether this influences consumers' expenditure other than for those expecting to hold a lower stock of housing in the future (e.g. those near retirement).

If the expansionary monetary policy results in a fall in the exchange rate then foreign-denominated assets held by domestic residents increase in value in terms of the domestic currency, and this may lead to increased spending (although evidence on this is scant)[11].

The above 'wealth effects' involve a *revaluation* of existing holdings of assets and must be distinguished from the wealth effects in §§1.4 and 5.2.7–5.2.10 which involve changes in the outstanding stock of *nominal* wealth (with a fixed price level). In practice both types of wealth effect occur.

As discussed above, if wage increases lag behind price increases, or government welfare payments and tax allowances and rates are not fully adjusted for inflation, then in the short run real incomes are squeezed which almost certainly leads to a reduction in consumers' expenditure and aggregate demand.

All of the above effects also have a feedback into the balance of payments. Any subsequent rise in prices tends to nullify the expenditure switching effect of the initial depreciation, while changes in aggregate demand directly influence imports. In the short run the precise effect on output, the exchange rate and the balance of payments of monetary and fiscal policy depends on all the coefficients and may be very sensitive to slight changes in the parameters of the model (for example, see the simulations reported in Wallis 1985, 1986) and can only be examined case by case. Thus we can at this stage only provide a list of positive and negative feedbacks on output and prices. The *net* effect of all of these factors requires the use of macroeconometric (or simulation) models.

5.3   The Current Account Monetary (CAM) Model

In the early 1970s a flex-price model of the open economy emerged known as 'current account monetarism' (occasionally, also referred to as the Chicago view because its main progenitors were associated with the University of Chicago). Reduced to its bare essentials the key elements are that (i) price arbitrage in a 'perfect goods' market yields purchasing power parity (PPP) together with (ii) the assumption of a (simple) stable demand for money function. The CAM model implies that, under fixed exchange rates, domestic inflation is determined solely by foreign prices and hence is 'imported'. The payments position is determined *solely* by the expansion in the domestic money supply. The main novelty, however, occurs with a flexible-exchange-rate regime where domestic inflation is determined by the domestic money supply and the exchange rate by the domestic *relative to* the 'foreign' rate of monetary expansion, this gives the model its monetarist flavour. Another monetarist element is the assumption that output is determined by 'the neoclassical supply side' model and is therefore at the full-employment level in the long run.

5.3.1 Purchasing Power Parity (PPP)

If domestic tradeable goods are perfect substitutes for foreign goods and the goods market is 'perfect' (i.e. there are low transactions costs, perfect information, perfectly flexible prices, no artificial (government) restrictions on trading), then 'middlemen' (arbitrageurs) will ensure that the price is equalized in a common currency. The PPP view of price determination assumes that domestic (tradeable) goods prices will be subject to arbitrage so as to equal the price in domestic currency of foreign goods. If the foreign currency price is P^* (say dollars) and the exchange rate measured as the domestic currency per unit of foreign currency (say sterling per dollar) is S, then the price of a foreign import in domestic currency is (SP^*). Domestic producers of a close (perfect) substitute for the foreign good and arbitrageurs in the market will ensure that *domestic* prices P equal SP^*:

$$P = SP^* \quad \text{(strong form)} \tag{5.19}$$
$$\dot{P} = \dot{S} + \dot{P^*} \quad \text{(weak form).}[12] \tag{5.20}$$

If domestic prices were higher than P^*S, then domestic producers would be priced out of the market and if they sold at a price lower than SP^* they would lose profits since they believe they can sell all they can produce at the going price. This is the usual perfect competition assumption, here applied to domestic and foreign firms. Observationally, the PPP idea gives a similar view of inflation under fixed exchange rates to the Phillips curve approach discussed above. However, the mechanisms that ensure PPP are very different in the two approaches.

The inflationary mechanism for fixed exchange rates in the CAM model involves domestic (tradeable) prices being arbitraged upwards after a devaluation or a rise in foreign prices, one for one. Inflation is therefore 'imported' and closely follows the world (foreign) rate of inflation. Devaluation does not alter price competitiveness and hence is ineffective in altering the trade balance in the long run. If we extend the CAM model slightly and recognize that the domestic aggregate price level also comprises non-tradeable goods (e.g. domestic internal transport), which are likely to be influenced by productivity (i.e. the Nordic model, see Cuthbertson 1979 for an overview) or by domestic excess demand (unemployment) then the association between the CAM model and the above Phillips curve approach under fixed exchange rates is even more apparent. However, although the conclusions on inflation and devaluation under fixed exchange rates are similar in the two models the transmission mechanisms are obviously very different.

In the CAM model, under fixed exchange rates, only an increase in the (domestic component of the) money supply leads to an increase in the demand for foreign goods and assets (via the familiar real balance effect) and hence causes a payments deficit on current and capital accounts combined. Excess demand 'spills over' or is 'exported' via the balance of payments. This contrasts with a neo-Keynesian model where fiscal policy and other domestic factors would also be allowed to influence the price level.

Note that in the CAM model it is not the absence of expenditure switching that is crucial in nullifying the long-run effects of step devaluation but the assumption of equilibrium in asset (money) stocks. The balance of payments is a flow and there cannot be asset stock equilibrium until flows are zero. A temporary payments surplus after a devaluation increases the money supply (via changes in foreign exchange reserves, ΔR) and this real balance effect tends to reduce the surplus. It is not possible for the authorities to offset the increase in the foreign component of the money supply and hence ensure a permanent surplus? Sales of government debt to the domestic NBPS, equal to the change in R (i.e. $\Delta D = -\Delta R$) would prevent the total money supply increasing: this is a policy of *sterilization*. However, as argued in §5.2.3 sterilization is not feasible in the long run with high capital mobility.

5.3.2   The CAM Model for Flexible Exchange Rates

For flexible exchange rates the CAM model may be used to explain the stylized facts of the behaviour of the inflation rate and the nominal exchange rate in small open economies. For example, countries with relatively high rates of monetary growth such as the UK and Italy in the early 1970s are expected to have high rates of inflation and depreciating exchange rates. The converse also applies, as was broadly typical of Germany, Switzerland and Japan in the early 1970s.

The CAM model relies on the PPP condition and a stable demand for money. The (logarithm) of the demand for money may be assumed to depend on (the logarithm of) real income, y, the price level, p, and the level of the (bond) interest rate, r. We assume a similar foreign demand-for-money function (foreign variables are starred below). Monetary equilibria in the domestic and foreign country are

$$m^s = p + \phi y - \lambda r \tag{5.21}$$
$$m^{s*} = p^* + \phi^* y^* - \lambda^* r^*. \tag{5.22}$$

In the CAM model the domestic interest rate is exogenous/fixed – a rather peculiar property. This is not due to the liquidity trap or an infinitely elastic investment schedule. It arises because the domestic interest rate is rigidly linked to the exogenous world interest rate because of the assumption of 'perfect capital mobility' and a zero expected change in the exchange rate. We discuss this 'uncovered interest parity' condition further in a section on capital account monetarism. Given that output is also assumed fixed at the full-employment level (the neoclassical supply curve) then any excess money can only influence the 'perfectly flexible' domestic price level, one for one: the neutrality proposition holds.

Equilibrium in the traded goods 'market' (i.e. the current account) ensues when there are no further profitable incentives for trade flows to occur – that is, when prices in a common currency are equalized: in short when PPP holds. Using lower-case letters to denote logarithms, the PPP condition is:

$$s = p - p^*. \tag{5.23}$$

The world price, p^*, is exogenous to the domestic economy, being determined by the world money supply. The domestic money supply determines the domestic price level and hence the exchange rate is determined by *relative* money supplies. Algebraically, substituting (5.21) and (5.22) into (5.23) gives

$$s = (m^s - m^{s*}) - \phi y + \phi^* y^* + \lambda r - \lambda^* r^*. \tag{5.24}$$

Possible transmission mechanisms underlying (5.24) are: (i) an increase in the domestic money supply leads to an increased demand for *foreign* goods (and assets), an excess demand for foreign currency and a depreciation in the domestic currency (the latter increases import prices in domestic currency and domestic producers 'arbitrage' domestic prices upwards to match the new level of import prices of tradeable goods); alternatively, (ii) excess money balances, which cause an excess demand for *domestic* goods, followed by a rise in domestic prices via the Phillips curve. This is followed by a switch to relatively cheaper foreign goods causing downward pressure on the domestic exchange rate. It is probably (i) that is closest to the spirit of the CAM price arbitrage approach.

It is worth noting that the effect of output and the domestic interest rate on the exchange rate in the CAM model are contrary to those found in a 'Keynesian' model. In the latter a higher level of output or lower domestic interest rates lead to a payments deficit and a depreciation in the domestic currency. In contrast, in the CAM model these effects increase the domestic demand for money, allow a lower domestic price level to achieve money market equilibrium, and hence result in an *appreciation* in the exchange rate (see, for example, Frenkel et al. 1980, Gylfason and Helliwell 1983). Now, a rise in nominal interest rates may ensue because of a tight monetary policy or because of an increase in the expected rate of inflation, π. The Fisher hypothesis states that real rates of interest ψ are constant[13] in the long run:

$$r = \psi + \pi. \tag{5.25}$$

Adding this relationship to the CAM model of equation (5.24) we see that a high expected rate of domestic inflation is associated with a high nominal interest rate and a low domestic exchange rate (i.e. S has a 'high' value). Thus the interest-rate–exchange-rate relationship appears somewhat less perverse when the Fisher hypothesis is added to the CAM model to yield what one might term the *hyper-inflation – CAM model*. The latter terminology arises because r is dominated by changes in π in hyper-inflations (e.g. as in Germany in the 1920s). This is all very well but one might be more disposed to view the rate of depreciation (i.e. the *change* in S rather than the level of S) as depending on the expected rate of inflation and this is investigated in §5.5.1 when discussing the Frankel (1979) 'real-interest' CAM model.

We noted above that a rise in r in the CAM model cannot be due to tight money, since r is rigidly linked to r^* because of perfect capital mobility and the assumption that the exchange rate is expected to remain constant. We are able to relax this very restrictive assumption when discussing capital account monetary (KAM) models in the next section.

The CAM model as presented here may be tested by estimating equations of the form (5.24) for the exchange rate or by investigating the stability of the PPP relationship and the demand for money functions. As far as equation (5.24) is concerned it worked reasonably well empirically in the early 1970s' floating period for a number of bilateral exchange rates (see Bilson 1978), but in the late 1970s the relationship performed badly other than for countries with high inflation (e.g. Argentina and Brazil). The increase in *capital* mobility in the 1970s and its cursory treatment in the CAM model may account for the failure of the latter and we discuss this in §5.4. Although there are difficulties in testing the PPP relationship, it too does not appear to hold in the latter half of the 1970s (Frenkel 1981).

5.3.3   *A Synthesis of Mundell–Fleming and Capital Accounts Monetarist (CAM) Models: Floating Exchange Rate*

Our MF model with the addition of a PEAPC (i.e. MF + PEAPC) allows output and price changes in the short run, but the long-run vertical PEAPC implies that output ultimately remains at the NAIRU, $y = \bar{y}$ (or natural rate), and PPP holds (other than for 'push factors', see equation (5.16)). The interest rate and output are endogenous in the MF model but exogenous in the CAM model and, in the latter, government expenditure plays no role. Hence the CAM model would appear to be a restrictive version of MF + PEAPC. For ease of exposition we only discuss the two models with respect to the flexible-exchange-rate case (after which the link between the two approaches is easy enough for the reader to deduce in the fixed-rate case).

Consider the impact of changes in the money supply in the MF + PEAPC model. The long-run vertical Phillips curve is represented by the vertical aggregate supply curve as in figure 5.9 and for illustrative purposes we assume perfect capital mobility (the latter assumption is not crucial in what follows). An increase in the money supply increases aggregate demand (A to B) and puts upward pressure on prices via the Phillips curve. The rise in prices reduces the real money supply and aggregate demand falls back to A. At A, $r = r^*$, $y = \bar{y}_f$ and $\Delta m^s = \Delta p$; hence we have money market equilibrium. Since r and y are unchanged, goods market equilibrium requires a depreciation of the domestic currency (s increases) to maintain a constant level of the real exchange rate and net trade demand. Hence PPP holds. Algebraically, with $y = \bar{y}_f$, the open-economy IS curve is

$$\bar{y}_f = \delta(s + p^* - p) - \sigma r + \gamma \bar{y}_f - w \bar{y}_f + \gamma^* \qquad (5.26)$$

where σr, $\gamma \bar{y}_f$, $w \bar{y}_f$ and γ^* represent investment, consumption, imports and exogenous expenditures, respectively. The LM curves for the domestic and foreign economies are

$$p = m^s + \lambda r - \phi \bar{y}_f \qquad (5.27)$$
$$p^* = m^{s*} + \lambda^* r^* - \phi^* \bar{y}_f^* \qquad (5.28)$$

Substituting for p and p^* from (5.27) and (5.28) in (5.26) and rearranging we obtain

$$s = (m^s - m^{s*}) + \lambda r - \lambda^* r^* - \phi \bar{y}_f + \phi^* y_f^* + \delta^{-1} [\sigma r + (1 - \gamma + w) \bar{y}_f - \gamma^*]. \qquad (5.29)$$

Now equation (5.29) is very similar to the CAM exchange rate equation (5.24). There is homogeneity with respect to relative money supplies. Ignoring the last term in (5.29) the relationship between s and r, r^*, $\bar{y}_f$, y^* is the same as in the CAM model. Note, however, that in deriving our 'CAM-like' equation (5.29) we have not used the balance-of-payments equilibrium

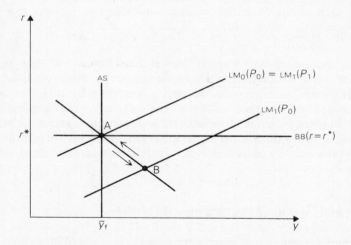

Figure 5.9 Monetary policy MF + PEAPC, flexible exchange rates

equation (i.e. the BB line) of the MF model and this emphasizes the fact that the CAM model can only be reconciled with the MF approach if there is perfect capital mobility and static expectations (i.e. the BB line becomes $r = r^*$). If foreign and domestic goods are close substitutes then δ will be large and the last term in (5.29) will be negligible. Thus the CAM model assumes perfect goods substitutability and as $\delta \to \infty$ then (5.29) reduces to (5.24).[14]

Turning now to fiscal policy in the MF + PEAPC model, fiscal policy is completely crowded out because the appreciation in the exchange rate at B (figure 5.10) causes a fall in real net trade, shifting the IS curve back to A. (Note that we could *not* end up at C after an induced price rise because capital mobility requires $r = r^*$.) Hence, for 'full employment' and perfect capital mobility the usual MF result of complete crowding out applies and this is consistent with the CAM result that fiscal policy does not influence output or the price level.

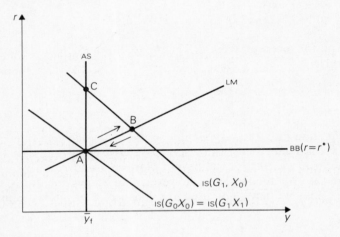

Figure 5.10   Fiscal policy, MF + PEAPC, flexible exchange rates $(G_1 > G_0,\ X_0 > X_1)$

To summarize, the MF + PEAPC model is more general than the CAM approach and to obtain the latter we need to add the restrictive assumptions of (i) a full-employment level of output, (ii) perfect substitutability between foreign and domestic goods (i.e. $\delta \to \infty$) and (iii) perfect capital mobility (i.e. $r = r^*$). Note that both models assume static expectations about the exchange rate and therefore do not explicitly model expectations formation in any meaningful way. The latter defect is remedied in KAM models to which we now turn.

5.4   Capital Account Monetarist (KAM) Models

In the latter half of the 1970s the CAM model ceased to provide an accurate description of the behaviour of exchange rates for a number of small open economies. For example, in the UK over the period 1979–81 the sterling *nominal* effective exchange rate (i.e. the rate against a basket of currencies) appreciated substantially even though the UK money supply grew rapidly relative to the growth in the 'world' money supply. However, more startling, the *real* exchange rate (i.e. price competitiveness or the terms of trade) appreciated by about 40 per cent over this period and this was followed by an equally sharp fall over the 1981–4 period. The CAM model can only explain changes in the real exchange rate by *differential short-run lags* in the response of the nominal exchange rate and the domestic (and foreign) price level to changes in relative money supplies. Faced with the kind of evidence cited above these lags appeared to be variable or, in other words, the CAM model failed to explain this phenomenon adequately. Large volatile swings in the real exchange rate may lead to large swings in net trade (i.e. real exports less real imports) with consequent multiplier effects on domestic output and employment. In the CAM model, output is determined outside the model and unless the model is extended it is incapable of explaining changes in real output. KAM models provide an explanation of exchange rate 'overshooting' together with short-run changes in real output, as for example occurred in the very severe recession of 1979–82 in the UK. The seminal paper of Dornbusch (1976) provides a starting point for our analysis of KAM models.

KAM models are also able to resolve the conundrum found in CAM models where one obtains the counter-intuitive result that a rise in domestic interest rates leads to a depreciation in the domestic currency. In the KAM approach if the rise in the nominal interest rate reflects a higher expected domestic rate of inflation, then the CAM result holds; but if the rise in nominal rates is unexpected and hence constitutes a rise in *real* interest rates the conventional result, namely an appreciation in the exchange rate, ensues. The extension by Frankel (1979) of the Dornbusch (1976) approach reconciles these two viewpoints.

It is widely thought that the appreciation of sterling over the 1976–9 period had something to do with the emergence of sterling as a petro-currency as North Sea Oil came rapidly on-stream. We can extend the Dornbusch (1976) KAM model to analyse the effects of a tradeable resource discovery on the exchange rate.

As KAM models are relatively sophisticated it is perhaps worthwhile briefly summarizing their key elements before proceeding to a detailed analysis.

Like the CAM models the KAM models as usually presented are 'monetarist' in the sense that the neutrality of money is preserved in the long run by invoking a vertical neoclassical supply curve for output (or equivalently the vertical long-run Phillips curve). However, PPP holds only in the long run and hence short-run changes in the real net trade balance are allowed. Key elements in KAM models are the assumption of a conventional, stable demand for money function and the so-called uncovered-interest-parity (or open-arbitrage) condition. In the 1970s the gradual removal of exchange controls and the lowering of transactions costs in switching between domestic and foreign assets due to improved technology (e.g. computers and telecommunications) led to increased capital mobility and an emphasis on the exchange rate as the 'price' that 'jumps' to clear the capital account. A view gradually emerged that capital account transactions, potential and actual, are more important than current account flows in determining movements in exchange rates particularly in the short run. In modelling capital account transactions the KAM models frequently invoke the simplifying assumption of perfect capital mobility and 'risk-neutral' speculators. Agents in the foreign exchange market are concerned only with the expected return from speculation and disregard any risk attached to their transactions. Hence expected returns from investing in domestic and foreign assets are equalized: that is, the so-called open-arbitrage condition holds. Agents in the foreign exchange market are assumed to form (Muth-) rational expectations about the future path of the exchange rate: they immediately act on any new information and this is what makes the exchange rate 'jump' and undergo frequent changes. In addition, in KAM models the capital account and the money market 'clear' in all periods, but the goods market, where prices are sticky, does not. It is this combination of 'flex-price' and 'fix-price' markets that can produce exchange rate overshooting.

Thus KAM models extend the MF and CAM approach by explicitly modelling expectations about the exchange rate and in allowing prices to be endogenous. In the versions of the KAM approach discussed below we exclude 'wealth effects' of any kind, as the analysis then becomes overly complex (Nguyen and Turnovsky 1980, 1983).

5.4.1   The Dornbusch Exchange Rate Overshooting Model

We present a simplified account of the Dornbusch (1976) model beginning with a description of the main behavioural assumptions, followed by an analysis of the impact of a tight monetary stance on the economy. The details of the mathematics and the rational-expectations solution of the model are relegated to appendix 5.1.

The *uncovered-interest-parity* (open-arbitrage) relationship expresses the condition for equilibrium in the capital account. Foreign exchange speculators investing abroad *expect* a return of $r^* + \dot{S}^e$ per cent where $r^* =$ foreign interest rate, $\dot{S}^e =$ expected *appreciation* of the *foreign* currency (depreciation in the domestic currency). Risk neutrality (by definition) implies that agents are indifferent to the riskiness of the transaction and are concerned only with the expected return from their investments. Hence with perfect capital mobility, equilibrium in the capital account requires equality of expected returns:

$$r = r^* + \dot{S}^e = r^* + \mu \qquad (5.30)$$

where $\mu = \dot{S}^e$ is used for ease of exposition.

Any deviation from this open-arbitrage condition will be immediately met by potential or actual capital flows.[15] As agents attempt to exploit expected profitable opportunities the open-arbitrage condition is continuously re-established. For example a rise in r^* leads to a capital outflow, downward pressure on domestic bond prices and a rise in r, or, alternatively, an expectation of an appreciation in the domestic currency.

Expectations about the exchange rate are assumed to be regressive. If the actual rate lies below the long-run equilibrium rate, $\bar{s}$, then agents expect the actual rate to rise towards the long-run rate; that is, for the domestic rate to *depreciate*,

$$\mu = \theta(\bar{s} - s) \qquad 0 < \theta < 1 \tag{5.31}$$

where s and $\bar{s}$ are in logarithms. This expectations generating equation may be made fully consistent with rational expectations in that the regressive formula allows expectations to be correct *ex post*, given the other equations in the Dornbusch model (see appendix 5.1). Equilibrium in the money market implies

$$m^s = -\lambda r + \phi y + p. \tag{5.32}$$

In the goods market, aggregate demand AD (i.e. the IS curve) is given by

$$AD = \delta(s - p + p^*) - \sigma r + \gamma y + \gamma'. \tag{5.33}$$

The first term represents the impact of the real exchange rate on *net* trade volumes, the second $(-\sigma r)$ the investment schedule, the third (γy) the consumption function *and* expenditure effects on imports and the final term (γ') exogenous demand factors such as government expenditure. The 'supply side' is represented by a vertical long-run Phillips curve: the rate of inflation responds to excess demand in the goods market; prices adjust slowly to equilibrium $(0 < \Pi < 1)$,

$$\dot{p} = \Pi(AD - \bar{y}) = \Pi[\delta(s - p + p^*) - \sigma r + \gamma y + \gamma' - \bar{y}] \tag{5.34}$$

where $\bar{y}$ is the full-employment level of output.[16]

Flexible Prices: Long Run   Consider a reduction of one per cent in the money supply. If the latter is perfectly anticipated (expected) and prices perfectly flexible, a fall of one per cent in the price level will restore money market equilibrium. In addition, if the exchange rate also immediately appreciates by one per cent, the *real* exchange rate remains constant and real aggregate demand continues to match aggregate supply. Since there has been no change in the interest rate, real investment is unchanged and uncovered interest parity still holds: immediately after the instantaneous appreciation, the exchange rate is *expected* to remain constant. Thus in this case the exchange rate immediately attains its long-run equilibrium value: there is no 'overshooting'. As prices in KAM models are *not* sticky *in the long run*, the above scenario reflects long-run equilibrium in the Dornbusch model.

Fixed Prices: Overshooting

In contrast, now assume prices and output are sticky in the short run. With y and p 'sticky', a decrease in the money supply requires a rise in the bond rate, r, to 'clear' the money market ($dr = -(1/\lambda)\ dm^s$, equation (5.32)). The rise in r causes a potential capital inflow, which can be arrested only if the domestic exchange rate is expected to depreciate, thus re-establishing uncovered interest parity. According to equation (5.31) an *expected* depreciation of the domestic currency requires the *actual* spot rate immediately to appreciate above its long equilibrium value; hence the exchange rate 'overshoots' its long-run value.

It is useful at this stage to present a very simplified account of the mathematics behind this result (a more general formulation is given in appendix 5.1). Because of the vertical Phillips curve, output is fixed in the long run and the neutrality of money implies $dp = dm$. As PPP also holds in the long run, $d\bar{s} = dp = dm^s$ (where a bar over a variable indicates its long-run value).[17] Turning to the short run, assume p and y are fixed so that any short-run disequilibrium in the money market is taken up by adjustments in r:

$$dr = -dm^s/\lambda. \tag{5.35}$$

To preserve uncovered interest parity in the short run the *expected* appreciation in the exchange rate $d\mu$ must equal the interest differential dr (note that $dr^* = 0$):

$$d\mu = dr = -dm^s/\lambda \tag{5.36}$$

From the expectations equation (5.31) and using (5.36) above, the *short-run* change in the exchange rate is

$$ds = d\bar{s} - d\mu/\theta = [1 + (\theta\lambda)^{-1}]\ dm^s. \tag{5.37}$$

Since $\theta\lambda > 0$ the initial change in the spot rate of $[1 + (\theta\lambda)^{-1}]\ dm^s$ exceeds the 'unit' long-run change: $d\bar{s} = dm^s$.

It is clear that 'overshooting' is in part due to the restrictive channels through which monetary policy is forced to operate. Initially all adjustment in the money market is via the interest rate and only in the long run does the price level equilibrate the money market and the interest rate return to its original level. Although it is not immediately apparent from the above analysis, the assumption of perfect capital mobility (and risk neutrality) is of equal importance in this respect. Note that, in contrast to the prediction of the CAM model, the response of the exchange rate to the interest rate is as one might intuitively expect: an unanticipated jump in the interest rate consequent on a fall in the money supply leads to an appreciation of the domestic currency. We now wish to repeat the above analysis while also allowing prices to change 'slowly' in the short run via the Phillips curve. Do we still get overshooting if prices are *partly* flexible? The answer is yes. We demonstrate this using a reasonably simple approach, which utilizes the equations as deviations from some long-run equilibrium and allows one to use a graphical exposition. (The full rational-expectations solution is given in appendix 5.1.) For analytical simplicity we hold output constant in the short run.

Overshooting: Fixed Output, Partly Flexible Prices We wish to examine the short- and long-run behaviour of prices and the spot rate (with output fixed, $y = \bar{y}$) after a reduction in the money supply. First consider the relationship between $p - \bar{p}$ and $s - \bar{s}$ when we impose money market, and bond market (i.e. uncovered-interest-parity, equation (5.30)) equilibrium and also utilize the expectations equation (5.31) for the exchange rate: we call these three conditions 'asset market equilibrium'. In static (long-run) equilibrium $\mu = 0$, $r = r^*$, $s = \bar{s}$, $y = \bar{y}$, $p = \bar{p}$ and hence money market equilibrium yields

$$m^s - \bar{p} = -\lambda r^* + \phi \bar{y}. \tag{5.38}$$

In the *short run*, using

$$m^s - p = -\lambda \theta (\bar{s} - s) - \lambda r^* + \phi \bar{y} \tag{5.39}$$

and subtracting (5.39) from (5.38) we obtain our *asset market equilibrium* locus AA' (figure 5.1) given by

$$p - \bar{p} = -\lambda \theta (s - \bar{s}). \tag{5.40}$$

The economics behind this negative relationship is that a rise in p (m^s fixed) leads to a rise in r to equilibrate the money market. The latter requires an expectation of a depreciation (equation (5.30)) to preserve uncovered interest parity; but because of the way expectations are formed (equation (5.31)) the latter requires s to fall below $\bar{s}$ (s then rises towards $\bar{s}$ – that is, there is a *depreciation*). Note that AA' shifts to the right if m^s increases.

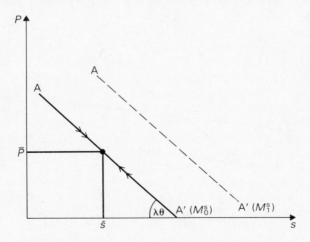

Figure 5.11 The asset market equilibrium locus, AA'

Goods market equilibrium is given by the Phillips curve when $\dot{p}=0$. To obtain a relationship between $p-\bar{p}$ and $s-\bar{s}$ we first need to eliminate r from equation (5.34) by substituting from the money market equilibrium equation (5.32). Hence, noting our fixed-output assumption, $y=\bar{y}$, we obtain

$$\dot{p}=\pi\left[\delta(s-p+p^*)+(\sigma/\lambda)(m^s-p)-q\bar{y}+\gamma'\right] \tag{5.41}$$

where $q=[(\phi\sigma/\lambda)+(1-\gamma)]$. Long-run equilibrium with m^s, $\gamma'p^*$ (and $\bar{y}$) held constant arises with $\dot{p}=0$, $s=\bar{s}$ and $p=\bar{p}$; hence, from (5.41) we have

$$0=\pi\left[\delta(\bar{s}-\bar{p}+p^*)+(\sigma/\lambda)(m^s-\bar{p})-q\bar{y}+\gamma'\right]. \tag{5.42}$$

Subtracting (5.42) from (5.41) gives the *goods–money (G–M) equilibrium* locus (in terms of *deviations* from long-run equilibrium values, $\bar{p}$, $\bar{s}$):

$$\dot{p}=\pi\left[\delta(s-\bar{s})+(\delta+\sigma/\lambda)(\bar{p}-p)\right]. \tag{5.43}$$

For $\dot{p}=0$, equation (5.43) implies a positive relationship between p and s; on rearranging we obtain

$$p-\bar{p}=\frac{\delta}{\delta+\sigma/\lambda}\,(s-\bar{s})=\frac{1}{1+\sigma/\lambda\delta}\,(s-\bar{s}) \tag{5.44}$$

with the slope $\partial p/\partial s$ less than unity (*G–M* in figure 5.12). The economics behind this result is as follows. A rise of one per cent in the price level leads via the money market (m^s fixed) to a rise in r. In the goods market the latter causes a fall in investment demand while the rise in the price level worsens

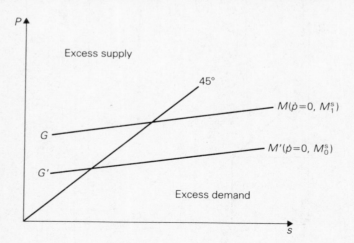

Figure 5.12   The goods-market–money-market equilibrium locus, *G–M*

competitiveness and net export demand also falls. The fall in demand puts downward pressure on prices. In the long run, a depreciation of one per cent (i.e. rise in s) would nullify the competitiveness effect, but because of the additional induced fall in investment demand the exchange rate must depreciate by more than one per cent to give a further positive stimulus to real net trade. Hence, for aggregate demand to remain unchanged (and $\dot{p} = 0$), a rise in p must be accompanied by a rise in s that is more than proportionate – hence the flattish $G–M$ schedule in figure 5.12. The $G–M$ schedule shifts to the left after an increase in the money supply: lower interest rates stimulate real investment and therefore the exchange rate must appreciate (i.e. s must fall) or prices rise, so net trade falls to keep aggregate demand constant.

We are now in a position to analyse 'overshooting' when prices are partly flexible in the short run (but output is constant). We begin at E_0 (figure 5.13) with equilibrium in all markets. After a reduction in the money supply the AA schedule shifts to the left and the $G–M$ schedule downwards: the new long-run equilibrium is on the 45° line at E_3 since we know that PPP holds (i.e. $\mathrm{d}p = \mathrm{d}s = \mathrm{d}m$). Agents must immediately jump onto the new A'A' schedule, since asset market equilibrium is continuously maintained, but they may slowly move towards the new $G'–M'$ schedule as prices are 'sticky'. If prices are absolutely rigid in the short run, we move to E_1 with exchange rate s_1 (this is the case analysed at the beginning of this section). If prices are partly flexible we immediately move to E_2 (with values s_2, p_2), with the (unique saddle-path) trajectory to equilibrium between E_2 and E_3. Along $E_2 E_3$ there is an excess supply of goods (we are above the new $G'–M'$ schedule), which causes prices to fall monotonically. However, in contrast

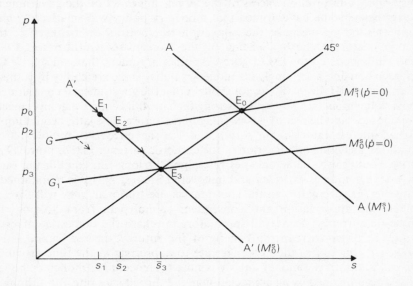

Figure 5.13 Contractionary monetary policy: exchange rate overshooting

the exchange rate overshoots its long-run equilibrium value $\bar{s}_3$ by the amount $s_2 - \bar{s}_3$.

The degree of overshooting clearly depends on the shape of the AA and G–M curves. The 'flatter' the G–M and AA curves are, the greater the degree of overshooting. It is shown in appendix 5.1 that under RE the parameter θ (and hence the slope of AA') depends on other parameters in the model, in a rather complex way. The conclusion reached is that the degree of overshooting is larger, when the competitiveness (δ) and interest elasticities (σ) of aggregate demand are smaller and when the interest elasticity of money demand (λ) is smaller. To see this, note that as λ becomes smaller we require a large change in interest rates to equilibrate the money market after a change in the money supply. To preserve uncovered interest parity then requires a large actual change in the spot rate. However, if σ and δ are 'small' there is little change in prices via the Phillips curve. Hence less of the disequilibrium in the money market is taken up by the price level and more by the interest rate. The latter then leads to overshooting as described above.

5.4.2   Extensions and Elaborations

Dornbusch-type models (see, e.g., Buiter and Miller 1982) have been used to analyse the qualitative movements in the UK exchange rate, particularly over the 1976–81 period which involved a rapid appreciation in the nominal and real (effective) exchange rate of sterling.

Was a tight monetary policy the cause of overshooting in the UK? Over the 1979–81 period of rapid appreciation the broad money supply £M3 grew very rapidly and well in excess of the target ranges set by the government. Nevertheless some have argued that monetary policy was relatively 'tight' over this period because the relaxation of controls on banks (i.e. the Supplementary Deposits Scheme or the Corset; see Cuthbertson 1985) artificially boosted the £M3 figures. Another argument that can square the appreciation and a seemingly lax monetary policy is the credibility hypothesis (Currie 1984). If the private sector thought that the governments' commitment to its stated monetary targets was strong then it would expect that any current overshoot would be met by a tightening in the future. The latter would imply higher interest rates *in the future* and via the uncovered-interest-parity condition an actual appreciation of the domestic currency in the future. (The latter would push the actual spot rate above its long-run equilibrium rate, so a depreciation is *expected* and uncovered interest parity is maintained.) However, if speculators in the spot market are 'rational' they will foresee this future appreciation and consequent capital gain from holding the domestic currency. Hence all speculators purchase the domestic currency *today*, in order to reap the benefit of the future expected capital gain. However, this causes the exchange rate to appreciate at the time at which the overshoot in the money supply is noted. Hence a lax monetary policy will be accompanied by an appreciation in the current spot rate if it is thought that the authorities will stick to their medium-term monetary targets. Finally, note that although £M3 grew rapidly, UK interest rates increased dramatically over this period and if they were considered to be a better indicator of the stance of monetary policy this would be consistent with overshooting in the exchange rate.

We have already noted that with perfectly flexible prices an (anticipated) change in the money supply does not cause 'overshooting'. Let us now consider the implications for overshooting of the degree of capital mobility. Risk-aversion models (Tobin 1956) suggest that the demand for assets depends on relative yields with the parameters of the demand functions determined by the risk characteristics (e.g. variances and covariances of returns; see Cuthbertson 1985) of the assets. Risk aversion implies that uncovered interest parity does not hold and hence equilibrium on the current plus capital account is given by

$$B = \delta(s - p + p^*) + \alpha(r - r^* + s^e - s) = 0 \tag{5.45}$$

where we have ignored income effects on trade flows. As $\alpha \to 0$ we have zero (low) capital mobility and $\alpha \to \infty$ leads to the uncovered-interest-parity condition. Frenkel and Rodriguez (1982) demonstrate that *undershooting* in the exchange rate is more likely for lower degrees of capital mobility and larger elasticities of trade flows with respect to competitiveness (δ). To take an extreme case, if $\alpha = 0$ the direct link between a tight monetary policy, the interest rate and the foreign exchange market is severed. To maintain continuous payments equilibrium the real exchange rate ($s - p + p^*$) must remain constant (at any given level of output). Hence p must adjust in line with s, and there is no overshooting. Even with a low (but non-zero) degree of capital mobility, after a reduction in the money supply any potential overshooting of Dornbusch type will cause a change in the trade balance, which tends to offset the inflow into the capital account; hence the tendency to overshooting is mitigated if the net trade flows are price-elastic.

There are no additional problems in analysing fiscal policy in the Dornbusch model. An increase in government expenditure, for example, leads to upward pressure in interest rates (the usual IS–LM case) which in turn triggers off overshooting if prices (and output) are sticky.

The impact of a resource discovery such as oil, or oil price changes, on a small open economy is a complex one, but of obvious importance in analysing the Dutch economy of the 1970s and the UK economy after about 1977. Obvious effects of an oil price rise include the redistribution of resources (income) from oil users to oil producers: asymmetry in spending patterns may then imply a fall in world trade and the demand for exports of our small open economy. In addition a country that is self-sufficient in oil may be perceived as a 'low-risk' area for portfolio investment and may induce a capital inflow and upward pressure on the exchange rate. To the extent that oil is used as an intermediate good a rise in its price requires a fall in real product wages if 'classical' unemployment is to be avoided. However, the resource re-allocation issues that arise on the production side (Forsyth and

Kay 1980, Brooks et al. 1986) lie outside our brief, and within the framework of the Dornbusch model we can only deal with demand side effects of an oil discovery. Oil resources constitute wealth which may be 'transferred' into an annuity or permanent income by, for example, investing oil receipts in foreign assets. An increase in permanent income may raise consumption (the life cycle hypothesis) and the demand for money. If f is the (log of the) annuity value of oil reserves that accrues in foreign currency (oil is priced in dollars on world markets) then (the logarithm of) *real* domestic permanent income is $f + s - p$. Broadly speaking, this variable is usually added to the aggregate demand and money demand equations of the Dornbusch model (see, e.g., Neary and van Wijnbergen 1984, Eastwood and Venables 1982).

The analysis of overshooting proceeds as follows. The annuity income from the oil discovery increases the transactions demand for money (i.e. the LM curve moves to the left) and has a direct impact on expenditure (i.e. the IS curve shifts to the right). Both of these effects tend to push up interest rates and hence lead to a sharp appreciation in the exchange rate to maintain uncovered interest parity. It may be shown that if the income from North Sea oil (NSO) is immediately paid out, then the direct expenditure effects outweigh any reduction in output caused by a short-run loss of competitiveness and an expansion occurs. However, the authorities, who receive the major portion of NSO wealth in the form of tax receipts, may either spend it or redistribute it in the form of tax cuts to the private sector or retire outstanding government debt. In the first two cases there is a direct demand effect, but in the latter case, which appears to be that taken by the UK government, there is not. Under such circumstances the fall in net trade caused by the appreciation in the exchange rate will lead to a recession in the short run. How long the recession lasts depends of course on the parameters of the model and the lag between the receipt of NSO taxes by the government and any disbursement in the form of tax cuts or increased expenditure. In appendix 5.2 we analyse the effects of a natural resource discovery using a simplified version of the model of Buiter and Miller (1981).

5.5   Interest Rates and the Exchange Rate

Is the relationship between domestic interest rates and the exchange rate positive or negative? If the authorities 'lean into the wind' then when the exchange rate depreciates they will tend to raise interest rates, hence $\partial r / \partial s > 0$ (remember, an increase in s is a depreciation of the domestic currency). However, we wish to exclude the possibility of such a reaction function for the authorities and concentrate on a 'clean float'. The CAM model somewhat counter-intuitively predicts a depreciation when interest rates rise ($\partial s / \partial r > 0$), because the latter reduces the demand for money and excess money spills over into foreign purchases (§5.3). However, if the rise in interest rates is due to upward revision concerning expectations about inflation, π, the hyper-inflation – CAM model predicts the opposite, namely $\partial s / \partial r < 0$.

In the Dornbusch model a rise in the interest rate signifies a tight monetary policy and in this 'portfolio' model (implicit in the uncovered-interest-parity condition) this causes an appreciation. Thus, there is no real conflict between these approaches; one (Dornbusch) assumes expected inflation does not affect interest rates and the demand for money; the other model does. It is the recognition that a change in the interest rate may be due either to anticipated events (e.g. a change in π) or to unanticipated events (e.g. an unexpected monetary contraction) that provides an insight into the interest-rate–exchange-rate link under a clean float. Two different approaches that embody this crucial distinction are the Frankel (1979) model and the Dornbusch (1980) 'news' model. We deal with each of these in turn.

5.5.1   The Frankel Model

Frankel (1979) provides a general model for analysing the impact of changes in the interest rate on the exchange rate and he refers to this as the 'real interest differential model'. It provides a Dornbusch relationship with respect to the nominal interest rate ($\partial s/\partial r < 0$) and a hyper-inflation–CAM solution with respect to the expected rate of inflation ($\partial s/\partial \pi > 0$). Also, the exchange rate may overshoot its equilibrium value.

Frankel's model assumes uncovered arbitrage but modifies the Dornbusch expectations equation for the exchange rate by adding a term reflecting relative expected secular inflation ($\pi - \pi^*$). The expectations equation is

$$s^e - s = \theta(\bar{s} - s) + (\pi - \pi^*) \tag{5.46}$$

and uncovered interest parity yields

$$s^e - s = r - r^*. \tag{5.47}$$

The expected rate of depreciation ($s^e - s$) depends upon the deviation of the exchange rate from its equilibrium value, which as we know gives Dornbusch-type results. In addition, if $s = \bar{s}$, the expected rate of depreciation is given by the expected inflation differential between the domestic and foreign currency: as we shall see this term generates hyper-inflation–CAM results. Frankel asserts that the expectations equation is a plausible, expectations generating mechanism *per se* but it may also be shown to be consistent with *rational* expectations. (We do not deal with this aspect.)

Combining equations (5.46) and (5.47) and rearranging we have

$$\bar{s} - s = (1/\theta)[(r - \pi) - (r^* - \pi^*)]. \tag{5.48}$$

The movement in the spot rate around its equilibrium value is determined by the relative *real* interest differential. Further, in long-run equilibrium, $s = \bar{s}$, which implies $\bar{r} - \bar{r} = \pi - \pi^*$; hence, the term in square brackets may be rewritten as $[(r - r^*) - (\bar{r} - \bar{r}^*)]$. It is only when a tight monetary policy raises the nominal interest differential $(r - r^*)$ above its long-run level $(\bar{r} - \bar{r}^*)$, given by relative expected inflation, that the 'current' exchange rate appreciates above its long-run equilibrium level $(\bar{s} - s > 0)$.

We now assume that PPP holds in the long run and with the usual demand-for-money functions (with $\phi = \phi^*$, $\lambda = \lambda^*$ for simplicity) we obtain an expression for the long-run exchange rate (as in the CAM model):

$$\bar{s} = \bar{p} - \bar{p}^* = \bar{m} - \bar{m}^* - \phi(\bar{y} - \bar{y}^*) + \lambda(\bar{r} - \bar{r}^*)$$
$$= (\bar{m} - \bar{m}^*) - \phi(\bar{y} - \bar{y}^*) + \lambda(\pi - \pi^*) \qquad (5.49)$$

where we have used $\bar{r} - \bar{r}^* = \pi - \pi^*$ (an 'international Fisher effect' which is implicit in the hyper-inflation–CAM model).

The cucial elements in the Frankel model are the expectations equation (5.46) and the distinction between the short-run and long-run determinants of the exchange rate. The long run is pure CAM with PPP (equation (5.49)). In the short run s can differ from $\bar{s}$ because of the way expectations are formed, as represented in equation (5.50).

Substituting for $\bar{s}$ from (5.48) in (5.49) we obtain Frankel's ('reduced-form') exchange rate regression equation:

$$s = \bar{m} - \bar{m}^* - \phi(\bar{y} - \bar{y}^*) - (1/\theta)(r - r^*) + [(1/\theta) + \lambda](\pi - \pi^*) \qquad (5.50)$$
$$s = \bar{m} - \bar{m}^* - \phi(\bar{y} - \bar{y}^*) + \alpha(r - r^*) + \beta(\pi - \pi^*) \qquad (5.51)$$

where $\alpha = -(1/\theta)$ and $\beta = (1/\theta) + \lambda$.

We can now characterize our three competing models in terms of the parameters α and β.

Table 5.3   The Frankel real-interest-rate model

	Model	Parameters
	Frankel	$\alpha < 0, \beta > 0; |\beta| > |\alpha|$
'Chicago'	CAM	$\alpha > 0, \beta = 0$
	CAM–hyper-inflation	$\alpha = 0, \beta > 0$
'Keynesian'	Dornbusch	$\alpha < 0, \beta = 0$

It is evident from table 5.3 that in the Frankel model we obtain a Dornbusch-type result $(\partial s / \partial r < 0)$ if interest rates increase while inflation expectations remain constant. This situation is likely to correspond to an *unanticipated* change in the money supply which has an immediate impact on interest rates (to 'clear' the money market) but is not immediately perceived as permanent and hence does not influence π. On the other hand an *equal* increase in the nominal interest rate, r, and inflationary expectations π cause a depreciation in the exchange rate $(\beta + \alpha > 0)$ – a CAM-type result. Hence, by adding an ancillary assumption to the Dornbusch-type model, namely equation (5.46) an *anticipated* increase in the money supply becomes likely to lead to an expected depreciation and (the Frankel model then predicts) an actual depreciation. Implicitly the Frankel model highlights the possible differential response of the exchange rate to anticipated and unanticipated changes in the money supply and interest rates. Dornbusch (1980) explains our interest-rate–exchange-rate conundrum in terms of this anticipated–unanticipated distinction using only the uncovered-interest-parity (UIP) relationship and it is this we now explore.

5.5.2 The Dornbusch News Model

The UIP condition (Dornbusch 1980) may be written

$$E_{t-1}s_t = s_{t-1} + d_{t-1} \tag{5.52}$$

where $E_{t-1}s_t$ is the expected value of the exchange rate formed with information available at time $t-1$ and $d_{t-1} = (r - r^*)_{t-1}$ is the interest differential at time $t-1$.

Equation (5.52) predicts that a known high positive interest differential, $d_{t-1} > 0$, is associated with an increase in the spot rate $(s_t - s_{t-1} > 0)$, that is, a depreciation of the domestic currency. As noted above, this is contrary to the Dornbusch portfolio view but consistent with the CAM model. The paradox may be resolved as follows. Consider individuals at time $t-1$ with a *two*-period decision $(t-1$ to $t+1)$. Uncovered arbitrage gives

$$E_{t-1}s_{t+1} = E_{t-1}s_t + E_{t-1}d_t. \tag{5.53}$$

Substituting (5.52) in (5.53) gives

$$E_{t-1}s_{t+1} = s_{t-1} + d_{t-1} + E_{t-1}d_t. \tag{5.54}$$

For a *one*-period decision *at time t*, we have

$$E_t s_{t+1} - s_t = d_t. \tag{5.55}$$

Subtracting (5.55) from (5.54) and rearranging:

$$s_t - s_{t-1} = d_{t-1} + [(E_t s_{t+1} - E_{t-1} s_{t+1}) - (d_t - E_{t-1} d_t)]. \tag{5.56}$$

We may interpret equation (5.56) as follows: d_{t-1} reflects the rate of depreciation between $t-1$ and t that was expected at $t-1$ $(s_t^e - s_{t-1} = d_{t-1})$. The terms in square brackets represent 'news' or unexpected events that form the basis of the agent's forecast error. The term $d_t - E_{t-1}d_t$ is the unexpected component of the interest differential. The other term represents the revision to expectations formed at t about the exchange rate that is expected to prevail in period $t+1$. Equation (5.56) is an implication, solely, of the UIP condition and it is independent of any specific model of exchange rate determination.

According to (5.56) an *un*anticipated increase in the interest differential $d_t - E_{t-1}d_t$ leads to an appreciation in the exchange rate, while a known high interest differential d_{t-1} is associated with a depreciating exchange rate. (However, if an unanticipated increase in the differential at time t leads to a reappraisal concerning the expected rate then $E_t s_{t+1} - E_{t-1} s_{t+1}$ will change. In practice this may well occur and then the simple negative relation between $d_t - E_{t-1}d_t$ and s_t may not hold.) Disregarding the above caveat, if interest differentials at time $t-1$ reflect underlying inflationary expectations then we would expect a rise in interest rates to lead to a depreciation as in the CAM–hyper-inflation model. On the other hand, unanticipated reduction in the money supply, which causes an *unanticipated* increase in r will, according to equation (5.52) yield an appreciation in the exchange rate, as in the Dornbusch (1976) KAM model. Thus both the CAM–hyper-inflation model and the Dornbusch model may be accommodated in equation (5.56) which highlights the crucial distinction between anticipated and unanticipated events when interpreting movements in the exchange rate. If agents use rational expectations then *on average* the terms in square brackets will be zero. However, in any single period new information or news may have a major impact on the spot rate thus accounting for its extreme volatility: economic fundamentals such as relative money supplies may influence s_t via the interest differential d_{t-1} as in the Dornbusch and CAM models, but these may, on occasions, be dominated by news.

5.6   The Portfolio Balance Model

The current and capital account monetary models which have been the subject matter of the preceding sections make at least two important simplifying assumptions: domestic and foreign assets are perfectly substitutable (so that no distinction need be made between them) and the wealth effects of a current account surplus or deficit are negligible. The portfolio balance model of exchange rates explores the consequences of explicitly relaxing these assumptions (see, e.g., Branson 1977, Isard 1978, Dornbusch and Fischer 1980).

In common with the CAM and KAM models, the level of exchange rate in the portfolio balance model (PBM) is determined, at least in the short run, by supply and demand in the markets for financial assets. However, as we saw in our discussion of the Marshall–Lerner condition in §5.2.1, the exchange rate is a principal determinant of the current account of the balance of payments. Now, surplus (deficit) on the current account represents a rise (fall) in net domestic holdings of foreign assets which in turn affects the level of wealth, which in turn affects the level of asset demand, which again affects the exchange rate. Thus, the PBM is an inherently dynamic model of exchange rate adjustment which includes in its terms of reference asset markets, the current account, the price level and the rate of asset accumulation. Moreover, we can distinguish between *short-run* equilibrium (supply and demand equated in asset markets), and the dynamic adjustment to *long-run* equilibrium (a static level of wealth and no tendency of the system to move over time). We begin by analysing the short-run determination of the exchange rate.

5.6.1 Short-Run Exchange Rate Determination

In the short run (a period of, say, three months or so), the exchange rate is determined purely by the interaction of supply and demand in asset markets. During this period, the level of financial wealth (and the individual components of that level) can be treated as fixed. For simplicity, we shall treat the net financial wealth of the private sector as composed of three assets: money (M), domestically issued bonds (B) and foreign bonds denominated in foreign currency (F). B is essentially government debt held by the domestic private sector. F is the level of net claims on foreigners held by the private sector. Since, under a free float, a current account surplus on the balance of payments must be exactly matched by a capital account deficit (i.e. capital outflow and hence increase in net foreign indebtedness to the domestic economy), the current account must give the rate of accumulation of F over time.

With foreign and domestic interest rates given by r and r^* as before,[18] we can write down our definition of wealth and simple domestic demand functions for its components as follows:

$$W = M + B + SF \tag{5.57}$$
$$M = M(r, r^*)W \qquad M_r < 0,\ M_{r^*} < 0 \tag{5.58}$$
$$B = B(r, r^*)W \qquad B_r > 0,\ B_{r^*} < 0 \tag{5.59}$$
$$SF = F(r, r^*)W \qquad F_r < 0,\ F_{r^*} > 0. \tag{5.60}$$

Equation (5.57) is an identity defining wealth. The only noteworthy characteristics of equations (5.58)–(5.60) are that, as is standard in the PBM,

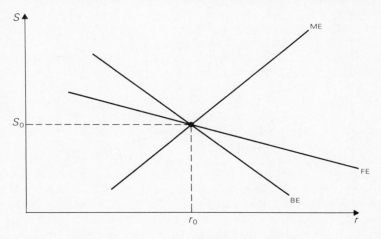

Figure 5.14 Short run equilibrium in the PBM

the scale variable is the level of wealth, W, and the demand functions are homogeneous in wealth; this allows them to be written in nominal terms (assuming homogeneity in prices and *real* wealth, prices cancel out) – see, e.g. Tobin 1969.

Figure 5.14 shows the short-run determination of the exchange rate diagrammatically in (S, r) space. The BE line in figure 5.14 gives the locus of points in (S, r) space at which, *ceteris paribus*, the supply and demand for domestic assets are equated. Similarly, the FE line gives the equilibrium locus along which the domestic demand for foreign assets is equal to the (short-run) fixed supply, and ME describes the money market equilibrium locus.

A depreciation in the exchange rate (rise in S) raises the domestic currency value of foreign assets F, and hence increases wealth, W. This raises the demand for both M and B. In order to maintain equilibrium in the money market, interest rates must rise – thus the ME schedule is upward-sloping in (S, r) space. Similarly, in order to maintain domestic bond market equilibrium, the domestic interest rate must fall – the BE schedule is downward-sloping.

As the domestic interest rate, r, rises, the domestic demand for foreign bonds falls as agents substitute domestic for foreign bonds in their portfolios. As foreign assets are sold, the foreign currency proceeds are converted into domestic currency thus bidding up the exchange rate (S falls) – hence FE is downward-sloping in (S, r) space. Since it seems reasonable to suppose that a given change in r will have a greater effect on domestic than foreign bond demand, the FE schedule is flatter than the BE schedule.

The intersection of the ME, BE and FE schedules gives the short-run equilibrium levels of the interest rate and the exchange rate. In fact, because of the 'adding-up' constraint (5.57), we know that equilibrium in any two markets implies equilibrium in the third, so our analysis of the PBM can in fact be conducted using any two of the three schedules.

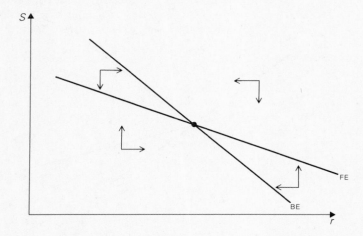

Figure 5.15   Global stability of short run equilibrium

However, before we proceed to analyse the short-run comparative statics of the model, it is as well to inquire as to its stability properties – i.e. does the equilibrium point in figure 5.14 represent a stable equilibrium? Consider any point to the right of the BE schedule. At such a point, we know that the domestic interest rate is too high, for the given level of S, for there to be domestic bond market equilibrium – i.e. there must be excess demand for the (short-run) fixed level of domestic assets. This excess demand will tend to depress r towards the BE line. A converse argument applies to any point to the left of the BE schedule, so we can draw in the horizontal arrows of motion as in figure 5.15.

Now consider any point above the FE schedule. At such a point, the level of S is too high, given r, for the domestic level of demand for foreign assets to be equal to the (short-run) fixed supply. This means that the domestic currency value of foreign asset holdings, SF, is too high. Thus, agents will attempt to sell foreign assets and convert the proceeds into domestic currency, causing the exchange rate to appreciate (S falls). Thus, at any point above FE, the vertical arrows of motion must point towards the FE schedule and, by a converse argument, at any point below FE, the vertical arrow of motion must point upwards, as in figure 5.15.

Combining these observations, we can see from figure 5.15 that at any point away from the intersection of the BE and FE schedules (i.e. the short-run equilibrium), the economy will tend to move towards the equilibrium – the system is globally stable.

We now consider the short-run comparative static effects of changes in the various components of net domestic wealth.

Increase in M Since in practice, and as we shall presently discuss, the authorities can (in this model) only bring about an increase in the amount of money held by redeeming public debt (i.e. reducing bonds B), in general, changes in M, ΔM, will be equal and opposite to changes in B, ΔB, i.e. $\Delta M + \Delta B = 0$. For the present case, however, we can think of a pure 'helicopter drop' of money.

As money holdings rise, agents attempt to rebalance their portfolios by buying both foreign bonds F and domestic bonds B. This will tend to depreciate the exchange rate (S rises) as agents buy foreign currency with which to purchase F, and depress the domestic interest rate, as domestic bond prices rise. Diagrammatically, this results in a shift to the left of the BE schedule, and an upward shift of the FE schedule, as in figure 5.16. The new short-run equilibrium must therefore be at a point such as B (figure 5.16) which is above and to the left of the initial equilibrium A – i.e. a pure increase in M leads to a reduction in the domestic interest rate and a depreciation of the exchange rate.

Increase in B Ignoring the effects of an open-market sale of domestic bonds on the level of the money supply, the effect of an increase in B is illustrated in figures 5.17 and 5.18. In order to induce domestic wealth holders to hold more domestic bonds, r rises (bond prices fall) for a given level of S – i.e. the BE schedule shifts to the right.

For a given level of r, the increase in wealth brought about by the rise in B leads to an increase in the demand for foreign assets – the concomitant purchase of foreign currency will tend to depreciate the exchange rate (S rises), i.e. FE shifts upward. If there is only a relatively small upward shift of FE, as in figure 5.17, the new equilibrium B will be below and to the right of the initial equilibrium – interest rates are higher and the exchange rate has

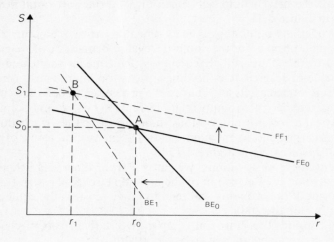

Figure 5.16   Increase in M

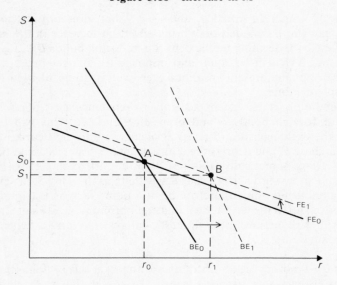

Figure 5.17   Increase in B, where domestic and foreign bonds are close substitutes

appreciated (*S* is lower). This would be the case if domestic and foreign assets were fairly close substitutes in domestic portfolios. The increase in wealth due to rise in *B* tends to raise the demand for foreign assets, but this is more than offset by a substitution effect towards domestic bond holding because of the rise in *r*. The net effect is a sale of domestically held foreign assets (and hence foreign currency) and the exchange rate appreciates. If, on the other hand, domestic and foreign assets were not viewed as closely substitutable by domestic wealth holders, the wealth effect would dominate the substitution effect, the demand for foreign assets (and hence foreign currency) would rise, and the exchange rate would depreciate (figure 5.18).

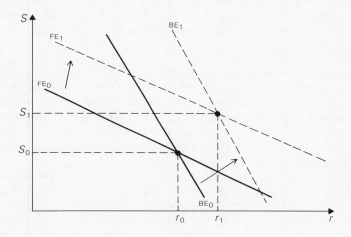

Figure 5.18 Increase in *B*, when domestic and foreign bonds are not close substitutes

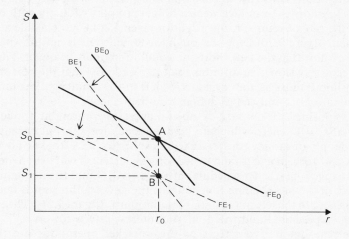

Figure 5.19 Increase in *F*

Thus, an increase in B will unambiguously raise the domestic interest rate, but the net effect on the exchange rate is ambiguous.

Increase in F   An increase in domestic holdings of net foreign assets, brought about by a current account surplus, will lead to an excess supply of domestically held foreign assets and thus foreign currency. As the exchange rate appreciates (i.e. S falls), the domestic currency value of foreign asset holdings, SF, rises. Clearly, S will continue to fall until the new value of foreign asset holdings ($S_1 F_1$ say) is just equal to the initial value ($S_0 F_0$), the initial level of wealth is restored and the domestic bond and money markets are unaffected. Thus, a rise in F leads to a fall in S (exchange rate appreciation) with r unchanged. Diagrammatically, this can be represented by a vertical downward movement of the short-run equilibrium, as in figure 5.19.

The Impact of Monetary Policy in the PBM   Having established the basic short-run comparative statics of the PBM, we are now in a position to examine the impact effects of monetary policy. As we noted above, the authorities can in general only affect the money supply through open-market operations. They can either effect a net repurchase of government debt from the private sector ($\Delta B + \Delta M = 0$), or else they can purchase foreign assets ($\Delta M + \Delta SF = 0$) (or some combination).

Consider first a net purchase of B by the authorities. Since this directly affects the money and domestic bond markets, it will be convenient to use the BE and ME schedules for our analysis.[19] The increase in private sector money holding can only be brought about by reducing the opportunity cost of money holding – i.e. r must fall for a given level of S (equivalently, the authorities drive up domestic bond prices and hence depress r in their attempts to repurchase). Thus the ME schedule must shift to the left (figure 5.20). Similarly, in order to induce wealth holders to part willingly with domestic assets, the rate of return, r, must fall for given S – the BE schedule also shifts to the left (figure 5.20). Now although the FE schedule is not drawn in figure 5.20, we know that the new short-run equilibrium must lie on FE. Thus, since FE is negatively sloped and flatter than BE, we know that the new short-run equilibrium B must be above and to the left of the initial equilibrium A – the interest rate falls and the exchange rate depreciates.

Now consider the impact of open-market operations in foreign assets ($\Delta M + \Delta SF = 0$). There will again be a tendency for r to fall because of the excess supply of money (the ME schedule shifts to the left). The government purchase of foreign assets (and hence foreign currency) will tend to depreciate the exchange rate (the FE schedule shifts upward). Since the new equilibrium must lie on the BE schedule (unchanged) the new equilibrium B must again be above and to the left of the initial equilibrium A (figure 5.21). The exchange rate has depreciated and the domestic interest rate is lower.

Thus, the qualitative effects of open-market operations are the same whether the government buys domestic or foreign assets. The quantitative effects are, however, different. In figure 5.20, the new equilibrium must lie on the unchanged FE schedule, whilst in figure 5.21, the new equilibrium must lie on the unchanged BE schedule. Since the FE schedule is flatter than the BE schedule, the change in the exchange rate $(S_1 - S_0)$ must be smaller in figure 5.20 than in figure 5.21, whilst the change in the interest rate must be larger. This is quite intuitive – open-market purchases of domestic assets affect r directly while open-market purchases of foreign assets affect S directly. Thus, the real impact of monetary policy on the tradeables-producing sector (through S) and the sector producing interest-sensitive durable goods will depend upon the mix of open-market operations.

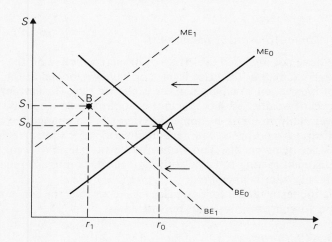

Figure 5.20 Increase in M; $\Delta M + \Delta B = 0$

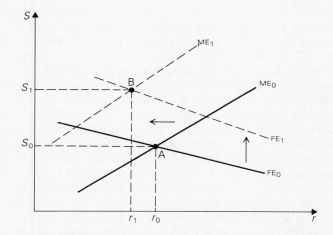

Figure 5.21 Increase in M; $\Delta M + \Delta SF = 0$

We can now summarize all the impact effects of changes in the components of wealth and monetary policy on the exchange rate and the domestic interest rate, as in table 5.4, before going on to examine dynamic adjustment to long-run equilibrium in the PBM.

Table 5.4   Impact effects in the PBM

Effect on	Changes in stocks			Open-market operations	
	ΔF	ΔM	ΔB	$\Delta M + \Delta B = 0$	$\Delta M + \Delta SF = 0$
S	$-$	$+$	?	$+$	$+$
r	0	$-$	$+$	$-$	$-$

5.6.2   Dynamic Adjustment in the PBM

So far we have not analysed the effect of monetary policy on the exchange rate through changes in the price level, nor have we looked at the dynamic stock flow interaction of changes in the exchange rate, the current account and the level of wealth. An increase in the money supply would be expected to lead eventually to a rise in domestic prices, but a change in prices will affect net exports and hence will have implications for the current account of the balance of payments. This in turn affects the level of wealth which, in the adjustment to long-run equilibrium, feeds back into asset market and hence exchange rate behaviour.

Holding the (exogenous) foreign price level constant, the current account balance (in foreign currency) can be written as

$$\text{CA} = N(S/P) + r^* F. \tag{5.61}$$

In equation (5.61), $N(.)$ represents the trade balance – this will improve as S rises and/or P falls (competitiveness improves for a given level of foreign prices). The term $r^* F$ represents net interest income from domestic holdings of foreign assets, F. If the economy has traditionally been a net capital exporter, so $r^* F$ is positive, then a balance on the current account requires a trade deficit. Since a non-zero current account implies changes in F and hence in wealth, such a deficit may be required in long-run equilibrium.

Now consider an increase in the money supply brought about by an open-market purchase of domestic bonds by the authorities.[20] As we saw above, the impact effect of this will be to cause an immediate depreciation of the exchange rate. This is not the end of the story, however. Suppose the economy was initially in equilibrium with a trade balance of zero and *net* foreign asset holdings of zero (and hence a current account balance of zero).[21] This is depicted in figure 5.22 at the points corresponding to time t_0. Figure 5.22 is drawn so that the initial values (at time t_0) of the price level and the exchange rate are normalized to unity, $P_0 = S_0 = 1$. The impact effect is a jump in the exchange rate S_0 to S_1 (AC). Moreover, assuming the Marshall–Lerner conditions hold, the improvement in competitiveness will improve the trade balance from zero to a positive amount (FG). This means that the current account goes into surplus and domestic residents begin to acquire net foreign assets (F accumulates). As we discussed above, an increase in F will tend to appreciate the exchange rate – S begins to fall from its new short-run equilibrium at C along CD, and the trade balance begins to worsen along GH. Meanwhile, the increase in the money supply will have begun to increase prices along the path AB towards the new long-run equilibrium price level P_1. This adds to the deterioration of competitiveness and hence the trade balance. At point E (time t_1) the exchange rate and the price level are equal in value and hence their ratio is unity ($S/P = 1$); but this is the same as the initial ratio at time t_0. Hence, the trade balance at time t_1 must be back to its original level – i.e. zero. However, this is no longer enough to restore long-run equilibrium. Domestic wealth holders have now acquired a positive level of net foreign asset holdings and will be receiving a stream of investment income r^*F. In order for the current account balance to be zero therefore, the trade balance must actually go into deficit. This requires a further appreciation of the exchange rate (fall in S) to its long-run equilibrium level S_2, by which time the price level has reached its long-run

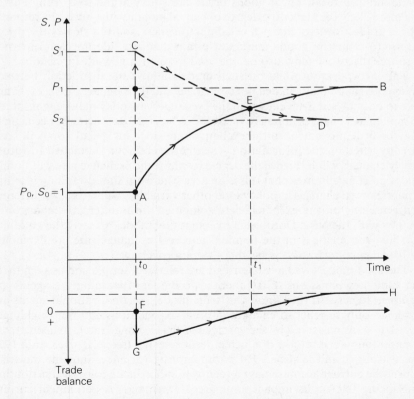

Figure 5.22 Dynamic adjustment in the PBM; increase in M with $\Delta M + \Delta B = 0$

equilibrium level P_1 and the current account just balances $(-N(S/P) = r^*F)$ so there is no further net accumulation of foreign assets.

Note that the PBM gives an alternative derivation of the overshooting result described in § 5.4 – the exchange rate (S) jumps immediately above its long-run level and then falls slowly.[22] Moreover, overshooting in the PBM does not rely solely on price level stickiness as in the Dornbusch overshooting model. Say, for example, the price level adjusted immediately to P_1, following the increase in the money supply, along AK in figure 5.22. So long as new short-run equilibrium exchange rate S_1 exceeds P_1, competitiveness will have increased, the trade balance will have gone into surplus and a slow appreciation to the long-run exchange rate level would ensue as above.

5.7   Summary

Capital account monetary models are able to explain the stylized facts of behaviour in some small open economies. In particular a tight monetary policy (or a jump in interest rates) can lead to exchange rate overshooting, and a trade-induced recession, if goods prices are sticky in the short run. This is the more likely the higher the degree of capital mobility, the lower the response of net trade flows to changes in competitiveness and the slower the prices adjust to clear the goods market. Certain demand side implications of a resource discovery may also be analysed in this framework (appendix 5.2).

The incorporation of RE in such models allows the distinction between anticipated and unanticipated policy changes and their impact on the exchange rate to be analysed. Movements in the exchange rate today may be in response to anticipated changes in policy variables. When the latter actually occur there may be little movement in the exchange rate since RE speculators will have already acted on the information. Clearly the credibility attached to future policy changes will influence the degree to which the exchange rate will 'jump' and it must be admitted that this is an area where our understanding is weak. Unanticipated changes in policy (and other variables) will have very different repercussions on the exchange rate compared with anticipated changes as we saw with the basic Dornbusch overshooting model. Clearly the volatility of short-run changes in the nominal and real exchange rate are explained in broad qualitative terms by the KAM approach.

The KAM models we have described are relatively simple and as such there are some key omissions. First, there is no model of learning: RE agents are *assumed* to act as if they know the 'true' model. Second, rational agents are assumed only to react to changes in point expectations and not to changes in risk (e.g. as measured by the variance of the exchange rate). Relaxing these assumptions is the subject of much current research (see, e.g., De Canio 1979 on 'learning', and Walshe 1984 on integrating variances into the models). Third, the current account plays a relatively subordinate role, its contribution only being felt via its impact on aggregate demand. A permanent current account surplus which leads to a *continuous* addition to wealth may arise but this has no impact elsewhere in the Dornbusch model, unlike in the portfolio balance model. Incorporating wealth effects (via the current account and the government budget constraint) in Dornbusch-type models usually results in analytically intractable solutions: a simulation model with 'representative' parameters has to be analysed, (e.g. Nguyen and Turnovsky 1980, 1983, Whittaker et al. 1986) or 'large-scale' econometric models constructed (Minford et al. 1984, Wallis 1985, 1986) and policy results are usually fairly sensitive to alternative parameter estimates.

Notes

1   The portfolio (stock) model may be represented as $K = K(r, W)$, assuming r^* is constant. Then $dK = K_r\, dr + K_W\, dW$ where $K_r = \partial K / \partial r$ etc. The first term indicates that a step change in r leads to a step increase in the *stock* of assets. In general K_W is a positive function of r. Hence, the higher the *level* of r, the larger K_W and dK, as long as $dW > 0$. For example if $K = r^a W^b$ then K_W is equal to $br^a W^{b-1} > 0$ and increases with the level of r. In addition, if $b > 1$, then K_W also increases as wealth grows.

2   Using (5.9) and setting $\Delta R = 0$ for payments equilibrium we have

$$r = r^* - (1/\alpha)[\,\delta(s + p^* - p) - \gamma y + q\,]\,).$$

In general, a change in s shifts the (r, y) locus (i.e. the BB line) but as $\alpha \to \infty$, $r = r^*$ and the new BB (horizontal) line is independent of s (as well as p^*, p, y and q).

3   Notice that we refer here to a *payments* surplus. A *trade* surplus may be willingly held in foreign assets – that is, matched by a capital outflow – in which case there is payments equilibrium and no change in the domestic money supply. Some empirical issues concerning sterilization and the money supply are dealt with in Taylor 1987e.

4   With zero capital mobility, $\alpha = 0$ and the change in the balance of payments is determined solely by the trade balance. For equilibrium on the trade account, using (5.9) we require

$$\delta(s + p^* - p) - \gamma y + q = 0$$

and y is completely determined by s, p, p^* and q which are constant by assumption, in our fixed-exchange-rate fix-price model.

5   We ignore, for the moment, any valuation changes in foreign assets in terms of the domestic currency, consequent on exchange rate changes.

6   Reverting to absolute values rather than logarithms, the change in wealth is given by

$$dW = dG - t_y\, dY - z_y\, dY \tag{i}$$

At C in figure 5.6, the change in output is given by the full Keynesian (open-economy) fix-price multiplier:

$$dY = dG / [\,1 - c_y(1 - t_y) + z_y\,]. \tag{ii}$$

At C, wealth is increasing if $dW>0$. Substituting (ii) in (i) we find that $dW>0$, if

$$(1-c_y)(1-t_y)>0$$

and

$$c_y(1-t_y)+z_y<1.$$

The latter is (always) assumed to be positive for stability of the multiplier process (see (ii)) and the former is positive under the usual assumption $0<c_y$, $t_y<1$.

7　Even this requires an additional assumption that the import content of government expenditure is equal to that for private expenditure. If the import content of government expenditure is less than that of private expenditure then the initial increase in G and fall in 'high'-import-content private expenditure (as T is increased to achieve a balanced-budget fiscal change) may directly reduce *net* imports (by more than the increase in imports due to any increase in Y consequent on the balanced-budget 'expansion'). Thus the trade balance *may* improve, and wealth increase and output rise (for a positive wealth effect) until increased imports and tax receipts match the initial trade surplus.

8　At C the full Keynesian multiplier applies. If the change in net trade due to the depreciation is $\delta\ ds$, the change in output at C is

$$dY=\delta\ ds/[1-c_y(1-t_y)+z_y]. \tag{i}$$

The change in wealth is

$$dW=\delta\ ds-t_y\ dY-z_y\ dY. \tag{ii}$$

Substituting (i) in (ii) we obtain $dW>0$ if

$$\delta(1-c_y)(1-t_y)>0$$

(which holds for $0<c_y,\ t_y<1$) and

$$c_y(1-t_y)+z_y<1.$$

9　Strictly speaking we are discussing factory-gate prices here. Consumer prices would have a *direct* import content (e.g. imported fresh fruit) as well as an indirect tax element (e.g. excise duties and VAT).

10　For convenience we implicitly assume that 'push factors' vary cyclically. For example, trade union 'power' is likely to be weak at high levels of unemployment and vice versa.

11　In part this may manifest itself in higher 'with-profits' payments from pensions and life assurance policies (and hence be counted as income). Pension funds and insurance companies hold a substantial amount of foreign assets on behalf of the holders of pensions and life assurance policies.

12　The 'weak form' allows a constant of proportionality k (representing, for example, transport costs) to drive a wedge between P and P^*S. Hence the 'weak form' of PPP in *levels* is $S=k(P^*S)$; equation (5.20) then follows directly.

13   The real rate of interest or real return on capital goods investment will vary with the secular rate of productivity growth in the economy but we ignore this complication here.

14   If foreign–domestic goods are perfect substitutes (i.e. $\delta \to \infty$), then our MF + PEAPC approach implies that PPP holds continuously and hence is consistent with the CAM model. To see this, rearrange the goods market equilibrium equation (5.26):

$$s + p^* - p = \delta^{-1}[\,\bar{y}_f(1 - \delta + w) - q + \sigma r\,].$$

As $\delta \to \infty$, goods market equilibrium requires $s + p^* - p = 0$, that is PPP.

15   No actual capital flows may take place. It is merely the *threat* of capital flows that may lead foreign exchange (FOREX) dealers to 'mark-up' sterling in their quotations over the telephone. See Taylor 1987f for evidence on the covered arbitrage condition.

16   It is easy enough to incorporate an open-economy PEAPC with the additional terms

$$+ b_1 \dot{p}^e + (1 - b_1)(\dot{p}^* + \dot{s})$$

added to the 'simple' Phillips curve of equation (5.34) and to make y endogenous. We refrain from doing so since the model is already complex enough for pedagogic purposes.

17   It is worth noting, in passing, that the econometric evidence is not generally supportive of PPP even as a *long-run* equilibrium condition – see e.g., Adler and Lehmann 1983, Darby 1980, Taylor 1987h, 1987i, although there is some evidence of it holding during certain historical periods (Taylor and McMahon 1987, Broadberry and Taylor 1987).

18   In the very simple PBM we are about to exposit, we are essentially assuming *static* expectations, so the expected rate of depreciation is zero, $\dot{s}^e = 0$. Note that this does not imply that the interest differential $(r - r^*)$ must be zero because the UIP relationship is now supplemented by a risk premium, ϱ, say:

$$\dot{s}^e = r - r^* + \varrho.$$

The existence of such a risk premium is merely one way of stating that domestic and foreign assets are no longer perfect substitutes (see, e.g., Taylor 1987j).

19   Recall that we are free to choose any two of three equilibrium loci for our analysis because of the adding-up constraint (5.57).

20   This avoids complications arising from interest income accruing to the government following a purchase of foreign assets from the private sector.

21   The reader can easily work through a similar analysis with different initial conditions.

22   The slow adjustment to long-run equilibrium may not, however, be monotonic – see Branson 1977.

23   The reader should verify that the case as depicted in figure 5.25 – i.e. a real exchange depreciation beyond the original level of competitiveness (i.e. $c > 0$) – is possible but not necessary.

Appendix 5.1   The Dornbusch Model

Full Solution of the Dornbusch Model   ($y = \bar{y}$, a constant; $\gamma^1 = 0$ for simplicity)

'Asset markets'

$$\dot{s}^e = \mu = r - r^* \qquad\qquad \text{UIP} \qquad\qquad\qquad (A5.1.1)$$
$$\dot{s}^e = \theta(\bar{s} - s) \qquad\qquad \text{expectations} \qquad\qquad (A5.1.2)$$
$$m^s - p = -\lambda r + \phi\bar{y} \qquad\qquad \text{money market} \qquad\quad (A5.1.3)$$
$$\dot{p} = \Pi[\delta(s - p + p^*) - \sigma r + (\gamma - 1)\bar{y}] \quad \text{Phillips curve.} \qquad (A5.1.4)$$

Substituting (A5.1.1) in (A5.1.2) and then (A5.1.2) in (A5.1.3) and rearranging we obtain

$$s - \bar{s} = -(1/\lambda\theta)(p - m^s - \lambda r^* + \phi\bar{y}). \qquad\qquad (A5.1.5)$$

In static equilibrium $\dot{s}^e = 0$; hence, from (A5.1.1), $r = r^*$, and from (A5.1.3)

$$\bar{p} = m^s + \lambda r^* - \phi\bar{y} \qquad\qquad\qquad (A5.1.6)$$

Substituting (A5.1.6) in (A5.1.5) for m^s we obtain the asset market equilibrium locus

$$s - \bar{s} = (-1/\lambda\theta)(p - \bar{p}) \qquad\qquad\qquad (A5.1.7)$$

with a negative slope: $\partial s/\partial p = -1/\lambda\theta$.

Goods-money equilibrium   Substituting for r from (A5.1.3) in (A5.1.4), setting $\dot{p} = 0$ in (A5.1.4) and rearranging we obtain the goods–money (*G–M*) equilibrium relation:

$$p = \left(1 + \frac{\sigma}{\delta\lambda}\right)^{-1}\left((s + p^*) + \frac{\sigma}{\delta\lambda}m^s + \frac{(\gamma - 1)\lambda - \sigma\phi}{\delta\lambda}\bar{y}\right) \qquad (A5.1.8)$$

where, $0 < \partial p/\partial s < 1$, and an increase in m^s leads to a shift to the left in the *G–M* schedule (($\partial p/\partial m^s) < 0$). This equation contains only s and p and exogenous variables and hence holds in the long run giving the long-run exchange rate $\bar{s}$ as:

$$\bar{s} = \left(1 + \frac{\sigma}{\delta\lambda}\right)\bar{p} - p^* - \frac{\sigma}{\lambda\delta}m^s - \frac{(\gamma - 1)/\lambda - \sigma\phi)}{\delta\lambda}\bar{y}. \qquad (A5.1.9)$$

Substituting for $\bar{p}$ from (A5.1.6) we obtain a reduced-form equation for the long-run equilibrium exchange rate, $\bar{s}$:

$$\bar{s} = m^s - p^* + \left(\lambda + \frac{\sigma}{\delta}\right) r^* - \left(\phi + \frac{(\gamma - 1)}{\delta}\right)\bar{y}. \tag{A5.1.10}$$

from (A5.1.10) and (A5.1.6) it is clear that $\partial\bar{s}/\partial m^s = \partial\bar{s}/\partial\bar{p} = 1$; that is, 'neutrality' and PPP hold in the long run. (Note also that the goods–market equilibrium equation (5.41) in the text may be derived by substituting for p^* from (A5.1.9) in (A5.1.8).)

Overshooting   The asset market equation (A5.1.7) holds continuously, and substituting for $\bar{s}$ from (A5.1.10) and $\bar{p}$ from (A5.1.6) yields

$$s = \left(\frac{1}{\lambda\theta} + 1\right)m^s - \frac{1}{\lambda\theta}p - p^* + \left(\lambda + \frac{\sigma}{\delta} + \frac{1}{\theta}\right) r^*$$
$$- \left(\phi + \frac{(\gamma - 1)}{\delta} + \frac{\phi}{\lambda\theta}\right)\bar{y}. \tag{A5.1.11}$$

If p and y remain constant in the short run, then

$$\partial s/\partial m^s = [1 + (\lambda\theta)^{-1}] > 1 \tag{A5.1.12}$$

and, since $\partial s/\partial m^s = 1$, overshooting occurs and is the larger, the smaller is the interest elasticity of the demand for money, λ.

Rational expectations   Asset market equilibrium (A5.1.7) and the Phillips curve equation (5.43) are

$$s - \bar{s} = -(\lambda\theta)^{-1}(p - \bar{p}) \tag{A5.1.7}$$
$$\dot{p} = \Pi\{\delta(s - \bar{s}) - [\delta + (\sigma/\lambda)](\bar{p} - p)\}. \tag{A5.1.13}$$

Hence the adjustment equation for prices is

$$\dot{p} = -v(p - \bar{p}) \tag{A5.1.14}$$
$$v = \Pi[(\delta + \sigma\theta)/\theta\lambda + \delta]. \tag{A5.1.15}$$

Differentiating (A5.1.7), substituting for $\dot{p}$ from (A5.1.4) and for $p - \bar{p}$ from (A5.1.7):

$$\dot{s} = -(\lambda\theta)^{-1}\dot{p} = (\lambda\theta)^{-1}v(p - \bar{p}) = v(\bar{s} - s). \tag{A5.1.16}$$

Thus the *actual* dynamic path for the spot rate given by the *whole* model is determined by all the parameters of the model embodied in v. However, in deriving this result we assumed expectations are determined by (A5.1.2):

$$\dot{s}^e = \theta(\bar{s} - s)$$

where θ is as yet an arbitrary parameter. If expectations formed using (A5.1.2) are to be consistent with the actual path of the exchange rate then $\dot{s}^e = \dot{s}$ and hence

$$\theta = \nu = \Pi[(\delta + \sigma\theta)/\theta\lambda + \delta].\tag{A5.1.17}$$

Equation (A5.1.17) is a quadratic equation in θ with the solution

$$\theta_{1,2} = \tfrac{1}{2}\Pi(\sigma/\lambda + \delta) \pm \tfrac{1}{2}[\Pi^2(\sigma/\lambda + \delta)^2 + 4\Pi\delta/\lambda]^{\frac{1}{2}}.\tag{A5.1.18}$$

It is easy to see that one root is negative and the other positive, and since θ in (A5.1.2) is expected to be positive we choose the positive root. RE therefore imposes a unique value for θ, the expectations adjustment parameter, in terms of all the other parameters of the model. The speed of adjustment of p and s to the steady state therefore depends on all the parameters of the model.

Dynamics – The Matrix Solution   Particularly in models with a relatively large number of endogenous variables a general RE solution using a matrix approach is often useful. We demonstrate this approach for our two-variable model. It is important to note at the outset that the expectations equation (A5.1.2) is not part of the model. Rational agents will form expectations of $\dot{s}$ as the predictions of the whole model. Thus the form of equation (A5.1.2) will be *derived* as the consistent solution of *the rest* of the model. We assume perfect foresight and therefore $\dot{s}^e$ is replaced by $\dot{s}$ in equation (A5.1.1). We retain the simplifying assumptions $y - \bar{y}$, $\gamma' = 0$.

If we can represent a dynamic two-variable model in the form

$$\begin{bmatrix} \dot{p} \\ \dot{s} \end{bmatrix} = \mathbf{A} \begin{bmatrix} p - \bar{p} \\ s - \bar{s} \end{bmatrix}\tag{A5.1.19}$$

where $\mathbf{A}$ is a 2×2 matrix of parameters, then the solution for both equations is of the form:

$$p - \bar{p} = a_1 \exp(\psi_1 t) + a_2 \exp(\psi_2 t)\tag{A5.1.20a}$$
$$s - \bar{s} = a_3 \exp(\psi_1 t) + a_4 \exp(\psi_2 t)\tag{A5.1.20b}$$

and in this model can be shown to satisfy the first-order differential equations

$$\dot{p} = \psi_1(p - \bar{p})\tag{A5.1.21a}$$
$$\dot{s} = \psi_1(s - \bar{s})\tag{A5.1.21b}$$

where ψ_1 is the stable root of the system (see below) and the a_i are constants. In fact ψ_1 is the stable eigenvalue of the $\mathbf{A}$ matrix. To put our model in the form (A5.1.19) note that from (A5.1.1) and '(A5.1.3) minus (A5.1.6)' we have *asset market equilibrium* when

$$r - r^* = (1/\lambda)(p - \bar{p}) = \dot{s}\tag{A5.1.22}$$

where we have assumed perfect foresight $(\dot{s} = \dot{s}^e)$. From (A5.1.4), in equilibrium (i.e. $s = \bar{s}$, $p = \bar{p}$, $r = r^*$),

$$0 = \Pi [\delta(\bar{s} - \bar{p} - p^*) - \sigma r^* + (\gamma - 1)\bar{y}] \qquad (A5.1.23)$$

Taking (A5.1.23) from (A5.1.4) and substituting from (A5.1.22) for $r - r^*$ we obtain *goods–money dynamic equilibrium*:

$$\dot{p} = \Pi\delta(s - \bar{s}) - \Pi(\delta + \sigma/\lambda)(p - \bar{p}). \qquad (A5.1.24)$$

Asset market equilibrium (A5.1.22) and goods–money equilibrium (A5.1.24) may be expressed in matrix form:

$$\begin{bmatrix} \dot{p} \\ \dot{s} \end{bmatrix} = \begin{bmatrix} -\Pi(\delta + \sigma/\lambda) & \Pi\delta \\ 1/\lambda & 0 \end{bmatrix} \begin{bmatrix} p - \bar{p} \\ s - \bar{s} \end{bmatrix} = \mathbf{A} \begin{bmatrix} p - \bar{p} \\ s - \bar{s} \end{bmatrix} \qquad (A5.1.25)$$

The eigenvalues ψ_i of $\mathbf{A}$ are obtained from $|\mathbf{A} - \theta\mathrm{I}| = 0$ where I is the identity matrix, that is

$$\begin{bmatrix} -\Pi(\delta + \sigma/\lambda) - \psi & \Pi\delta \\ 1/\lambda & -\psi \end{bmatrix} = 0 \qquad (A5.1.26)$$

$$\psi^2 + \Pi(\delta + \sigma/\lambda)\psi - \Pi\delta/\lambda = 0 \qquad (A5.1.27)$$
$$\psi_1, \psi_2 = -\tfrac{1}{2}\Pi(\delta + \sigma/\lambda) \pm \tfrac{1}{2}[\Pi^2(\delta + \sigma/\lambda)^2 + 4\Pi\delta/\lambda]^{1/2} \qquad (A5.1.28)$$

and clearly one root is positive, the other negative. Taking the solution for $s - \bar{s}$ in equation (A5.1.20b), a non-explosive solution requires $\psi_i < 0$; and hence we take the negative root, say ψ_1, and impose $a_2 = a_4 = 0$ to avoid an explosive solution. The unique stable saddle-path RE solution is then given by (A5.1.20a) and (A5.1.20b) with $a_2 = a_4 = 0$, and by differentiating (A5.1.20a) and (A5.1.20b) it is easy to see they satisfy (A5.1.21a) and (A5.1.21b) with $\psi_i = \psi_1$, the stable root. Note that in this particular case $\psi_1 = -\theta_1$.

Naturally the expression (A5.1.28) is the same as that derived earlier (A5.1.18) when we arbitrarily (but correctly) assume a particular form for the expectations equation for $\dot{s}$, namely the 'solution' (A5.1.21b). (See Blanchard and Kahn 1980 for further details of matrix solution methods.)

Note that from (A5.1.12) the degree of overshooting is smaller in θ. Using (A5.1.28), the degree of overshooting increases as $(\delta, \sigma, \Pi, \lambda) \to 0$.

Appendix 5.2   The Buiter–Miller Model

This appendix uses a much-simplified version of the Buiter and Miller (1981) overshooting model of the real exchange rate to analyse the effects of a natural resource discovery ('oil') on the real economy.

Since the model is (log–) linear, we can appeal to the so-called 'certainty equivalence' or 'separation' principle – namely that the solution to the model under the assumption of perfect foresight will be identical to that obtained under the assumption of rational expectations. We accordingly set down the model in perfect-foresight terms. The equations of the model are as follows:

$$y - \bar{y} = \delta(s - p - p^*) + \chi \varrho_\infty \tag{A5.2.1}$$
$$m - p = \varkappa(y + \varrho) - \lambda r \tag{A5.2.2}$$
$$\dot{p} = \phi(y - \bar{y}) + \pi \tag{A5.2.3}$$
$$\dot{s} = r - r^* \tag{A5.2.4}$$
$$\mu \equiv m - p \tag{A5.2.5}$$
$$c \equiv s - p + p^* \tag{A5.2.6}$$

where

y = domestic real income
$\bar{y}$ = full-employment level of domestic real income
s = nominal exchange rate (domestic price of foreign currency)
p = domestic price level
m = domestic money stock
π = rate of 'core' inflation $(= \dot{m})$
r = domestic interest rate
μ = real domestic money stock
c = real exchange rate ('competitiveness')
ϱ = flow of resource output
ϱ_∞ = permanent income equivalent of ϱ.

All variables are in logarithms except interest rates; a dot denotes a time derivative and an asterisk a foreign variable; δ, χ, $\varkappa$, λ and ϕ are positive constants.

Equation (A5.2.1) is the IS curve, (A5.2.2) the LM curve, (A5.2.3) a Phillips curve and (A5.2.4) the UIP condition, also (A5.2.5) and (A5.2.6) define the real money stock and the real exchange rate (or 'competitiveness') respectively. Now we wish to trace out the dynamics of the model in (c, μ) space. Differentiating (A5.2.5) with respect to time and using (A5.2.1) and (A5.2.3) and the fact that $\pi = \dot{m}$, we have

$$\dot{\mu} = -\phi(\delta c + \chi \varrho_\infty). \tag{A5.2.7}$$

Similarly, differentiating (A5.2.6) with respect to time (treating foreign prices as constant) and substituting from each of the other relations, we can obtain

$$\dot{c} = -\mu/\lambda + \delta(\varkappa/\lambda - \phi)c + (\varkappa/\lambda - \phi)\chi \varrho_\infty$$
$$+ (\varkappa/\lambda)(\bar{y} + \varrho) - (\pi + r^*). \tag{A5.2.8}$$

Writing (A5.2.7) and (A5.2.8) in matrix (i.e. 'state space') form:

$$\begin{bmatrix} \dot{c} \\ \dot{\mu} \end{bmatrix} = \begin{bmatrix} \delta(\varkappa/\lambda - \phi) & -1/\lambda \\ -\phi\delta & 0 \end{bmatrix} \begin{bmatrix} c \\ \mu \end{bmatrix} \tag{A5.2.9}$$
$$+ \begin{bmatrix} (\varkappa/\lambda - \phi)\chi \\ -\phi\chi \end{bmatrix} \varrho_\infty + \begin{bmatrix} (\varkappa/\lambda)(\bar{y} + \varrho) - (\pi + r^*) \\ 0 \end{bmatrix}.$$

If the system is to have a unique convergent saddle-path, we require the first coefficient matrix on the right-hand side of (A5.2.8) (the 'transition matrix') to have a negative determinant, which is easily seen to be satisfied $(-\phi\delta/\lambda < 0)$.

Setting $\dot{\mu} = 0$, we have

$$c|_{\dot{\mu}=0} = -\chi\varrho_\infty/\delta \tag{A5.2.10}$$

and, similarly, setting $\dot{c} = 0$,

$$\mu|_{\dot{c}=0} = \delta(\varkappa - \phi\lambda)c + (\varkappa - \phi\lambda)\chi\varrho_\infty + \varkappa(\bar{y} + \varrho) - \lambda(\pi + r^*). \tag{A5.2.11}$$

Consider now the situation before the natural resource is discovered, $\varrho = \varrho_\infty = 0$. Then

$$c|_{\dot{\mu}=0} = 0 \tag{A5.2.12}$$

$$\mu|_{\dot{c}=0} = \delta(\varkappa - \phi\lambda)c + \varkappa\bar{y} - \lambda(\pi + r^*). \tag{A5.2.13}$$

Solving (A5.2.12) and (A5.2.13) simultaneously gives the (pre-oil) long-run equilibrium:

$$(c, \mu) = (0, \varkappa\bar{y} - \lambda(\pi + r^*)). \tag{A5.2.14}$$

Relation (A5.2.14) is quite intuitive: $c = 0$ implies, via (A5.2.1) (with $\varrho = 0$), long-run full employment; with a constant level of competitiveness, and constant foreign prices, the nominal exchange rate must be depreciating at the core rate of inflation, which then, via the UIP condition and the LM curve, gives the long-run level of real money as in (A5.2.14).

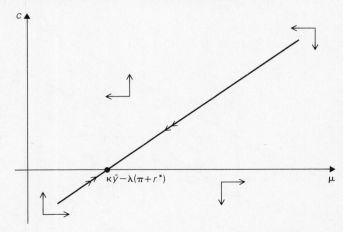

Figure 5.23 The phase diagram for the Buiter–Miller model

Relations (A5.2.10) and (A5.2.11) can be used to sketch the arrows of motion and hence the saddle-path in (c, μ) space, as in figure 5.23 (the reader should verify that the saddle-path is qualitatively unaffected by the sign of $(\varkappa - \phi\lambda)$).

Now consider the effects of the oil discovery $(0 < \varrho_\infty < \varrho)$. We can see immediately from (A5.2.10) that the equilibrium real exchange rate must now appreciate to $-\chi\varrho_\infty / \delta$. Substituting this value for c into (A5.2.11), we can see that the new (post-oil) long-run equilibrium is

$$(c, \mu) = (-\chi\varrho_\infty / \delta, \varkappa(\bar{y} + \varrho) - \lambda(\pi + r^*)). \tag{A5.2.15}$$

Comparing (A5.2.14) and (A5.2.15), we can see that the equilibrium real exchange rate has appreciated (c is lower), and the equilibrium level of the real money stock is higher. Intuitively, long-run competitiveness must have worsened because the permanent income value of current oil production affects the demand for non-oil output y, with $\bar{y}$ fixed (equation (A5.2.1)). For long-run equilibrium ($y = \bar{y}$), there must therefore be a worsening of competitiveness which provides an offsetting reduction in demand for non-oil output (see $y = \bar{y}$ in (A5.2.1)). This is the so-called 'Dutch disease' effect. Clearly, the long-run equilibrium real money stock must be higher (post-oil) because of the increased transactions component of the money demand ($\varkappa\varrho$).

The dynamics of the natural resource discovery are illustrated in figure 5.24. The system is initially in long-run equilibrium at point A. Following the resource discovery, the long-run equilibrium is at point D, and hence there is a shift in the saddle-path to pass through this point. The old equilibrium, A, is therefore no longer on the unique convergent saddle-path. Since, in the short run, nominal money balances and prices (and hence the

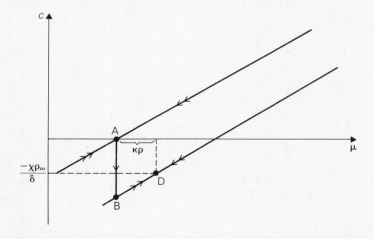

Figure 5.24   The overshooting effect of a natural resource discovery

real money stock) are fixed, all adjustment is borne by the nominal and hence the real exchange rate in order to place the economy on the new saddle-path – i.e. the real exchange rate immediately appreciates to point B. Since the real exchange rate has overshot its long-run (full-employment) level, there is a drastic fall in final demand (via a negative trade balance) and a short-term recession ensues. This causes inflation to fall below its core rate ($\dot{p} < \pi = \dot{m}$), the real money stock begins to rise ($\dot{\mu} = \dot{m} - \dot{p} > 0$), and the economy moves towards long-run equilibrium at point D. Thus, there is an initial overshoot of the real exchange rate by the vertical distance DB. Intuitively, the overshoot arises because the impact effect of the resource discovery is to raise the (transactions) demand for money. With (short-run) unchanged real money balances, this causes a jump in the domestic interest rate. Foreign capital then flows in and drives up the nominal exchange rate until the rate of depreciation is just equal to the interest differential (the real exchange rate jumps onto the new saddle-path).

Finally, consider what would happen in this model if agents actually knew that the resource discovery was finite and would therefore eventually be exhausted. For simplicity, assume that the natural resource discovery will be completely exhausted in exactly *T*-periods' time. Agents therefore know that the correct, stable position for the economy to be on immediately after the resource is exhausted is somewhere on the original saddle-path, through point A in figure 5.24.

Considering the arrows of motion of the *new* saddle-path in figure 5.25, it can be seen that if the economy moves to *any* point between A and B, it will eventually arrive back on the *original* saddle-path. However, there will

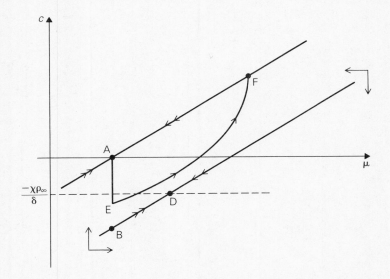

Figure 5.25 The effect of an exhaustible natural resource discovery

be a *unique* point between A and B (point E in figure 5.25) such that it takes exactly T periods to arrive back on the original saddle-path (at point F) (Wilson 1979). Thus, if the discovered resource will eventually be exhausted, the economy will eventually find itself in long-run equilibrium at point A.[23] In the short run, however, there will be a real exchange rate overshoot, albeit below what would have been the case if the resource had not been exhaustible.

6 Models and policy design

6.1 Introduction

In this chapter we shall demonstrate the relationship between the models discussed in previous chapters and 'real-world' econometric models and how the latter are used to analyse the economy taking the UK as our main example. Given the plethora of UK macroeconometric models and the speed with which their key behavioural equations are amended it becomes impossible to provide a detailed analysis here. Instead we give a schematic outline of the link between our analytic models and the main features of macroeconometric models in §6.2. We also explain how the models may be used to yield deterministic and stochastic simulations and discuss the problems of incorporating expectations variables. In §§6.3 to 6.5 we outline some issues in the design of policy, focusing on optimal control techniques. In §6.6 we return to the issue of expectations and extend our analysis of the Lucas critique (of §3.6) and discuss the problem of time inconsistency. The latter refers to the problem faced by the authorities when the private sector can react in advance to policy announcements. We end with a technical appendix on the optimal control problem.

6.2 Analytical and 'Real-World' Models

The reader might think that we have encountered enough technical problems and varieties of models in the preceding pages. However, moving from analytic models to real-world econometric models creates additional difficulties. For any economy there are likely to be a wide range of competing models each of which embodies different aspects of the analytic models discussed. Major distinctions between macroeconometric models centre on the degree to which they explicitly incorporate expectations (often the choice is between adaptive or rational expectations), and the speed with which markets 'clear' (particularly the labour and goods markets), or put another way, the sluggishness of price adjustment. We will discuss real-world models with reference to the UK (see Wallis 1985, 1986).

As far as the determinants of aggregate demand are concerned there is probably a reasonable amount of agreement between most UK modellers. Consumption is usually determined by income and some measure of wealth. Changes in wealth consist of additions to financial assets (i.e. saving), revaluations due to changes in bond and share prices (Pesaran and Evans 1984) and changes in the 'inflation loss' on liquid assets (Hendry and von-Ungern Sternberg 1979). Interest rate effects influence durable and non-durable consumer's expenditure (Cuthbertson 1980). Fixed investment and stock building are determined by output (i.e. the accelerator) and (particularly stock building) by interest rates (or the user cost of capital – see Jorgenson 1963). Trade flows (i.e. export and import volume) are determined by relative prices (or costs) and by home (imports) and world demand (exports).

On the supply side and the determination of employment, few macro-econometric models explicitly model the supply and demand for labour separately, together with a production function, to yield a 'full' neoclassical supply side model (although an exception here is the City University Business School, CUBS, model; see Wallis 1985, 1986). At present most models have the demand for labour determined by output and relative factor prices including the real wage. The 'supply side' may then be said to be modelled in the main via a wage–price model that in the long run yields a vertical PEAPC relationship (§3.4). Where this is the case, price and wage adjustment is usually sluggish and this allows considerable scope for changes in output and employment. This is as close as 'real-world' models get to the non-clearing models of chapter 2. Switches of regime are difficult to handle econometrically and as part of a complete model. Therefore, most 'real-world' models use somewhat ad hoc disequilibrium methods which allow price adjustment and quantity changes to take place simultaneously, but at different speeds of adjustment.

In chapter 5 we noted the importance of the exchange rate in the transmission mechanism of monetary and fiscal policy. Econometric models of the UK differ widely in their treatment of the exchange rate. Some assume uncovered interest parity (e.g. the Liverpool model; Minford et al 1984), while others (the National Institute of Economic and Social Research, NIESR; see Hall 1983) have a more eclectic 'single-equation' approach with the exchange rate depending on relative interest rates (capital flows), the current balance (trade flows) and a term representing the impact of North Sea Oil. In contrast HM Treasury (HM Treasury 1982) and the London Business School (LBS; see Keating 1985) have a portfolio model of the financial sector which can be solved for the exchange rate that clears the foreign exchange market (and simultaneously other financial markets – for example, the gilts market). This extreme diversity is in part due to the difficulty in successfully modelling changes in the UK exchange rate in the floating-rate period. It is in the foreign exchange (FOREX) market (and other financial markets) that one would expect continuous market clearing and also that agents might use consistent expectations (i.e. their expectations are the forecasts from their assumed model). As far as the FOREX market is concerned the Liverpool and LBS models may be solved under full (Muth-) rational expectations.

It is now becoming more commonplace to see explicit modelling of expectations in behavioural equations (see, e.g., Hall et al 1986a on stockbuilding, Hall et al 1986b on employment, Cuthbertson and Taylor 1987a, Spencer 1986, and Keating 1985 on financial assets). Equations with forward-looking variables in both the real and financial sectors are now appearing in UK models. The models may then be solved under either backward-looking schemes (e.g. adaptive expectations) or in a fully consistent (Muth-rational) manner. However, note that if the model in question involves RE in some sectors (e.g. the FOREX market) but sluggish adjustment in other sectors (e.g. goods and labour markets) we do *not* obtain the 'strong' New Classical results such as policy ineffectiveness. (See, e.g., the 'partly rational' models of §§3.8 and appendices 5.1 and 5.2).

Space precludes any discussion of policy simulations with specific UK macroeconometric models (see Wallis 1986). However, we hope we have said enough for the reader to realize that most of the analytic ideas discussed in previous chapters are incorporated in one or other of the UK macro-econometric models. Previous chapters therefore provide the basic building blocks for understanding the economic mechanisms involved in 'real-world' models and policy discussions. We now turn to the issues involved in using models for policy analysis.

6.2.1 Forecasting and Simulation

Most macroeconometric models consist of a set of behavioural equations (and identities) that yield a solution for the endogenous variables in terms of current and lagged values of the exogenous variables (e.g. world trade or policy instruments such as tax rates). Macroeconometric models contain variables in discrete time, and are dynamic and non-linear in the variables. Because of the non-linearities, the existence, uniqueness and stability of the solution of the model are determined by numerical (rather than analytic) methods. However, for expositional purposes we lose little by considering 'real-world' models as (approximated by) a *linear* simultaneous system.

By way of an example consider the fix-price, closed-economy IS–LM model of §1.2 and (equation (A1.1.7) of appendix 1.1) but with the addition of lags:

$$\begin{bmatrix} k & i_r \\ m_y & -m_r \end{bmatrix} \begin{bmatrix} Y \\ r \end{bmatrix}_t + \begin{bmatrix} a_{11} & a_{12} \\ a_{21} & a_{22} \end{bmatrix} \begin{bmatrix} Y \\ r \end{bmatrix}_{t-1} + \begin{bmatrix} -1 \\ -1 \end{bmatrix} \begin{bmatrix} G+X^* \\ M^s/P \end{bmatrix}_t = \begin{bmatrix} u_1 \\ u_2 \end{bmatrix}_t$$

(6.1)

where y = output, r = interest rate, G = government expenditure, X^* = exports, M^s = money supply, P = price level and u_{it} = random errors. All other terms are coefficients. The inclusion of the a_{ij} elements merely allows G, X^* and M^s/P to take several periods before their long-run impact on r and Y is achieved. (We could also have introduced lagged terms in G, X^* and M^s/P.) The above two-equation simultaneous system in the endogenous variables Y and r may be written in obvious matrix notation as

$$\mathbf{B}\,Y_t = \mathbf{A}\,Y_{t-1} + \mathbf{C}\,X_t + U_t \tag{6.2}$$

where $Y_t = (Y,r)_t'$, $X_t = (G+X^*, M^s/P)_t'$ and the known coefficient matrices are $\mathbf{B}$, $\mathbf{A}$, and $\mathbf{C}$ (e.g. $\mathbf{A} = -[a_{ij}]$). All (linear) simultaneous equation models (excluding for the moment any consideration of expectations) may be represented in the form (6.2) with the set of exogenous variables subsumed in the vector X. The complete model can then be 'solved' in a variety of ways.

In *deterministic forecasting* the error terms u_{it} are set to zero (in all time periods) and forecasts made for the exogenous variables. Knowing Y_0 and X_1, the deterministic forecast for the first time period is

$$\hat{Y}_1 = \mathbf{B}^{-1}\mathbf{A}\,Y_0 + \mathbf{B}^{-1}\mathbf{C}\,X_1. \tag{6.3}$$

Successive *forecasting values* of Y_t and known forecast values of X_t are then used to determine the whole forecast path of $\hat{Y}_t$:

$$\hat{Y}_t = \mathbf{B}^{-1}\mathbf{A}\,\hat{Y}_{t-1} + \mathbf{B}^{-1}\mathbf{C}\,X_t \qquad (t = 2, \ldots, H) \tag{6.4}$$

that is

$$\hat{Y}_t = \Pi_1 \hat{Y}_{t-1} + \Pi_2 X_t \qquad (t = 2, \ldots, H) \tag{6.5}$$

where $\Pi_1 = \mathbf{B}^{-1}\mathbf{A}$, $\Pi_2 = \mathbf{B}^{-1}\mathbf{C}$, and H is the forecast horizon.

Model-users frequently make residual or intercept adjustments. These 'add factors' are primarily used either because recent forecast errors (outside of the sample period of estimation) show a systematic pattern (e.g. they are all positive) or because 'special factors' not explicitly incorporated in the behavioural equations need to be considered (e.g. the impact of a revised corporation tax system on fixed investment). If the sequence of residual adjustments is $\bar{U}_t$ ($t = 1, \ldots, H$) then the adjusted solution incorporating the add factors is

$$\tilde{Y}_t = \Pi_1 \tilde{Y}_{t-1} + \Pi_2 X_t + \bar{U}_t$$

and the difference between the two solutions is

$$\begin{aligned}\tilde{Y}_t - \hat{Y}_t &= \bar{U}_t + \Pi_1 \bar{U}_{t-1} + \Pi_1^2 \bar{U}_{t-2} \ldots \\ &+ \Pi_1^{t-1}\bar{U}_t \qquad (t = 1, \ldots, H).\end{aligned} \tag{6.6}$$

If the residual adjustment is held constant ($U_t = \bar{U}$ for all t) the two solutions increasingly diverge (as $t \to H$) but at a decreasing rate[1]. Of course a constant adjustment $\tilde{Y}_t - \hat{Y}_t = U$ (for all t) is possible if we set

$U_1 = \bar{U}$, $U_t = (1 - \Pi_1)\bar{U}_1$ ($t = 2, \ldots, H$). In fact, one can apply a suitable residual adjustment to obtain *any* desired forecast value for Y_t (or a subset of the endogenous variables). This has become known as a 'type-1 (residual) fix'. Indeed it appears that for models with a broadly similar philosophy, 'residual adjustments' are a major source of differences between the rival forecasting groups (Wallis 1986). Also, residual adjustments in practice tend to offset the impact of inherent differences in structure between models, producing a set of 'consensus forecasts' by rival groups.

Policy or exogenous variable simulations consist of altering the exogenous variables X (e.g. a permanent step increase in government expenditure G of ten n per cent), usually one at a time, and noting the difference for all the endogenous variables Y_t (with $G_{1t} = 1.1G_{0t}$ for a change of ten per cent in G). (Residuals U_t are usually held constant at their base-run values, so they do not influence the differential effect on Y_t.) A variant on this theme, known as a 'type-2 fix' amongst UK modellers, is to alter a policy instrument (or set of policy instruments), like G_t, to achieve a *given target* for an endogenous variable (or variables), say output. Usually one is interested in whether the changes in the policy instrument appear feasible (e.g. large violent swings in G would probably be an administrative impossibility and certainly pose political problems) in order to achieve the desired target. A natural extension of this is to use the model to calculate the movements in several policy instruments to get 'close to' a set of targets. If it is not possible to achieve all the desired policy targets exactly (e.g. zero inflation and full employment), the policy maker must determine the relative costs and benefits of deviations in the variables from their target levels. The policy maker might also attach penalties to the changes in policy instruments required to achieve the targets. The problem is then reduced to one of constrained optimization of a dynamic system and optimal control techniques are required. We discuss the instruments and targets issue and optimal control in §§6.3–6.5.

So far we have been concerned with the deterministic properties (i.e. $U_t = 0$ for all t) of our simultaneous model. If the *estimated* residuals are zero-mean errors, then the expected value of Y_t, given $\hat{Y}_{t-1}$ and X_t, that is $E(Y_t | \hat{Y}_{t-1}, X_t)$, is just the deterministic solution (6.5) for a linear model. However, if the model is *non-linear* in the variables this is not the case (e.g. $E(\ln Y_t)$). In a large non-linear model it would be useful to know the error band in the forecast of the endogenous variables (e.g. GDP). This could then be compared with the impact of proposed policy changes. If the latter are small relative to the forecast error band for the model, one might take the view that the policy changes are not worth undertaking on macroeconomic grounds. It may also be the case that the deterministic forecast (i.e. $U_t = 0$) differs from the conditional expectation of the whole model and hence gives a *biased* estimate of likely outcomes. To assess the bias in a deterministic forecast and the error band of the forecast when using the whole model requires a *stochastic simulation* exercise. In a stochastic simulation exercise the model produces a series of forecast values $\tilde{Y}_t$ ($t = 1, 2, \ldots, H$) from

$$\tilde{Y}_t = \Pi_1 \tilde{Y}_{t-1} + \Pi_2 X_t + \mathbf{B}^{-1} U_t \tag{6.7}$$

where in each time period the error terms U_t are drawn from a distribution as near as possible to the estimated (or historical) distribution of the error terms. The forecast exercise is then repeated a large number of times (each with the same 'forecast values' for X_t) but each time a different set of values of U_t are drawn (from the fixed distribution). For each time period t we then have say 1000 values for $\tilde{Y}_t$ that is $\{\tilde{Y}_{ti}; i = 1, 2, \ldots, 1000\}$. The mean value 'at time t' is

$$\tilde{Y}_t^* = (\Sigma_i \tilde{Y}_{ti}/1000).$$

Given the deterministic solution $\hat{Y}_t$ we can compute the bias $(\hat{Y}_t - \tilde{Y}_t^*)$ for successive forecast horizons ($t = 1, 2, \ldots, H$). The variance of the forecast is given by

$$\mathrm{var}(\tilde{Y}_t) = \Sigma_i (\tilde{Y}_{ti} - \tilde{Y}_{ti}^*)^2/1000.$$

Tentative conclusions from two UK models (NIESR and LBS, see Wallis 1986) are that (i) the bias is relatively small, (ii) the variance in the forecast is large relative to possible plausible policy changes, (iii) the error band of one model easily overlaps the central deterministic forecast of the rival model and (iv) the bias and variance of the forecast increase absolutely and proportionately as the forecast horizon is extended. These results suggest that central deterministic forecasts are subject to relatively wide margins of error and even the direction of change of key endogenous variables is somewhat uncertain.

6.2.2. *Expectations*

A simultaneous equation model that explicitly incorporates (one-period-ahead) expectations may be written in matrix notation as

$$\mathbf{B} Y_t = \mathbf{A} Y_{t-1} + \mathbf{C} X_t + \mathbf{D} E(Y_{t+1}|\Omega_t) + U_t \tag{6.8}$$

or

$$Y_t = \Pi_1 Y_{t-1} + \Pi_2 X_t + \Pi_3 E(Y_{t+1}|\Omega_t) \tag{6.9}$$

where $E(Y_{t+1}|\Omega_t)$ is the expectation of Y at time $t+1$, formed with information Ω_t at time t, $\Pi_1 = \mathbf{B}^{-1} \mathbf{A}$ etc., and we have set $U_t = 0$.

The problem that arises in finding the solution for Y_t in (6.9) is that Y_t depends on the unknown $E(Y_{t+1}|\Omega_t)$: a problem we met in chapter 3 on RE solution methods. In analytic models it is usually possible to obtain the unique stable saddle-path solution. However, over a *finite* time horizon we cannot assume the model has reached this saddle-path solution and in any case in a large non-linear model we are unlikely to be able to determine the analytic solution. In this case, somewhat arbitrary terminal conditions must be imposed (and they might set GDP at a constant growth rate, or at a constant level).

There are a number of alternative algorithms for solving large non-linear RE models. By way of an example consider the following. Choose an arbitrary set of 'starting values', Y^e_{t+1} for the expectations term $E(Y_{t+1}|\Omega_t)$ in equation (6.8) for each time period. Since the $E(Y_{t+1}|\Omega_t)$ are now 'known', equation (6.8) can be solved in the usual way to obtain our forecasts for the endogenous variable $_1\tilde{Y}_{t+1}$ (given the X_t variables and setting $U_t = 0$ – its 'expected value'). $_1\tilde{Y}_{t+1}$ will generally not equal $_1Y^e_{t+1}$; that is, the forecasts are not consistent with the predictions of the model. We therefore take a new trial value for Y^e_{t+1}, namely

$$_2Y^e_{t+1} = {}_1Y^e_{t+1} + \gamma({}_1\tilde{Y}_{t+1} - {}_1Y^e_{t+1})$$

where γ is an 'adjustment factor' which varies according to the algorithm used. Using $_2Y^e_{t+1}$, we solve the model to yield new forecast values $_2\tilde{Y}_{t+1}$. We proceed until convergence is achieved, i.e. where $_j\tilde{Y}_{t+1}$ and $_jY^e_{t+1}$ differ by a 'small amount'. Then the predictions of the model are consistent with the expectations used in solving the model. Since the terminal condition is arbitrary (i.e. Y^e_{t+H} is arbitrary) then the model solution over the forecast period may be sensitive to the terminal condition chosen and the choice of terminal date, H. For one UK model at least (i.e. the Liverpool model; see Wallis 1985, 1986) different terminal conditions give rise to very different forecasts in the five years *preceding the terminal date*, indicating that these terminal conditions are a poor approximation to the stable saddle-path solution and forecasts over time periods close to H (like $H-5$, $H-4$, . . ., H) are of little use. However, forecasts for the 'early periods' are largely unaffected by a different choice of terminal conditions and are also unaffected as the terminal date is extended. Clearly, 'real-world' models with rational expectations yield additional technical problems, and these are the focus of much current research (see, for example, Hall 1985).

Finally, for completeness it is worth noting that if the expectations scheme chosen by the modeller is backward-looking (e.g. adaptive), that is $E(Y_{t+1}|\Omega_t)$ is just a function of past values of Y_t and possibly X_t, then the model in (6.8) reduces to (6.2) and may be solved in the usual way.

Having outlined the various ways in which real-world models may be used in forecasting and policy simulations, we now critically examine the formal techniques that have been used in policy design.

6.3 Models, Instruments and Targets

We can modify equation (6.2) slightly and express our (linear) macro-econometric model schematically as

$$\mathbf{B}Y_t + \mathbf{C}X_t + \mathbf{D}Z_t = U_t. \tag{6.10}$$

In (6.10), Y_t is a $T \times 1$ vector of target or 'state' variables that the government wishes to focus on in its macroeconomic policy, observed at time t. Examples of typical elements of Y_t might be the rate of inflation at a particular point in time, or the rate of national output, or the level of employment. X_t is an $I \times 1$ vector of instruments, or 'control' variables, which are under the control of the authories and which the government uses to pursue its targets. Typical elements of X_t might be the level of government expenditure at a point in time, or the level of taxes. Z_t is a $P \times 1$ vector of variables considered predetermined in the model. A predetermined variable is either a lagged variable (Y_{t-1}) or a truly exogenous variable such as the level of commodity prices on world markets. Finally, U_t is a $T \times 1$ vector of stochastic disturbances at time t. $\mathbf{B}$, $\mathbf{C}$ and $\mathbf{D}$ are matrices of estimated structural parameters, which determine the relationships between the variables – $\mathbf{B}$ is $T \times T$, $\mathbf{C}$ is $T \times I$ and $\mathbf{D}$ is $T \times P$. Thus, (6.10) is similar in form to (6.2), except that we have deliberately rearranged the system so that targets, instruments and predetermined variables appear separately. Hence (6.10) is just an alternative way of expressing the structural form.

Suppose that the government had a set of values of Y_{t+i} (Y_{t+i}^* say) which it wished to achieve in time period $t + i$ – for example, inflation of two per cent, unemployment of two per cent and a balance on the external account. The policy advisers would be unable to forecast the value of U_{t+i} at time t since the disturbance vector is, by definition, that part of the economy's behaviour that they cannot model (unless of course, U_t is serially correlated – a complication we ignore). Hence, the best they can do is to set U_{t+i} to a null vector:

$$\mathbf{B}Y_{t+i} + \mathbf{C}X_{t+i} + \mathbf{D}Z_{t+i} = 0. \tag{6.11}$$

Now, suppose that the policy advisers have available a set of forecasts on the exogenous variables at $t + i$, $\tilde{Z}_{t+i}$. They can, at least in principle, substitute these for Z_{t+i}, and Y_{t+i}^* in (6.11), and solve for the appropriate vector of control variables or instruments, X_{t+i}^* say, needed to attain the government's goals (this is the 'type-2 fix' discussed above):

$$X_{t+i}^* = -\mathbf{C}^{-1}\mathbf{B}Y_{t+i}^* - \mathbf{C}^{-1}\mathbf{D}\tilde{Z}_{t+i}. \tag{6.12}$$

This may strike the reader as rather glib since we have said nothing at all about whether or not $\mathbf{C}$ is a square matrix, let alone whether or not its inverse exists. This forms the basis of a problem originally analysed by Tinbergen (1952).

We defined $\mathbf{C}$ as a $T \times I$ matrix, where T is the number of state variables or targets and I is the number of control variables or instruments. There are, therefore, three logically possible relevant cases: either $T = I$ (number of targets is equal to the number of instruments), $T < I$ (more instruments than targets) or else $T > I$ (more targets than instruments). Let us examine the first of these, $T = I$.

If the number of instruments is exactly equal to the number of targets then **C** will be a square matrix. If all of the instruments are (linearly) dependent, i.e. the value of one or more instruments does not depend on the value of any other instrument, then, in matrix terminology, **C** will be of full rank and its inverse $\mathbf{C}^{-1}$ will exist. Thus, we can solve uniquely for X^*_{t+i} in exactly the way suggested by (6.12) and the government will attain its targets, subject only to any stochastic disturbances that may subsequently arise (i.e. U_{t+i}) or any errors in forecasting the exogenous variables.

Now consider the second case of more instruments than targets, $T < I$. Again, we assume all the instruments are independent of one another. Although **C** is no longer square, this raises no problem since a square, non-singular matrix can easily be obtained by deleting any $I - T$ rows of **C**. Thus, the government will again be able to achieve its targets subject only to stochastic disturbances and forecasting errors. Moreover, applying simple combinatorics (Chiang 1984) we can see that there will in general be $I! / [T!(I - T)!]$ ways of achieving this,[2] corresponding to the number of ways of choosing T instruments from a total of I.

Now, consider the final case where there are more targets than instruments, $T > I$. This is, as the reader might suspect, the case most closely corresponding to the real world, where the government has a large number of macro-economic policy targets, but only a very limited number of policy instruments under its control. In such a case, no solution such as (6.12) exists – the government cannot achieve all of its targets simultaneously. In these circumstances, the authorities will have to decide upon a trade-off between the various targets – e.g. by relaxing their inflation target a little in order to get nearer to their employment target. The formal theory underlying such policy trade-offs and the necessary adjustments that have to be made to the control variables is the subject matter of the theory of optimal control.

6.4 Optimal Control Theory

To simplify matters, we shall, at least initially, consider the system we are dealing with to be deterministic and ignore stochastic disturbances. We shall also simplify the system by ignoring truly exogenous variables and writing it in the form

$$Y_t = \mathbf{A} Y_{t-1} + \mathbf{C} X_t \tag{6.13}$$

where we have assumed that lagged values of the targets, i.e. state variables, partially determine the current values. **A** will be a $T \times T$ coefficient matrix. (This is in fact unrestrictive, since any model of the form (6.11) can be expressed in the form (6.13) by rearrangement and slightly redefining the variables (see Chow 1975).)

Now, suppose that the authorities have a target vector Y^* that they would like to achieve in the long run. In fact, because of costs involved in running the control variables or policy instruments at certain levels (e.g. extremely high levels of government expenditure involve administration and monitoring costs), the authorities may also have a desired level of the policy instruments that they would like to achieve, X^* say. If these two sets of objectives are to be consistent, they must satisfy the system

$$Y^* = A Y^* + C X^*. \tag{6.14}$$

Now, since we have assumed that $T > I$, there will in general be no way of achieving Y^* in any one period. In such a case we have to begin to make some assumptions about what trade-offs the authorities find acceptable. In particular, we shall assume that they try to keep the state variables as close to their desired values as possible over some finite period of time. Let us say that the authorities' planning horizon is H periods long. Then as a first step we can assume that it minimizes the weighted distance of the state variables from their desired values over the planning horizon by minimizing a quadratic loss function:

$$L = \sum_{t=1}^{H} (Y_t - Y^*)' M (Y_t - Y^*). \tag{6.15}$$

M is a $T \times T$ positive-semi-definite[3] matrix of weights, which encapsulates the authorities' attitudes towards the various trade-offs between the targets. As a simple example, suppose Y_t consisted of only two targets – inflation (p) and unemployment (u). For simplicity, assume M is diagonal with positive diagonal elements (m_1, m_2). Then we have

$$\sum_{t=1}^{H} (Y_t - Y^*)' M (Y_t - Y^*) = \sum_{t=1}^{H} [m_1(p_t - p^*)^2 + m_2(u_t - u^*)^2]$$

where p^* and u^* are the target levels of inflation and unemployment respectively. Clearly the greater p_t and u_t are above their target levels, the greater will be the loss. However, if the authorities put a greater emphasis on inflation than on unemployment, m_1 will be much larger than m_2. On the other hand, if the government is bent on reducing unemployment but is relatively unperturbed by high inflation, then m_2 will tend to be much larger than m_1.

Of course, equation (6.15) takes no account of deviations of the control variables from their desired levels. However, by defining an appropriate, positive-semi-definite, $I \times I$ weight matrix, N, this is relatively straightforward to incorporate:

$$L = \sum_{t=1}^{H} (Y_t - Y^*)' M (Y_t - Y^*) + \sum_{t=1}^{K} (X_t - X^*)' N (X_t - X^*). \tag{6.16}$$

If we denote deviations of the state and control variables from their desired values by lower-case letters, i.e. $y_t = Y_t - Y^*$ and $x_t = X_t - X^*$, then (6.16) may be written more compactly as

$$L = \sum_{t=1}^{H} (y_t' \mathbf{M} y_t + x_t' \mathbf{N} x_t). \tag{6.17}$$

Before proceeding, we should perhaps comment on the assumed form of the loss function, notably the fact that it is quadratic. This has the effect of making deviations from desired values contribute disproportionately more to the loss as the deviation gets larger. On the other hand, a major drawback is the symmetric way it treats positive and negative deviations. For example, if the desired level of inflation is two per cent, then inflation of one per cent contributes just as much to the loss as three per cent does. However, this is probably not greatly important so long as it is noted that the quadratic function is really only an approximation. In actual practice, computer algorithms may be available that only penalize positive deviations.

The policy-makers' problem should now be clear. The economic system is assumed to be of the form (6.13). Subtracting (6.14) from (6.13) and again using lower-case letters to denote deviations from desired values, policy makers wish to minimize

$$\sum_{k=1}^{H} (y_t' \mathbf{M} y_t + x_t' \mathbf{N} x_t)$$

subject to

$$y_t = \mathbf{A} y_{t-1} + \mathbf{C} x_t.$$

In appendix 6.1 we demonstrate the solution to this problem by dynamic programming methods. Essentially, this involves solving the intertemporal problem backwards, starting in period H. The loss in period H is minimized to yield the optimal level of the policy instruments or control variables, x_H, which is contingent upon the value of y_{H-1}: $\hat{x}_H = \mathbf{R}_H y_{H-1}$, say. This gives an optimized value for H-period loss:

$$\hat{L}_H = y_H' \mathbf{M} y_H + \hat{x}_H' \mathbf{N} \hat{x}_H.$$

Next we go to period $H-1$ and minimize

$$L_{H-1} = y_{H-1}' \mathbf{M} y_{H-1} + x_{H-1}' \mathbf{N} x_{H-1} + \hat{L}_H \tag{6.18}$$

with respect to x_{H-1}, to obtain the optimal level of x_{H-1}:

$$\hat{x}_{H-1} = \mathbf{R}_{H-1} y_{H-2}. \tag{6.19}$$

Now, given any particular value of y_{H-1} and $\hat{x}_H$, we must minimize the sum of the last-two-periods' loss. If we substitute (6.19) into (6.18) to obtain $\hat{L}_{H-1}$ and then minimize.

$$L_{H-2} = y'_{H-2} \mathbf{M} y_{H-2} + x'_{H-2} \mathbf{N} x_{H-2} + \hat{L}_{H-1}$$

we can determine a level of x_{H-2}, $\hat{x}_{H-2}$ say, such that $\hat{x}_{H-2}$, $\hat{x}_{H-1}$ and $\hat{x}_H$ minimize the sum of the last-three-periods' loss. Continuing in this fashion, we can obtain the full solution $\hat{x}_1, \hat{x}_2, \ldots, \hat{x}_H$ that minimizes (6.16) subject to (6.13).

In appendix 6.1 we show that this solution takes the form of an optimal feedback rule:

$$\hat{x}_t = \mathbf{R}_t y_{t-1} \tag{6.20}$$

where $\mathbf{R}_t$ is a non-linear matrix function of $\mathbf{M}$, $\mathbf{N}$, $\mathbf{A}$ and $\mathbf{C}$, and varies from period 1 to period H. This solution relies on Bellman's optimality principle, which states that 'An optimal policy has the property that, whatever the initial state and decision (i.e. control) are, the remaining decisions must constitute an optimal policy with regard to the state resulting from the first decision' (Bellman 1957). Perhaps a slightly clearer way of expressing the optimality principle is to say that the dynamic programming solution is optimal because, at the beginning of each period, whatever the initial conditions, all future policies are optimal (see Chow 1975 or Astrom 1970 for further details).

Expression (6.20) is an example of a 'closed-loop' control rule. This terminology, and indeed much of the theory of optimal control, is borrowed from the control engineering literature. A closed-loop control rule is contingent upon the state of the system at the relevant point in time – for example, the optimal boost for a rocket will depend upon its current coordinates and velocity, if the objective is a successful lunar landing. This is in contrast to an 'open-loop' control rule where the values of the control variables are determined in advance and there is no feedback from the state variables. A very simple example of an open-loop rule is a Friedmanite fixed-money-growth rule.

We should also point out that the problem we are analysing (i.e. the linear–quadratic control problem) satisfies what is known as 'certainty equivalence'. That is to say, the optimal feedback rule (6.20) would be identical even if the system were stochastic (see Chow 1975).[5] Thus, our simplifying assumption at the beginning of this section that the system is deterministic is in fact non-restrictive. Once we relax the assumption that the system is deterministic, we can, however, no longer write down at the beginning of time period 1 the optimal time path for $\hat{x}_t$, from $t = 2$ to H. This is because $\hat{x}_t$ depends upon y_{t-1}, and if the system is stochastic, $\hat{x}_t$ only becomes known after y_{t-1} is actually observed.[6] However, the policy rule (6.20) remains optimal since by Bellman's optimality principle we known that at each time t, whatever the initial conditions, all future policies are optimal.

6.5   Optimal Control in Practice: A Comparative Simulation Exercise

Craine et al (1978) examine the conduct of monetary policy in the context of optimal control and other rules over the period third quarter 1973 to second quarter 1975, using the large MIT-Penn-SSRC (MPS) macroeconometric model of the US economy. The study was carried out when all data for this period had actually been collected, although the optimal policy for each period was calculated using only information known at that time, so it provides a proper test of *'ex ante'* optimal control.

Craine et al's study involves three target variables – unemployment (u_t), inflation (p_t) and changes in the Treasury Bill rate (Δr_t) – and one instrument – the level of the money stock (M_t). The specific loss function they use is

$$L = \sum_{t=1}^{H} [2(u_t > 4.8)^2 + 1(p_t > 2.5)^2 + 5(|\Delta r_t| > 1.5)^2$$
$$+ 0.0001(M_t - 1.051^{t/4}M_0)^2].$$ (6.21)

The target for inflation, 2.5 per cent, was chosen on the basis of the Nixon Administration's announced policy objective in 1973 to reduce inflation to the 2–3 per cent range. The unemployment target of 4.8 per cent is equal to the long-run or natural rate of unemployment in the MPS model at the time. Since they were working with quarterly data, the last bracketed term in (6.21) penalizes growth of the money stock (demand deposits and currency) above 5.1 per cent per annum. This is within the target range made public in 1975 and is consistent with the inflation and unemployment target paths – i.e. the loss function takes a value of zero in stead-state (non-stochastic) equilibrium. The discontinuous penalty on Δr_t penalizes large quarterly changes in the Treasury Bill rate, on the supposition that this is disruptive to financial markets.

Although the chosen weights are somewhat arbitrary, they were felt to reflect the mood of policy prevailing at the time. Also, Craine et al carried out an analysis of the sensitivity of their results to changes in the targets and weights.

As a benchmark, Craine et al first of all derived the perfect-foresight optimal control solution, i.e. the optimal control solution using the actual rather than the forecasted values of all exogenous variables. Their method is as follows. They derived the optimal rule for the first quarter given by optimizing the loss function over eight successive quarters. The money stock is then set at this level and the model is simulated for one quarter, given the historical exogenous variables and errors, to calculate the endogenous variables. At the beginning of next quarter, the realizations of the exogenous variables and errors (i.e. equation residuals) become known and a new eight-quarter optimization is carried out. This 'rolling horizon' method is repeated until the first quarter of the eight-quarter horizon becomes 1975ii.

This process was then carried out for the *'ex ante'* optimal control solution – i.e. optimal control as it could have been carried out in practice, with the optimal forecasts of the exogenous variables used at each step, using information only up to that quarter.

In addition, Craine et al computed the value of the loss function over the period obtained by applying a number of ad hoc feedback and fixed rules

Table 6.1 Loss for alternative policies

Fixed 5.1% money growth	Actual monetary policy	Optimal control	Perfect-foresight optimal control
619.9	613.1	677.8	600.8

to the model. The two we shall discuss are actual monetary policy as it was conducted over the period (i.e. the value of the loss obtained by feeding the actual time path of the money stock into the model), and a Friedmanite fixed-money-growth rule (i.e. the value obtained by allowing money to grow at an annual rate of 5.1 per cent, come what may).

The values of the loss function obtained for these four policies are reported in table 6.1. By construction, the loss for the perfect-foresight optimal control rule defines the lower bound. Somewhat surprisingly perhaps, the *'ex ante'* optimal control solution fares the worst among these four policies, with actual monetary policy doing best but only by a short lead over the Friedmanite fixed-money-growth rule.

This result is quite instructive for a number of reasons. One should perhaps expect an optimal feedback rule to outperform a fixed rule since observed errors can be offset rather than having a permanent effect. However, given uncertainty concerning the structure of the economy (even though the model was given, the equation residuals were not) and future events, there is in fact no guarantee that performance will be improved. Indeed, it is precisely because of such uncertainties (as well as the additional uncertainty that follows from not knowing the 'true' model) that Friedman advocated fixed rules in the first place (Friedman 1961). However, even the fixed-growth rule was beaten by actual monetary policy. Craine et al note that actual monetary policy suffers from at least one major advantage relative to the optimal control policy, but also a major disadvantage. The advantage is that policy was not fixed for a quarter at a time, but could be continuously modified as new information became available. The disadvantage was that the money supply was not perfectly controllable, so the actual path of the money supply was not in fact identical to the targeted path.

In attempting to explain the poor performance of the optimal control solution, Craine et al examined the loss function and carried out a sensitivity analysis of their results to changes in the parameters (i.e. both the targets and the weights). However, their finding was that the effect on 'the loss' of changes in the weights was heavily dominated by the effect of uncertainty in the forecasts of the exogenous variables. Moreover, they found that changes of up to 100 per cent in target paths and weights do not alter the ranking in table 6.1. In conclusion, Craine et al attribute this result to the unusually turbulent period used for the simulations. The period covered a number of exogenous shocks – including the first oil price shock, various financial crises such as the failure of Herstatt Bank, Soviet crop failures, midwestern US floods, and so on. This led to very poor exogenous variable forecasts which effectively sabotaged the optimal control solution. They conclude: 'when predictive tools suddenly begin to miss badly, they have to be corrected (and the proper corrections were not apparent in early 1974) or the forecasting structure must be heavily discounted in policy decisions'.

6.6 Policy Optimization with Rational Expectations

So far, our discussion of policy optimization has ignored the possibility that agents may be endowed with forward-looking or more particularly rational expectations. Once we allow this possibility, a number of problems are introduced. The first problem is that if agents alter their behaviour according to the particular policy regime in force, then the structure of the model may itself alter across different policy regimes. This is the basis of the so-called Lucas critique which we discussed briefly in chapter 3. The second problem that may arise is that it may no longer be possible to design a policy that is consistently optimal at all points in time – this is the time-inconsistency problem.

6.6.1 The Lucas Critique

The Lucas (1976) critique of policy evaluation makes the point that many of the estimated equations in macroeconometric models may in fact be a mixture of the true, time-invariant parameters that describe agents' behaviour (the 'deep parameters') and parameters that are contingent upon the particular economic environment prevailing during the estimation period, and that may alter as the policy regime alters. In general, there will be no way of unravelling the estimates to work out how they would change when the economic environment changes. If this is the case, macroeconometric models are only useful for predicting the future on the assumption of unchanged policies. In particular, they cannot be used to evaluate alternative policies since, had a different policy regime been in force when the estimation was carried out, the estimates would have been different.

A simple example should help to illustrate the argument. Suppose agents' choose the value of an economic variable x_t depending on the value of another variable y_t and the one-step-ahead ration expectation of a third variable, z_t, plus a stochastic disturbance η_t:

$$x_t = \alpha y_t + \beta E(z_{t+1}|\Omega_t) + \eta_t \tag{6.22}$$

where Ω_t is the information set available at time t. Suppose further that z_t follows some sort of autoregressive process, say a second-order process:

$$z_t = \phi_1 z_{t-1} + \phi_2 z_{t-2} + \epsilon_t \tag{6.23}$$

where ϵ_t is white noise and, in particular, $E(\epsilon_t|\Omega_{t-i})=0$, $i>0$. Clearly, the rational expectation of z_{t+1} given (6.23) is

$$E(z_{t+1}|\Omega_t)=\phi_1 z_t+\phi_2 z_{t-1}. \tag{6.24}$$

Substituting (6.24) into (6.22):

$$x_t=\alpha y_t+\beta(\phi_1 z_t+\phi_2 z_{t-1})+\eta_t. \tag{6.25}$$

Now, if (6.25) describes the behaviour of z_t over the period of estimation, the economic modeller may estimate an equation of the form:

$$x_t=\alpha y_t+\gamma_1 z_t+\gamma_2 z_{t-1}+\eta_t. \tag{6.26}$$

Unknown to the modeller, however, the estimates of γ_1 and γ_2 are in fact estimates of non-linear functions of the 'deep parameter' β and the historically contingent, possibly policy-dependent parameters ϕ_1 and ϕ_2, since $\gamma_1=\beta\phi_1$ and $\gamma_2=\beta\phi_2$.

Now suppose that an equation of the form (6.26) formed part of an econometric model. The policy advisers may wish to simulate on the model the effect of a change in policy, say a switch from monetary targeting to interest rate targeting. Such a switch may in fact alter the form of (6.24), say to

$$z_t=z_{t-1}+\epsilon_t. \tag{6.27}$$

(For example, z_t may be the money supply, so switching to interest rate targeting means allowing money to follow a random walk.) In this case, the policy advisers *should* be working with an equation of the form

$$x_t=\alpha y_t+\beta z_t+\eta_t. \tag{6.28}$$

However, by continuing to work with (6.26) when simulating the new policy, they will draw erroneous conclusions.

A possible solution to the Lucas critique is to try to model agents' expectations formation processes directly, without mixing them up during estimation (see, e.g., Hansen and Sargent 1980). For example, Cuthbertson and Taylor (1987a) postulate that agents' desired money holdings at any point in time will be of the form:

$$M_t^*=\alpha Y_t \tag{6.29}$$

where M_t^* denotes desired money holdings and Y_t is nominal income (in fact, Cuthbertson and Taylor use prices, real income and interest rates, but considering only one explanatory variable will suffice to illustrate the argument). Furthermore, agents are endowed with rational expectations and incur costs both of holding money balances different to the desired level, and costs of adjusting money balances. This is summarized by assuming that they minimize a quadratic loss function of the form

$$L = E \sum_{t}^{\infty}_{i=1} D^i [a_1 (M^*_{t+i} - M_{t+i})^2 + a_2 (M_{t+i} - M_{t+1-i})^2] \tag{6.30}$$

where E denotes $E(.|\Omega_t)$, D is a discount factor ($0 < D < 1$), and M_t is actual money holdings. Expression (6.30) is in fact just a multi-period extension of the one-period loss functions often used to derive familiar equations for estimating partial adjustment (see, e.g., Chow 1966). The 'deep parameters' that we are interested in are α, the 'long-run' income elasticity, as well as a_1 and a_2, the loss function weights. Minimization of (6.30) with respect to M_t yields (see 'B3' in appendix 4.1 which uses the Sargent (1979) forward-lag operator method):

$$M_t = \lambda M_{t-1} + (1 - \lambda)(1 - \lambda D) \sum_{i=0}^{\infty} (\lambda D)^i \alpha E_{t} Y_{t+i} \tag{6.31}$$

where λ is the 'stable root' of the system ($0 < \lambda < 1$) and is a function of a_1, a_2 and D. Now suppose that Y_t follows a simple first-order autoregressive process (Cuthbertson and Taylor in fact use a fourth-order vector autoregression):

$$Y_t = \phi_1 Y_{t-1} + \epsilon_t \qquad |\phi_1| < 1 \tag{6.32}$$

where ϵ_t is again white noise. From (6.32) we have

$$E(Y_{t+1}|\Omega_t) = \phi Y_t.$$

However, by the chain rule of forecasting

$$E(Y_{t+2}|\Omega_t) = E(\phi E(Y_{t+1}|\Omega_t)|\Omega_t) = \phi^2 Y_t$$

and, in general,

$$E(Y_{t+i}|\Omega_t) = \phi^i Y_t. \tag{6.33}$$

Substituting (6.33) into (6.31):

$$M_t = \lambda M_{t-1} + (1 - \lambda)(1 - \lambda D) \sum_{i=0}^{\infty} \alpha (\lambda D)^i \phi^i Y_t$$

or

$$M_t = \lambda M_{t-1} + \frac{(1 - \lambda)(1 - \lambda D)}{1 - \lambda D \phi} \alpha Y_t. \tag{6.34}$$

Equations (6.32) and (6.34) can be estimated jointly by non-linear estimation techniques (for a given D), either imposing the cross-equation restriction (that ϕ appears in both equations) or estimating the two equations separately without the restriction. A test of the validity of the cross-equation restrictions can then be undertaken in the manner described in §4.5 (for the policy ineffectiveness proposition). Estimates of α and λ are obtained that are not dependent on ϕ. Moreover, if it can be ascertained how a particular policy may alter the process governing Y_t (e.g. the parameter ϕ falls by 50 per cent, or the process becomes of higher order), then (6.34) can be altered accordingly and a correct forecast of M_t obtained under the new regime. Of course, in practice, such a procedure may be of limited use to the policy adviser (e.g. would the money supply switch to a third-order autoregression if the authorities switched to monetary targeting?), but it is an important first step. Moreover, such a method yields estimates of the deep parameters that may not otherwise be available, and that may be of interest in themselves for determining long-run policy.

6.6.2   The Time Inconsistency of Optimal Plans

The above discussion of optimal control was deliberately couched in terms of a so-called 'causal' or backward-looking model:

$$Y_t = \mathbf{A} Y_{t-1} + \mathbf{C} X_t + U_t. \tag{6.35}$$

That is to say, the current state, Y_t, is a function only of the past state and the current values of the so-called 'forcing variables' (i.e. the control or instrumental variables, the exogenous variables and the disturbance term). In particular, the current state does not depend upon the expected value of future states. Any expectations variables that do occur in causal models are backward-looking (e.g. adaptive expectations), so they can be 'solved out' as a function of past states and current forcing variables. This is not so in 'non-causal' or forward-looking models, which are of the form

$$Y_t = \mathbf{A} Y_{t-1} + \mathbf{C} X_t + \mathbf{D} E(Y_{t+1}|\Omega_t) + U_t. \tag{6.36}$$

In (6.36) the current state Y_t depends partly upon the expected or anticipated value of future states, $E(Y_{t+1}|\Omega_t)$. By repeatedly substituting out for $E(Y_{t+1}|\Omega_t)$ using the chain rule of expectations, Y_t can be expressed as a function of the current and anticipated future values of the instruments (control variables), of the exogenous variables and of the disturbances. This highlights the crux of the problem of time inconsistency. The current state depends upon expectations formed in the current period of future *instruments*, $E(X_{t+1}|\Omega_t)$ etc., or, to put it another way, the *present* depends upon expected *future* policy. It is this that makes it difficult to design a policy that is time-consistent in the sense that at each point in time it is the best policy, given the current situation.

The problem is in fact quite intuitive. Kydland and Prescott (1977), who originated the idea of the time inconsistency of optimal plans, give a simple example involving patent policy, which may help to illustrate the argument. In order to provide incentives for research and development, the government offers patent protection, equivalent to a monopoly for a certain period, on new inventions. Before an invention has been made this is the optimal policy. Once the invention has been made, however, the optimal policy now is not to offer patent protection, since monopolies cause all sorts of welfare distortions, and after all the inventor can hardly 'de-invent' his or her brainchild. Hence, what starts off as an optimal policy (i.e. patent protection) is not consistently so through time. Of course, the inventor's activity almost certainly depends upon his or her expectations of future policy, namely that patent protection will be extended. In this case, the objective functions of the authorities and the representative individual (in this case the inventor) are different – the optimal but time-inconsistent policy of promising patent protection but then withdrawing it may benefit society as a whole, but makes the inventor worse off. This is not, however, a necessary characteristic of the problem, as is shown in an example due to Fischer (1980). Imagine a two-period economy in which people inherit a capital stock in the first period, supply labour in both periods and save in the first period. The only way of saving is by investing in the capital stock. The government distributes a 'public good', the revenue for which it obtains by raising taxes. The government's objective is to maximize the representative individual's objective (i.e. utility) function. The government then has to decide the optimal mix for taxes on labour and capital in both periods. Consider the optimal mix for the second period. Agents' behaviour in the first period will depend upon anticipated policy in the second period. For example, if capital is expected to be heavily taxed in the second period then this may discourage first-period saving. On the other hand, if labour is expected to be more heavily taxed in one period, then this may lead to intertemporal distortions in the labour market as people try and sell more labour in the other period (see, e.g., Lucas and Rapping 1969). It would therefore seem that the optimal policy would be to announce some mix of taxes on both capital and labour in both periods. However, once the second period arrives, the capital stock is given – i.e. supplied inelastically. Now it is a well known result of optimal tax theory that it is generally better to tax goods supplied inelastically, since, by definition, their supply cannot be altered. Hence, the optimal policy once the second period has arrived is to tax capital heavily. Thus, the overall optimal policy is time-inconsistent.

We can begin to analyse more formally what is causing the problem by examining Kydland and Prescott's definition of 'time-consistent policy' more closely. This can be paraphrased as: 'A sequence of policy actions is time consistent if, for each time period, the policy action in that period maximises the objective function, taking as given all previous policy actions and private agents' decisions and that all future policy actions will be similarly determined' (Buiter 1981). However, this is just a restatement of Bellman's optimality

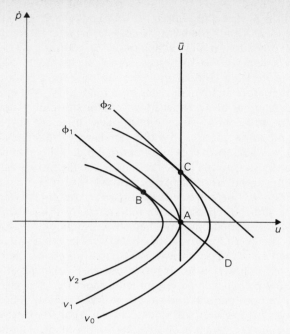

Figure 6.1   The time-inconsistency of optimal plans

principle, which is relied upon to demonstrate the optimality of the dynamic programming solution in causal models. The dynamic programming solution to the optimal control problem in causal or backward-looking models works by not forcing us to choose a policy for a future period until that period arrives (although a rule is determined in advance, the policy chosen will depend upon the inherited state of the system, according to (6.20)). However, if the model is non-causal, or forward-looking, then the dynamic programming solution will fail to allow for the effect of anticipated future instrument values (i.e. policy) on current and past states. Since not allowing for these expectations effects further circumscribes the government's behaviour, one should expect a better policy (i.e. one that achieves a higher value of the objective function) to exist: the dynamic programming solution in a non-causal framework will be sub-optimal.

Of course, if agents are rational, and they realize that the government has an incentive to renege on its announced policies at some future stage, then they will modify their behaviour accordingly. Moreover, the government will realize this, and take it into account in deciding its policy. In fact, this is really a problem in game theory, and the outcome will be an equilibrium where each of the 'players' (the government and the representative individual) correctly anticipates the other's behaviour – a so-called non-cooperative or 'Nash' equilibrium.

Take the inflation–unemployment example discussed by Kydland and Prescott 1977, Barro and Gordon 1983a,b and Barro 1985. Consider an expectations-augmented Phillips curve of the form

$$u_t = \bar{u} + \alpha(\dot{p}^e_t - \dot{p}_t) \qquad \alpha > 0 \qquad (6.37)$$

where u_t is the level of unemployment, $\bar{u}$ is the natural rate of unemployment, $\dot{p}_t$ is the rate of inflation and $\dot{p}^e_t$ is the expected rate of inflation. This is plotted in figure 6.1 where the vertical line at $\bar{u}$ represents the long-run Phillips curve ($\dot{p}_t = \dot{p}^e_t$) and ϕ_1 and ϕ_2 represent short-run Phillips curves ($\dot{p}_t \neq \dot{p}^e_t$). Also in figure 6.1 we have plotted curves v_0, v_1 and v_2, along which the points represent equal-social-welfare (equivalently, equal-loss) combinations of inflation and unemployment. Social welfare rises as we get nearer to the origin, so v_2 dominates v_1 which dominates v_0. We assume that the government uses the money supply as a control variable to influence the current state (levels of inflation and unemployment).

Consider point A, where the government sets inflation to zero and the economy settles down at the natural rate of unemployment. At A, however, the government will be tempted to gain a short-term advantage by unexpectedly raising inflation and trading along the short-run Phillips curve ϕ_1 to point B. However, economic agents realize this and increase their expectations of inflation accordingly, and so the short-run Phillips curve shifts up. The authorities may then be able to steal a short-term reduction in unemployment by trading along the new short-run Phillips curve; but, of course, agents realize this and so their inflation expectations rise again. Eventually an equilibrium will be achieved at a point such as C where the short-run Phillips curve ϕ_2 is tangential to the iso-welfare contour v_0. At C, the authorities have no incentive to expand (or reduce) inflation since if they did they would have to move to an iso-welfare contour further from the origin than v_0, and social welfare would fall. Thus, the monetary policy necessary to reach point C is the time-consistent policy. It is the only policy that is incentive-compatible in the sense of being consistent with the authorities' desire to maximize social welfare at each point in time, taking the initial state as given. Thus, although the authorities retain the power to fool people via inflation surprises in any period, they are not motivated to exercise it. For this to be the case, the marginal benefit of inflation surprises must be just equal to the marginal cost of inflation – i.e. the iso-welfare contour must be tangential to the short-run Phillips curve. This condition, plus the rational expectations equilibrium condition, which requires that agents' expectations of inflation are correct on average, together ensure that point C represents the time-consistent equilibrium policy.

However, a higher level of social welfare could have been achieved by sticking at point A! Thus, although A is time-inconsistent, if the government can convince people that it is not going to renege at some future point, then the government would be better off pursuing an optimal, time-inconsistent, zero-inflation strategy.

One way achieving the necessary credibility of precommitment to locate at A is via reputation effects. For example, the government can attempt to raise the political costs of reneging by repeatedly making public statements ('there is no alternative', 'no U-turn'). This may eventually raise the costs of reneging to such a point where, viewed from the perspective of the government, point A is in fact incentive-compatible in the sense that any short-term gains to be had from a quick 'dash for growth' are likely to be offset by political costs. Of course, problems may arise as the administration faces the run-up to an election. The temptation to pursue an 'end-game' strategy in order to try to obtain just enough short-term gain to increase the probability of being re-elected will be high, but of course agents will to some extent realize this, so the exact, game-theoretic solution may be hard to determine (see, e.g., Barro and Gordon 1983a).

6.7   Summary and Conclusion

We have demonstrated that the 'small' analytic models of previous chapters form the basic building blocks of some UK macroeconometric forecasting models. It is only by analysing these 'simple' models that we can begin to disentangle the major principal influences at work in complex large-scale models. We then moved on to analyse how large-scale models may be used in forecasting and policy analysis. In particular we noted the strengths and limitations of various forecasting models and the application of optimal control techniques. When RE are incorporated into the model we encounter additional problems, namely, the choice of terminal conditions, the Lucas policy evaluation problem and the problem of time inconsistency. Ultimately the importance of both is an empirical matter, but they further reinforce the argument for a cautious approach to policy changes.

Notes

1   For $U_t = \bar{U}$, for all t, we have

$$\tilde{Y}_t - \hat{Y}_t = (I - \Pi_1)^{-1}(I - \Pi_1')\bar{U}$$

which will converge on $(I - \Pi_1)^{-1}\bar{U}$ for high values of t, so long as the system is stable in the sense that the roots of $|I - \Pi_1 z| = 0$ (where z is a real scalar) lie outside the unit circle. The latter is the usual (matrix) diffferential equation condition for dynamic stability.

2   $n! = n(n-1)(n-2)$, . . ., 1. For example, $3! = 3 \times 2 \times 1 = 6$.

3   See Chiang 1984 for a discussion of positive-semi-definiteness. The principle characteristic of a positive-semi-definite matrix is that its diagonal elements are non-negative. In the present context, this means that target deviations cannot reduce the loss.

4 Sometimes, in the literature and below, reference is made to 'maximizing the authorities' objective function'. In this case, the objective function would be simply $-L$.

5 This is only true if the disturbances are additive. If the stochastic disturbances enter multiplicatively, the solution may be slightly different – see, e.g., Turnovsky 1977, ch. 14.

6 In fact, under certainty, the optimal closed-loop linear feedback solution and the optimal open-loop solution coincide.

Appendix 6.1   Solution to the Linear–Quadratic Control Problem by Dynamic Programming

The problem is to minimize

$$L = \sum_{t=1}^{H} (y_t'\mathbf{M}y_t + x_t'\mathbf{N}x_t) \qquad \text{(A6.1.1)}$$

subject to

$$y_t = \mathbf{A}y_{t-1} + \mathbf{C}x_t. \qquad \text{(A6.1.2)}$$

The method of dynamic programming works recursively. First we optimize the loss in the last period, contingent upon y_{H-1}. Then we optimize the sum of the loss in the last-but-one period plus the optimized last-period loss, contingent upon y_{H-2}, and so on. In the last stage the optimal x_1 for period 1 is found, contingent upon the known value of the initial state y_0. Note that the method works recursively, or back in time. At each step, we determine the optimal value of x_t. Hence, the problem of H unknown values of x_t ($t = 1, \ldots, H$) is transformed into H problems, each involving one unknown, x_t. Bellman's optimality principle (see, e.g., Chow 1975) states that this will yield the optimal solution. That this is so is quite intuitive. Whatever the value of y_{H-1}, we choose an optimal value of x_H, $\hat{x}_H$ say, for the last period. Given this, we go to period $H-1$ and choose $\hat{x}_{H-1}$ such that $\hat{x}_{H-1}$ and $\hat{x}_{H-2}$ are together optimal for periods $H-1$ and H, given any particular value of y_{H-2}. Proceeding in this fashion, we eventually end up with a set of H $\hat{x}_t$'s, $\hat{x}_1, \hat{x}_2, \hat{x}_3, \ldots, \hat{x}_H$, which are jointly optimal for periods 1–H, given the known value of y_0.

We shall now illustrate how Bellman's optimality principle can be used to derive optimal feedback rules of the form described within the chapter.

We define

$$\hat{L}_H = y_H'\mathbf{M}y_H + \hat{x}_H'\mathbf{N}\hat{x}_H \qquad \text{(A6.1.3)}$$

i.e. $\hat{L}_H$ is the optimized value of period-H loss, L_H. Then

$$L_{H-1} = y_{H-1}'\mathbf{M}y_{H-1} + x_{H-1}'\mathbf{N}x_{H-1} + \hat{L}_H$$

or, in general,

$$L_t = y_t' \mathbf{M} y_t + x_t' \mathbf{N} x_t + \hat{L}_{t+1} \qquad (A6.1.4)$$

for $t = 1, \ldots, H - 1$.

First, we write down period-H loss after substituting in from (A6.1.2):

$$L_H = (y_{H-1}' \mathbf{A}' + x_H' \mathbf{C}') \mathbf{M} (\mathbf{A} y_{H-1} + \mathbf{C} x_H) + x_H' \mathbf{N} x_H. \qquad (A6.1.5)$$

Differentiating with respect to x_H:

$$\partial L_H / \partial x_H = 2(\mathbf{N} + \mathbf{C}' \mathbf{MC}) x_H + 2\mathbf{C}' \mathbf{MA} y_{H-1}. \qquad (A6.1.6)$$

Setting (A6.1.6) equal to zero and solving for $\hat{x}_H$:

$$\hat{x}_H = -(\mathbf{N} + \mathbf{C}' \mathbf{MC})^{-1} (\mathbf{C}' \mathbf{MA}) y_{H-1} = \mathbf{R}_H y_{H-1} \text{ say.} \qquad (A6.1.7)$$

Expression (A6.1.7) is an optimal feedback rule giving the optimal value for x_H, given y_{H-1}, which will be the result of optimal policies pursued in periods 1 to $H - 1$.

Substituting (A6.1.7) into (A6.1.5) gives the optimized value of period-H loss:

$$\hat{L}_H = y_{H-1}' [(\mathbf{A} + \mathbf{CR}_H)' \mathbf{M} (\mathbf{A} + \mathbf{CR}_H) + \mathbf{R}_H' \mathbf{NR}_H] y_{H-1}. \qquad (A6.1.8)$$

Substituting (A6.1.8) into (A6.1.4):

$$L_{H-1} = y_{H-1}' \mathbf{S}_{H-1} y_{H-1} + x_{H-1}' \mathbf{N} x_{H-1} \qquad (A6.1.9)$$

where

$$\mathbf{S}_{H-1} = \mathbf{M} + (\mathbf{A} + \mathbf{CR}_H)' \mathbf{M} (\mathbf{A} + \mathbf{CR}_H) + \mathbf{R}_H' \mathbf{NR}_H. \qquad (A6.1.10)$$

Substituting (A6.1.2) into (A6.1.9):

$$L_{H-1} = (y_{H-2}' \mathbf{A}' + x_{H-1}' \mathbf{C}') \mathbf{S}_{H-1} (\mathbf{A} y_{H-2} + \mathbf{C} x_{H-1}) + x_{H-1}' \mathbf{N} x_{H-1}.$$

Differentiating with respect to x_{H-1}:

$$\frac{\partial L_{H-1}}{\partial x_{H-1}} = 2(\mathbf{N} + \mathbf{C}' \mathbf{S}_{H-1} \mathbf{C}) x_{H-1} + 2\mathbf{C}' \mathbf{S}_{H-1} \mathbf{A} y_{H-1}. \qquad (A6.1.11)$$

Setting (A6.1.11) equal to zero and solving for $\hat{x}_{H-1}$:

$$\hat{x}_{H-1} = -(\mathbf{N} + \mathbf{C}' \mathbf{S}_{H-1} \mathbf{C})^{-1} (\mathbf{C}' \mathbf{S}_{H-1} \mathbf{A}) y_{H-1}$$
$$= \mathbf{R}_{H-1} y_{H-1} \text{ say.} \qquad (A6.1.12)$$

Note that (A6.1.12) is identical in form to (A6.1.7) if we write $\mathbf{M}=\mathbf{S}_H$. It should therefore be clear that repeating this process to minimize L_{H-2} will yield a feedback rule of the form

$$\hat{x}_{H-2}=-(\mathbf{N}+\mathbf{C}'\mathbf{S}_{H-2}\mathbf{C})^{-1}(\mathbf{C}'\mathbf{S}_{H-2}\mathbf{A})y_{H-2}=\mathbf{R}_{H-2}y_{H-2} \text{ say}$$

where

$$\mathbf{S}_{H-2}=\mathbf{M}+(\mathbf{A}+\mathbf{CR}_{H-1})'\mathbf{S}_{H-1}(\mathbf{A}+\mathbf{CR}_{H-1})+\mathbf{R}'_{H-1}\mathbf{NR}_{H-1}.$$

(The reader may wish to verify this.) Continuing in this fashion back to period 1, the general solution emerges:

$$\hat{x}_t=\mathbf{R}_t y_{t-1} \qquad t=1, \ldots, H$$

where

$$\mathbf{R}_t=-(\mathbf{N}+\mathbf{C}'\mathbf{S}_t\mathbf{C})^{-1}(\mathbf{C}'\mathbf{S}_t\mathbf{A})$$

and

$$\mathbf{S}_t= \begin{cases} \mathbf{M} & t=H \\ \mathbf{M}+(\mathbf{A}+\mathbf{CR}_{t+1})'\mathbf{S}_{t+1}(\mathbf{A}+\mathbf{CR}_{t+1})+\mathbf{R}'_{t+1}\mathbf{NR}_{t+1} & t<H. \end{cases}$$

References

Adler M and Lehmann B (1983) Deviations from Purchasing Power Parity in the Long Run. *Journal of Finance*, **38**, 1471–1487.

Akerlof G and Miyazaki H (1980) The Implicit Contract Theory of Unemployment Meets the Wage Bill Argument. *Review of Economic Studies*, **47**, 109–128.

Anderson L C and Jordan K M (1969) A Monetarist Model for Economic Stabilization. *Federal Reserve Bank of St Louis Review*, **52**, 7–25.

Ando A and Modigliani F (1963) The Life Cycle Hypothesis of Saving: Aggregate Implications and Tests. *American Economic Review*, **53**, 55–84.

Arrow K J (1971) *Essays in the Theory of Risk Bearing*. Chicago: Markham.

Arrow K J (1985) The Economics of Agency. In: Pratt J W and Zeckhauser R (eds) *Agency: The Structure of Business*. Cambridge, Mass: Harvard Business School Press.

Astrom K J (1970) *Introduction to Stochastic Control Theory*. New York: Academic Press.

Attfield C L F, Demery D and Duck N W (1981a) A Quarterly Model of Unanticipated Monetary Growth, Output and the Price Level in the UK 1963–78. *Journal of Monetary Economics*, **8**, 331–350.

Attfield C L F, Demery D and Duck N W (1981b) Unanticipated Monetary Growth, Output and the Price Level: UK, 1946–77. *European Economic Review*, **16**, 367–385.

Azariadis C (1975) Implicit Contracts and Underemployment Equilibria. *Journal of Political Economy*, **83**, 1183–1202.

Azariadis C (1982) Employment with Asymmetric Information. *Quarterly Journal of Economics*, **98**, Supplement, 157–172.

Azariadis C and Stiglitz J E (1983) Implicit Contracts and Fixed Price Equilibria. *Quarterly Journal of Economics*, **98**, Supplement, 1–22.

Baily M N (1974) Wages and Employment Under Uncertain Demand. *Review of Economic Studies*, **41**, 37–50.

Ball R J, Burns T and Laury J S E (1977) The Role of Exchange Rate Changes in Balance of Payments Adjustment – the United Kingdom Case. *Economic Journal*, **87**, 1–29.

Barro R J (1974) Are Government Bonds Net Wealth? *Journal of Political Economy*, **82**, 1095–1117.

Barro R J (1976) Rational Expectations and the Role of Monetary Policy. *Journal of Monetary Economics*, **2**, 1–33.

Barro R J (1977a) Long-term Contracting Sticky Prices and Monetary Policy. *Journal of Monetary Economics*, **3**, 305–316.

Barro R J (1977b) Unanticipated Money Growth and Unemployment in the United States. *American Economic Review*, **67**, 101–115.

Barro R J (1978) Unanticipated Money, Output and the Price Level in the United States *Journal of Political Economy*, **86**, 549–570.

Barro R J and Fischer S (1976) Recent Developments in Monetary Theory. *Journal of Monetary Economics*, **2**, 133–167.

Barro R J and Gordon D (1983a) Rules, Discretion and Reputation in a Model of Monetary Policy. *Journal of Monetary Economics*, **12**, 101–211.

Barro R J and Gordon D (1983b) A Positive Theory of Monetary Policy in a Natural Rate Model. *Journal of Political Economy*, **91**, 589–610.

Barro R J and Rush M (1980) Unanticipated Money and Economic Activity. In: Fisher S (ed.) *Rational Expectations and Economic Policy*. Chicago: University of Chicago Press for NBER.

Baumol W J (1977) *Economic Theory and Operations Analysis*. London: Prentice-Hall.

Begg D K H (1982a) *The Rational Expectations Revolution in Macroeconomics: Theories and Evidence*. Deddington, Oxford: Philip Allan.

Begg D K H (1982b) Rational Expectations, Wage Rigidity, and Involuntary Unemployment: A Particular Theory. *Oxford Economic Papers*, **34**(2), 23–47.

Bellman R (1957) *Dynamic Programming*. Princeton, NJ: Princeton University Press.

Benassy J P (1977) On Quantity Signals and the Foundations of Effective Demand Theory. *Scandinavian Journal of Economics*, **79**, 147–168.

Bilson J F O (1978) The Monetary Approach to the Exchange Rate: Some Empirical Evidence. *IMF Staff Papers*, **25**, 48–77.

Bilson J F O (1980) The Rational Expectations Approach to the Consumption Function. *European Economic Review*, **13**, 273–299.

Blanchard O J (1979) Wage Indexing Rules and the Behaviour of the Economy. *Journal of Political Economy*, **87**, 798–815.

Blanchard O J (1981) Output, the Stock Market and Interest Rates. *American Economic Review*, **71**, 132–143.

Blanchard O and Kahn C M (1980) The Solution of Linear Difference Models Under Rational Expectations. *Econometrica*, **48**, 1305–1311.

Blinder A S and Fischer S (1981) Inventories, Rational Expectations and the Business Cycle. *Journal of Monetary Economics*, **8**, 277–304.

Blinder A S and Solow R M (1973) Does Fiscal Policy Matter?. *Journal of Public Economics*, **2**, 319–337.

Blume L E M, Bray M M and Easley D (1982) Introduction to the Stability of Rational Expectations Equilibrium. *Journal of Economic Theory*, **26**, 313–317.

Borch K (1962) Equilibrium in a Reinsurance Market. *Econometrica*, **30**, 424–444.

Branson W H (1977) Asset Markets and Relative Prices in Exchange Rate Determination. *Sozial Wissenschaftliche Annalen*, Band 1.

Bray M M and Savin N E (1986) Rational Expectations Equilibria, Learning and Model Specification. *Econometrica*, **54**, 1129–1160.

Brooks S, Cuthbertson K and Mayes D G (1986) *The Exchange Rate Environment*. London: Croom Helm.

Buiter W H (1980) Monetary, Financial and Fiscal Policies under Rational Expectations. *IMF Staff Papers*, **27**, 785–813.

Buiter W H (1981) The Superiority of Contingent Rules over Fixed Rules in Models with Rational Expectations. *Economic Journal*, **91**, 647–670.

Buiter W H (1983) Real Effects of Anticipated Money: Some Problems of Estimation and Hypothesis Testing. *Journal of Monetary Economics*, **11**, 207–224.

Buiter W H and Miller M (1982) Real Exchange Rate Overshooting and the Output Cost of Bringing Down Inflation. *European Economic Review*, **18**, 83–130.

Calvo G A and Phelps E S (1977) Indexation Issues: Appendix. *Journal of Monetary Economics*, Supplementary Series, **5**, 160–168.

Carlson J A and Parkin J M (1975) Inflation Expectations. *Economica*, **42**, 123–138.

Carlton D W (1986) The Rigidity of Prices. *American Economic Review*, **76**, 637–658.

Chiang A C (1984) *Fundamental Methods Of Mathematical Economics*. 3rd edn, Tokyo: McGraw-Hill.

Chick V (1977) *The Theory Of Monetary Policy*. London: Grey Mills.

Chow G C (1975) *Analysis and Control of Dynamic Economic Systems*. New York: John Wiley.

Christ C F (1986) A Simple Macroeconomic Model with a Government Budget Restraint. *Journal of Political Economy*, **76**, 53–67.

Christ C F (1978) Sure Dynamic Theory of Macroeconomic Policy Effects on Income and Prices Under the Government Budget Constraint. *Journal of Monetary Economics*, **4**, 45–70.

Christ C F (1979) On Fiscal and Monetary Policies and the Government Budget Restraint. *American Economic Review*, **69**, 147, 526–538.

Clower R (1965) The Keynesion Counterrevolution: A Theoretical Appraisal. In: Hahn F and Brechling F (eds) *The Theory of Interest Rates*. London: Macmillan.

Craine R, Havenner A and Berry J (1978) Fixed Rules vs Activism in the Conduct of Monetary Policy. *American Economic Review*, **68**, 769–783.

Currie D (1984) Monetary Overshooting and the Exchange Rate. *The Manchester School*, **102**, 28–48.

Cuthbertson K (1979) *Macroeconomic Policy*. London: Macmillan.

Cuthbertson K (1980) The Determination of Expenditure on Consumer Durables. *National Institute Economic Review*, **94**, 62–72.

Cuthbertson K (1982) The Measurement and Behaviour of the UK Saving Ratio in the 1970s. *National Institute Economic Review*, **99**, 75–84.

Cuthbertson K (1985) *The Supply and Demand for Money*. Oxford: Basil Blackwell.

Cuthbertson K (1986) Price Expectations and Lags in the Demand for Money. *Scottish Journal of Political Economy*, **119**, 1–21.

Cuthbertson K (1987) The Demand for M1: A Forward-Looking Buffer Stock Model. *Oxford Economic Papers*, forthcoming.

Cuthbertson K and Taylor M P (1986) Monetary Anticipations and the Demand for Money in the UK: Testing the Rationality of Buffer Stock Money. *Journal of Applied Econometrics*, **1**, 355–365.

Cuthbertson K and Taylor M P (1987a) The Demand for Money: A Dynamic Rational Expectations Model. *Economic Journal*, Supplement, **97**, 65–76.

Cuthbertson K and Taylor M P (1987b) On the Short Run Demand for Money: The Case of the Missing Money and the Lucas Critique. *Journal of Macroeconomics*, forthcoming.

Cuthbertson K and Taylor M P (1987c) Monetary Anticipations and the Demand for Money: Some UK Evidence. *Empirical Economics*, (forthcoming).

Cuthbertson K and Taylor M P (1987d) Buffer Stock Money: An Assessment. In: Goodhart C A E, Currie D A and Llewelyn D (eds) *The Operation and Regulation of Financial Markets*. London: Macmillan.

Darby M R (1980) Movements in Purchasing Power Parity: The Short and Long Runs. In: Darby M R and Lothian J R (eds) *The International Transmission of Inflation*. Chicago: University of Chicago Press.

Davidson J E H (1984) Monetary Disequilibrium: An Approach to Modelling Monetary Phenomena in the UK. London School of Economics, mimeo.

Davidson J E H, Hendry D F, Srba F and Yeo S (1978) Econometric Modelling of the Aggregate Time Series Relationship Between Consumers' Expenditure and Income in the UK. *Economic Journal*, **88**, 661–691.

Davidson R and MacKinnon J G (1982) Some Non-Nested Hypothesis Tests and the Relation Among Them. *Review of Economic Studies*, **69**, 551–565.

De Canio S (1979) Rational Expectations and Learning From Experience. *Quarterly Journal of Economics*, **93**, 47–57.

Dickenson D G, Driscoll M J and Ford J L (1982) Rational Expectations, Random Parameters and the Non-Neutrality of Money. *Economica*, **49**, 241–248.

Dixit A K (1978) The Balance of Trade in a Model of Temporary Keynesian Equilibrium. *Review of Economic Studies*, **45**, 393–404.

Dornbusch R (1976) Expectations and Exchange Rate Dynamics. *Journal of Political Economy*, **84**, 1161–1176.

Dornbusch R (1980) Exchange Rate Economics: Where Do We Stand? *Brookings Papers in Economic Activity*, **1**, 143–185.

Dornbusch R and Fischer S (1980) Exchange Rates and the Current Account. *American Economic Review*, **85**, 960–971.

Drazen A (1980) Recent Developments in Macroeconomic Disequilibrium Theory. *Econometrica*, **48**, 283–306.

Eastwood R K and Venables A J (1982) The Macroeconomic Implications of a Resource Discovery in an Open Economy. *Economic Journal*, **92**, 285–229.

Fair R C (1979) An Analysis of a Macroeconomic Model with Rational Expectations in the Bond and Stock Market. *American Economic Review*, **69**, 539–552.

Feige E and Pearce D (1976) Economically Rational Price Expectations. *Journal of Political Economy*, **84**, 499–522.

Figlewski S and Wachtel P (1981) The Formation of Inflationary Expectations. *Review of Economics and Statistics*, **58**, 1–10.

Fischer S (1977) Long-Term Contracts, Rational Expectations and the Optimal Money Supply. *Journal of Political Economy*, **85**, 187–209.

Fischer S (1980) Dynamic Inconsistency, Co-Operation and the Benevolent Dissembling Government. *Journal of Economic Dynamics and Control*, **2**, 93–107.

Fisher I (1911) *The Purchasing Power of Money*. New York: Macmillan.

Fisher P G, Holly S and Hughes-Hallett A J (1985) Efficient Solution Techniques for Dynamic Non-Linear Rational Expectations Models. ESRC Macroeconomic Modelling Bureau Discussion Paper 4, University of Warwick.

Fleming J M (1962) Domestic Financial Policies under Fixed and Floating Exchange Rates. *IMF Staff Papers*, **9**, 369–379.

Flemming J R (1976) *Inflation*. Oxford: Oxford University Press.

Forsyth P J and Kay J A (1980) The Economic Implications of North Sea Oil Revenues. *Fiscal Studies*.

Frenkel J A (1979) On the Mark: A Theory of Floating Exchange Rates Based on Real Interest Differentials. *American Economic Review*, **69**, 4, 610–622.

Frenkel J A (1981) The Collapse of Purchasing Power Parity During the 1970s. *European Economic Review*, **16**, 145–165.

Frenkel J A, Gylfason T and Helliwell J F (1980) A Synthesis of Monetary and Keynesian Approaches to Short Run Balance of Payments Theory. *Economic Journal*, **90**, 582–592.

Frenkel J A and Rodriguez C A (1982) Exchange Rate Dynamics and the Overshooting Hypothesis. *IMF Staff Papers*, **29**, 1–29.

Friedman B M (1979) Optimal Expectations and the Extreme Information Assumptions of 'Rational Expectations' Macro Models. *Journal of Monetary Economics*, **5**, 23–41.

Friedman M (1961) The Lag in the Effect of Monetary Policy. *Journal of Political Economy*, **69**, 447–466.

Friedman M (1968) The Role of Monetary Policy. *American Economic Review*, **58**, 1–17.

Gale D (1978) A Note on Conjectural Equilibrium. *Review of Economic Studies*, **45**, 319–338.

Goodhart C A E, Gowland D and Williams D (1976) Money Income and Causality: the UK Experience. *American Economic Review*, **66**, 417–423.

Grandmont J M and G Laroque (1976) On Temporary Keynesian Equilibria. *Review of Economic Studies*, **43**, 53–67.

Granger C W J and Newbold P (1977) *Forecasting Economic Time Series*. New York: Academic Press.

Grossman S J and Hart O D (1981) Implicit Contracts, Moral Hazard and Unemployment. *American Economic Review*, **71**, 301–307.

Grossman S J and Hart O D (1983) Implicit Contracts Under Asymmetrical Information, *Quarterly Journal of Economics*, **98**, Supplement, 123–156.

Gylfason T and Helliwell J F (1983) A Synthesis of Keynesian, Monetary and Portfolio Approaches to Flexible Exchange Rates. *Economic Journal*, **93**, 820–831.

Hahn F (1977) Exercises in Conjectural Equilibria. *Scandinavian Journal of Economics*, **79**, 210–226.

Hall R E (1978) Stochastic Implications of the Life Cycle – Permanent Income Hypothesis: Theory and Evidence. *Journal of Political Economy*, **86**, 971–987.

Hall R E and Lilien D M (1979) Efficient Wage Bargains Under Uncertain Supply and Demand. *American Economic Review*, **69**, 868–879.

Hall S G (1983) The Exchange Rate. In: Britton A J C (ed.) *Employment, Output and Inflation*. London: Heinemann.

Hall S G (1985) On the Solution of Large Economic Models with Consistent Expectations. *Bulletin of Economic Research*, **37**, 157–161.

Hall S G, Henry S G B and Wren Lewis S (1986a) Manufacturing Stocks and Forward-Looking Expectations in the UK. *Economica*, **53**, 447–466.

Hall S G, Henry B, Payne J and Wren-Lewis S (1986b) Forecasting Employment: The Role of Forward Looking Behaviour. *International Journal of Forecasting*, **2**, 435–445.

Hannan E J (1970) *Multiple Time Series*. New York: John Wiley.

Hansen L P and Sargent T J (1980) Formulating and Estimating Dynamic Linear Rational Expectations Models. *Journal of Economic Dynamics and Control*, **2**, 7–46.

Hart O D (1982) A Model of Imperfect Competition with Keynesian Features. *Quarterly Journal of Economics*, **97**, 109–138.

Hart O D (1983) Optimal Labour Contracts Under Asymmetric Information: An Introduction. *Review of Economic Studies*, **50**, 3–35.

Harvey A C (1981) *Time Series Models*. Deddington, Oxford: Philip Allan.

Hendry D F (1983) Econometric Evaluation of Linear Macro-Econometric Models. Nuffield College Oxford, mimeo.

Hendry D F and von Ungern Sternberg T (1979) Liquidity and Inflation Effects on Consumers' Expenditure. In: Deaton A S (ed.) *Essays in the Theory and Measurement of Consumers' Behaviour*. Cambridge: Cambridge University Press.

Hicks J R (1937) Mr Keynes and the "Classics": a Suggested Interpretation. *Econometrica*, **5**, 147–159.

Hines A G (1971) *On the Reappraisal of Keynesian Economics*. London: Martin Robertson.

H M Treasury (1982) *Macroeconomic Model Technical Manual*. H M Treasury.

Holden K and Peel D A (1977) An Empirical Investigation of Inflationary Expectations. *Oxford Bulletin of Economics and Statistics*, **39**, 291–299.

Holden K, Peel D A and Thompson J L (1985) *Expectations Theory and Evidence*. Basingstoke: Macmillan.

Isard P (1978) Exchange Rate Determination: a Survey of Popular Views and Recent Models. *Princeton Studies in International Finance*, no. 42.

Jorgensen D W (1963) Capital Theory and Investment Behaviour. *American Economic Review, Papers and Proceedings*, **53**, 247–259.

Keating G (1985) The Financial Sector of the LBS Model. mimeo, LBS Centre for Economic Forecasting.

Kelly C M (1985) A Cautionary Note on the Interpretation of Long-run Equilibrium Solutions in Conventional Macro Models. *Economic Journal*, **95**, 1078–1086.

Kennally G (1983) Some Consequences of Opening the Keynesian Model. *Economic Journal*, **93**, 390–410.

Kennally G (1985) Committed and Discretionary Saving of Households. *National Institute Economic Review*, **12**, 35–40.

Kennan J (1979) The Estimation of Partial Adjustment Models with Rational Expectations. *Econometrica*, **47**, 1441–1455.

Keynes J M (1936) *The General Theory of Employment, Interest and Money*. London: Macmillan.

Killingsworth M R (1983) *Labour Supply*. Cambridge: Cambridge University Press.

King R G (1982) Monetary Policy and the Information Content of Prices. *Journal of Political Economy*, **90**, 247–279.

Kydland F E and Prescott E C (1977) Rules Rather than Discretion: The Inconsistency of Optimal Plans. *Journal of Political Economy*, **85**, 473–491.

Laidler D E W (1968) The Permanent Income Concept in a Macroeconomic Model. *Oxford Economic Paper*, **20**, 11–23.

Laidler D E W (1973) Expectations, Adjustment and the Dynamic Response of Income to Policy Changes. *Journal of Money Credit and Banking*, **4**, 157–172.

Laidler D E W (1982) *Monetarist Perspectives*. Philip Allan. Oxford: Deddington.

Laidler D E W (1985) *The Demand for Money: Theories, Evidence and Problems*. New York: Harper and Row.

Laidler D E W and O'Shea P (1980) An Empirical Macromodel of an Open Economy under Fixed Exchange Rates: the UK, 1954–70. *Economica*, **47**, 141–158.

Laider D, Bentley B, Johnson D and Johnson S T (1983) A Small Macroeconomic Model off an Open Economy: the Case of Canada. In: Claasen E and Salin P (eds) *Recent Issues in the Theory of Flexible Exchange Rates*. Amsterdam: North Holland.

Laider D E W and Bentley B (1983) A small Macro-Model of the Post-War United States. *Manchester School*, **5**, 317–340.

Lawson T (1980) Adaptive Expectations and Uncertainty. *Review of Economic Studies*, **67**, 305–320.

Layard R and Nickell S (1985) The Causes of British Unemployment. *National Institute Economic Review*, **111**, 62–85.

Leiderman L (1980) Macroeconometric Testing of the Rational Expectations and Structural Neutrality Hypothesis for the United States. *Journal of Monetary Economics*, **6**, 69–82.

Leijonhufvud A (1968) *On Keynesian Economics and the Economics of Keynes*. Oxford: Oxford University Press.

Lucas R E Jr (1972) Expectations and the Neutrality of Money. *Journal of Economic Theory*, **4**, 103–124.

Lucas R E Jr (1973) Some International Evidence on Output-Inflation Trade-offs. *American Economic Review*, **63**, 326–334.

Lucas R E Jr (1975) An Equilibrium Model of the Business Cycle. *Journal of Political Economy*, **83**, 1113–1144.

Lucas R E (1976) Econometric Policy Evaluation: A Critique. In: Brunner K and Meltzer A H (eds) *The Phillips Curve and Labour Markets*. Carnegie Rochester Conferences in Public Policy, 1, 19–46, Amsterdam: North Holland.

Lucas R E and Rapping L A (1969) Real Wages, Employment and Inflation. *Journal of Political Economy*, **77**, 721–754.

Matthews K G P and Ormerod P (1978) St Louis Models of the UK Economy. *National Institute Economic Review*, **2**, 65–69.

McCallum B T (1978) Dating Discounts and the Robustness of the Lucas-Sargent Proposition. *Journal of Monetary Economics*, **4**, 121–129.

McCallum B T (1980) Rational Expectations and Macroeconomic Stabilisation Policy. *Journal of Money, Credit and Banking*, **12**, 716–746.

McCallum B T (1983) On Non-Uniqueness in Rational Expectations Models: An Attempt at Perspective. *Journal of Monetary Economics*, **11**, 139–168.

McCallum B T and Whittaker J K (1979) The Effectiveness of Fiscal Feedback Rules and Automatic Stabilisers Under Rational Expectations. *Journal of Monetary Economics*, **5**, 171–186.

MacDonald R and Taylor M P (1988) Recent Developments in Empirical Exchange Rate Economics. In: Pearce D W and Rau N J (eds) *Economic Perspectives*. London: Harwood.

Minford A P L and Peel D A (1981) On the Role of Monetary Stabilisation Policy Under Rational Expectations. *The Manchester School*, **69**, 39–50.

Minford A P L and Peel D A (1982) The Phillips Curve and Rational Expectations. *Weltwirtschaftliches Archiv*, **118**, 456–478.

Minford P, Marwaha S, Matthews K G P and Sprague A (1984) The Liverpool Macroeconometric Model of the United Kingdom. *Economic Modelling*, **1**, 24–62.

Minford A P L, Matthews K G P and Marwaha S (1979) Terminal Conditions as a Means of Ensuring Unique Solutions of Rational Expectations Models with Forward Expectations. *Economics Letters*, **4**, 117–120.

Mishkin F S (1982a) Does Anticipated Monetary Policy Matter? An Econometric Investigation. *Journal of Political Economy*, **90**, 22–50.

Mishkin F S (1982b) Does Anticipated Aggregate Demand Policy Matter? Further Econometric Results. *American Economic Review*, **72**, 788–802.

Mishkin F S (1983) *A Rational Expectations Approach to Macroeconometrics*. Chicago: University of Chicago Press for NBER.

Muellbauer J (1983) Surprises in the Consumption Function. *Economic Journal*, **93**, Supplement, 34–50.

Muellbauer J and Portes R (1978) Macroeconomic Models with Quantity Rationing. *Economic Journal*, **88**, 788–821.

Mundell R A (1963) Capital Mobility and Stabilisation Policy under Fixed and Flexible Exchange Rates. *Canadian Journal of Economics and Political Science*, **29**, 475–485.

Muth J F (1960) Optimal Properties of Exponentially Weighted Forecasts. *Journal of the American Statistical Association*, **55**, 299–306.

Muth J F (1961) Rational Expectations and the Theory of Price Movements. *Econometrica*, **29**, 315–335.

Myerson R (1979) Incentive Compatibility and the Bargaining Problem. *Econometrica*, **47**, 61–74.

Neary J P (1980) Non-traded Goods and the Balance of Trade in a Neo-Keynesian Temporary Equilibrium. *Quarterly Journal of Economics*, **94**, 403–429.

Neary P and Stiglitz J E (1983) Towards a Reconstruction of Keynesian Economics: Expectations and Constrained Equilibria. *Quarterly Journal of Economics*, **98**, Supplement, 199–228.

Neary J P and van Wijnbergen S (1984) Can an Oil Discovery Lead to a Recession? Comment on Eastwood and Venables. *Economic Journal*, **94**, 390–395.

Nguyen, Duc-Tho and Turnovsky S J (1980) Perfect Myopic Foresight and the Effects of Monetary and Fiscal Policy in a Simple Inflationary Model. *European Economic Review*, **14**, 237–290.

Nguyen Duc-Tho and Turnovsky S J (1983) The Dynamic Effects of Fiscal and Monetary Policies Under Bond Financing. *Journal of Monetary Economica*, **11**, 45–71.

Nickell S J (1984) The Modelling of Wages and Employment. In: Hendry D F and Wallis K F (eds) *Econometrics and Quantitative Economics*. Oxford: Basil Blackwell.

Nickell S J (1985) Error Correction, Partial Adjustment and all That: An Expository Note. *Oxford Bulletin of Economics and Statistics*, **47**, 119–130.

Patinkin D (1956) *Money, Interest and Prices*. New York: Harper and Row.

Patterson K D (1985) The Development of Expectations Schemes that are Asymptotically Rational. Bank of England Discussion Paper Technical Series No 12.

Pesaran M H (1981) Identification of Rational Expectations Models. *Journal of Econometrics*, **16**, 375–398.

Pesaran M H (1982) A Critique of Proposed Tests of the Natural Rate – Rational Expectations Hypothesis. *Economic Journal*, **92**, 529–554.

Pesaran M H and Evans R A (1984) Inflation, Capital Gains and UK Personal Savings, 1953–81. *Economic Journal*, **94**, 237–257.

Phelps E S and Taylor J B (1977) The Stabilising Powers of Monetary Policy under Rational Expectations. *Journal of Political Economy*, **85**, 163–190.

Pigou A C (1943) The Classical Stationary State. *Economic Journal*, **53**, 343–351.

Rees R (1985a) The Theory of Principal and Agent: Part I. *Bulletin of Economic Research*, **36**, 3–26.

Rees R (1985b) The Theory of Principal and Agent: Part II. *Bulletin of Economic Research*, **37**, 77–95.

Samuelson P A (1947) *Foundations of Economic Analysis*. Cambridge, Mass: Harvard University Press.

Sargent T J and Wallace N (1975) Rational Expectations, the Optimal Monetary Instrument and the Optimal Money Supply Rule. *Journal of Political Economy*, **83**, 241–254.

Sargent T J (1976) The Observational Equivalence of Natural and Unnatural Rate Theories of Macroeconomics. *Journal of Political Economy*, **84**, 631–640.

Sargent T J (1978) Estimation of Dynamic Labour Demand Schedules under Rational Expectations. In: Lucas R E Jr and Sargent T J (eds) *Rational Expectations and Econometric Practice*. London: George, Allen and Unwin.

Sargent T J (1979) *Macroeconomic Theory*. New York: Academic Press.

Sheffrin S M (1983) *Rational Expectations*. Cambridge: Cambridge University Press.

Sims C A (1972) Money, Income and Causality. *American Economic Review*, **62**, 540–552.

Spencer P D (1986) *Financial Innovations, Efficiency and Disequilibrium*. Oxford: Oxford University Press.

Sutton J (1979) Comment on Azariadis' Paper. In: Hornstein A, Grice J and Webb A (eds) *The Economics of the Labour Market*. London: HMSO.

Taylor C T and Threadgold A R (1979) 'Real' National Savings and its Sectoral Composition. Bank of England Discussion Paper No 6.

Taylor J B (1977) Conditions for Unique Solutions to Macroeconomic Models with Rational Expectations. *Econometrica*, **45**, 1377–1385.

Taylor M P (1984) *Approaches to Balance of Payments Adjustment: History, Theory and Empirical Analysis*. Ph.D. thesis, University of London.

Taylor M P (1987a) What do Investment Managers Know? An Empirical Study of Practitioners' Predictions. *Economica* (forthcoming).

Taylor M P (1987b) Learning and Rationality: An Empirical Study of Investment Managers' Stock Market Predictions. *Annales d'Economie et de Statistique*, (forthcoming).

Taylor M P (1987c) On Long-Run Solutions to Dynamic Econometric Equations Under Rational Expectations. *Economic Journal*, **97**, 215–218.

Taylor M P (1987d) The Simple Analytics of Implicit Labour Contracts. *Bulletin of Economic Research*, **39**, 1–28. (Reprinted as Chapter 7. In: Hey J D and Lambert P J (eds) *Surveys in the Economics of Uncertainty*. Oxford: Basil Blackwell.

Taylor M P (1987e) Further Developments in the Theory of Implicit Labour Contracts. Chapter 8. In Hey J D and Lambert P J (eds) *Surveys in the Economics of Uncertainty*. Oxford: Basil Blackwell.

Taylor M P (1987f) On Granger Causality and the Monetary Approach to the Balance of Payments. *Journal of Macroeconomics*, (forthcoming).

Taylor M P (1987g) Covered Interest Parity: A High-Frequency, High-Quality Data Study, *Economica* (forthcoming).

Taylor M P (1987h) An Empirical Examination of Long-Run Purchasing Power Parity Using Cointegration Techniques. *Journal of Applied Econometrics* (forthcoming).

Taylor M P (1987i) On Unit Roots and Real Exchange Rates: Empirical Evidence and Monte Carlo Analysis. Bank of England, mimeo.

Taylor M P (1987j) A DYMIMIC Model of Forward Foreign Exchange Risk, With Estimates for Three Major Exchange Rates. *The Manchester School* (forthcoming).

Taylor M P and McMahon P C (1987) Long-Run Purchasing Power Parity in the 1920s. *European Economic Review* (forthcoming).

Tinbergen J (1952) *On the Theory of Economic Policy*. Amsterdam: North-Holland.

Tobin J (1969) A General Equilibrium Approach to Monetary Theory. *Journal of Money Credit and Banking*, **1**, 15–29.

Tobin J (1956) The Interest Elasticity of the Transactions Demand for Cash. *Review of Economics and Statistics*, **38**, 241–247.

Tobin J (1958) Liquidity Preference as Behaviour Towards Risk. *Review of Economic Studies*, **25**, 65–86.

Tucker D (1966) Dynamic Income Adjustment to Money Supply Changes. *American Economic Review*, **56**, 433–449.

Turnovsky S J (1970) Empirical Evidence on the Formation of Price Expectations. *Journal of the American Statistical Association*, **65**, 210–50.

Turnovsky S J (1977) *Macroeconomic Analysis and Stabilisation Policy*. Cambridge: Cambridge University Press.

Wallis K F (ed) (1985) *Models of the UK Economy: A Second Review by the ESRC Macroeconomic Modelling Bureau*. Oxford: Oxford University Press.

Wallis K F (ed) (1986) *Models of the UK Economy: A Third Review by the ESRC Macroeconomic Modelling Bureau*. Oxford: Oxford University Press.

Walshe C E (1984) Interest Rate Volatility and Monetary Policy. *Journal of Money, Credit and Banking*, **16**, 133–150.

Weiss A (1980) Job Queues and Layoffs in Labor Markets with Flexible Wages. *Journal of Political Economy*, **88**, 526–538.

Weiss L (1980) The Role for Active Monetary Policy in a Rational Expectations Model. *Journal of Political Economy*, **88**, 221–233.

Whiteman C H (1985) *Linear Rational Expectations Models: A User's Guide*. Minneapolis: University of Minnesota Press.

Whittaker R, Wren-Lewis S, Blackburn K and Currie D (1980) Alternative Financial Policy Rules in an Open Economy Under Rational and Adaptive Expectations. *Economic Journal*, **96**, 680–695.

Wickens M R and Molana H (1983) Stochastic Life Cycle Theory with Varying Interest Rates and Prices *Economic Journal*, **94**, Supplement, 133–147.

Wold H (1954) *A Study in the Analysis of Stationary Time Series*, 2nd edn; Stockholm: Almquist and Wiksell.

Wren-Lewis S (1984) Omitted Variables in Equations Relating Prices to Money. *Applied Economics*, **16**, 483–496.

Author Index

Adler M., 229
Akerlof, G., 152
Anderson, L. C., 14
Ando, A., 17
Arrow, K. J., 143, 157
Astrom, K. J., 250
Attfield, C. L. F., 108
Azariadis, C., 136, 145, 149, 160, 162, 173

Baily, M. N., 136
Ball, R. J., 194
Barro, R. J., 38, 81, 101, 102, 105, 108, 259, 260
Baumol, W. J., 169
Begg, D. K. H., 84, 103
Bellman, R., 250, 257, 261
Benassy, J. P., 77
Bentley, B., 13
Bilson, J. F. O., 108, 200
Blanchard, O. J., 84, 102, 113, 116, 120, 124, 134, 233
Blinder, A. S., 20, 40, 112
Blume, L. E. M., 81
Borch, K., 143
Branson, W. H., 216, 229
Bray, M. M., 111
Broadberry, S., 229
Brooks, S., 84, 211
Buiter, W. H., 38, 42, 102, 107, 125, 210, 212, 257

Calvo, G. A., 160
de Canio, 5, 81, 111, 226
Carlson, J. A., 80
Carlton, D. W., 75
Chiang, A. C., 40, 44, 45, 48, 49, 128, 129, 260
Chick, V., 37, 45
Chow, G. C., 247, 250, 255, 261
Christ, C., 19, 40
Clower, R., 54, 55
Craine, R., 250
Currie, D. A., 210
Cuthbertson, K., 14, 38, 111, 122, 132, 196, 198, 210, 211, 240, 241, 254

Darby, M. R., 229
Davidson, J. E. H., 13, 124, 195
Dickenson, D. G., 101
Dixit, A., 72
Dornbusch, R., 113, 115, 119, 124, 177, 203, 204, 213, 215, 216
Drazen, A., 76

Eastwood, R. K., 212
Edgeworth, F. Y., 54
Evans, A., 240

Fair, R. C., 120
Feige, E., 81
Figlewski, S., 89
Fischer, S., 101, 102, 112, 161, 257
Fisher, I., 29, 101
Fisher, P., 124
Fleming, J. M., 176

Flemming, J. S., 80, 110, 121
Forsyth, P. J., 212
Frankel, J. A., 177, 200, 203, 213
Frenkel, J. A., 199, 200, 211
Friedman, B., 120
Friedman, M., 33, 34, 75, 124, 252

Gale, D., 76
Goodhart, C. A. E., 14, 115
Gordon, R. J., 259, 260
Grandmont, J. M., 76
Granger, C. W. J., 121
Grossman, S. J., 156, 160, 173
Gylfason, T., 199

Hahn, F., 76
Hall, R. E., 102, 108
Hall, S. G., 124, 132, 241
Hannan, E. J., 127
Hansen, A., 132, 254
Hart, O. D., 76, 132, 156, 254, 160, 173
Harvey, A. C., 109, 121
Helliwell, J. F., 199
Hendry, D., 111, 195, 240
Hicks, J. R., 3, 53
Hines, A. G., 53
Holden, K., 80, 84, 89, 99

Isard, P., 216

Jordan, K. M., 14
Jorgenson, D. W., 240

Kahn, R., 134, 233
Kay, J. A., 212
Keating, G., 240, 241
Kelly, C. M., 132
Kennally, G., 73, 196
Kennan, J., 132
Keynes, J. M., 53
Killingsworth, M. R., 25
King, R. G., 100
Kydland, F. E., 257

Laidler, D. E. W., 13, 38, 40
Laroque, G., 76
Lawson, T., 122
Layard, R., 36, 41
Lehmann, B., 229
Leiderman, Y., 108
Leijonhufuod, A., 54, 76
Lilien, D. M., 102
Lucas, R. E., 25, 81, 83, 90, 93, 109, 112, 253

McCallum, B., 99, 100, 101, 118
MacDonald, R., 84
McKinnon, R. I., 124
McMahon, 229
Marshall, 54
Matthews, K. G. P., 14
Minford, A. P. L., 93, 94, 101, 128, 227
Mishkin, F. S., 108
Miyazaki, H., 152
Modigliani, F., 17

Molana, H., 108
Muellbauer, J., 56, 108
Mundell, R. A., 176
Muth, J. F., 80, 81, 121, 125, 126
Myerson, R., 168

Neary, J. P., 73, 104, 212
Newbold, P., 121
Nguyen, D., 204, 227
Nickell, S. J., 36, 41, 132

Ormerod, P., 14

Parkin, J. M., 80
Patinkin, D., 55
Patterson, K. D., 121
Pearce, I., 81
Peel, D., 80, 93, 94, 101
Pesaran, M. H., 107, 108, 240
Phelps, E. S., 101, 160
Pigou, C., 15
Portes, R., 56
Prescott, E. C., 257, 259

Rapping, L. A., 25, 93
Rees, A., 157
Rodriguez, C. A., 211
Rush, M., 105

Samuelson, P., 42
Sargent, T. J., 81, 84, 90, 107, 112, 125, 129, 130, 131, 132, 166, 254, 255
Savin, N. E., 111
Shaw, G. K., 53
Sheffrin, S. M., 89
Sims, C. A., 14, 115
Solow, R. M., 20, 40
Spencer, P. D., 241
Stiglitz, J. E., 104, 149, 168
Sutton, J., 166

Taylor, M. P., 38, 73, 84, 89, 101, 129, 132, 166, 229
Threadgold, A. R., 38
Tinbergen, J., 246
Tobin, J., 14, 79, 211
Tucker, D., 40
Turnovsky, S. J., 40, 80, 204, 227, 261

von Ungern Sternberg, T., 195, 240

Venables, A. J., 212

Wachtel, P., 89
Wallace, N., 81, 84, 90
Wallis, K. F., 196, 227, 240, 241, 244, 245
Walshe, C. E., 123, 226
Weiss, A., 162
Weiss, L., 100
Whiteman, C. H., 134
Whittaker, R., 99, 227
Wickens, M. R., 108
van Wijnbergen, S., 212

Subject Index

Accelerationalist Hypothesis, 33, 36
Acceptance Wage, 144, 161–2, 165
Adaptive Expectations, 40, 120–2, 239, 241
  First Order, 121
  Hypothesis (AEH), 79, 110
Adverse Selection in the Labour Market, 161–6
Aggregate
  demand, 4, 75, 205
  demand curve, 23, 32
  supply, 25, 26, 40–2
  supply curve, 3, 21, 22, 23, 27
Algebra of IS-LM and AS-AD models, 39–42
Analytic Models, 239–45
Anticipated Changes in Policy, 113, 119
Arrow-Pratt measure of risk aversion, 147
Asset-Market Equilibrium, 117
Asymmetric Information, 34, 94, 160,
  161, 167–73

Balance of Payments (BB Locus), 179–81
Balance of Trade, 72, 180
Balanced Budget, 188–9, 192
BB Locus, The, 179–81
Bond Finance, 17
  instability, 17, 18, 20
  pure, 19
Bond Rate, 180
Bonds, 217
  domestic, 219, 221
  foreign, 218–19, 221
Boom State, 137, 139, 141, 144
Bootstraps Effect, 57, 70–2, 75, 76, 77, 104
Bretton-Woods system, 176
Bubbles, 129
Budget Deficit, 15, 16
Buiter-Miller Model, The, 233–8
Business Cycle, 84, 123, 136, 147

Capital Account, 204, 217
Capital Account Monetarist (KAM) Models,
  177, 202–12, 216
Capital Flows, 180
Capital Mobility, 204
Certainty Equivalence, 250, 131
Chain Rule of Forecasting, 88, 128
Chicago View, 196–7
Classical Dichotomy, 27
Classical Unemployment, 64–5, 82
Closed Loop Policy Rule, 96, 99, 250
Co-Insurance, 159
Comparative Statics, Method of, 42, 48, 50
  IS-LM Model, 46–8
Competitiveness, 177, 178, 182, 197, 209, 229
Conditional Mathematical Expectation, 85
Conjectural Equilibria, 76
Conjecture Function, 76
Consistency, 85, 87–8, 122
Consistent Expectations, 80
Consumption, 61, 240
Consumption Function, 68, 70, 108
  labour rationed, 68, 72, 77
  sales rationed, 77
Contingent Rule, 96

Contract Model, 94–5
Correspondence Principle, 37, 42–3, 45,
  48–50
Counter Inflationary Monetary Policy, 83
Cramer's Rule, 44
Credibility, 210, 260
Cross Equation Restrictions, 106, 132, 256
Crowding Out, 2, 3, 4, 40, 50–2, 83, 184,
  188, 202
  full, 12
  partial, 10
  physical, 27, 42
Current Account, 217, 224–5, 233
Current Account Monetarist (CAM) Model,
  176–7, 196–202, 212, 216

Demand for Labour, 23, 240
Demand for Money, 40, 198, 203
  effective, 74
  notional, 74
Deterministic Forecasting, 242, 243
Devaluation, 197
Difference Equation, 126
Discrete Labour Supply, 152
Discretionary Policies, 83, 100
Disequilibrium Monetary Models, 13
Dornbusch Exchange Rate Overshooting, 204,
  205, 230–3
  Model, 204, 205
  Solution, 230–1
Dual Decision Hypothesis, 54–67, 74
Dutch Disease, 236
Dynamic Programming, 261–3

Efficiency, 84, 86–7
Efficiency Units of Labour, 161–2
Efficient Markets Hypothesis, 84
Elasticity
  of exports, 179
  of imports, 179
Endogenous Prices, 75–6
Endogenous Variables, 241, 243
Equilibrium
  in money and goods markets, 8, 9, 114,
    115
  stability of, 219
  temporary, 75
  Walrasian, 62, 63, 65, 66, 72, 77, 104
Equities, 113, 114
Euler Equation, 131
Ex ante, 54, 61, 63, 76
Ex post, 149, 151, 152, 159, 167
Exchange Rate, 175, 180, 212–16
  nominal and effective, 203
  overshooting, 177, 203, 226
Exogenous variables, 241, 243
Expectational Errors, 35
Expectations, 244–5
  see also rational expectations
Expected Money Supply, 98
Expected Real Profit, 139, 144
Expected Utility, 139, 144
Expenditure Switching, 176, 179, 194

False Trading, 32, 56, 76
Feasible Contract, 139, 146
Fiscal Policy, 10, 32, 82, 96, 101, 113, 118, 193
  exchange rates and, 184, 185–6
  impotent, 11, 12
  M-F model and, 183, 187–8
Fisher Hypothesis, 199–200, 214, 215
Fixed Exchange Rate System, 176
Fixed Price Model, 23
Floating Exchange Rate, 200
Flow Equilibrium Condition, 37
Forecast Errors, 82
  see also real expectation forecasting errors
Foreign Exchange (FOREX) Market, 240
Foreign Exchange Reserves, 181, 198
Foresight, perfect, 234, 251
  see also rational expectations
Forward Looking Expectations, 127–9, 133
Forward Operator, 129, 132
Full Employment, Automatic, 29–32
Full Money Multiplier, see multiplier

Game Theory, 258
General Theory, The, 52, 63

High Powered Money, 17
HM Treasury, 240
Hyper-inflation CAM model, 200, 212

Imperfect Competition, 76
Implicit Contract Theory, 136–61
Implicit Dynamics, 45, 49
Implicit Function Theorem, 43
Incentive Compatibility, 167–71, 259–60
Indifference Curve Analysis, 69
Indirect Tests of REH, 89
Inelastic demand for money, 40
Inelastic investment expenditure, 30
Inelastic investment schedule, 40
Inflation
  accelerating, 35, 72
  differential, 213
  loss, 38, 195, 196
Instability, 127
Instruments, 247
Interest elasticity, 2, 7, 10
  differential, 213
  inelasticity, 11, 30
  rate, 4–5, 212, 216
Intertemporal Substitution, 90, 93
Intertemporal Supply Hypothesis, 93
IS-curve, 5, 7, 13, 19, 205
IS/LM Model
  analysis, 2, 3–8, 14, 22, 29, 51, 96, 110, 114
Iso profit line, 142

J-Curve Effect, 179
Joint tests of neutrality, 108
Joint tests of RE, 108

KAM models, see Capital Account Monetarist Models
Keynesian Aggregate Supply, 113
Keynesian Consumption Function, 77
Keynesian Demand Side Multiplier, 64
Keynesian Economics, 1, 2, 97
  versus Classical, 21, 29

Keynesian Unemployment, 63, 64, 67, 69, 70, 71, 77, 104
Kuhn Tucker Conditions, 171–2

Labour Constraint, 58
  demand for, 23, 240
Labour Endowment, 162–3
Labour Endowment Distribution, 162
Labour Heterogeneity, 161
Labour Market, 26, 136, 161
Labour Productivity, 27, 36
Lay offs, 135, 136, 140–1, 147–9, 150, 159, 165–6
Learning, 89, 111, 118, 121, 226
Leisure
  work choice, 141, 150
Life-Cycle Hypothesis, 17
Linear Quadratic Control Problem, 261–3
Liquid Assets, 114
Liquidity Trap, 9, 10, 14, 30
Liverpool Model, 240
LM Curve, 6, 7, 8, 10, 11, 13, 19, 27, 125
Loanable Funds, 29
London Business School (LBS), 240
Long-Run AS Curve, 97
Long-Run Equilibrium, 114–15
Loss Function, 252
Low Capital Mobility, 185
Lucas Critique, 83, 109–11, 239, 253–6
Lucas Model, 90, 93, 94

Marginal Costs, 21, 23, 32
Marginal Expected Profit of Wages, 142
Marginal Expected Utility, 143, 159, 172
Marginal Physical Product of Labour, 24, 152
Marginal Propensity to Consumer (MPC), 64, 67
Marginal Rate of Substitution, 142, 143, 158
Market Clearing, 25, 26
Market Clearing Price Vector, 55
Mark-Up, 217
Marshall-Lerner Condition, 176, 178–9, 180, 182, 224
Mean Square Errors, 121
Min Condition, 61, 62, 63
Minford-Peel Model, 94–5
Minimum Variance, 92
Monetary Feedback Rule, 109
Monetary Policy and Exchange Rates, 9, 32, 82, 101, 113, 118, 184, 192–3, 226
  in a Closed Economy with Wealth Effects, 20, 21
  impotent, 9
  ISLM Fixed Price Model, 9–14
  M-F model, 183, 187
  PBM Model, 222–4
Money, 217
  demand for, 40, 74, 198, 203
Money Financed Deficit, 19
Money Illusion, 166
Money Supply, 96, 98, 217, 224
  sterilisation, 182–3
  variance, 99–198
Moral Hazard, 157
Moving Average, 121
Multipliers
  Fiscal, 39
  Full Keynesian Fiscal, 11
  Full Money, 12
  Money Supply, 39

Mundell-Fleming (M-F) Model, 176, 178–96
  with fixed prices, 193–5
Muth-RE, 80, 84, 85, 96, 100, 113, 119, 120,
  122, 204, 241
Muthian Solution, 130, 133

NAIRU, *see* Non-Accelerating Inflation Rate
  of Unemployment
Nash Equilibrium, 258
National Institute of Economic and Social
  Research (NIESR), 240
Natural Rate, 27
  of output, 39, 82, 97, 112
  see also unemployment
Neoclassical Labour Market, 25–6, 27, 34
  Market Clearing, 31, 54–67
  Model, 30, 81
  Supply Curve, 26, 203
  Supply Model, 240
  Synthesis, 53, 76
von Neumann Utility Function, 138, 157
Neutrality
  of debts, 39
  of money, 27, 29, 39, 41, 42, 203
  proposition, 2, 21, 104, 199
New Information, 8, 7, 88
  see also news
News, 86, 215
  model, 215
  see also new information
Nominal Interest Rate, 199
Nominal Wage Rate, 24, 25
Nominal Wages, 31, 161
Non-Accelerating Inflation Rate of
  Unemployment (NAIRU), *see*
  unemployment
Non Contingent Policy Rule, 96
Non Market Clearing, 31, 54–67
  RE model, 103–4
Non Uniqueness, 127–8
Nordic Model, 198
North Sea Oil, 203, 212, 240

Observational Equivalence, 104–5, 106–8
Oil, 236
  see also North Sea Oil and Resource Discovery
Open Arbitrage Condition, 203, 204
Open Economy, 15, 72–3
Open Loop Policy Rule, 96, 99, 250
Optimal
  Control, 243, 247–53
  risk sharing, 142, 158
Optimality principle, 250, 257, 261
Orthogonality, 84, 86–7
Over-identification, 106
Overlapping wage in contract models, *see*
  Wage Contract Models
Overshooting, 113, 115, 177, 205, 210, 226, 230–3

Paradox of Thrift, 48, 71
Pareto Optimal, 140
Partial Adjustment Equation, 130
Partly Rational Models, 84, 113–20
Price Expectations Augmented Phillips Curve
  (PEAPC), 2, 32–6, 40–2, 79, 89–95, 100,
  109, 123, 176, 194, 203, 205, 229, 240
  Vertical, 2, 32, 36, 82, 100

Perfect Capital Mobility, 180, 188
  with fixed exchange rates, 189–90
  with flexible exchange rates, 190–1, 199, 206
  with M-F model, 183, 184–5
Perfect Foresight, 80
Perfect flexibility of
  prices, 26, 82, 96
  wages, 26
Perfect substitutes, 180
Permanent Income, 30
Perpetuity, 38
Persistence Effect, 111–13
Phase Diagrams, 115–13
Phillips Curve, *see* PEAPC
Pigou Effect, 15
  see also Real Balance Effect
Policy Evaluation Proposition, 83–4
Policy Ineffectiveness, 82, 84, 95–108, 125
  Robustness of, 99–100
  Tests of, 104–5
Policy Optimisation
  with RE, 253–60
Policy Simulations, 243
Portfolio
  Balance Model, The, 216–26, 240
  Investment, 175
  Theories, 180
Price Competitiveness, 175, 17
Price Level, 22
Price Surprises, 34
Price Vector, 54, 85
Principal Agent Relationship, 157, 161
Production Function, 23, 240
Productivity, 161
Profit Margin, 94
Profit Maximising, 138, 139, 140
Psuedo Dynamics, *see* Implicit Dynamics
Purchasing Power Parity, 195, 197–8, 200

Quadratic Cost Function, 130
Quadratic Loss Function, 243, 244
Quantity Constrained Models, 104
Quantity Rationing, 56–60
  Firm, 59–60
  Household, 56–59
Quantity Signals, 56

Rate of Inflation, 195
  expected, 28
Rational Expectations, 79, 83–9, 134, 175,
  205, 226, 231, 239
  forecasting errors, 86
  hypothesis, 80–4, 87
  model solutions, 124–34
  policy optimisation, 253–60
Rationing, 55, 56
  manipulable and non-manipulable, 77
  of labour, 62
Raw Material Prices, 32
Real Balance Effect, 14–21, 28, 70, 198
  see also Pigou effect
Real Exchange Rate, 177, 178, 203, 205, 210, 236
Real Interest Rate, 28, 195, 213
Real Wage, 23, 24, 28, 34, 240
  resistance, 32
Real World Markets, 239–45
Reduced Form Equation, 39, 43, 105

Redundancy Pay, *see* Unemployment Compensation
Regressive Expectations, 122, 205
Relative Price, 91, 178
Replacement Ratio, 105
Repressed Effects, 260
Residual Adjustments, 242, 243
Resource Discovery, 203, 211, 233
Revaluation Effect, 195
Revelation Principle, 168
Ricardian Equivalence Theorem, 38
Rigid Nominal Wages, 31
Risk aversion, 18, 136–7, 157
    neutrality, 136–7, 138, 140, 144, 157, 204
Risk-Averse firms, 156–9, 167
Risk Sharing Equilibrium, 140

Saddle Path, 117, 119, 237, 244
Samuelson's Correspondence Principle, 37, 42, 43, 46, 48–50
Sargent's solution method, 130–2
Sargent-Wallace (SW) surprise supply function, 84, 89, 94, 96, 97, 101, 114
Say's Law, 74, 76
Separation Principle, 131, 233
Share Prices, 114, 240
Signal Extraction, 92
Simple Open Economy Model, 72, 73
Simultaneous System, 242
Slump State, 137, 141, 144, 145, 148, 149, 150
Small Open Economy, 175
Speculative Bubbles, 117
Speculative Demand, 6
Spillover Effects, 32
Spot Rate, *see* exchange rate
Stability, 129, 141
Stabilisation Policy, 103
Stagflation, *see* classical unemployment
    substitutes, 221
Standard Production Function, 138
State Invariant
    employment, 144
    real wage, 139, 143, 152
States of Nature, 136–7
State Variable Wage, 139, 146
Static Expectations, 244–5
Sterilisation of Money Supply, 182, 198
Sticky Price Model, 102, 125
Sticky Wages, 31–2, 104, 135–6, 160, 165–6
Stochastic Simulation, 243
Stock Equilibrium, 37, 46, 51
Structural Form, 43
Substitution Effects, 25
Super Neutrality of Money, 42
Supplementary Deposits Scheme, 210
Supply Curve, 21–9
Supply Curve for Labour, 24–5
Surprise Supply Function, 84, 89–95
    see also Sargent-Wallace supply function
Survey data, 83, 85, 88, 89
Systematic Policy Rule, 82, 95

Targets, 247
Taxes on Labour, 28

Terminal Condition, 128, 245
Terms of Trade, 178, 182
Time Inconsistency, 239, 256–60
Trade Balance, 225
Trade Offs, 248
Trade Surplus, 192, 227
Tradeable goods, 197
Tradeable prices, 197
Transactions, 6
    demand, 8
Transversality condition, 128
Two-step estimates, 105
Type 1 fix, 243
Type 2 fix, 243, 246

Unanticipated Changes
    in money supply, 82–83, 115, 118
    in policy, 113
Unbalanced budget, 189
Unbalanced budget expansion, 17, 192
Unbiasedness Property, 84–86
Uncovered Arbitrage, 213
Uncovered Interest Parity, 199, 203, 204, 210, 215, 240
Underconsumption, 66–7
Under employment premium, 145
Under employment marginal premium, 145, 146
Undershooting, 211
Unemployment, 26, 34, 145, 164
    benefit, 141
    classical, 64, 82
    compensation, 147, 150, 151, 156, 159
    frictional, 26
    involuntary, 26, 31, 103, 149, 151
    Keynesian, 63, 64, 67, 69, 70, 71, 77, 104
    natural rate, 26, 33, 35
    see also NAIRU
    voluntary, 90
    Walrasian, 149, 152, 156
Uniqueness, 129, 241
Utility, 58, 59

Valuation Changes, 175
Variability of Wages, 137–40
Variables
    control, 246
    forcing, 256
    predetermined, 246
    state, 246
Variance, 92, 93
Variance of Local Prices, 92
Vector Autoregressive Expectations, 132
Voluntary Unemployment, 90

Wage Contract Models, 101–2
Walrasian Equilibrium, *see* equilibrium
Wealth Effects, 14–21, 50–2, 53, 70, 176
    in Open Economy, 188
Welfare Benefits, 25
Welfare Payments, 32
White Noise, 88
Wold Decomposition Theorem, 126